MW01000291

# The Wisdom Books

---

## THE COMPLETE PORTRAIT
### OF THE MESSIAH

Volume 5

Other volumes in The Complete Portrait of the Messiah series

Also available from Time to Revive and Laura Kim Martin

*reviveDAILY: A Devotional Journey from Genesis to Revelation, Year 1*
*reviveDAILY: A Devotional Journey from Genesis to Revelation, Year 2*

# The Wisdom Books

## THE COMPLETE PORTRAIT OF THE MESSIAH

Volume 5

Kyle Lance Martin

Time to Revive and reviveSCHOOL

time to
**revive**
Richardson, Texas

*The Wisdom Books*

Published in conjunction with
Iron Stream Media
100 Missionary Ridge
Birmingham, AL 35242
IronStreamMedia.com

Library of Congress Control Number: 2023907192

978-1-63204-114-2 (hardback)
978-1-63204-104-3 (eBook)

1 2 3 4 5—27 26 25 24 23

# DEDICATION

Greetings friends and colaborers of the Lord Jesus Christ!

I am writing to you with an excitement that is beyond words. For I would like to dedicate this book to individuals like yourselves whose desire to grow closer to Jesus and go deeper in the Word of God brings such JOY to my heart. And my prayer for each one of you is that the Holy Spirit will reveal more of Himself to you in this in-depth time of studying the Word of God daily. Jesus said, "Blessed are those who hunger and thirst for righteousness, for they will be satisfied" (Matthew 5:6 NASB). So as you embark on this journey of studying each book of the Bible, may you experience a freshness and a fulfillment that can only come from the Spirit of God. You will have days that you won't want to wake up early and read. There will be moments when life throws you a situation that delays your personal devotional time with Him. But please press in and allow the Holy Spirit to strengthen your every step. This will allow you to exercise your faith muscles and walk out what you are learning in this. From my experience, obedience will bring education to life!

It will be quite a strenuous commitment, yet it's a part of an intentional strategy to equip the saints for His return. And your participation with revive-SCHOOL is a unique part of this preparation.

May the Lord receive all the glory, honor, and fame in this pursuit of righteousness.

Praying,
Dr. Kyle Lance Martin

# Contents

## WEEK 56

## WEEK 57

## WEEK 58

## WEEK 59

**WEEK 64**

**WEEK 65**

**WEEK 66**

**WEEK 67**

# reviveSCHOOL History and Introduction

In January of 2015, our ministry, Time to Revive, was invited from our home base in Richardson, Texas, to Goshen, Indiana, to help equip the local church to learn how to go out and share the gospel in their community. We called it reviveINDIANA. During this frigid first trip in January, our intention was to help facilitate a week of prayer and outreach as a form of training, which we hoped would lead to an intentional week of outreach later that year. Little did we know that God had other plans.

The week of prayer and outreach started with about 450 people from various churches in the community and, to our surprise, quickly swelled to over 3,000. And by the end of that first week, the Holy Spirit confirmed to a group of us, including local pastors, that the Time to Revive team should stay for 52 straight days! Imagine the phone calls we had to make to our spouses telling them we were going to stay a "little" longer.

Over the course of these seven weeks, the local church witnessed God move in mighty ways, and each person involved could tell you miraculous testimonies of how they witnessed, firsthand, how God was moving. The 52 days culminated on March 4 of that year where an estimated 10,000 people showed up to brave the cold temperatures and go out and share the love of Jesus Christ.

All the while, word of this was spreading throughout the state, and it led to the Time to Revive team being invited to seven different cities in Indiana over the course of the next seven months. We continued to witness the local body of believers in these various communities encouraged and equipped to continue to take out their faith and share with others. The gospel wasn't intended to stay only in the church building. Jesus commissioned each one of us to go and make disciples in our own Jerusalem, Judea, and Samaria and to the ends of the earth. Back in Goshen, the local body continued to go out regularly after those initial 52 days while keeping track of the days since that first amazing week. A couple of years later in 2017, the local believers invited our team to celebrate their 1,000th day of outreach in their community. It was during that time when a local man shared with us a dream he had, which led us to start a two-year Bible study in the community. Similar to the Apostle Paul as he taught 12 disciples in Ephesus to study the Word of God on a daily basis, Time to Revive's desire was to also provide in-depth teaching that would focus on where the Messiah is found in every book of the Bible from Genesis to Revelation. We knew this would deepen their commitment to sharing the gospel as well as deepen their relationship with the Lord and with those whom they were discipling.

> But when some became hardened and would not believe, slandering the Way in front of the crowd, he withdrew from them and met separately with the disciples, conducting discussions every day in the lecture hall of Tyrannus. —Acts 19:9

This local Bible study started with 12 men who signed up and committed to study the Word of God in a barn on a county road in Goshen, Indiana. And on January 1, 2018, we launched reviveSCHOOL with 54 men in this initial group. They studied the Scriptures daily, using the online resources, then gathered in the barn to discuss them in person. Each student studied the Bible daily using these resources:

- a Scripture reading plan to stay on track,
- a 29-minute teaching video (by Kyle Lance Martin, Indiana pastors, and TTR teachers),
- a devotion (written by Laura Kim Martin),
- reading guide questions to help facilitate discussion and critical thinking,
- lesson plans to summarize the daily teaching, and
- a painting of each book of the Bible by Mindi Oaten.

Upon the completion of the two-year study in the Word, Time to Revive celebrated over 200 students who had joined reviveSCHOOL with a graduation ceremony in January 2020. Plans were made for these individuals to take the Word and launch reviveSCHOOL groups not only in the United States but also throughout various nations. However, with worldwide travel restrictions due to the COVID-19 pandemic, this travel didn't happen. Thankfully, God had another plan, His plan was "above and beyond" all that Time to Revive could ask or think of (Ephesians 3:20–21).

With all the reviveSCHOOL materials already available online, the Holy Spirit spread the word to pastors and leaders of nations all throughout the world. Believers were hungry for biblically sound teaching and resources to grow closer to the Lord. As exemplified in Acts 19 with Paul and the disciples, and all the people of Asia, the Word of God through reviveSCHOOL truly spread—from a barn in Indiana to the nations.

> And this went on for two years, so that all the inhabitants of Asia, both Jews and Greeks, heard the message about the Lord. —Acts 19:10

By God's grace, reviveSCHOOL has become an outlet for individuals to gain fresh insight into the Messiah all throughout the Scriptures, as well as to develop an understanding of the role of Israel from a biblical perspective.

I am humbled and honored that you would select reviveSCHOOL for your learning. When we started with 12 guys in a Bible study, we had no idea that reviveSCHOOL would be as far reaching as it has become. Our team would delight in knowing that you are studying the Word of God and using the resources with reviveSCHOOL. We pray that through these resources you will grow closer to the Lord and that you are inspired to walk out the plans that God has for your life by exposing others to the love of Christ.

To God be the glory!
Dr. Kyle Lance Martin

For further information about how to sign up for this two-year study in the Word of God or if you would like to launch a reviveSCHOOL group in your community, state/province, or country, please go online to www.reviveSCHOOL.org.

# How to Use this Bible Study Series

The Complete Portrait of the Messiah Bible study series contains multiple components for each lesson. These components work together to provide an in-depth study of how Jesus is revealed throughout the whole of Scripture. Below is a description of each component and how you can use each one to maximize your study experience.

## Teaching Notes and Video Lessons
The teaching notes summarize the main points of each video lesson and include a QR code to access the video teaching. If you have access to the internet via your phone, you can scan the QR code to watch the video lesson.*

## The Daily Word Devotional
Dig deeper into personal application for each lesson through *The Daily Word* devotional. This day-by-day devotional encourages you with thoughts for application and further Scripture readings.

## Reading Guide Questions
These questions will guide you into a more detailed exploration of each lesson's content. Examine the concepts of the daily Scripture readings in more detail.

## The Bible Art Collection
This Bible study series is augmented by a one-of-a-kind, especially inspired series of original artwork created by artist Mindi Oaten. These 66 acrylic paintings creatively depict the revelation of Christ in each book of the Bible. Viewing each of these original art pieces will inspire your understanding and further enrich your understanding of Jesus throughout all of the Scriptures. These can be found at https://www.mindioaten.com/pages/mindi-oaten-art-bible-art-collection or https://www.reviveschool.org/

# About the Cover

*Psalms*
"Our Prayer & Song"

Artist Notes: Mindi Oaten

It was difficult to wrap up the magnitude of Psalms in one painting, so I did the best I could. I tried to create a composition encompassing elements that signify Jesus and our praise to the *King* of kings. The sky is dark and stormy representing lament, as well as sunny and blue representing brighter days in our songs of deliverance and praise. The rock represents Christ as our *Rock* and *Redeemer* with elements of who He is and our response of praise to Him.

## Sky / Landscape / River

"There is a river—its streams delight the city of God, the holy dwelling place of the Most High." (Psalm 46:4)

I wanted the background to reflect God's glory in nature. He is with us in both bright days and darker days. The river was important to show Christ as the living water running through the painting.

## Harp

"Rejoice in the LORD, you righteous ones; praise from the upright is beautiful. Praise the LORD with the lyre; make music to Him with a ten-stringed harp. Sing a new song to Him; play skillfully on the strings, with a joyful shout" (Psalm 33:1–3).

The harp symbolizes songs of praise, prayers that ascend to heaven, and are woven throughout the book. Most people, when they think of Psalms, think of praise and singing to God.

## Blue Birds and the Branches

"The birds of the sky live beside the springs; they sing among the foliage" (Psalm 104:12).

I painted five blue birds to symbolize the five books that make up the Psalms. The birds also symbolize the songs and worship of this collection. Five is often associated with grace.

## The Rock

"The Lord is my rock, my fortress, and my deliverer, my God, my mountain where I seek refuge, my shield and the horn of my salvation, my stronghold" (Psalm 18:2). "He alone is my rock and my salvation, my stronghold; I will never be shaken" (Psalm 62:2).

I prayed about the way to incorporate many of the elements, and I felt it was fitting to place them all on the rock. The rock is mentioned several times in Psalms and represents Jesus Christ, our *Rock* and *Redeemer*.

## Scrolls and Sheet Music

On the rock, I painted the five scrolls (sheet music), another representation of the five books of Psalms.

## Olive Branches

"But I am like a flourishing olive tree in the house of God; I trust in God's faithful love forever and ever" (Psalm 52:8).

Here the olive tree is mentioned as a metaphor (Israel flourished under David, a godly leader). The olive branches I painted are a symbol of the anointing and an element of the garden.

## Gold Horn

"He has raised up a horn for His people, resulting in praise to all His godly ones, to the Israelites, the people close to Him. Hallelujah!" (Psalm 148:14).

The horn symbolizes strength, victory, glory, power, and authority. The horn of His people, the horn of the Lord's *Anointed One*, and the horn of salvation is Yeshua.

> We often see the horn in Scripture as a symbol of salvation. Psalm 18:2 says, "The Lord is my rock and my fortress and my deliverer, my God, my rock, in whom I take refuge, my shield, and the horn of my salvation, my stronghold." In the New Testament, Jesus is the horn of salvation (Luke 1:68–69). Thus, a title applied to Yahweh is also applied to Jesus; they are both called "the horn of salvation."

The very name *Jesus* means "The Lord Is Salvation." The salvation Jesus offers is strong, triumphant, and powerful. Just like the horns on the altar offered refuge and atonement, Jesus offers clemency and cleansing through His death on the cross. However strong our spiritual foe, the horn of our salvation is stronger still. (Got Questions; https://www.gotquestions.org/horn-of-salvation.html)

## Torah

"How happy are those whose way is blameless, who live according to the LORD's instruction!" (Psalm 119:1).

I painted a Torah to show the significance of God's law to the Israelites and how they were to obey and love the law. If you love the Lord, you will want to obey His commands. Psalm 119 is a beautiful poem in reverence of God's law.

## Red Apple

"I call on You, God, because You will answer me; listen closely to me; hear what I say. Display the wonders of Your faithful love, Savior of all who seek refuge from those who rebel against Your right hand. Protect me as the pupil of Your eye; hide me in the shadow of Your wings from the wicked who treat me violently, my deadly enemies who surround me" (Psalm 17:6–9).

I included a red apple that can be viewed as a symbol in two ways: the apple of God's eye (God's love for His children) and the sinful nature of men (referencing the apple in the fall at the beginning of Creation).

## Red Ribbon

"You do not delight in sacrifice and offering; You open my ears to listen. You do not ask for a whole burnt offering or a sin offering. Then I said, 'See, I have come; it is written about me in the volume of the scroll. I delight to do Your will, my God; Your instruction lives within me.' I proclaim righteousness in the great assembly; see, I do not keep my mouth closed—as You know, LORD. I did not hide Your righteousness in my heart; I spoke about Your faithfulness and salvation; I did not conceal Your constant love and truth from the great assembly" (Psalm 40:6–10).

These verses predict that a day will come when Deity will dwell with men. The red ribbon signifies a foreshadowing of the blood of Christ that will be shed for our salvation. We know from the New Testament it is a gift from God, so I chose the ribbon to represent this gift. The blood given as a gift covers or cancels the law; it is fulfilled. We are passed over by the covering from the Messiah who shed his blood for us all.

## Flowers—Messianic Crown

To show the coming messianic kingdom, I painted the crown, as in other paintings, to represent the crown of David's bloodline all the way to Jesus, who will reign as the *Eternal King*. On the crown is the rose of Sharon and the lily of the valley as my flowers from the garden.

*In reviveSCHOOL, the theme name for Jesus in Psalms is *King of Glory*.

# Lesson 1: Job 1

*The Promised Redeemer:* Job and His Family

## Teaching Notes

### Intro

Today we start a new book of the Bible—Job—and a new division of the Bible—the Wisdom Books, or the poetical books. Also, this is our 365th lesson today, so we are exactly halfway through our study. The title of the book bears the name of the major character in the book, Job. MacArthur states, "This name might have been derived from the Hebrew word for *persecution*, thus meaning 'persecuted one,' or from an Arabic word meaning 'repent,' thus bearing the name 'repentant one.'"[1] Throughout this book, we will see the theme of persecution and the need to repent in the process. The author was not Job "because the book's message rests on Job's ignorance of the events that occurred in heaven as they related to his ordeal."[2] Some scholars suggest Moses could have written the book because he spent 40 years in Midian, land adjacent to Uz where Job was living. A second possible author was Solomon because he authored the book of Ecclesiastes, which bear similarities to Job, as well as other Wisdom books. Other possibilities include: Elihu, Isaiah, Hezekiah, Jeremiah, and Ezra.[3]

Some scholars suggest Job is the oldest book in the Bible. MacArthur states the book may have been written well after the events within the book took place based on: (1) Job's age when the book took place (Job 42:16); (2) Job's life lasted 200 years (42:16), which puts him in the patriarchal period; (3) the social unit during Job's time was the patriarchal family; (4) the Chaldeans who murdered Job's servants (1:17) were described as nomads, not city dwellers; (5) Job's wealth was counted in livestock only, not in precious metals (1:3; 42:12); (6) Job served as a priest within his family (1:4–5); and (7) the book is silent on things like the Abrahamic covenant, the nation of Israel, the Exodus journey, and the Law of Moses. MacArthur concludes that "the features found in the book appear to place

---

[1] John MacArthur, *The MacArthur Bible Commentary* (Nashville: Thomas Nelson, 2005), 563.

[2] MacArthur, 563.

[3] MacArthur, 563.

the events chronologically at a time probably after [the Tower of] Babel (Genesis 11:1–9), but before or contemporaneous with Abraham (Genesis 11:27ff.)."[4]

The Wisdom Books include Job, Psalms, Proverbs, Ecclesiastes, and the Song of Songs. These books are not national in intention but are personal in nature. In some of the books, the meaning of life is discussed, while in others the practicality of living life is outlined. Our phrase for the book of Job is *The Promised Redeemer*. Amid Job's pain and suffering, God's promise was to provide a redeemer (Job 19). MacArthur points out that God allows His children to walk in suffering and pain, sometimes as the result of personal sin, sometimes as the process of discipline for strengthening the individual, sometimes as the opportunity to reveal God's comfort and grace in our lives, and sometimes it is just unknowable.[5]

## Teaching

*Job 1:1–5*: Job is introduced in verse 1 as a man from Uz with "perfect integrity, who feared God and turned away from evil." Job's character was impeccable. Uz was in northern Arabia, close to Midian. Job's description does not mean he was perfect, because no human being is perfect (6:24; 7:21; 9:20). Job was wealthy and had been enormously blessed with seven sons and three daughters, a large estate, and thousands of livestock and animals (vv. 2–3a; 42:13). "Job was the greatest man among all the people of the east" (v. 3b). Job's sons would give banquets at their homes and invite their sisters, having family time (v. 4). After each banquet was over, Job would purify his children with burnt offerings, just in case his children had sinned in their hearts (v. 5a). This had become Job's regular practice—to act as a priest for the family (v. 5b).

*Job 1:6–12*: The "sons of God" were angelic hosts who reported to God on their ministries around the world (v. 6). *Nelson's Commentary* describes the sons of God as "a heavenly council over which the Lord sits as Supreme King."[6] There is the image here of a courtroom. Satan, a fallen angel, came with them, so he had not yet faced his final banishment from God's court.[7] God asked Satan where he had come from, and Satan said he had been roaming through the earth and walking on it (v. 7). MacArthur states that, "Emboldened by the success he had with the unfallen Adam in paradise, [Satan] was confident that the fear of God in Job, one of the fallen race, would not stand his tests, for he had fallen himself."[8] Obviously,

---

[4] MacArthur, 563.

[5] MacArthur, 565.

[6] Earl D. Radmacher, Ronald B. Allen, and H. Wayne House, eds., *Nelson's New Illustrated Bible Commentary* (Nashville: Thomas Nelson, 1999), 616.

[7] Radmacher et al., 616.

[8] MacArthur, 569.

God knew where Satan had been and what he had been doing. God presented his servant Job to Satan as a man of perfect integrity who turns away from evil (v. 8). Satan asked, "Does Job fear God for nothing?" (v. 9). Satan pointed out that Job had good reason to fear God because God had blessed him so abundantly (v. 10). Satan challenged God to take everything away from Job, and then he would see Job curse the Lord (v. 11). God put everything Job owned under Satan's power, but would not let him touch Job himself (v. 12). Satan left to confront Job. In this courtroom setting, Job didn't even know that his life was being discussed by God's council. Four disasters were about to quickly come Job's way.

*Job 1:13–19*: Satan's goal is to always take people's vision and perspective off of the Lord. Job's sons and daughters were at another banquet (v. 13), and a messenger came to Job and reported the Sabeans had taken away the oxen and donkeys in the field and killed all the servants except the messenger (vv. 14–15). Then, a second messenger came while the first was still speaking and reported that lightning struck from heaven and burned up the sheep and all the servants except for him (v. 16).

Then, a third messenger came while the second was still speaking and reported that the Chaldeans had taken away the camels and killed the servants (v. 17). Then, a fourth messenger came while the third messenger was speaking and reported that Job's sons and daughters were killed in the oldest brother's house when a powerful wind collapsed the house upon them, and he alone had escaped (vv. 18–19).

*Job 1:20–22*: Job tore his robe and shaved his head in mourning, but he fell to the ground and worshipped the Lord, acknowledging that everything he had was God's to give and to take away (vv. 20–21). "Throughout all this Job did not sin or blame God for anything" (v. 22).

## Closing

We are to submit to trials and still worship God, not because we know the "why" but because God wills them for His own reasons.

### The Daily Word

Job lived in the country of Uz and was known as the greatest man among all the people of the East. He feared God, turned from evil, and lived with perfect integrity. As Satan roamed the earth, he asked God for permission to attack Job. The Lord granted his request but restricted Satan from laying a hand on Job himself. So Satan brought four specific disasters that resulted in the destruction of Job's animals, his servants, and even his children. In the midst of this great suffering, Job fell to the ground and worshipped God: "The Lord gives, and the Lord takes away. Praise the name of Yahweh." Through this testing, Job continued to walk in integrity, without sin, and did not blame the Lord for anything.

As believers, you will endure suffering. Even today, the enemy prowls, seeking to steal, kill, and destroy. When you lay with your face to the ground, crying out to the Lord in pain and agony, the Lord promises He is with you. God gives you a reason to hope in the midst of disaster. Keep your eyes on *the Promised Redeemer, Jesus Christ.* The Lord gives and takes away. Even so, will you continue to say, "Praise the name of the Lord"? Choose to praise the Lord even in the midst of suffering. Yes, it's painful, but choose hope moment by moment. The Lord promises He will personally restore, establish, strengthen, and support you after your season of suffering. Hold on to His promises.

**Naked I came from my mother's womb, and naked I will leave this life. The LORD gives, and the Lord takes away. Praise the name of Yahweh. Throughout all this Job did not sin or blame God for anything. —Job 1:21–22**

Further Scripture: 1 Samuel 2:6–7; 1 Peter 1:6–7; 5:10; 1 Peter 5:10

## Questions

1. As a parent, what did Job do in Job 1:5? If you are a parent, how do you intercede on behalf of your children?

2. When the angels or "sons of God" came to present themselves to the Lord, God asked Satan where he had come from. Since God is omniscient (all-knowing), why did He ask?

3. Satan told the Lord he came from roaming about on the earth and walking around on it. According to 1 Peter 5:8, what is Satan doing as he roams?

4. Describe whether it seems out of character for God to bring up Job for Satan to consider.

5. How did Job respond when he lost his wealth and offspring within a few hours? How does this reveal Job's character? How do you respond when things go badly, and what does your response reveal about your character?

6. What did the Holy Spirit highlight to you in Job 1 through the reading or the teaching?

# Lesson 2: Job 2—3

*The Promised Redeemer*: Satan's Second Test

## Teaching Notes

### Intro

The phrase for the book of Job is *The Promised Redeemer*. Some say Job is the oldest book in the Bible, having possibly been written before Moses wrote the five books of the Law. Chronologically, it takes place just after the Tower of Babel in Genesis 11 and before or during the time of Abraham in Genesis 12. In chapter 1, Job was hit by four devastating disasters. Two of the disasters came from earth; enemies who raided his herds and killed his servants. Two of the disasters came from heaven in the form of a lightning storm and a powerful wind that killed animals, servants, and his children. As a result of the four disasters, he lost everything he possessed—his livestock, his servants, and even his seven sons and three daughters. At the end of Job 1, Job responded to these disasters with these words: "The LORD gives, and the LORD takes away. Praise the name of Yahweh" (v. 21). Despite his pain and his suffering, Job still recognized God was in charge. MacArthur points out that God allows His children to walk in suffering and pain, sometimes as the result of personal sin, sometimes as the process of discipline for strengthening the individual, sometimes as the opportunity to reveal God's comfort and grace in our lives, and sometimes it is just unknowable.[1] In the courtroom setting of Job 1, Satan was given permission to take away the things Job owned, but he was not allowed to touch or harm Job in any way. Chapter 1 concludes with these words: "Throughout all this Job did not sin or blame God for anything" (v. 22). That gives us the transition into chapter 2 where the conversation between God and Satan about Job continues, and Job will remain unaware of the battle being fought over him.

### Teaching

*Job 2:1–10*: Again, the sons of God came before the Lord, and Satan came with them (v. 1). God asked Satan where he had been, and Satan responded just as

---

[1] John MacArthur, *The MacArthur Bible Commentary* (Nashville: Thomas Nelson, 2005), 563.

he had in chapter 1—from roaming and walking on the earth (v. 2). God again brought Satan's attention to His servant Job and pointed out that Job had retained his integrity, even though he had been attacked by Satan "without just cause" (v. 3). *Nelson's Commentary* explains, "'Without cause' translates the same Hebrew word Satan used in insinuating that Job did not serve God 'for nothing.'"[2]

Job remained the same person he had been, despite what had happened to him in this season of his life. This is really the question for all of us—do we remain the same people we've always been when things are good or when we go through a difficult, even disastrous season? Do we find a coping mechanism that we do not want anyone else to know about? Or do we turn to the Lord and worship Him in all things? Satan constantly comes against us to "steal, kill, and destroy" (John 10:10) and to take our eyes off God.

*Nelson's Commentary* provides these characteristics of Satan. Satan remains accountable to God and he is not all-powerful. He is a created being and does not have the ability to be in more than one place at a time, so he must depend on other fallen angels to help him do his work on earth. Further, Satan cannot read our minds or know our futures. In fact, "Satan can do nothing without God's permission,"[3] and God will not permit us to "be tempted beyond what [we] are able" (1 Corinthians 10:13). In Job 42, God delivered Job because God will always find a way out for us—through *The Promised Redeemer*.

Satan pushed again, crying out "Skin for skin!" Satan said Job would not keep his integrity if his body was struck down (vv. 4–5). *Nelson's Commentary* explains the phrase "Skin for skin" may have come from "the practice of bartering animal skins . . . [or] the phrase is similar to the proverb 'life for life, eye for eye, tooth for tooth.'"[4] God gave His permission again but told Satan he could not take Job's life (v. 6). Satan left the Lord and infected Job with painful boils from the top of his head to the bottom of his feet (v. 7). Job sat among the ashes and used a broken pottery shard to scrape the boils (v. 8). Wiersbe points out that the symptoms were horrific: "Severe itching (Job 2:8), insomnia (7:4), running sores and scabs (7:5), nightmares (7:13–14), bad breath (19:17), weight loss (19:20), chills and fever (21:6), diarrhea (30:27), and blackened skin (30:30)."[5]

Wiersbe points out that four different voices were heard in Job 2—3. First was "the voice of the accuser," to whom, sadly, we give too much credence and

---

[2] Earl D. Radmacher, Ronald B. Allen, and H. Wayne House, eds., *Nelson's New Illustrated Bible Commentary* (Nashville: Thomas Nelson, 1999), 618.

[3] Radmacher et al., 617.

[4] Radmacher et al., 618.

[5] Warren W. Wiersbe, *Be Patient: Waiting on God in Difficult Times* (Colorado Springs: David C. Cook, 1991), 22–23.

power and see ourselves as victims (2:1–8).[6] The second voice was "the voice of the quitter"[7] (2:9) and belonged to Job's wife who told him he should curse God and die. Job responded that she spoke foolishly because he could not accept good from God without also accepting the adversity (2:10a). Again, Job did not sin in what he said (2:10b).

*Job 2:11–13*: The third voice was "the voice of the mourners" (2:11–13) who were Job's three friends.[8] The friends heard what had happened to Job and came to see him and comfort him (v. 11). From a distance, they barely recognized Job. The friends wept aloud, tore their robes, and threw dust into the air and on their heads in response (v. 12). The friends sat with him for seven days and nights without speaking because Job's suffering was so intense (v. 13).

The three friends were Eliphaz, Bildad, and Zophar. Eliphaz was the eldest, his speeches in the book were longer and more mature, and he heard directly from God. Eliphaz was either from Edom or Arabia. Bildad was the second oldest and was possibly related to Shuah, Abraham's youngest son (Genesis 25:2). Zophar, the youngest of the three, possibly came from the Judean town of Naamah[9] Constable asked, "How many friends do you have that would travel a long distance to visit you in an illness and sit with you silently for seven days out of respect for your pain?"[10]

## Closing

At this point in the story, the voices of the accuser and the quitter were not good. But the voices of the mourners, Job's friends, were good. They cared for Job and came to comfort him and care for him. This should be the mentality of the body of Christ—that people's needs are being met and that people are being cared for. They sat in silence for seven days, just to be there for him. In Job 3, the fourth voice was heard—"the voice of the sufferer."[11] It is OK to voice how we are feeling when we suffer. Regardless of the symptoms, God will give us people who will walk through these times with us and who will listen to our voices during the journey.

---

[6] Wiersbe, 22.

[7] Wiersbe, 23.

[8] Wiersbe, 24.

[9] Thomas L. Constable, *Expository Notes of Dr. Thomas Constable: Job*, 30, https://planobiblechapel.org/tcon/notes/pdf/job.pdf.

[10] Constable, 31.

[11] Wiersbe, 25.

## The Daily Word

Again, the Lord gave Satan permission to attack Job. This time Satan could strike Job physically as long as he spared Job's life. Satan thought Job would surely curse God when his body was attacked with boils from top to bottom. However, Job proved Satan wrong. Through this attack, Job pressed on, living with integrity. He said to his wife, who wanted him to curse God, "Should we accept only good from God and not adversity?" In contrast, Job's three friends traveled to spend time with Job. Upon seeing their good friend in great agony, the friends wept together and sat with Job in silence for seven days.

When you see someone suffering, it can be awkward when you don't know exactly what to do or say. You can be the voice of an accuser, saying: "Go ahead and quit, you have every right to give up." Or you can be a sympathetic voice—a friend who sits with someone else in their pain. You may not know what to do for your friend going through cancer, a job loss, or depression. Sometimes you get stuck and just don't do anything. Today, *ask the Lord for wisdom*. He may just lead you to sit in silence in your car outside their home and pray for them. Or perhaps you give them a hug and sit in the hospital waiting room in silence. Any act of kindness is an expression of God's love. Today, go and show kindness to someone the Lord places on your heart.

**Then they sat on the ground with him seven days and nights, but no one spoke a word to him because they saw that his suffering was very intense. —Job 2:13**

Further Scripture: Job 2:11; Proverbs 17:17; Colossians 3:12

## Questions

1. In Job 2:9, how did Job's wife react to his suffering? Why do you think she reacted this way?

2. In Job 3:13, 17–18, Job described death with these descriptions: quiet, restful, and at ease. Job 3:26 (NASB) contrasts this with his present state: "I am not at ease, nor am I quiet, and I am not at rest, but turmoil comes." Do you think Job had an inaccurate view of death? When you have dealt with suffering, have you felt like Job? Or how might you have viewed things differently?

3. Job mentioned the thing he feared had come upon him, and what he dreaded had befallen him. Explain whether you think Satan knew what Job feared and attacked in that way or if you think Job's statement was a generalization.

4. What did the Holy Spirit highlight to you in Job 2—3 through the reading or the teaching?

# Lesson 3: Job 4

*The Promised Redeemer:* Eliphaz Speaks

## Teaching Notes

### Intro

The Lord gave Satan permission to attack everything belonging to Job in chapter 1. Later, Satan was given permission to attack Job's health. In spite of his health troubles and everything he lost, Job refused to turn away from God. Job's wife tried to convince him to turn away from God. Job's friends came and sat with him in silence for seven days because they saw how much he suffered. Finally, Job vented to his friends in chapter 3 who sat and listened. Job 4 is the first speech of one of Job's friends. These speeches will make up much of the rest of the book, and we will see Job's relationship with his friends take a bit of a turn. Who were Job's friends?

1. Eliphaz—served as something of a mystic. He spoke with the most respect and restraint. Eliphaz's speeches were based on his understanding of God as an "inflexible lawgiver."
2. Bildad—functioned as an attorney. Bildad was very direct in what he said and was less courteous than Eliphaz.
3. Zophar—functioned more dogmatically. Zophar was blunt and came across harshly, "like a schoolmaster addressing a group of ignorant freshmen."[1]

### Teaching

*Job 4:1–4:* While a counselor is meant to comfort and listen to the heart, Bildad tried to heal Job's heart with logic. Bildad never dealt with Job's feelings and, as a result, did not show love to Job. None of Job's friends will demonstrate love to him. Instead, they will show themselves to be religious guys who wanted to show Job how much they knew. They failed to live out Ephesians 4:15: "But speaking the truth in love, let us grow in every way into Him who is the head—Christ."

---

[1] Warren W. Wiersbe, *Be Patient: Waiting on God in Difficult Times* (Colorado Springs: David C. Cook, 1991), 31–32.

These verses show us Eliphaz's approach to Job's situation. Eliphaz practiced a kind of "reprimand sandwich." He began with a compliment, brought his criticism, then softened it at the end.[2] Eliphaz tried to be positive and gentle while complimenting what Job had done for others. One of Eliphaz's compliments to Job was about how Job had helped people who were struggling, probably by offering encouragement. Wiersbe observed, "The right words, spoken at the right time, and with the right motive, can make a tremendous difference in the lives of others,"[3] and that was exactly what Job had done.

*Job 4:5–11*: After he complimented Job for his past actions, Eliphaz now brought his accusation against Job.[4] Eliphaz's first question to Job in verses 5–6 implied that if Job had been living a godly life then he would have nothing to fear from God. In Eliphaz's mind, Job could only have suffered all his calamities if he brought them on himself through sin. Each of Job's friends will make a similar argument. For them, any explanation for Job's situation, except that he had sinned and brought it on himself, was unthinkable.

Old Testament Scholar Kent Hughes outlined four signs of Eliphaz's bad theology:

1. Eliphaz believed "God is absolutely in control." In principle, we agree with this idea. But the way Eliphaz built on it would become a problem.
2. Eliphaz believed "God was absolutely just and fair." The problem with Eliphaz's second belief was that God's idea of fairness may not match ours.
3. Eliphaz believed "God always punished wickedness and blessed righteousness." According to Eliphaz's theology, if God ever failed to punish wickedness or bless righteousness, He would be unjust. This is where the points of Eliphaz's theology went bad. God does not always have to punish wickedness nor does He always have to bless righteousness.
4. Eliphaz believed that if a person suffered, he/she must have sinned and was being punished justly for that sin.[5]

The judgment Eliphaz expected for a person's sin could come upon the sinner gradually like a crop that was planted (v. 8) or quickly like a storm or an attack from a lion (vv. 9–11), but judgment for sin would surely come.[6] Yes, these

[2] Wiersbe, 35.

[3] Wiersbe, 36.

[4] Wiersbe, 36.

[5] Christopher Ash, *Job: The Wisdom of the Cross*, Preaching the Word, ed. R. Kent Hughes (Wheaton, IL: Crossway, 2014), 90.

[6] Wiersbe, 36.

things can be true. God can punish a person for sin and that punishment could come either gradually or quickly. We could be attacked suddenly as though a lion attacked us, so we should regularly ask the Lord for protection (Psalm 91).

*Job 4:12–21*: Now Eliphaz brought Job his argument.[7] The "word . . . brought to me in secret" (v. 12) could have been a vision of some kind, but we don't know from where the message came. Eliphaz described the circumstances around this vision in verses 13–15 in an attempt to build credibility for his point. Eliphaz then described a message from "a figure" that stood before him in the night (vv. 16–21). This figure spoke a message to Eliphaz pointing out that God put "no trust" in angels and asked why He would then trust men who were much weaker.

Eliphaz did not tell the whole story about God and men. Yes, mankind is feeble and limited, especially in comparison to God or angels. But Eliphaz left off the final compliment in his reprimand sandwich. He started with encouragement, he brought his criticism, then he failed to point out that mankind was made in God's image. He failed to point out that the God who made himself and Job is a God of grace and justice. It seemed like Eliphaz just wanted to vent and one-up Job in an attempt to prove himself right.

## Closing

Eliphaz approached his suffering friend in an overly religious spirit. In the midst of Job's suffering, Eliphaz could only deal with the situation in a logical way. Instead of showing love to his suffering friend, Eliphaz was more concerned with proving himself right and justifying his own theology. We cannot heal the heart with logic, only with love. We are to speak "the truth in love" (Ephesians 4:15). This approach is always concerned with helping the other person love God more and not concerned with proving ourselves right. Eliphaz felt that if he was always right, then God would always bless him. But this is simply not true.

## The Daily Word

After seven days of sitting with Job in his misery, the first of Job's three friends spoke up. Eliphaz brought accusations and arguments against Job because of what had happened to him. As the first to speak, Eliphaz had an agenda. Instead of conveying brotherly love, Eliphaz spoke out of his own wisdom.

You may see things frwom a different perspective as you observe a friend going through a time of suffering. However, as a friend, truly seek the heart of the Lord for wisdom before blurting out what you think about the situation.

---

[7] Wiersbe, 36.

*Be slow to speak.* Then, when you do say something, speak from a pure heart, not with ulterior motives. Ask the Lord to help you communicate truth in love at the proper time. Your friend may not be ready to hear the insight you feel you have from the Lord, so pray. Pray for your suffering friend. Ask the Lord to cover your words of truth in His love. Ask the Lord to confirm your words to your friend with a supporting Scripture. Above all, walk it out in obedience, and trust the Holy Spirit to move in ways beyond human words.

**In my experience, those who plow injustice and those who sow trouble reap the same. —Job 4:8**

Further Scripture: Ephesians 4:15, 29; 1 Peter 1:22

## Questions

1. Do you think Job 4:12–14 refers to a vision Eliphaz had? If so, was it from God?

2. In Job 4:15, Eliphaz spoke of a spirit that had passed before him. Where do you believe this spirit came from? Was it from God, Satan, or the flesh?

3. Was Eliphaz implying that good and innocent people never suffer in Job 4:7 (Psalm 73; Luke 16:19–31)?

4. Do you believe people are punished for their sins (Numbers 27:12–14; 2 Samuel 12:11–14)? If so, has God ever punished you for something you did wrong?

5. What did the Holy Spirit highlight to you in Job 4 through the reading or the teaching?

# Lesson 4: Job 5—6

*The Promised Redeemer*: Job Responded

## Teaching Notes

### Intro

Job is considered one of the oldest books of the Bible and is classified as wisdom literature. Job is filled with practical information about how to navigate a difficult situation. The primary question of the book of Job is, "Do you depend on the Lord in the midst of suffering?" But Job also raises the question of why we experience suffering. Some say it's because of sin, others for disciplining, still others consider suffering an opportunity for God to show us His grace and comfort.

In yesterday's lesson, Eliphaz, one of Job's three friends who came to visit him when he heard Job had lost everything and that his health had also been taken from him, began to respond to Job's venting about his situation in chapter 3. In the first part of his response, Eliphaz stated his belief that God punishes the wicked but rewards the righteous, implying Job experienced his calamity because of his own personal sin. In today's lesson, Eliphaz continues his first response to Job, and Job begins his response. However, *Nelson's Commentary* pointed out, "The dialogue is not so much a conversation between friends as it is a speech contest."[1]

### Teaching

*Job 6:1–7*: This section highlights Job's reasons for complaining.[2] Job pointed out he had lost everything: his family, his possessions, and his health. Now Job's situation is a perfect picture of Proverbs 27:3: "A stone is heavy and sand, a burden, but aggravation from a fool outweighs them both." Eliphaz was a fool. Job having to deal with him was a much heavier burden than Job's actual sufferings. Eliphaz, and later all of Job's friends, did not feel the heaviness of his suffering.[3]

---

[1] Earl D. Radmacher, Ronald B. Allen, and H. Wayne House, eds., *Nelson's New Illustrated Bible Commentary* (Nashville: Thomas Nelson, 1999), 620.

[2] Thomas L. Constable, *Expository Notes of Dr. Thomas Constable: Job*, 43, https://planobiblechapel.org/tcon/notes/pdf/job.pdf .

[3] Warren W. Wiersbe, *Be Patient: Waiting on God in Difficult Times* (Colorado Springs: David Cook, 1991), 39.

Job modeled the type of dependence on God during suffering that Jesus encouraged (Matthew 11:28–29). This attitude was the opposite of Eliphaz.

Job described his feelings as "the arrows of the Almighty have pierced me" (v. 4). Arrows can be symbolic of judgment. Job's use of this imagery might indicate he had been somewhat influenced by Eliphaz's belief that God always punishes wickedness and always rewards righteousness, at least temporarily. Job's heaviness in his suffering had turned into bitterness in suffering.[4] He listed a variety of foods that were tasteless before concluding, "I refuse to touch them; they are like contaminated food" (v. 7). *Nelson's Commentary* notes that this statement was a rejection of Eliphaz's "tasteless counsel."[5]

*Job 6:8–13*: This section highlights Job's desperate condition. Wiersbe noted that Job's language conveyed a sense of hopelessness.[6] Job expressed his desire for God to "crush me" and "cut me off" (v. 9). At this point in Job's suffering, this "would still bring me comfort" (v. 10). Job had not denied God, but neither could he deny his level of suffering. *Nelson's Commentary* observes that Job was "more concerned to preserve his relationship with the Holy One than for God to remove his pain and anguish through death."[7] A shift began to occur in Job's speech beginning in verse 11. Job shifted from responding to Eliphaz to speaking a prayer.

*Job 6:14–23*: Job expressed his disappointment with his friends. Job compared his friends to a wadi, a streambed that was full in the rainy season but completely dry in the summer.[8] Like travelers who passed by these wadis in the summer and were frustrated to find them completely dry, Job's friends frustrated him by failing to offer him relief from his suffering with their words and actions. Leonard Ravenhill said, "You can have all of your doctrines right—yet still not have the presence of God."[9] Somewhere along the way, Job's friends allowed their relationship with God to become more about law, regulations, and rules rather than the Lord Himself. Their hearts grew far from Him, and they dried up. Job's friends needed to return to the Lord and allow Him to fill them (Jeremiah 24:7; Zechariah 1:3; James 4:8). However, at this point, they did not know the Lord was not with them, similar to Samson not realizing the Lord had left him (Judges 16:20).

---

[4] Wiersbe, 39.

[5] Radmacher et al., 621.

[6] Wiersbe, 39.

[7] Radmacher et al., 621.

[8] Constable, 44.

[9] Leonard Ravenhill (@DailyRavenhill), "You can have all of your doctrines right," Twitter, December 21, 2015, 4:49 a.m., https://twitter.com/dailyravenhill/status/678889975564382209.

*Job 6:24–30*: Job asked his friends to teach him, to help him understand what he did wrong. He demonstrated incredible humility to his friends who had insulted him, but he also reminded them that his "righteousness is still the issue" (v. 29). Job implied he could discern whether the disaster that came upon him was the result of his own sin in the same way he could distinguish different tastes on his tongue (v. 30).[10]

## Closing

Job was not passive aggressive as he expressed his disappointment with his friends. During his suffering, Job found his friends to be dry with nothing to offer him instead of a refreshing spring in the midst of a desert. If you find yourself dry before the Lord, return to Him. Allow Him to fill you so that you have something to offer others.

---

### The Daily Word

Job responded honestly to his friend Eliphaz. He shared that he was indeed suffering. Because Job was suffering, he was weighed down and heavy-laden. He admitted the boils on his body caused him pain. And yet, despite feeling the bitterness of suffering, despite not agreeing with his friend's response, *Job turned to the Lord in prayer.*

Sometimes it's hard to admit you carry heavy burdens. It's difficult to be vulnerable with family and friends and admit, "I am weary and worried." This admission requires honesty and humility. However, as a believer, you walk with a Savior, a King, and a Friend named Jesus who reaches out His hand and says, "Come to Me, all of you who are weary and burdened, and I will give you rest." Jesus says, "I am your rest." Friend, rest in Jesus. First, admit your burden. Take a deep breath in and breathe out. As you breathe out, say, "God, take this burden from me. I'm worn out from carrying it. I trust You to carry it for me." Now, lift your hands in the air with your palms up as a sign of releasing the burden. He's got it. He is able to carry it, and He is able to equip you with grace and power to walk through this season. *Rest in Him.*

**If only my grief could be weighed and my devastation placed with it in the scales. For then it would outweigh the sand of the seas! That is why my words are rash. —Job 6:2–3**

Further Scripture: Psalm 62:5–8; 91:1–2; Matthew 11:28–30

---

[10] Constable, 45.

## Questions

1. Do you feel like Eliphaz spoke arrogantly and acted as though he knew everything about God in Job 5 (1 Corinthians 13:12)?

2. Eliphaz said, "We have investigated this, and it is true" (Job 5:27). Who do you think he was referring to when he said, "We"?

3. Job was clearly angry with Eliphaz in chapter 6 for accusing him of sin without naming what he had done wrong. What did Jesus say about this (Matthew 7:3; Romans 12:15)?

4. Is it possible Eliphaz was afraid that what happened to Job might happen to him because of some hidden sin in his own life (Romans 6:21)? Was Job's dilemma a result of sin in his life, as his friends assumed? Have you ever been guilty of finding fault in someone else while overlooking the sin in your own life?

5. What did the Holy Spirit highlight to you in Job 5—6 through the reading or the teaching?

# Lesson 5: Job 7—8

*The Promised Redeemer*: The Threat of Traditions

## Teaching Notes

### Intro

So far, we have looked at Job's suffering and a lot of people who were not OK with Job's suffering. Job didn't like the suffering either, but he wanted everyone to understand that his suffering was not necessarily because he had sinned. Job's friends were some who were more vocal about why they thought he was in the situation he was in. So far, we've already looked at his friend Eliphaz's response. Job then responded to Eliphaz in chapters 6—7. Next, Job's second friend, Bildad, addressed Job. Our phrase for Job is *The Promised Redeemer*, and that promise will get Job out of the situation he had been drawn into.

### Teaching

*Job 8:1–7*: Bildad, a relative of Abraham, charged Job of being a "blow-hard."[1] *Nelson's Commentary* explains Bildad's comment as telling Job he was "full of hot air."[2] Bildad could not accept that Job was receiving anything from God that he did not deserve (vv. 1–3). Bildad stated Job's children had been punished because they had rebelled against God (v. 4). These words had to have been shocking to Job, who had done everything to guard his children's walk with God. Bullock points out, "Obviously the friends' theology was far more important than Job."[3] Then Bildad told him to do two things—earnestly seek God asking for His mercy and be pure and upright so God would restore his prosperity (vv. 5–7). This again shows Bildad's bad theology, believing that if Job did certain things, God would automatically bless him because of what he had done.

---

[1] Thomas L. Constable, *Expository Notes of Dr. Thomas Constable: Job*, 48, https://planobiblechapel.org/tcon/notes/pdf/job.pdf.

[2] Earl D. Radmacher, Ronald B. Allen, and H. Wayne House, eds., *Nelson's New Illustrated Bible Commentary* (Nashville: Thomas Nelson, 1999), 622.

[3] C. Hassell Bullock, *An Introduction to the Poetic Books of the Old Testament* (Chicago: Moody, 1979), 34.

*Job 8:8–10*: Bildad then moved on to support his argument with evidence from history. Bildad pointed to the earlier generation and what their fathers had discovered (v. 8). Yet Bildad acknowledged that he knew nothing (v. 9). *Nelson's Commentary* points out how little Bildad really knew and states, "One purpose of the Book of Job is to challenge the traditional dogmas of the past—particularly the retribution dogma."[4]

What does Scripture say about tradition? Traditions are not bad as long as they are based on Christ.

- Stand firm and hold to traditions (2 Thessalonians 2:15).
- See to it that no one takes you captive by philosophizing (Colossians 2:8).
- Why break a commandment for the sake of tradition (Matthew 15:3)?
- We remember Christ in everything and maintain traditions (1 Corinthians 11:2).
- For the sake of your tradition, you made void the Word of God (Matthew 15:6).
- Hold to the tradition of the elders (Mark 7:3–9).

Regarding traditions, "Bildad's position is that what is true is not new, and what is new is not true."[5] Historian Jaroslav Pelikan explains, "Tradition is the living faith of the dead; traditionalism is the dead faith of the living."[6] What does it look like to have truth over tradition? God's truth trumps man's traditions:

1. Jesus' claims outweighed man's authority (John 7:48–49). The Pharisees didn't believe in who Jesus was.
2. Jesus' deeds (such as casting out demons) outraged the religious rulers (Matthew 12:23–24).
3. Jesus was a threat to their religious system (John 2:13–17). He showed that threat when He flipped over the tables in the temple.
4. Jesus was a threat to the religious system's way of life.
5. The people Jesus socialized with outraged the religious rulers (Matthew 11:19; Luke 7:39).
6. Jesus had a lack of respect for their traditions (Mark 3:4–5).

---

[4] Radmacher et al., 623.

[5] Samuel Rolles Driver and George Buchanan Gray, *A Critical and Exegetical Commentary on the Book of Job*, International Critical Commentary Series (Edinburgh: T&T Clark, 1921), 78.

[6] Warren W. Wiersbe, *Be Patient: Waiting on God in Difficult Times* (Colorado Springs: David C. Cook, 1991), 47.

Job is an incredible foreshadow of the coming Christ.

*Job 8:11–18*: Bildad used a series of illustrations from nature to support his understanding of how God punishes the wicked and blesses the righteous (vv. 11–12). Each was dependent upon an outside source to thrive. Bildad pointed out that the godless would perish because they had forgotten they needed God (v. 13). The one who forgets God tries to trust a fragile spider web that is not strong enough to support him (vv. 14–15). Then Bildad compared Job to a well-watered plant who abandoned everything to which he had been rooted and now did not know God (vv. 16–18). Implied in these verses is that Job was depending upon his possessions instead of God.

*Job 8:19–22*: Regardless of all Job had experienced, Bildad pointed out there was hope of God's blessing (v. 19). But then Bildad placed judgment on Job, stating God would never reject a person of integrity (v. 20). Throughout his experiences, Job had clung to the fact he was a man of integrity. Yet God could still bring joy into Job's life (v. 21), and Job's enemies would be clothed with shame (v. 22).

## Closing

Constable writes, "People with problems get little help from rigid, closed-minded Bildads who refuse to reevaluate their theories in the light of new evidence but simply reaffirm traditional answers. We must always stay open to new evidence, new insights, and the possibility that not only we ourselves but those we follow may have interpreted the facts incorrectly."[7] Anderson explains, "Bildad's assertion that God will not reject a blameless man makes him the precursor of those who mocked Jesus with the same logic: 'He trusts in God; let God deliver him' (Matthew 27:43). Job has a lesser Calvary, and each person has his own. But when we know about God's rejection of Jesus, our dereliction can never again be as dark as Job's."[8] Be careful of the Bildads.

## The Daily Word

Bildad examined Job's season through the lens of tradition. Without really knowing what caused Job's pain and suffering, Bildad responded with the traditional thought: *If you earnestly seek God, then ask Him for mercy. If you are pure and upright, then God will respond.* Bildad implied that because God wasn't releasing Job from the pain, then something must be wrong with Job. Job responded to

[7] Constable, 51.

[8] Francis I. Andersen, *Job*, Tyndale Old Testament Commentaries (Leicester, UK, and Downers Grove, IL: InterVarsity Press, 1976), 142–43.

Bildad's reasoning by proclaiming God as a sovereign God. Sometimes both the blameless and the wicked endure pain and disaster. Even so, all things point back to God. He alone is God, and He alone is sovereign.

Allow Bildad's response to serve as a reminder to not get stuck in tradition looking at every situation the same. Each painful situation will not always make sense. It may not always fit in a specific category. *And yet God remains in control.* He sees the heart. He sees the motives. He carries all understanding. In the New Testament, God sent the Holy Spirit to guide, counsel, and grant you understanding. Therefore, as you walk through life upholding Scripture to be true, also seek the Holy Spirit for help in each situation. As the Holy Spirit moves in your life, He will grant you patience and wisdom for His glory and for lives to enter His kingdom. In each new situation, ask the Lord for help and guidance, and trust Him to lead you in all your ways.

**For ask the previous generation, and pay attention to what their fathers discovered, since we were born only yesterday and know nothing. Our days on earth are but a shadow. —Job 8:8–9**

Further Scripture: Mark 7:5; John 16:13; Colossians 2:8

## Questions

1. By chapter 7, Job had asked to die, and now he felt like there was no purpose. No one else has been tested as Job was. Do you think his tests and trials were for our benefit also? Why or why not?

2. Have you ever been to such a low point in your life that you felt completely hopeless and that God had forsaken you? What was the outcome? What got you through that time?

3. In Job 7:17, Job asked "What is man, that You think so highly of him?" Where else do we hear the same question being asked (Psalm 8:4)? What do you think the answer is to that question?

4. In Job 8, Bildad spoke to Job. Do you think he was being a good friend to Job? Why or why not?

5. In Ephesians 4:29, we are told to speak only that which will build up and not tear down. After reading Job 8, do you feel Bildad is a good example of that verse? What do you think the issue was for Bildad and Job's other friends (Isaiah 55:8–9)? Do you have friends like Bildad? Who could you reach out to and encourage today?

6. What did the Holy Spirit highlight to you in Job 7—8 through the reading or the teaching?

# Lesson 6: Job 9—10

*The Promised Redeemer:* Needing a Mediator

## Teaching Notes

### Intro

Mindi's painting for the book of Job is darker than some of the others. It definitely directs us to the suffering Job experienced and how we question why bad things happen to us. It also points us to the phrase for the book—*The Promised Redeemer.* Amid the storm, there is always hope. We have already seen Job's friends with him. Today, we'll be focusing on Bildad's explanation of what was happening to Job and Job's response to Bildad in chapters 9—10.

### Teaching

*Job 9:1–13*: Job acknowledged Bildad made some good points (vv. 1–2).[1] However, Job pointed out that anyone taken to court before God would be unable to answer God's charges even once out of a thousand times (v. 3), because God is wise and all-powerful (v. 4). Job said no one had ever opposed God and come out unharmed. Zuck gives four reasons why Job felt it was useless to take God to court: (1) God is so mighty (9:3–14); (2) God could ignore his cries and be against him (9:15–19); (3) God has the power to destroy both the innocent and the wicked (9:20–24); (4) and even if Job tried to forget his problems or confess his sins, God would still find him guilty (9:25–32).[2] Job continued by describing God's power to move mountains without their knowledge and to shake the earth to its core (vv. 5–6). God has power over the sun and the stars, over the heavens and the waves of the sea, and over the constellations in the sky (vv. 7–9). God does unbelievable things that fill us with wonder (v. 10). God passes by us, but we don't recognize Him and cannot stop Him from doing anything (vv. 11–12). God also does not hold back His anger and can cause people to cringe in fear (v. 13).

---

[1] Earl D. Radmacher, Ronald B. Allen, and H. Wayne House, *Nelson's New Illustrated Bible Commentary* (Nashville: Thomas Nelson, 1999), 623.

[2] Roy B. Zuck, *Job*, Everyman's Bible Commentary (Chicago: Moody, 1978), 47.

*Job 9:14–24*: In light of all God's greatness, Job questioned how he could even have an argument with God (v. 14). Even though Job was righteous, he knew he could not answer God (v. 15). If Job summoned God, he didn't believe God would hear what he said but would instead batter him with a whirlwind (vv. 16–17). Job said if he tried to confront God, it wouldn't go well—God would soak him with bitter experiences (v. 18). Job again pointed out God's strength and justice and said his own mouth would condemn him as guilty before the Almighty God (vv. 19–20).

Job explained he was blameless but that his life no longer mattered when confronted with the power of God (v. 21) who destroys both the blameless and the wicked (v. 22). Job stated that when disaster brings sudden death, God mocks the innocent (v. 23). The earth would be given to the wicked and God would blindfold its judges (v. 24).

*Job 9:25–35*: Job described how his life was flying by without seeing any good (vv. 25–26). He said that if he tried to forget about all he had gone through, he would live in terror of his pains because he knew God would not acquit him (vv. 27–28), and he would be found guilty (v. 29). Job stated that his filth before the Lord was so bad his clothes would despise him (vv. 30–31). Job understood that God was not a man like he was, so there was no one who could judge between them (vv. 32–33). There was no bridge between God and Job. Job wanted God's rod taken away from him so God's terror would no longer frighten him. Job was alone with no mediator to support his case (vv. 34–35). Praise God that amid our despair He gave us a mediator, and it is Jesus (1 Timothy 2:5).

## Closing

Why do we need a mediator and how is God's mediator described in Scripture?

- *1 Timothy 2:5–6*: God's mediator was Jesus Christ who became human and gave Himself as our ransom. We will all face the courtroom and be represented by our mediator, Jesus.
- *Isaiah 64:6*: We have all become something unclean and polluted, and our sins carry us like the wind from place to place.
- *Hebrews 9:15*: Jesus mediates a new covenant that promises eternal inheritance because death has been replaced by redemption.
- *1 Peter 3:18*: Jesus suffered for all our sins to bring us to God.

If we had to go before a court to make our case for our salvation, we have a path we can follow:

- Romans 3:23: All are guilty and fall short of the glory of God. We will never meet God's status.
- Romans 6:23: The wages of sin is death, but the gift of God is eternal life.
- Romans 5:8: But God showed His great love for us in that Christ died for us while we were still sinners.
- Ephesians 2:8–9: We are saved by God's grace, not by anything we do.
- Romans 10:9–10: When we confess with our mouths and believe in our hearts that Jesus Christ is Lord, we will be saved and will have complete access to God.
- 2 Corinthians 5:21: Jesus was without sin but took on our sin so we could be the righteousness of God in Him.

How has God changed your life through His mediator? Hebrews 8:6 says Jesus is the superior mediator of a better covenant and has enacted better promises.

## The Daily Word

Job replied to Bildad as he persevered through suffering. Job asked the question: "How can a person be justified before God?" And then, even in the midst of his pain, Job proceeded to recognize God's attributes—God is wise and all-powerful. He removes mountains without their knowledge. He alone stretches out the heavens and treads on the waves of the sea. He does great and unsearchable things—wonders without number. Even in the midst of suffering, Job spoke forth the greatness of God.

If God is such a magnificent God, *then how are you justified before Him?* How do you get to God? *The answer is Jesus, our Promised Redeemer.* Jesus is your mediator. He came to earth so that you don't have to defend yourself before God. Jesus came to set you free from sin. He came as a gift from God for you to receive. As you receive Jesus into your life, walk with Him, fix your eyes on Him, and He will transform your life. If you haven't received Jesus as your Savior and Lord but believe you have sinned and want to be justified freely by Christ, receive Him today. Say to the Lord, "I believe in You, Jesus, the resurrected Messiah, and I give You my life. I receive You as my Savior and Mediator." When you ask Jesus to take control of your life, even in the midst of suffering, you will be able to stand with His hope in you and praise the Lord for His mighty attributes.

**Yes, I know what you've said is true, but how can a person be justified before God? —Job 9:2**

Further Scripture: Romans 3:23–24; 1 Timothy 2:5–6; Hebrews 9:15

## Questions

1.  How does the Bible speak of righteousness in a relative sense and a legal sense (Genesis 7:1; Job 1:1; Romans 5:19)?

2.  How did Job feel about God in Job 9:9–11, despite understanding Him as creator? When are the times in your life God seemed distant?

3.  Where in chapter 9 do you see Job, seemingly, longing for Jesus? What does Jesus do as the mediator between God and man (John 14:7–11; 1 Timothy 2:5; 1 Peter 3:18)?

4.  How does Job 10 make it clear that God created us? Where else does the Bible make it plain (Psalms 119:73; 139:13)? How does knowing this fact comfort you?

5.  Have you ever felt like Job did in Job 10:15–22? What promises from God can you cling to during these times (Hebrews 13:5)?

6.  What did the Holy Spirit highlight to you in Job 9—10 through the reading or the teaching?

# Lesson 7: Job 11—12

## *The Promised Redeemer:* You Deserve Worse

## Teaching Notes

### Intro

It has been a full week of suffering, complaining, and bad friends. Guess what is going to happen today? Another friend will tell Job he doesn't like him. Remember, the first guy we talked about was Eliphaz, and then we heard from Job's friend Bildad. Keep in mind at this point in Scripture that Job was covered in boils, sores, and had shared his feelings with his friends. In the following passage, we will see how Zophar responded.

Zophar gave two speeches in the book of Job. MacArthur wrote, "The first speech tells Job to get right with God (11:1–20). The second speech accuses Job of rejecting God by questioning His justice (20:1–29)."[1] He also wrote, "Zophar the Naamathite now stepped in to interrogate Job. He was quite close to his friends and chose to assault Job with the same law of retaliation. Job must repent, he said, not understanding the heavenly reality."[2]

### Teaching

*Job 11:1–6:* Job is a hard book to study. We are looking at human suffering and Job's friends telling him over and over again he had done wrong. It gets old. At some point, you think surely someone would comfort Job. But no! Constable writes, "Four things about Job that bothered Zophar: his loquacity (v. 2), his boasting (v. 3), his self-righteousness (v. 4), and his ignorance (v. 5)."[3]

It is important to note that Job did remain innocent of any great transgression throughout the entire book. It is not that he was perfect (Job 7:21; 13:26). Job didn't play that card. Zophar was playing the role of the judge and ruling that Job was guilty.

---

[1] John MacArthur, *The MacArthur Bible Commentary* (Nashville: Thomas Nelson, 2005), 578.

[2] MacArthur, 577.

[3] Thomas L. Constable, *Expository Notes of Dr. Thomas Constable: Job*, 57, https://planobiblechapel.org/tcon/notes/pdf/job.pdf.

*Job 11:7–12*: Zophar gave praise for God's wisdom.[4] I think the questions he asked in these Scripture verses were weird because nobody could or can understand these things. Zophar was so self-righteous he thought he understood God's plans, His reasoning, and His logic. Zophar had sound doctrine and theology but had incorrect application, as he showed no love for Job. All he wanted to do was show Job how much he knew about God. Zophar indirectly called Job stupid. *Nelson's Commentary* states, "He could be implying that Job's 'empty talk' indicates that he is empty-headed (vv. 2–12)."[5] Who was this guy anyway? So far, he had been the worst to Job.

*Job 11:13–20*: Zophar appealed to Job.[6] In other words, if Job wanted to change, he needed to do four things that would lead to a radical change and repentance. When I look at these things, it is hard to take them as truth and principal because it came from someone of his stature. He was right about these things, although they came from a wrong attitude. Here are the four things Job needed for repentance:[7]

1. *"Re-direct you heart to God."* Another way of putting this is to devote your heart to God. How do you devote your heart to God? Give up control of your life to God (Proverbs 3:5–6). When you trust in God, you are no longer relying on your own understanding, you are no longer trying to figure things out on your own. I think it is funny for Zophar to make this point while the whole time he had been trying to figure out God's plan by playing judge.
2. *"Stretch your hands to Him in prayer and forgiveness."* When you pray do you lift up your hands? I am going to try it! As crazy and self-righteous as Zophar was, he did speak truth about ways to keep your eyes on the Lord. Lifting your hands is a sign of release and submission.
3. *"Put your sin far away."* If there is sin in your life, remove it! We can all decide if we want to hold onto sin or not. For some reason in the church culture, we think we can hide our sin.
4. *"Don't allow sin in your tent."* Do a walk-through of your house and question things that are not of God. Listen to the Holy Spirit.

Lift your hands to God! Don't feel silly. We need to get over what people think of us and praise the Lord. Although these are great simple principles, I don't like

---

[4] Constable, 58.

[5] Earl D. Radmacher, Ronald B. Allen, and H. Wayne House, eds., *Nelson's New Illustrated Commentary* (Nashville: Thomas Nelson, 1999), 624.

[6] Constable, 58–59.

[7] MacArthur, 578.

that Zophar implied works-based faith. Which implies if you do 1, 2, 3 you get 1, 2, 3. But let's look at the benefits of these principles. Constable wrote, "These benefits were a clear conscience, faithfulness, and confidence (v. 15); forgetfulness of his troubles (v. 16); joy (v. 17); hope and rest (v. 18); and peace, popularity, leadership, and security (v. 19)."[8] I don't know why people wouldn't want these benefits as they are reflections of the Almighty Himself. I want to read a great quote from MacArthur that sums up these verses concisely.

> If Job didn't repent, he would die. Zophar was right that the life of faith in God is based on real confession of sin and obedience. He was right that God blesses people with hope, security, and peace. But, like his friends, he was wrong in not understanding that God allows unpredictable and seemingly unfair suffering for reasons not known on earth. He was wrong in presuming that the answer for Job was repentance.[9]

Zophar closed out his arguments by indirectly calling Job wicked. Constable wrote, "Whereas Eliphaz's authority was personal experience, and Bildad's was tradition, Zophar's seems to have been intuition (cf. 20:1–5)."[10] His intuition was wrong.

## Closing

The story of Job is a crazy story! I want to say that these three friends had good and right intentions, but their efforts sure did come out wrong. They based all of their accusations and advice on logic, not love. Ephesians 4:15 says, "But speaking the truth in love, let us grow in every way into Him who is the head—Christ." That is how we grow to become like Christ!

## The Daily Word

Job's third friend, Zophar, responded to Job's pain and suffering with wise, biblical truth. However, Zophar did not know that Job didn't need to repent. Zophar didn't know Job's heart. Only the Lord knew Job's heart and what caused his suffering.

Only the Lord knows your heart. He sees the pain and knows your thoughts. Even so, if you find yourself in a season of suffering, Zophar gave some practical encouragement to consider. *Ask the Lord if these practical steps are for you.* Redirect

---

[8] Constable, 58.

[9] MacArthur, 578.

[10] Constable, 59.

your heart to God. Literally lift your hands up in the air as an outward expression of surrender and submission to the Lord. Remove any sin in your life and put it far away. Don't allow any temptation to sin in your home. Today, take time to process through these and act on them as the Lord leads you. As you do this, the Lord will walk with you. Although you may still endure suffering, even through the hard days, you will find hope, joy, confidence, and freedom as you seek the Lord with a pure heart.

**As for you, if you redirect your heart and lift up your hands to Him in prayer—if there is iniquity in your hand, remove it, and don't allow injustice to dwell in your tents—then you will hold your head high, free from fault. You will be firmly established and unafraid. —Job 11:13–15**

Further Scripture: Psalm 28:2; 2 Timothy 2:21; 4:5

## Questions

1. How was Zophar's doctrine correct but his application wrong (Job 42:7)? What did he and the other two originally set out to do, according to Job 2:11? What could Zophar have said or done differently?

2. What was the hope that Zophar described to Job? What did Zophar say Job had to do to get the blessings described in Job 11:13–20? Was this advice right or wrong according to Job's situation?

3. How does the mocking of an innocent Job point to the mocking of an innocent Jesus (Matthew 27:29, 41; Mark 15:27–31)?

4. What was Job's understanding of God and His sovereignty as it relates to nations and kings (Daniel 2:20–22; Acts 17:24–28)? Are there any other times in Scripture when man tried to build something without God (Genesis 4:16–18; 11:1–9; Psalm 127:1)? What was the result?

5. What did the Holy Spirit highlight to you in Job 11—12 through the reading or the teaching?

# Lesson 8: Job 13

*The Promised Redeemer*: Job's Initial Response to Zophar

## Teaching Notes

### Intro

We have only had one full week in our study of Job, but it feels as though we've been here for at least a month. It feels repetitive to me as I study. It sounds like the story of the Israelites who kept their eyes on God until they turned away from Him. It's that same ongoing cycle in Job, based on Job's three friends who kept saying the same things over and over, with just a slight difference in attitude. Job's ongoing dialogue with his friends is recorded in chapters 3—31. Job's friends were Eliphaz, Bildad, and Zophar. Wiersbe points out that in chapter 13, "Job first expressed his *disappointment* in his three friends (vv. 1–12), then his *declaration* of faith in the Lord (vv. 13–17), and finally his *desire* that God come to him and get the issue settled once and for all (vv. 18–28)."[1]

### Teaching

*Job 13:1–12*: Job shared his disappointment with his friends because he didn't need them to explain what he already understood. MacArthur points out that Job "wanted to take his case before God."[2] *Nelson's Commentary* states, "The irony is that neither Job nor his friends know very much because they all assume an inflexible dogma of retribution."[3] Their theory was based on the idea that a good person would always be blessed while a wicked person would always bring wickedness onto his life. As the three friends watched Job, they concluded he was no longer blessed and had, therefore, become wicked. Job wanted to speak directly to God (v. 3). In verse 4, his friends were whitewashing and spreading their lies of retribution to keep their traditional views (Psalm 119:69). Because they were

[1] Warren W. Wiersbe, *Be Patient: Waiting on God in Difficult Times* (Colorado Springs: David C. Cook, 1991), 64.

[2] John MacArthur, *The MacArthur Bible Commentary* (Nashville: Thomas Nelson, 2005), 579.

[3] Earl D. Radmacher, Ronald B. Allen, and H. Wayne House, eds., *Nelson's New Illustrated Bible Commentary* (Nashville: Thomas Nelson, 1999), 625.

worthless in understanding what was going on in Job's life, he told them to be quiet and not speak (v. 5).

Job began his argument in verse 6 and questioned if his friends were testifying deceitfully about God (v. 7). MacArthur interprets Job's question in verse 8 as, "Are you wise enough to argue in God's defense?"[4] Job pointed out that his friends would have been unable to deceive God, and if they tried to deceive him, God Himself would rebuke their actions (vv. 9–10). Job told his friends their words not only offended God but were completely ineffective and worthless (vv. 11–12). All the disappointment Job felt with his friends would also be acknowledged by God's disappointment of them in Job 42:7–8.

*Job 13:13–17*: Job then began his *declaration* of faith. Job told them to listen to his words and that he would take responsibility for his words and his life (vv. 13–14). Regardless of the consequences of his actions, Job's hope was found in the Lord (v. 15) (Daniel 3:16–18). Job anticipated his deliverance as a godly man (v. 16). Therefore, his friends should pay attention to his words and his faith (v. 17).

*Job 13:18–28*: Job moved on to his *desire* for God to be in his life. Job had prepared his case and knew God would vindicate him (vv. 18–19). MacArthur explains Job "would defend his innocence before God and was confident that he was truly saved and not a hypocrite."[5] In verse 20, Job switched from his argument with his friends into a prayer to God. Job requested two things. First, he asked God to remove His hand—the actual pain Job was experiencing. Second, he asked God to not let His terror frighten him (vv. 20–21). This second request was about his relationship with God. He didn't want to be so afraid of God that he ran from Him. Job desired for God to call him and to speak to him (v. 22) (Jeremiah 33:3; Matthew 7:7; 21:22; Luke 18:1; John 14:13; Philippians 4:6; Hebrews 4:16; James 4:3). Job then asked God to reveal all his sins to him (v. 23). MacArthur explains Job wanted to hear his list of sins so "he could determine if his measure of suffering matched the severity of his sin, and he could then repent for sins about which he was unaware."[6] Then Job asked why God considered him an enemy and why did He hold past sins against him (vv. 24–26). Job was saying God wasn't acting the way Job understood Him to be (v. 27). Verse 28 is best understood with Job 14:1: "Man . . . is short of days and full of trouble." The condition of man is difficult. Job had experienced severe suffering and couldn't accept that these symptoms and pains had been caused by his own sins.

---

[4] MacArthur, 579.

[5] MacArthur, 579.

[6] MacArthur, 579.

## Closing

What I love about Job in this book is that he never stopped loving God. He never blamed God for his suffering. Job always wanted to be restored into relationship with God.

## The Daily Word

Job was covered with boils from head to toe when he responded to his three friends. He had listened to their logic and truth. He understood them and yet believed he was not inferior to them. As Job saw into their hearts and motives, he believed they were missing something in their counsel to him. At one point, Job told Zophar: "If only you would shut up and let that be your wisdom!"

Many families or schools have rules against saying the phrase "Shut up." In most cultures, this phrase comes across as impolite and crass in its direct approach of telling someone to stop talking. However, Job directed the phrase at his three friends, equating shutting up with wisdom. Yes, sometimes keeping your mouth closed and not offering advice is indeed the best wisdom. Today, be intentional and don't say everything you think, even on your social media comments, posts, or text messages. Before you say something, pause, close your mouth, and listen longer than you normally would. Rest in the fact you don't have to get your point across. God is sovereign. God is in control. When you exercise self-control with your words, you allow the Lord to move in the situation. So do as Job said, "Shut up and let that be your wisdom."

**If only you would shut up and let that be your wisdom! —Job 13:5**

Further Scripture: Proverbs 17:28; 18:2; James 1:19

## Questions

1. In Job 13:4, Job called his friends worthless physicians. What do you think he meant by this?

2. In Job 13:8 (NASB), Job asked his friends, "Will you contend for God?" Do you think God needs anyone to contend for Him? Why or why not? Have you ever found yourself doing this?

3. Job made a powerful statement in Job 13:15 when he said, "Even if He kills me, I will hope in Him." What does this say about Job's faith? Do you think this statement proved Satan wrong when he made the accusation against Job back in Job 2:5: "But stretch out Your hand and strike his flesh and bones, and he will surely curse You to Your face"? If all this happened to you, could you make the same statement that Job did?

4.  Referring to Job 13:24, how do you handle a situation when it seems God is silent? When you cry out to Him for answers? Do you feel like God considers you an enemy like Job did?

5.  What did the Holy Spirit highlight to you in Job 13 through the reading or the teaching?

# Lesson 9: Job 14

*The Promised Redeemer:* Losing Hope

## Teaching Notes

### Intro

Yesterday, we looked at Job's response to Zophar that turned into a prayer (Job 13). In chapter 14, Job's conversation with God continued. Constable explains that Job's words in chapter 14 were "really his answer to the major argument and several specific statements all three of his companions had made so far."[1]

### Teaching

*Job 14:1–6:* Job continued discussing the brevity of life in Job 14:1 and said it was "short of days and full of trouble." Then Job described life as a wilting flower and a fleeting shadow (v. 2). Job asked for grace (v. 3) and wondered if anyone could create something pure out of something already impure (v. 4). We are all born in a state of impurity, and we are all sinners (1 Kings 8:46; Psalm 14:1, 3; Ecclesiastes 7:20; Isaiah 64:5; Romans 3:10, 23). The blood of Christ, our mediator, is the only one who can take this on. Job next described man as a hired man whose days had already been numbered (vv. 5–6).

*Job 14:7–17:* Job moved from the brevity of life to the finality of death (vv. 7–17). A chopped down tree has the ability to sprout again and will not die (vv. 7–9) (Isaiah 6:13). The tree had more hope for life than Job. The "holy seed" was still within the tree stump.[2] This is a prophetic picture that leads to Jesus. But man had no such hope and was more like the water that evaporated completely in the soil (vv. 10–11). Job stated that when man lay down in death, there was no assurance he would live again (v. 12). However, Job asked God to hide him in death until His anger was over (v. 13). MacArthur states Job was requesting that, after God's anger was done, he "be raised to life again when God called him

---

[1] Thomas L. Constable, *Expository Notes of Dr. Thomas Constable: Job*, 64, https://planobiblechapel.org/tcon/notes/pdf/job.pdf.

[2] Earl D. Radmacher, Ronald B. Allen, and H. Wayne House, eds., *Nelson's New Illustrated Bible Commentary* (Nashville: Thomas Nelson, 1999), 626.

back."[3] Job wondered if resurrection was possible (v. 14). Job thought that if God brought him back to life, He could then count Job's days without looking at his sin, and that God would cover his sin (vv. 15–17).

Job was asking if a person could live again. The psalmist said God would not abandon him in Sheol (Psalm 16:9–11) and that he would see God's face when he "awoke" (Psalm 17:15; Isaiah 26:19; Daniel 12:2). Job had hope that if he died, he would live again. Job 19:25–26 speaks of *The Promised Redeemer* that gives hope in death. God has power over the finality of death, and everyone will stand before him (Acts 24:15; Hebrews 9:27). Which side will you fall on? The side of shame or of eternal life? The New Testament also speaks of a person being able to live again. Jesus promised that Lazarus would live again (John 11:23–27). We do not have to fear the finality of death because Jesus has abolished it (2 Timothy 1:10).

*Job 14:18–22*: Although Job had maintained his hope in God up until this point, these last verses show a distinct absence of hope. MacArthur explains, "Job returned to his complaint before God, and reverted to a hopeless mood, speaking about death as inevitable and causing separation. He was painfully sad to think of it."[4] Job described his loss of hope as a collapsed and crumbling mountain or torrents of water that wash away soil in its wake (vv. 18–19). Job told God: "You destroy a man's hope. You completely overpower him, and he passes on; You change his appearance and send him away" (vv. 19b–20). Hope is the only thing that gets us through difficult times and friends who do not support us. Hope is the major weapon against anything we face in life (Hebrews 6:19). Our hope must be tethered to Christ Himself. *Nelson's Commentary* emphasizes, "The OT believer admits that he sees little evidence for a blessed afterlife. This is the importance of Jesus' resurrection. He promises, 'Because I live, you will live also.'"[5] Belief in Christ means we are rooted in Him as our Living Hope (1 Peter 1:3). Job concluded that without hope, a man would find no honor in what happens to his own life or to the lives of others (vv. 21–22).

## Closing

Charles Allen said, "When you say a situation or a person is hopeless, you are slamming the door in the face of God." Our hope comes from the Lord. "Now may the God of hope fill you with all joy and peace as you believe in Him so that you may overflow with hope by the power of the Holy Spirit" (Romans 15:13).

---

[3] John MacArthur, *The MacArthur Bible Commentary* (Nashville: Thomas Nelson, 2005), 580.

[4] MacArthur, 580.

[5] Radmacher et al., 627.

No matter what you are going through right now, you have purpose in Christ, and you can find your hope in Him.

## The Daily Word

Job continued to respond to his friends' advice. In his response, his hopelessness is palpable. He was weary in the suffering. Eventually he began asking God all kinds of questions. As Job's pain intensified, he even questioned life after death.

What do you do when you are at the end of your rope? Do you think about death more than you think about life? You may ask yourself: *Is there really anything to hope for? What is my purpose here on earth?* Here's the answer. Hope remains. Hope lives on. You have *The Promised Redeemer*, the hope of this world, Jesus Christ. He is the anchor for your soul. He is safe and secure. Allow the Holy Spirit to fill you up with this hope found in Christ. He fills you with joy and peace as you believe in Christ Jesus. Then, through believing in Jesus, you will have eternal life. If you are questioning life right now, listen to these words for you: You have purpose. You are worthy of Jesus coming to earth just for *you.* You are loved. You are not alone. You have hope. Hold on to the *hope* found in Jesus, and ask the Holy Spirit to fill you up. Today, you may need to pray this moment by moment, trusting that the Lord hears you and will answer you.

**When a man dies, will he come back to life? If so, I would wait all the days of my struggle until my relief comes. You would call, and I would answer You. You would long for the work of Your hands. —Job 14:14–15**

Further Scripture: Romans 15:13; 2 Timothy 1:10; Hebrews 6:19

## Questions

1. In your opinion, how could Job know God has appointed a specific number of months for each person's life (Job 14:5; Psalm 139:16)?

2. In Job 14:12, Job spoke as though he knew there would be a resurrection. How could Job know this? What are some other examples in the Bible where the Old Testament speaks of a resurrection (Job 19:26; Isaiah 25:8–9; 26:19; Daniel 12:2)?

3. What did the Holy Spirit highlight to you in Job 14 through the reading or the teaching?

# Lesson 10: Job 15

*The Promised Redeemer*: Curses for the Wicked

## Teaching Notes

### Intro

Eliphaz, Bildad, and Zophar had all spoken one round of letting Job know that they didn't like who he had become. Today's chapter begins the friends' second round of speeches to Job. Eliphaz again went first. After delivering his first speech in Job 4—5, Eliphaz was ready to elaborate on his disagreement with Job. MacArthur observed, "Job's resistance to their [Eliphaz, Zophar, and Bildad] viewpoint and his appeals energized them to greater intensity in their confrontation."[1]

### Teaching

*Job 15:1–6*: Eliphaz held onto a dogma of retribution that led him to believe that wicked people deserved bad things while good people would receive blessings. Constable noted that the friends' first speeches were more intellectual and logical while their second speeches were more emotional as they sought to convict Job's conscience.[2]

Eliphaz accused Job of being full of hot air as his friend probably had trouble breathing because of his various afflictions. Wiersbe noted that Job's situation offered a great theological challenge to his friends. If Job had not sinned and was not being punished by God, "Then what motive would people have for obeying God?"[3] Eliphaz's theology was works-based. If Job did the right things, then God would owe him for the good things, and he was in control of avoiding the bad things. This type of theology doesn't serve God at all. As Wiersbe concluded, this type of belief "is only a pious system for promoting selfishness and not glorifying God."[4] In order for us to rise above this type of religion, we actually have to love

---

[1] John MacArthur, *The MacArthur Bible Commentary* (Nashville: Thomas Nelson, 2005), 580.

[2] Thomas L. Constable, *Expository Notes of Dr. Thomas Constable: Job*, 65, https://planobiblechapel.org/tcon/notes/pdf/job.pdf.

[3] Warren W. Wiersbe, *Be Patient: Waiting on God in Difficult Times* (Colorado Springs: David C. Cook, 1991), 72.

[4] Wiersbe, 73.

God (Deuteronomy 6:4–6; 7:7–9). Eliphaz rebuked Job's attitude, but the attitude he rebuked was actually Job's love for God.

Verses 5 and 6 were a kind of ironic agreement with something Job said in 9:20: "Even if I were in the right, my own mouth would condemn me; if I were blameless, my mouth would declare me guilty." Eliphaz twisted Job's words just enough to twist his meaning.

*Job 15:7–13*: Eliphaz started a series of questions, about claims that Job never actually made, to rebuke his attitude. Eliphaz's question to Job in verse 9, "What do you know that we don't?" seems to be in response to Job's statement in 13:2, "Everything you know, I also know; I am not inferior to you." In verse 10, Eliphaz accused Job of rejecting the wisdom of his elders.[5] Later, Job would observe, "It is not only the old who are wise or the elderly who understand how to judge" (Job 32:9). In verse 12, Eliphaz wondered why Job had shown some anger toward him. In Eliphaz's mind, he was being completely reasonable and rational.

*Job 15:14–16*: Eliphaz continued his attack on Job by pointing out that no one on earth was righteous, so Job himself couldn't possibly be, in this extreme instance. The reference to "the holy ones" God "puts no trust in" could be a reference to angels who fell.[6]

*Job 15:17–35*: Having established Job's sinfulness in his own mind, Eliphaz devoted this section of his speech to outlining the fate of the wicked.[7] Eliphaz's qualifications to speak into Job's situation was based on his own experience (v. 17) and the tradition of men (v. 18). While his first speech outlined the blessings of the godly person, now Eliphaz switched to highlighting the seven curses of the wicked, all of which he implied Job would experience if he did not repent:

1.  They experience pain (v. 20a)—Job was experiencing plenty of physical pain because of his boils and health struggles.
2.  They die early (v. 20b)—Job was still alive but had expressed his desire to die.
3.  They have irrational fears (v. 21a).
4.  They suffer destruction while at peace (v. 21b).
5.  They experience torment from a guilty conscience (v. 22a).
6.  They are hunted people (v. 22b).
7.  They are always hungry and looking for basic needs (v. 23a).

---

[5] MacArthur, 580.

[6] MacArthur, 580.

[7] Constable, 67.

8. They are distressed and in anguish (vv. 23b–24).[8]

God's reasons for judgment are based on a person's rebellion (vv. 25–26) and self-indulgence (vv. 27–28). After outlining these causes, Eliphaz gave Job seven more judgments facing the wicked:

1. They will not prosper (v. 29).
2. They will die (v. 30a).
3. Their works will fail (v. 30b).
4. They will suffer prematurely (vv. 31–32a).
5. Their wealth will fail (vv. 32b–33).
6. They will experience barrenness (v. 34).
7. They deceive themselves (v. 35).

Eliphaz called Job hypocritical and ungodly in a passive-aggressive way. He never once specified that Job was experiencing all his sufferings because he was personally ungodly, but Eliphaz's entire speech made it clear that was precisely what he thought. However, Eliphaz's theology was not always true. God "causes his sun to rise on the evil and the good and sends rain on the righteous and the unrighteous" (Matthew 5:45). God "is patient with you, not wanting any to perish but all to come to repentance" (2 Peter 3:9), whether we have done either good or bad.

## Closing

Paul wrote in Romans 2:4, "God's kindness is intended to lead you to repentance." God does not want to judge us or destroy us, even when we deserve it, but He is willing to allow us to experience suffering in order to draw us closer to Himself (1 Peter 1:6–8). God may want to take you through a period of suffering to teach you to hold onto hope and to hold onto Him (Romans 8:18–20).

## The Daily Word

Job's friends began a second round of responses. Eliphaz went first, and this time he intensified his comments, almost rebuking Job. He responded to Job's suffering with a works-based perspective, believing Job surely did something wicked to earn the suffering he was experiencing.

Here's the deal. *You cannot earn your way to God.* God's love and mercy are a free gift. He is kind and patient. It's not based on what you do or don't do. Yes,

---

[8] Constable, 67.

there are times you may have consequences to your choices or sin. However, as you go through trials, understand that God's ways are not your ways. The Lord is a God of grace and mercy. Yes, as believers, the Lord promises you will endure suffering. Everyone. However, hope remains by understanding even if you suffer from various trials, as you keep your eyes on Jesus, you will come out refined by the fire. You will be purified as gold, resulting in praise, glory, and honor to Jesus. *Ask the Lord for endurance and strength.* May the Lord cover you with His love and allow His kindness to wash over you today.

**Listen to me and I will inform you. I will describe what I have seen.
—Job 15:17**

Further Scripture: Romans 2:4; 1 Peter 1:6–7; 2 Peter 3:9

## Questions

1. What was Eliphaz's response to Job's reliance on God? How did he accuse Job?

2. Why do you think Job's three friends were so adamant about thinking Job was suffering because of his sin? Is obedience to the Lord a guarantee of health and/or wealth? Explain (Matthew 26:39; Luke 9:58; Philippians 2:8; Hebrews 5:8).

3. Was Job a man of prayer (Job 1)? Eliphaz told Job that he cast off fear and that he restrained prayer before God (Job 15:4 NKJV). How does someone restrain prayer before God?

4. Compare the words of Eliphaz's first speech (Job 5:17–26) to the speech in Job 15:17–35. How were the two different?

5. What sin did Eliphaz accuse Job of in 15:34–35? How would you handle these friends if you were Job? Have you ever been falsely accused of something? How did you handle it?

6. What did the Holy Spirit highlight to you in Job 15 through the reading or the teaching?

# Lesson 11: Job 16

## *The Promised Redeemer*: Miserable Comforters

## Teaching Notes

### Intro

We just finished Eliphaz's verbal vomit! He supplied 16 consequences for the wicked (implying Job). Job was forced to give rebuttal to Eliphaz a second time. He had to rebut all of his friends multiple times.

### Teaching

*Job 16:1–5*: In these verses, we see what Constable describes as "Job's disgust with his friends."[1] *Nelson's Commentary* paraphrases the verses in this way: "Speaking of trouble, rather than comforting me in my troubles as a good counselor should, you have increased my trouble despite your claims to the contrary."[2]

Do you remember what Job called his friends a couple of chapters ago? He called them worthless doctors. They had done nothing up to this point but ridicule, judge, and discourage. In verse 2, Job called his friends "miserable comforters." MacArthur wrote, "Job's friends had come to comfort him. Despite seven blissful days of silence at the outset, their mission had failed miserably, and their comfort had turned into more torment for Job. What started out as Eliphaz's sincere efforts to help Job understand his dilemma had turned into rancor and sarcasm."[3] Let's go back to Job 6:15; 8:2; and 13:4 and look at all the names Job called his friends.

Job pointed out that he could judge and shake his head at his friends, as in Psalm 22:7, if they were in his position. But Job would rather encourage and assuage their pain. How would you treat someone in Job's position? To see how to encourage and help others, it is important to understand Matthew 7:12. In that passage we see that we should treat others how we want to be treated. This verse

---

[1] Thomas L. Constable, *Expository Notes of Dr. Thomas Constable: Job*, 69, https://planobiblechapel.org/tcon/notes/pdf/job.pdf.

[2] Earl D. Radmacher, Ronald B. Allen, and H. Wayne House, eds., *Nelson's New Illustrated Bible Commentary* (Nashville: Thomas Nelson, 1999), 627.

[3] John MacArthur, *The MacArthur Bible Commentary* (Nashville: Thomas Nelson, 2005), 581.

is also referred to as "the golden rule." Author Greg Faulls identifies five ways to live out the golden rule.

Here are the five ways:[4]

1. *Forgive as you wish to be forgiven* (Matthew 6:12; Colossians 3:13). For Job to encourage his friends, he would have to forgive them for constantly bombarding him with negativity. Forgiveness is something we really don't want to do. We would rather move on from a hurt or slight rather than stick it out and forgive. We need to forgive each other.

2. *Help as you wish to be helped* (Colossians 3:13). This is all about accepting one another. If you see another person in need you should desire to help them. We need to help each other.

3. *Encourage as you wish to be encouraged* (Hebrews 3:13). Job should probably stop calling his friends names. I don't think you can encourage if you can't forgive. Faulls wrote, "Ben Franklin once said, 'Most men die from the neck up at age twenty-five because they stop dreaming.'" This happens because people stop encouraging each other.

4. *Understand as you wish to be understood* (John 8:7). Job's friends showed no understanding or empathy for Job. They had no desire to understand Job.

5. *Look for things to do to lift and bless those around you* (Philippians 2:4). How do you get to the point where you can encourage those who have hurt you? You must go out of your way to show that you value and care for people. Look at a situation and ask: How can I help?

*Job 16:6–17*: Constable refers to these verses as "Job's distress at God's hand."[5] Job's perspective of God was that God had been angry with him, and he was being punished. Job actually referred to God as his enemy. MacArthur writes, "Job refers to God as 'my adversary,' who has shattered, shaken, shot at and sliced him (vv. 12–14)."[6] Wiersbe writes that "Job's response [to Eliphaz and his friends] is to utter three heartfelt requests: first, a plea to his friends for sympathy (Job 16:1–14); then, a plea to God for justice (vv. 15–22); and finally, a plea to God to end his life and relieve him of suffering (17:1–16)."[7]

---

[4] Greg Faulls, "Five Ways to Live Out the Golden Rule," Prevailing Life with Greg Faulls, March 3, 2014, http://prevailinglife.com/five-ways-to-live-out-the-golden-rule/.

[5] Constable, 69.

[6] MacArthur, 581.

[7] Warren W. Wiersbe, *The Bible Expository Commentary: Job–Song of Solomon* (Colorado Springs: David C. Cook, 2004), 33–34.

As Job pleaded for God's justice, he compared himself to a wounded animal. Job had no one left to turn to so he put on sackcloth, buried his face in the dust and wept with humiliation and contrition. This seems like a hopeless situation.

*Job 16:18—17:2*: Constable refers to these verses as, "Job's desire for a representative in heaven."[8] Job had no friends and felt as though God had abandoned him. Constable writes, "Job called on the earth not to cover his blood (v. 18)—so it might cry to God for vindication (Genesis 4:10). Job did not want people to forget his case when he died. He wanted someone to answer his questions and to vindicate his innocence even if he was not alive to witness it."[9] Even though Job was in distress, he could only turn to God.

MacArthur writes that Job's "pleading would be for a verdict of innocent on behalf of a friend or neighbor in a court setting before the judge/king."[10] Job was asking for an intercessor, for someone to defend him to God. God provided that intercessor through Christ (1 Timothy 2:5).

## Closing

Job needed an advocate, an intercessor, and a mediator. God provided these things through Christ.

*1 John 2:1–2*: "My little children, I am writing you these things so that you may not sin. But if anyone does sin, we have an advocate with the Father—Jesus Christ the Righteous One. He Himself is the propitiation for our sins, and not only for ours, but also for those of the whole world."

*Romans 5:8*: "But God proves His own love for us in that while we were still sinners, Christ died for us!"

*Hebrews 7:25*: "Therefore, He is always able to save those who come to God through Him, since He always lives to intercede for them." Jesus becomes the fulfillment of Job 16:21. Jesus is able to save anyone who comes through Christ. He wants to give every single one of us life!

## The Daily Word

Job replied to Eliphaz's second, more blunt comments directed toward his suffering. Job responded honestly and shared how Eliphaz didn't encourage him.

[8] Constable, 70.

[9] Constable, 70.

[10] MacArthur, 581.

He called Eliphaz's words empty, just a string of words together. Job even said if Eliphaz was the one suffering, Job would offer him more encouragement and more encouraging words resulting in relief to the soul rather than discouragement.

Your words are important. They matter and have impact. Are you an encouraging friend? Or are you the one who quickly points out the problems and criticizes the situation? The Lord says to treat others the way you want to be treated. As you receive love from your heavenly Father, pour His love out to others. Forgive as you want to be forgiven. Help as you want to be helped. *Encourage as you want to be encouraged.* Be the friend you would like to have. When in doubt, remember love is patient, kind, not envious, not boastful, not conceited, doesn't act improperly, is not selfish, and not provoked to do something wrong. Instead, love rejoices in truth and never ends. Today, ask the Lord for an encouraging, loving word to share with a friend. Then deliver the message with love and watch God show up!

**If you were in my place I could also talk like you. I could string words together against you and shake my head at you. Instead, I would encourage you with my mouth, and the consolation from my lips would bring relief. —Job 16:4–5**

Further Scripture: 1 Corinthians 13:4–6; Colossians 3:13–14; Hebrews 3:13

## Questions

1.  Job called his friends "miserable comforters." What was the most comforting thing his friends had done up to this point (Job 2:11–13)?

2.  Contrast how Job spoke of God in Job 13:15–18 and 19:25 to how he spoke of Him in verses 16:9–14. Does it seem as though Job was wrestling with God just like Jacob in Genesis 32:22–32? What was the difference between the two struggles?

3.  How did Job physically respond to God's "attack"? What was his deep spiritual conviction (Job 16:19–21)?

4.  When things aren't going your way, who is your advocate (1 John 2:1–2)? Who is your interceding High Priest (Hebrews 2:17–18; 4:14–16)? Who wants to perfect you in the will of God (Hebrews 13:20–21)?

5.  What did the Holy Spirit highlight to you in Job 16 through the reading or the teaching?

# Lesson 12: Job 17—18

## *The Promised Redeemer*: Death Is Not the End

## Teaching Notes

### Intro

Job responded to Eliphaz in chapter 16. In Chapter 18, Bildad gave his second speech. Bildad's first speech was in Job 8. Bildad's basic argument throughout this speech was, "Job, you've got to come to your senses."

### Teaching

*Job 18:1–4*: Constable points out that these verses contain Bildad's criticism of Job.[1] Both Job and his friends believed the other had spoken too much. Neither group liked the attitude of the other, and they expressed their disappointment (v. 2). Neither group seemed to care much for the other. Bildad was mad because he thought Job called him cattle (v. 3) (12:7–9) and became scornful. He didn't appreciate being called an animal nor did he appreciate being called stupid. The first four verses of this chapter are laced with sarcasm. Then Bildad's speech turned to fear as things got more serious.

*Job 18:5–21*: Constable highlights that these verses were Bildad's warning concerning the wicked.[2] Bildad set forth four pictures of death as a warning to Job[3]:

1. *A light put out* (vv. 5–6)—"The Lord's lamp sheds light on a person's life, searching the innermost parts" (Proverbs 20:27).

2. *A traveler trapped* (vv. 7–10)—Six Hebrew synonyms for "net" and "trapped" were used to describe this point. A net was spread to catch him, a snare covered over a pit with branches, a trap using a noose that sprung when touched, a robber, a snare hidden on the ground, and a trap, a generic term for any

---

[1] Thomas L. Constable, *Expository Notes of Dr. Thomas Constable: Job*, 73, https://planobiblechapel.org/tcon/notes/pdf/job.pdf.

[2] Constable, 73.

[3] Constable, 74.

device used to catch prey.[4] Bildad used all these images to convey fear that wickedness would lead to death. Wiersbe noted that fear is a normal human emotion that can motivate us to take good, healthy actions. However, the fear that Bildad seemed to want to instill in Job was a hopeless fear of death.[5]

3. *A criminal pursued* (vv. 11–15)—Bildad referenced "the king of terrors" in verse 14. This was most likely death,[6] but it could also be Satan. John Burns suggests this could be "a reference to Namtar, the Mesopotamian god of pestilence and a vizier of the underworld."[7]

4. *A tree rooted up* (vv. 16–21)—Job had previously expressed that, despite calamity, a tree retained some form of hope (14:7–9). Bildad argued that once the roots of a tree dried up, there was no hope for any part of the tree, whether it be above or below ground. This image brought to mind a family tree. Once a wicked man came to his end, all of the branches would also fall.[8]

As Bildad wrapped up his speech to Job, he went to drastic lengths to refute Job's claim of innocence. Bildad argued that Job's situation, in which he found himself with no children, no heritage, and nothing left of all his possessions, were the marks of an "unjust man," and were evidence of a person "who does not know God" (v. 21).

In their more recent speeches, both Eliphaz and Bildad described the wicked with some commonalities[9]:

| Eliphaz | The wicked . . . | Bildad |
|---|---|---|
| 15:22–23, 30 | experience darkness | 18:5–6, 18 |
| 15:30b, 32–33 | are like unhealthy plants | 18:16 |
| 15:30, 34 | are destroyed by fire | 18:15 |
| 15:27–31 | lose their influence | 18:7, 15–16 |
| 15:21, 24 | are terrified by anguish | 18:11, 14 |
| 15:34 | lose their homes | 18:6, 14–15 |

---

[4] Warren W. Wiersbe, *The Bible Expository Commentary: Job–Song of Solomon* (Colorado Springs: David C. Cook, 2004) 37–38.

[5] Wiersbe, 37.

[6] Wiersbe, 38.

[7] John Barclay Burns, "The Identity of Death's First-Born (Job XVIII 13)," *Vetus Testamentum* 37:3 (July 1987): 362–64.

[8] Wiersbe, 38.

[9] Constable, 73–74.

| Eliphaz | The wicked . . . | Bildad |
|---|---|---|
| 15:4, 13, 25–26 | oppose or do not know God | 18:21 |
| 15:13 | are ensnared | 18:8–10 |

## Closing

Wiersbe observes, "Death is an enemy to be feared by all who are not prepared to die."[10] In many ways, Job's life was like ours. Satan threw many negative messages against Job, and he does the same thing to us every day to try to get us to fall. But if we believe in and hold fast to Christ, all of Satan's attacks mean nothing. Jesus said, "I assure you: Anyone who hears My word and believes Him who sent Me has eternal life and will not come under judgment but has passed from death to life" (John 5:24).

We have nothing to fear in this life when we belong to Christ. For us, death actually means life. Death means that we get to go home and be with the Father instead of being separated from God.

## The Daily Word

As Job spoke in frustration and helplessness for his situation, his friend Bildad responded for the second time. This time he responded with such criticism toward Job it was almost to the point of death and destruction. Bildad warned Job about what happened to the wicked, the one who does not know God. But here's the truth: *Job knew God.*

Can you imagine getting these harsh words from a friend as you walked through the most intense suffering and pain of your life? It may seem rare to have a friend like this. However, the enemy prowls around daily, seeking to bring about a similar destruction and death to your life. He comes to steal your joy and break up your relationships. He even speaks lies to you, leaving you feeling depressed, helpless, and hopeless. But here's the deal. You have the power within you to stop the lies. Jesus has won the battle. Remember, through the power of the Holy Spirit, you have everything you need to fight back. Take every thought captive by gaining control over what you think about yourself and believe God's truth. Lift up your shield of faith. Don't allow yourself to fall into the traps the enemy places in your life. Walk with victory because the battle belongs to the Lord! So press on in great faith, believing God's promises.

---

[10] Warren W. Wiersbe, *The Wiersbe Bible Commentary: Old Testament* (Colorado Springs: David C. Cook, 2007), 841.

**Indeed, such is the dwelling of the unjust man, and this is the place of the one who does not know God. —Job 18:21**

Further Scripture: Deuteronomy 20:4; 2 Corinthians 10:4–5; 1 John 5:4

## Questions

1. How did Job's description of himself in Job 17:6 point to the Messiah (Isaiah 53:3, 4b; Luke 18:32)? Who is the one credited for smiting both Job and the Messiah (Job 6:4; Isaiah 53:10)?

2. Bildad believed Job regarded him and the other two friends as "beasts." According to the following scriptures, what would that actually mean: Job 18:3; Psalms 49:20; 57:4; 73:22; Ecclesiastes 3:18; and Titus 1:12?

3. As Bildad shared his theology about the wicked in Job 18, what were the elements of truth that lined up with Scripture, and where was he in error (Psalms 11:6; 37:10; 73; 1 Peter 2:21–23; 3:17)?

4. What did the Holy Spirit highlight to you in Job 17—18 through the reading or the teaching?

# Lesson 13: Job 19

*The Promised Redeemer:* A Living Redeemer

## Teaching Notes

### Intro

Every book of the Bible should ultimately point us to Jesus. Jesus Himself said He didn't come "to destroy the Law or the Prophets . . . but to fulfill" them (Matthew 5:17). Job 19 will point us directly to the Messiah by expressing Job's hope for a redeemer. After losing his family, all his possessions, his health, and in the midst of struggling with his friends, Job looked forward to his *Promised Redeemer* as he responded to Bildad's speech recorded in chapter 18.

### Teaching

*Job 19:1–4*: Constable observes that these verses highlight "the hostility of Job's accusers."[1] Job reached a point where he was tired of his friends' complaints. Their words had crushed him (v. 2), and he felt humiliated by their treatment (v. 3). Job argued that even if he had sinned it would have been no concern to his friends.

*Job 19:5–12*: Job brought forth seven images to describe the trials of his life. These images marked a transition from Job describing the hostility of his friends to Job describing the hostility of God.[2] Warren Wiersbe composed a list of what Job was feeling:

1. He felt like a trapped animal (v. 6).
2. He felt like a criminal in court (v. 7).
3. He felt like a traveler fenced in (v. 8). Job felt like his path had been filled with darkness by the Lord. In contrast, Isaiah prophesied, "Who among you fears the LORD, listening to the voice of His Servant? Who among you walks

---

[1] Thomas L. Constable, *Expository Notes of Dr. Thomas Constable: Job*, 75, https://planobiblechapel.org/tcon/notes/pdf/job.pdf.

[2] Constable, 76.

in darkness, and has no light? Let him trust in the name of Yahweh; let him lean on his God" (Isaiah 50:10).

4.   He felt like a king dethroned (v. 9).

5.   He felt like a structure destroyed (v. 10).

6.   He felt like a tree uprooted (v. 10b). In 14:7, Job said there was hope for a tree that was cut down because "its roots would not die." But there is no hope for a tree that is uprooted. Job saw no hope in his situation.

7.   He felt like a besieged city (v. 12).[3]

*Job 19:13–22:* This section of Job's speech describes the hostility Job faced from his other acquaintances.[4] Job complained that everyone close to him, including those he considered his "brothers," his acquaintances, his family, and even his servants had all abandoned him (vv. 13–16). His family now found him repulsive (v. 17). Things had gotten very dark for Job. Oswald Chambers wrote, "Oh, the unspeakable benediction of the 'treasures of darkness'! It is not the days of sunshine and splendor and liberty and light that leave their lasting and indelible effect upon the soul, but those nights of the Spirit in which, shadowed by God's hand, hidden in the dark cleft of some rock in a weary land, He lets the splendors of the outskirts of Himself pass before our gaze."[5]

Even young people began to mock Job (v. 18). The treatment Job experienced resembled that of a leper. No one wanted anything to do with him and they kept him at a distance. His friends and those he loved turned against him. Job's experience was remarkably similar to what the Messiah would endure. Isaiah prophesied, "He was despised and rejected by men, a man of suffering who knew what sickness was. He was like someone people turned away from; He was despised, and we didn't value Him" (Isaiah 53:3).

Job described the frailty of his current physical condition (v. 20). MacArthur noted Job "had escaped death by a very slim margin."[6] After experiencing such radical suffering, Job appealed again to his friends to "have mercy on me" (v. 21).

*Job 19:23–29:* Now, after outlining all the ways God and his acquaintances had been against him, Job began to express his confidence in God.[7] MacArthur wrote,

---

[3] Warren W. Wiersbe, *The Bible Exposition Commentary: Job–Song of Solomon* (Colorado Springs: David C. Cook, 2004), 39–40.

[4] Constable, 77.

[5] Oswald Chambers; quoted in Wiersbe, 39.

[6] John MacArthur, *The MacArthur Bible Commentary* (Nashville: Thomas Nelson, 2005), 582.

[7] Constable, 77.

"At the point of Job's greatest despair, his faith appeared at its highest."[8] Job knew God would redeem him. Other pictures of God being viewed as a living Redeemer are provided in the Old Testament:

- Therefore tell the Israelites: I am Yahweh, and I will deliver you from the forced labor of the Egyptians and free you from slavery to them. I will redeem you with an outstretched arm and great acts of judgment" (Exodus 6:6).
- "May the words of my mouth and the meditation of my heart be acceptable to You, LORD, my rock and my Redeemer" (Psalm 19:14).
- "He will redeem them from oppression and violence, for their lives are precious in his sight" (Psalm 72:14).
- "This is what the LORD, your Redeemer, the Holy One of Israel says: Because of you, I will send to Babylon and bring all of them as fugitives, even the Chaldeans in the ships in which they rejoice" (Isaiah 43:14).

Job believed he would see and experience *The Promised Redeemer* (v. 27). In the midst of all of the chaos, Job remembered the promise of the living Redeemer.

## Closing

Job may not have known what he was doing, but his expression of hope in a living Redeemer was an expression of hope in the coming Messiah, Jesus. No matter how desperate our situation may be, Jesus can redeem any of us: "They are justified freely by His grace through the redemption that is in Christ Jesus" (Romans 3:24).

### The Daily Word

Job responded to Bildad with exhaustion, saying: How long will you torment me and crush me with words? . . . He has removed my brothers from me; my acquaintances have abandoned me. . . . My breath is offensive to my wife, and my own family finds me repulsive.

Nevertheless, even in the midst of despair and exhaustion, Job found hope, saying: "But I know my living Redeemer, and He will stand on the dust at last." Yes, Job knew the living Redeemer, the one who was still to come, *The Promised Redeemer*, Jesus. Job found hope.

Each day, you will walk through situations that may bring discouragement: spilled coffee on your computer, a lost phone, infertility, a friend who won't speak

---

[8] MacArthur, 582.

to you, being confined to bed or your house . . . there are so many situations on any given day that can lead to discouragement. As you walk through these difficult moments, remember there is always a *but*. There is always the truth. *You have a living Redeemer, Jesus Christ.* He gave His life in order to set you free from sin and death. And now, your Redeemer lives. Even at the end of a difficult day, choose to say: "*But* I know my Redeemer lives." Now you can face tomorrow, because your Redeemer lives. God's got you, friend. Hang on to the hope in Christ.

**But I know my living Redeemer, and He will stand on the dust at last. Even after my skin has been destroyed, yet I will see God in my flesh. —Job 19:25–26**

Further Scripture: Isaiah 43:1; Romans 8:1–2; Ephesians 1:7–8

## Questions

1.  Job was tired of being insulted by Bildad (Job 19:1–5). It seems Bildad was more concerned about Job's sins than his own. Where in Scripture do we find a proper response to another's sin (Matthew 7:3–5)? Do you know someone like this?

2.  In Job 19:13–20, Job listed his woes. What did he list more than once?

3.  At the end of Job 19, Job said, "Yet as for me, I know that my Redeemer lives" (ESV). How powerful was that statement? Do you think you could have suffered as Job and still praised God, knowing you would see him?

4.  What did the Holy Spirit highlight to you in Job 19 through the reading or the teaching?

# Lesson 14: Job 20

*The Promised Redeemer:* The Wicked Will
Not Prosper

## Teaching Notes

### Intro

In the previous chapter, Job expressed his hope in a living Redeemer who would ultimately save him. Now, Zophar offered his second speech in response to Job. The other two friends, Bildad and Eliphaz, had each given their second speeches, and Zophar wanted his turn. Zophar's previous speech was in chapter 11. In this speech, Zophar "admonished Job to reconsider the fate of the wicked."[1] Zophar's second speech would hurt Job more than any other thus far.[2]

### Teaching

*Job 20:1–3*: These verses clearly portray Zophar's anger.[3] Zophar asserted Job's rebuke had upset him, so he felt compelled to reply. This was probably in response to Job's statement in 16:3, "Is there no end to your empty words? What provokes you that you continue testifying?" Phillip Brooks wrote, "The truest help we can render an afflicted man is not to take his burden from him, but to call out his greatest strength that he may be able to bear it."[4]

*Job 20:4–11*: Zophar outlined the brief prosperity of the wicked.[5] He believed the joy wicked people experienced came and went quickly, similarly to Job's happiness that was now gone. Ash reminds us that, even in the midst of what can feel repetitive in these friends' speeches, we can depend on the promise of 2 Timothy 3:16–17: "All Scripture is inspired by God and is profitable for teaching, for

---

[1] John MacArthur, *The MacArthur Bible Commentary* (Nashville: Thomas Nelson, 2005), 582.

[2] Thomas L. Constable, *Expository Notes of Dr. Thomas Constable: Job*, 80, https://planobiblechapel.org/tcon/notes/pdf/job.pdf.

[3] Constable, 81.

[4] Phillip Brooks; quoted in Warren W. Wiersbe, *The Bible Exposition Commentary: Job–Song of Solomon* (Colorado Springs: David C. Cook, 2004), 42.

[5] Constable, 81.

rebuking, for correcting, for training in righteousness, so that the man of God may be complete, equipped for every good work."[6]

The book of Job, and especially these chapters that repeat the warnings against wickedness from Eliphaz, Bildad, and Zophar, is beneficial for three reasons:

1.  *They terrify us and move us to warn unbelievers that unless they repent, this will indeed be their destiny.* Consequences for our sin, ultimately including death, are real. Eliphaz, Bildad, and Zophar were at least aware of the eternal consequences of wickedness.

2.  *They help us grasp the depth of darkness and suffering that the Lord Jesus experienced on the cross.* When we go through periods of darkness and suffering, we must consider that the Lord may be trying to speak to us through it. Christ took on suffering and darkness so we could have life (2 Corinthians 5:21). Job painted a picture of the depth of darkness and suffering Jesus took upon himself to give us life.

3.  *If it is true that disciples of Christ in this age do have, in some measure, to drink the cup that He drank, then we do suffer with Him in order that in the end we may be glorified with Him.*[7] Because of the eternal life that we will inherit through Christ, there is a measure of suffering in this life that we must embrace. Romans 8:17 says, "And if children, also heirs—heirs of God and coheirs with Christ—if indeed we suffer with him so that we may also be glorified with him."

Zophar continued to explain the fate of the wicked. In Zophar's opinion, the wicked would quickly disappear, his children would become beggars, and he would ultimately meet an early death.

*Job 20:12–19*: Zophar outlined his belief in the certain punishment of sin. *Nelson's Commentary* notes, "Though evil may be sweet to the wicked for a while, the certain consequences of their behavior will bring about their downfall."[8] Proverbs 20:17 says, "Food gained by fraud is sweet to a person, but afterward his mouth is full of gravel." While Zophar's main point that God will judge the wicked was true, its application was twisted because he and his friends insisted Job was wicked and sinful.

---

[6] Christopher Ash, *Job: The Wisdom of the Cross*, ed. R. Kent Hughes (Wheaton: Crossway, 2014), 219.

[7] Ash, 220.

[8] Earl D. Radmacher, Ronald B. Allen, and H. Wayne House, eds., *Nelson's New Illustrated Bible Commentary* (Nashville: Thomas Nelson, 1999), 628.

*Job 20:20–29*: Finally, Zophar outlined his belief in "God's swift judgment of the wicked." Zophar's bottom-line admonition to Job was for Job to repent or face the loss of everything he had.

## Closing

While persecution may be coming to believers, that does not mean it is God's judgment. While Zophar's theology was wrong, he did remind us to be willing to consider death, to remember the depth of darkness and suffering experienced by Christ, and he admonished us to be willing to drink the cup of suffering to share in God's eternal glory.

## The Daily Word

Zophar responded to Job a second time. This time Zophar's unsettled thoughts forced him to angrily answer Job. Zophar strongly explained how the joy of the wicked would be brief and how happiness for the godless would only last a minute. He went on to say that the wicked person's appetite would never be satisfied.

Those without Jesus, who are without the presence of the living God inside them, will search and search for meaning and fulfillment in their lives, but they will never find satisfaction. They will chase after everything they desire but never truly find peace. However, in Christ's presence, there is fullness of joy. Even when life is dry and parched, He will be your living water. He will be your strength. He will forgive your sins and heal your diseases. He will redeem your life from the pit and satisfy you with goodness. As you delight in the Lord, He will give you the desires of your heart and will give you the strength you need for every situation. Christ is enough. When you hunger and thirst for life with Christ, you will be filled. Stop chasing after the things of the world. *Only Christ can give complete satisfaction.*

**Because his appetite is never satisfied, he does not let anything he desires escape. —Job 20:20**

Further Scripture: Psalm 103:2–5; Isaiah 58:11; Matthew 5:6

## Questions

1. Zophar said his spirit prompted him to reply (Job 20:3). In your opinion, which spirit was he listening to: Holy Spirit or a spirit of the enemy?
2. Do you think Zophar spoke to Job in love? Tough love? Where in Scripture did Jesus tell us what love is and what it should look like (Proverbs 17:17; John 15:12; Romans 13:10)?

3. Throughout all of Job 20, Zophar said "he," "him," and "they." Was the tone of the chapter a generality, or did Zophar attack Job, claiming he was a hypocrite, serpent, and evil?

4. What did the Holy Spirit highlight to you in Job 20 through the reading or the teaching?

# Lesson 15: Job 21

*The Promised Redeemer:* Waiting on the Lord

## Teaching Notes

### Intro

Waiting on the Lord has always been difficult. In this chapter, Job responds to Zophar's second speech. Job's speech in this chapter was a response to Zophar, but it also spoke to the bigger picture of what was going on.

### Teaching

*Job 21:1–3*: Job desperately wanted his friends to hear his words, to stop judging his conduct, and hear his heart in his suffering. He wanted his friends to sympathize with him. Job began this speech with a restatement of the sentiment in 13:5: "If only you would shut up and let that be your wisdom!" Job admonished his friends to listen to him for just a moment before rushing to speak again.

*Job 21:4–16*: Constable points out that Job simply wanted to be heard by his friends.[1] Job was desperate for someone to hear him because he felt even God wasn't listening to him. However, his friends were more concerned with trying to get him to repent of sin they were sure he had committed.

Beginning in verse 7, Job spoke about how wicked people experience continued prosperity.[2] The wicked experience good things while refusing to acknowledge God at all. Wiersbe calls this "practical atheism."[3] The wicked simply didn't care about God but were still prosperous. This truth undermined his friends' entire theology of God always punishing the wicked and always rewarding the godly.

---

[1] Thomas L. Constable, *Expository Notes of Dr. Thomas Constable: Job*, 84, https://planobiblechapel.org/tcon/notes/pdf/job.pdf.

[2] Constable, 84.

[3] Warren W. Wiersbe, *The Wiersbe Bible Commentary: Old Testament* (Colorado Springs: David C. Cook, 2007), 845.

*Job 21:17–26:* Job argued that God chose how and when the wicked prospered. In Job's mind, life was not as simple as his friends made it out to be. Sometimes God allowed the wicked to prosper and the righteous to suffer. At other times, God might punish the wicked and prosper the righteous. The issue was much more mysterious and less formulaic than his friends made it out to be. Job's argument refuted the idea of karma. Doing good things, including obeying God, did not mean he was due to receive good things. Nor did doing bad things, including sinning, mean he was necessarily due to receive bad things.

*Job 21:27–34:* Job offered more examples to refute his friends' theology of retribution. He asked them to simply walk around and observe how wicked people lived securely in their houses, experienced peaceful burials with people watching over their graves, and saw their children live on after them. In Job's mind, his friends needed to open their eyes to the world around them to see their argument didn't hold water.

In Job 21:4, Job struggled to wait on God during his suffering and in the middle of everything going wrong. Linda Green offers ten suggestions for things we can do while we wait on the Lord:

1. *Believe that the God who saved you hears your cries.* No matter what situation you have found yourself in, whether you are alone or with others, you must understand God hears you. "But I will look to the LORD; I will wait for the God of my salvation. My God will hear me" (Micah 7:7).

2. *Watch with expectancy, but be prepared for unexpected answers.* "In the morning, LORD, you hear my voice; in the morning I lay my requests before you and wait expectantly" (Psalm 5:3 NIV). God will answer our prayers, but He might not answer them in the way that we think He will.

3. *Put your hope in His Word.* We can put our hope in many things, but Psalm 130:5–6 says, "I wait for Yahweh; I wait and put my hope in His word. I wait for the Lord more than watchmen for the morning—more than watchmen for the morning."

4. *Trust in the Lord, not in your own understanding.* "Trust in the LORD with all your heart, and do not rely on your own understanding; think about Him in all your ways, and He will guide you on the right paths" (Proverbs 3:5–6). None of the things we can do to settle our minds in the midst of struggles ultimately work. We only find the relief we seek when we resolve to place our trust in the Lord.

5. *Resist fretting, refrain from anger, be still, and choose patience.* "Be silent before the Lord and wait expectantly for Him; do not be agitated by one who prospers in his way, by the man who carries out evil plans. Refrain from anger and give up your rage; do not be agitated—it can only bring harm" (Psalm 37:7–8).

6. *Be strong and take courage.* "I am certain that I will see the Lord's goodness in the land of the living. Wait for the Lord; be strong and courageous. Wait for the Lord" (Psalm 27:13–14).

7. *See it as an opportunity to experience God's goodness.* "The Lord is good to those who wait for Him, to the person who seeks Him" (Lamentations 3:25).

8. *Wait for God's promise instead of going your own way.* "While He was together with them, He commanded them not to leave Jerusalem, but to wait for the Father's promise" (Acts 1:4).

9. *Continue steadfastly in prayer, being watchful with thanksgiving.* "Devote yourselves to prayer; stay alert in it with thanksgiving" (Colossians 4:2).

10. *Remember the blessings yet to come.* "Therefore the Lord is waiting to show you mercy, and is rising up to show you compassion, for the Lord is a just God. All who wait patiently for Him are happy" (Isaiah 30:18). We may receive the blessings of the Lord in the here and now, or we may receive them eternally. Either way, God promises to bless us as we wait for Him.[4]

## Closing

These ten truths help us understand how we can wait on the Lord in the middle of suffering. They aren't a process or a formula, but holding on to these truths will ensure we get to the other side of any situation that requires us to wait on the Lord.

## The Daily Word

Job responded to his friends' reasoning about why he was experiencing this time of suffering, living day and night with painful boils. Job's thoughts and emotions had been up and down, and yet he continued to wait upon the Lord for the day when he would be free from the suffering. *Waiting.* When you walk in the Spirit, the Lord will fill you with patience. In contrast, when you walk in your flesh, you will naturally grow impatient, experience worry and fear, get irritated, and lose perspective. Whether you are waiting for coffee to brew, the line at the

[4] Linda Green, "What to Do While You're Waiting on God," Open the Bible with Pastor Colin Smith, August 31, 2017, https://unlockingthebible.org/2017/08/what-to-do-while-youre-waiting-on-god/.

grocery store to move, or traffic to clear, everyday situations may cause you to grow impatient. Waiting for a health test result over the weekend or for a loved one to get out of surgery can really cause unrest in your heart. However, the Lord says those who wait upon the Lord will renew their strength. No matter what you are waiting for, you can release your prayers to the Lord and wait expectantly, trusting that He hears you! As you wait for something in your life today, believe one thing—*the Lord knows*. He hears you. So trust His timing even through traffic. Wait with thanksgiving. Rest in His promises. Resist the urge to fear and fret. *The Lord your God is with you through the waiting.*

**As for me, is my complaint against a man? Then why shouldn't I be impatient? Look at me and shudder; put your hand over your mouth. —Job 21:4–5**

Further Scripture: Psalm 5:3; Isaiah 40:31; Micah 7:7

## Questions

1. What was the one consolation Job said his friends could give him? Do you struggle to listen to others? How can you become a better listener instead of the one giving your opinion?

2. At whom was Job's real complaint aimed? Do you see this as a bad thing? Explain.

3. What were the three main points of Zophar and his friends that Job refuted (Job 21:7, 17, 22–26)?

4. What was Job's position on the thought that the punishment for parents' sins falls on their children (Deuteronomy 24:16; Ezekiel 18:1–20; John 9:1–3)?

5. Read 21:7–16. Do you ever catch yourself envying or admiring those who reject God yet seem to live a trouble-free and prosperous life? How do you share the gospel with people who seem to have everything?

6. What did the Holy Spirit highlight to you in Job 21 through the reading or the teaching?

# Lesson 16: Job 22—23

*The Promised Redeemer:* The Bottom Line

## Teaching Notes

### Intro

We all have to deal with the ideas of loss, pain, and suffering. As we encounter these situations, we have to determine for ourselves what we will hold on to that will get us through them. In a way, we must determine what truth we will believe. Job is something of a philosophy lesson for us. Philosophy is derived from two Greek words that mean "love" and "wisdom," so "philosophy" is "the love of wisdom."

In today's chapters, Eliphaz gave his third response to Job, and Job again responded to Eliphaz. Eliphaz had bravado. He wanted to be the one to get to the bottom line of what was going on.

### Teaching

*Job 22:1–4*: Eliphaz essentially asked, "What do you get the guy who has everything?" In Eliphaz's mind, God was omniscient, omnipotent, and omnipresent. There simply was nothing else any human being could offer God that He did not already have. This was the heart cry of a humanity that walked in the physical without seeing the spiritual. Eliphaz could conceive of ways his own wisdom or righteousness could better his life, but none of those things could add to God.

*Job 22:5–9*: Eliphaz brought a series of accusations against Job, but they feel general in nature. Eliphaz tried to show Job some of the situations in which he might have sinned.

*Job 22:10–20*: Eliphaz argued that because Job was a man like everyone else and had surely sinned in some general way, "sudden dread" had come upon Job. Sometimes the good things we experience in life come from the general grace of God. When those things are taken away, we can wonder what we did to cause God to remove them from our lives; their loss feels like "sudden dread."

Eliphaz acknowledged the wicked could have their time in the sun but again asserted his belief they would be "snatched away before their time" (v. 16).

*Job 22:21–30*: Eliphaz encouraged Job, "Come to terms with God and be at peace" (v. 21), which meant to acknowledge his own sin and God's justice in judging him. According to Eliphaz, if Job would simply humble himself in this way, God would be gracious to him again.

"Now without faith it is impossible to please God, for the one who draws near to Him must believe that He exists and rewards those who seek Him" (Hebrews 11:6). To please God, we must believe in the things that He has said are true and that He will reward those who walk in obedience to Him.

"Therefore, since we have been declared righteous by faith, we have peace with God through our Lord Jesus Christ. We have also obtained access through Him by faith into this grace in which we stand, and we rejoice in the hope of the glory of God. And not only that, but we also rejoice in our afflictions, because we know that affliction produces endurance, endurance produces proven character, and proven character produces hope. This hope will not disappoint us, because God's love has been poured out in our hearts through the Holy Spirit who was given to us" (Romans 5:1–5). God can be found in the low points. When He is found in the low points, we learn to trust Him more while the Holy Spirit gives us the hope and the perseverance to wait on the things to come.

*Job 23:1–7*: Job looked for hope but didn't know where to turn. He wanted to stand before God, but he didn't know where to find God anymore. Despite this, Job knew that if he were able to stand before God that God would treat him differently than his friends. God would strengthen Job, and Job would be able to "reason with Him" (v. 7), unlike Zophar, Bildad, and Eliphaz. Job knew God was not out to prove a point to humanity but wanted to bring His answers to humanity so humanity could understand its existence in light of Him.

*Job 23:8–12*: Job stated his belief that "when He has tested me, I will emerge as pure gold" (v. 10). Job didn't despise his suffering. He didn't believe it was anti-God for him to have to walk through a period of suffering. Job seems to have understood he would experience God more deeply in his suffering.

*Job 23:13–17*: Job believed God would always do what He wanted, including working out whatever it was He was doing through Job's current situation. In light of this, Job expressed he was "terrified in His presence" and that he was "afraid of Him" as a result (v. 15). Job knew who God was but acknowledged he could have undersold the scope of God's power and plan for him. Job believed God to be limitless in power. Job believed God to be omnipresent. Job believed

God to have all wisdom. When he considered all these things, he came to a place of awe, a holy reverence for God's power and wisdom.

## Closing

Understanding the bottom-line truth of who God is enables us to overcome any trial or tribulation in life. The one place in which we must be satisfied is knowing God and knowing He knows us.

---

## The Daily Word

Once again Job heard from his friend Eliphaz, who questioned the reasons for Job's suffering. Eliphaz offered answers to Job, essentially saying: If only Job would work on X-Y-Z, then his suffering would stop. However, Job understood that life doesn't happen like a formula. Job admitted he couldn't find God anywhere from the north, south, east, or west, and *yet* Job kept his faith saying, "*Yet* He knows the way I have taken; when He has tested me, I will emerge as pure gold." Job acknowledged he was terrified and afraid of God, and *yet* Job held onto hope saying: "*Yet* I am not destroyed by the darkness, by the thick darkness that covers my face."

Today, you may be in the middle of a trial like Job. You can't see God's hand in your life anywhere, and *yet* you know He is with you. You may be terrified, and *yet* you trust and are not destroyed. You have faith and hope carrying you through the difficult, painful days. Remember, through the affliction, the Lord is producing endurance, character, and hope in you. Today, as you walk through the darkness, God knows the way you have taken. You are not destroyed. You will emerge like pure gold. Press on in faith, and hold on to the hope within you.

**When He is at work to the north, I cannot see Him; when He turns south, I cannot find Him. Yet He knows the way I have taken; when He has tested me, I will emerge as pure gold. —Job 23:9–10**

Further Scripture: Isaiah 48:10; Romans 5:3–5; Hebrews 11:6

---

## Questions

1. Eliphaz asked if a person could do anything to help God (Job 22:2). What do you think? Does God need our help?

2. What does it look like for you to "submit to God" in your life (Job 22:21–22)? Where else are we told to "submit to God" (James 4:7–10)? What are some of the differences between these verses? Similarities?

3.  In Job 23:3, Job said, "If I only knew how to find Him." Job felt he could not reach God. Have you ever felt you could not reach God—that He was far from you? What were some things you did to draw closer to God? What does Scripture say (Deuteronomy 4:29; Jeremiah 29:13)? Are there times when God intentionally withdraws for a season to test us?

4.  What did the Holy Spirit highlight to you in Job 22—23 through the reading or the teaching?

# Lesson 17: Job 24

*The Promised Redeemer:* Injustice Everywhere

## Teaching Notes

### Intro

In the middle of all the chaos in Job's life, he held on to hope in his *Promised Redeemer* (Job 19:25–26). Today's chapter is a continuation of Job's response to Eliphaz, but more broadly it was a speech directed to all three of his friends. Wiersbe points out that a good summary statement on the content of this chapter from Job's perspective could be, "God perplexes me."[1]

### Teaching

*Job 24:1–11:* Wiersbe observes that these verses contain Job's complaint about injustices in Israel that seem to have gone unpunished. At the forefront of his complaint, Job wondered why God didn't have specific days in which to hold court and hear people's complaints and give judgments.[2]

In verses 2–8, Job listed three types of sins committed in rural areas[3] that God seemed to leave unpunished:

1. The wicked displaced boundary markers (v. 2). This was the same thing as stealing land in ancient Israel. *Nelson's Commentary* points out the seriousness of this crime in Israel. Those found guilty of moving boundary stones were considered to be under a divine curse:[4]

   - "You must not move your neighbor's boundary marker, established at the start in the inheritance you will receive in the land the LORD your God is giving you to possess" (Deuteronomy 19:14).

---

[1] Warren W. Wiersbe, *The Wiersbe Bible Commentary: Old Testament* (Colorado Springs: David C. Cook, 2007), 849.

[2] Wiersbe, 849.

[3] Wiersbe, 849.

[4] Earl D. Radmacher, Ronald B. Allen, and H. Wayne House, eds., *Nelson's New Illustrated Bible Commentary* (Nashville: Thomas Nelson, 1999), 630.

- "The one who moves his neighbor's boundary marker is cursed" (Deuteronomy 27:17).
- "Don't move an ancient boundary marker that your fathers set up" (Proverbs 22:28).

MacArthur notes that land markers would be moved by corrupt landowners to "increase their holdings, particularly where the land was owned by bereaved widows."[5]

2. The wicked mistreated the weak (v. 3–8). The wicked ran off donkeys owned by the fatherless and took animals belonging to others. Without the means to provide for themselves, they were forced to forage for food and went without clothing. MacArthur points out that taking a person's outer garment as a pledge was a common practice in the Old Testament. However, the Law "forbade keeping the garment at night since its owner could get cold and sick."[6]

- "When you make a loan of any kind to your neighbor, do not enter his house to collect what he offers as security. You must stand outside while the man you are making the loan to brings the security out to you. If he is a poor man, you must not sleep in the garment he has given as security. Be sure to return it to him at sunset. Then he will sleep in it and bless you, and this will be counted as righteousness to you before the LORD your God" (Deuteronomy 24:10–13).

3. The wicked cause chaos in the land (v. 9–11). The wicked seized children as collateral on loans, caused the poor to go without clothing, and didn't pay workers their wages.

*Job 24:12–17*: Job moved on to observe crimes in cities that God left unpunished.[7] Job listed murder, theft, and adultery as sins specific to his complaint.

*Job 24:18–25*: Wiersbe observes that after listing unpunished sins in the country, then in the city, Job pronounced a curse on the wicked.[8] Job's language in this section was similar to his friends'. Job may have attempted to sound like his friends in order to further refute their viewpoint. In the midst of his suffering, Job was able to see the suffering of others. Wiersbe points out, "Too often, personal suffering can make us selfish and even blind us to the needs of others, but

---

[5] John MacArthur, *The MacArthur Bible Commentary* (Nashville: Thomas Nelson, 2005), 584.

[6] MacArthur, 584.

[7] Wiersbe, 849.

[8] Wiersbe, 849.

Job was concerned that God help others who were hurting."[9] Job's friends treated the suffering of others as an abstract concept while Job sought to view them from a personal perspective. Job wanted to be part of the solution despite the greatness of his own suffering.

# Closing

Hampton Keathley IV notes three actions the Good Samaritan took in response to the suffering man he found on the roadside. They are helpful for us as we consider serving those who are suffering:

1. *He had compassion.* The Samaritan took the initiative to move toward the man who was suffering.
2. *He cared.* The Samaritan took time to reach out.
3. *It cost him.* The Samaritan used his own money to care for the man. He sacrificed to show his care for someone else.[10]

If we functioned like the good Samaritan, we might get the point of Job's complaint and be able to be part of the solution in other people's suffering.

## The Daily Word

As Job responded to his friends, he brought attention to others suffering around him: the injustices happening, the crimes in the city, and the curses on the wicked. Rather than just focusing on his own suffering, Job noticed how the orphans, the widows, and other misfortunate, helpless people needed help, hope, and love.

In the midst of your own suffering, *take your eyes off yourself and look at others around you.* You may be in the hospital for treatment or at an insurance office making a claim for an accident, but for a moment, open your eyes to see those around you. As a believer in Jesus, you are called to love God and love others—and not just when things in your life are going smoothly. Who knows, maybe in the midst of sickness or loss, the Lord wants to use you to bring hope to another person. You never know how the Lord will move when you take your eyes off yourself and show someone compassion and love. Even when you feel weary and have nothing left to give, God's grace is sufficient and will give you strength. Love others even through the pain. It may be just what you need to get through your own painful situation.

---

[9] Wiersbe, 849–50.

[10] Hampton Keathley IV, "The Good Samaritan," Bible.org, August 17, 2004, https://bible.org/seriespage/4-good-samaritan.

They prey on the childless woman who is unable to conceive, and do not deal kindly with the widow. Yet God drags away the mighty by His power; when He rises up, they have no assurance of life. He gives them a sense of security, so they can rely on it, but His eyes watch over their ways. —Job 24:21–23

Further Scripture: Ephesians 5:2; Philippians 2:3–4; 1 John 4:19–21

## Questions

1. In chapter 24, Job asked an age-old question about why the wicked were not punished. If Job had asked you that question, how would you have answered?

2. Could Job 24 describe the world today? Why or why not? In what ways?

3. Job spoke about sinners having no assurance of life (Job 24:22). What does Jesus say about this assurance (Romans 5:8; 10:9–10)?

4. What did the Holy Spirit highlight to you in Job 24 through the reading or the teaching?

# Lesson 18: Job 25—26

*The Promised Redeemer*: Relationship,
Not Righteousness

## Teaching Notes

### Intro

These chapters wrap up the third cycle of speeches in Job. Throughout each speech, each person had pushed their viewpoint, and no one had given an inch. Bildad spoke for the last time in chapter 25. Bildad's position had been consistent throughout all his speeches. He routinely called on Job to repent and be saved. Job consistently claimed his innocence, to which Bildad replied once more.

### Teaching

*Job 25:1–6*: Bildad's final response to Job highlights his traditionalist understanding of God and sin. McKenna observes, "Tradition has no answer for radical changes in the circumstances of life."[1] Job challenged his friends in chapter 24 to prove his claims about the injustices in the world being untrue. Instead of responding directly to Job, Bildad's comments were brief, focused on God, and summed up his previous conclusions. Bildad had no real answer to Job's observations and claims.

Bildad's final response is a doxology of praise to God. Every attribute of God he highlighted was true, but each attribute was also incomplete. The God Bildad praised was in a box. God was powerful, God was perfection, and God was pure, but God didn't resemble the God of Job who offered His presence through interaction.

Bildad asked, "How can one born of woman be pure" (v. 4)? The answer was simply that we couldn't be born pure. Interestingly, this was a conclusion Job reached all the way back in chapter 14: "Who can produce something pure from what is impure? No one!" (Job 14:4). Isaiah also wrestled with this question: "All of us have become like something unclean, and all our righteous acts are like a polluted garment; all of us wither like a leaf, and our iniquities carry us away like

---

[1] David L. McKenna, *Job*, vol. 12 of The Preacher's Commentary (Nashville: Thomas Nelson, 1986), 180–81.

the wind" (Isaiah 64:6). Isaiah also saw the Savior that bridged the gap between man and God: "We all went astray like sheep; we all have turned to our own way; and the LORD has punished him for the iniquity of us all" (Isaiah 53:6).

Bildad contended that man was unable to stand before God, which was closer to the truth than Job's position that he would be able to stand before God because of his righteousness. Bildad had an unmovable, fixed image of an impassable God who could never stoop to meet man, whereas Job had a dynamic faith in which he learned more about God through his suffering as God met him in the midst of it. McKenna noted, "Although [Job] has a problem of his own righteous conceit, he has demonstrated that he is open to change. If Bildad and Job were alive at the advent of Christ, we could expect that Bildad would side with the Pharisees while Job would cry, 'Lord, be merciful to me a sinner.'"[2]

To conclude his doxology, Bildad drew a comparison between God and man by comparing man to "a maggot" and "a worm." While his friend sat before him during unspeakable suffering, Bildad's final word to him was to call him a maggot and a worm. David wrestled with the same understanding of man in comparison to God: "When I observe the heavens, the work of Your fingers, the moon and the stars, which You set in place, what is a man that You remember him, the son of man that You look after him? You made him little less than God and crowned him with glory and honor" (Psalm 8:3–5). David's questions were similar to Bildad's, but he came to a completely opposite conclusion. Bildad believed man to be a worm while David saw the glory of being created in God's image.[3]

*Job 26:1–4*: Job's tone changed in his response to Bildad. As his frustration mounted with his friends over how they chose to pontificate on their beliefs rather than listen and respond to his complaint, Job became sarcastic. Bildad was the friend who was known for his wisdom, yet he failed Job. McKenna observed, Job "resents the hostile tone of voice that reflects not the spirit of God but the spirit of a self-defensive man tainted with a touch of the demonic."[4] McKenna proposed that Job paused after speaking the first four verses to allow his friends an opportunity to respond. Neither Zophar, Bildad, or Eliphaz had anything further to say, so Job's speech continued.[5]

*Job 26:5–14*: Job pointed out that death was a reality mankind faced, but God's power in heaven and on earth extends into what is beyond death. Mankind will not be able to hide from God, even in death, because God will judge us: "And just as it is appointed for people to die once—and after this, judgment" (Hebrews 9:27).

---

[2] McKenna, 180–81.

[3] McKenna, 180–81.

[4] McKenna, 180–81.

[5] McKenna, 180–81.

In light of this, Job praised God for His power in creation. Job used a series of word pictures to describe God as a divine architect. God "stretches the northern skies" (v. 7), "wraps up the water in His clouds" (v. 8), "obscures the view of His throne" (v. 9), "laid out the horizon on the surface of the waters" (v. 10), causes the pillars that hold up the sky to shake when He rebukes them (v. 11), stirs up the sea (v. 12), and "by His breath, the heavens gained their beauty" (v. 13). After listing the evidences for God's power, Job bowed in humility before God: "These are but the fringes of His ways; how faint is the word we hear of Him! Who can understand His mighty thunder?" (v. 14).

## Closing

Job would continue to wrestle with his own righteousness. He still didn't understand how and why all that had happened to him. But he began to understand it was somehow about being in relationship with God.

---

### The Daily Word

Bildad spoke to Job again, this time calling Job a maggot and a worm. Bildad's advice and comments were not likely what Job needed to hear. Job responded strongly to Bildad with a series of direct questions. Job put his foot down and said to Bildad, "I have heard enough from you." And then, in the midst of his own personal misery and suffering, Job focused on Who he knew was certain—the God who created the universe and all creation. "He stretches the northern skies over empty space; He hangs the earth on nothing. . . . He laid out the horizon on the surface of the waters."

Today, as you press on through the Lord's plan for your day—whether it's a day filled with joy and delight or a day filled with heartache and unknowns—*give thanks to God, the creator of heaven and earth*. Praise the Lord for His power that stirs the sea. Praise the Lord for His breath that gives the heavens their beauty. Open a window, walk outside, breathe in the fresh air, let the sun soak your face or the raindrops drench your hair, and give thanks to the Lord for His mighty, powerful creation. The same God who created the universe longs for a relationship with you. The God of miracles and wonders loves you. Stop and pause at His wonders today.

**He stretches the northern skies over empty space; He hangs the earth on nothing. He wraps up the waters in His clouds, yet the clouds do not burst beneath their weight. —Job 26:7–8**

Further Scripture: Psalm 104:24–25; John 1:3; Romans 1:20

---

# Questions

1. Bildad asked two questions. First, "how can a person be justified before God?" How would you answer this question (Romans 3:26; 10:9–10; Philippians 3:9; 1 John 2:1)? Second, "how can anyone born of woman be pure?" How would you answer? How does this point to *The Promised Redeemer*?

2. To what did Bildad equate man (Job 25:6)? Does this line up with the rest of Scripture? Does this foreshadow the Messiah (Psalm 22:6)?

3. Job responded to Bildad in chapter 26. The chapter concludes with a question. Restate this question in your own words. What Scripture would you use to answer it?

4. What did the Holy Spirit highlight to you in Job 25—26 through the reading or the teaching?

# Lesson 19: Job 27

## *The Promised Redeemer*: Hold Fast

## Teaching Notes

### Intro

Job was able to endure all his suffering because he looked forward to his living Redeemer (Job 19:25–26). Ultimately, this Redeemer was Jesus who took on our sin and our suffering and gave us hope to endure. Job's three friends repeatedly told him he was wicked. Job had to hold on to *The Promised Redeemer*. Today's chapter is a continuation of Job's response to Bildad's final speech in which Job moved to more generally defending his righteousness.

### Teaching

*Job 27:1–6*: Wiersbe observes Job taking an oath when he began this speech with the phrase, "as God lives." To this point, God had not answered Job even though Job asked God to declare him righteous.[1] In spite of the quietness of God, Job was resolute that his "lips will not speak unjustly," and he would not lie (v. 4). Job was serious about his oath. Wiersbe points out, "Among Eastern people in that day, taking an oath was a serious matter. It was like inviting God to kill you if what you said was not true."[2]

MacArthur notes, "God did not speak to declare Job innocent," similarly to how Isaiah described Christ's treatment: "He was taken away because of oppression and judgment; and who considered His fate? For He was cut off from the land of the living; He was struck because of my people's rebellion" (Isaiah 53:8).[3]

While under his oath, Job vowed he would never affirm his friends' viewpoint. Job knew he had nothing to be afraid of because he had done nothing wrong. Job determined to "cling to my righteousness" (v. 6). The New American

---

[1] Warren W. Wiersbe, *The Bible Exposition Commentary: Job–Song of Solomon* (Colorado Springs: David C. Cook, 2004), 54.

[2] Wiersbe, 54.

[3] John MacArthur, *The MacArthur Bible Commentary* (Nashville: Thomas Nelson, 2005), 585.

Standard Bible translates "cling to" as "hold fast." Michael Bradley lists four points on holding fast:[4]

1. *Hold fast to the Lord.* Without an initial confession of faith in the Lord, we will have nothing to hold on to. The author of Hebrews admonished: "Let us hold on to the confession of our hope without wavering, for He who promised is faithful" (Hebrews 10:23). God's faithfulness to us should motivate us to hold fast to who He is.

   "But Christ was faithful as a Son over His household. And we are that household if we hold on to the courage and the confidence of our hope" (Hebrews 3:6). Our confidence comes from Jesus' status as the One over our household.

   "Watch out, brothers, so that there won't be in any of you an evil, unbelieving heart that departs from the living God. But encourage each other daily, while it is still called today, so that none of you is hardened by sin's deception. For we have become companions of the Messiah if we hold firmly until the end the reality that we had at the start" (Hebrews 3:12–14). Job knew he was clinging to God's righteousness, and he would not let anyone keep him from that.

   "So don't throw away your confidence, which has a great reward. For you need endurance, so that after you have done God's will, you may receive what was promised" (Hebrews 10:35–36).

2. *Be faithful until death.* Once we are confident of our foundation in Christ, we have the ability to remain faithful throughout our lives.

   "Don't be afraid of what you are about to suffer. Look, the Devil is about to throw some of you into prison to test you, and you will have affliction for 10 days. Be faithful until death, and I will give you the crown of life" (Revelation 2:10).

   Paul admonished the Corinthian church to "Be alert, stand firm in the faith, act like a man, be strong" (1 Corinthians 16:13).

   "If indeed you remain grounded and steadfast in the faith and are not shifted away from the hope of the gospel that you heard. This gospel has been proclaimed in all creation under heaven, and I, Paul, have become a servant of it" (Colossians 1:23).

3. *Be an overcomer in the Lord.* Job knew in whom his faith was placed, and he resolved to be faithful to the Lord no matter what happened. He understood that the rewards were both in this life and still to come eternally.

---

[4] Michael Bradley, "Holding Fast to the Lord," BibleKnowledge.com, February 23, 2021, https://www.bible-knowledge.com/holding-fast/.

"The one who is victorious and who keeps My works to the end: I will give him authority over the nations" (Revelation 2:26).

"The victor: I will give him the right to sit with Me on My throne, just as I also won the victory and sat down with My Father on His throne" (Revelation 3:21).

"I have fought the good fight, I have finished the race, I have kept the faith" (2 Timothy 4:7).

"For God is not unjust; He will not forget your work and the love you showed for His name when you served the saints—and you continue to serve them. Now we want each of you to demonstrate the same diligence for the final realization of your hope , so that you won't become lazy but will be imitators of those who inherit the promises through faith and perseverance" (Hebrews 6:10–12).

4. *Jesus is the author and finisher of our faith.* "Therefore, since we also have such a large cloud of witnesses surrounding us, let us lay aside every weight and the sin that so easily ensnares us. Let us run with endurance the race that lies before us" (Hebrews 12:1).

"I am sure of this, that He who started a good work in you will carry it on to completion until the day of Christ Jesus" (Philippians 1:6). What Christ has started in you, He will finish. We must hold on.

## Closing

God has not promised that our road will be easy. We must cling to His righteousness, His promises, and the eternal knowledge that He will not let us go.

## The Daily Word

Job's friends didn't offer Job much hope as he pressed on through suffering. Even so, Job affirmed his commitment to the Lord, to his integrity, and to holding on, clinging to hope. He stated to his friends, "I will never affirm that you are right." Then Job expressed he would "cling to [his] righteousness and never let it go."

To *cling* means to hold fast, to persevere, to not quit, to hold on to what God has asked you to do. Imagine plastic wrap—they kind you use for leftovers. The purpose of it is to keep two pieces connected as they cling to each other, oftentimes covering a dish of food. Plastic wrap's purpose fails when it stops clinging to the side of a container of food. The spaghetti sauce may slip out, causing a mess. In the same way, you must hold fast and cling to the Lord so His purposes and plans for you are carried out to completion. The Lord will give you strength as you hold fast to His love and grace in your life by faith. Don't lose hope, even when bumps in the road come. Instead, *cling to the hope you have in Christ.* The Lord is faithful to fulfill His promises as you hold fast to Him.

> **I will never affirm that you are right. I will maintain my integrity until I die. I will cling to my righteousness and never let it go. My conscience will not accuse me as long as I live! —Job 27:5–6**
>
> Further Scripture: Philippians 1:6; Hebrews 10:23; Revelation 2:10

## Questions

1. How does Job 27:4 point to Christ (Isaiah 53:7, 9b; 1 Peter 2:22b)?

2. Read Job 27:8. How should this encourage you to share the good news with those you know or meet, especially those whom you identify as "wicked" or "godless"? What Scriptures can you use to support your answer?

3. Who was Job's audience in Job 27:12? What was Job claiming that they had seen? How were they acting foolishly? How do you sometimes act or behave contrary to the truths you know and proclaim?

4. What did the Holy Spirit highlight to you in Job 27 through the reading or the teaching?

# Lesson 20: Job 28—29

*The Promised Redeemer*: The Mystery of Wisdom

## Teaching Notes

### Intro

In today's chapters, Job continues to wrestle with both what had happened to him and how his friends had responded to him. Job's responses were both specific to things his friends had said to him and general about the nature of life and suffering.

### Teaching

*Job 28:1–11*: Job described the processes for obtaining precious metals from the earth, including silver, gold, iron, and copper. He highlighted that mankind had developed knowledge to mine beneath the earth's surface to bring out needed materials. In the process, mankind had seen and walked in places no other creature in the world had ever seen or walked. Humanity's knowledge is so developed he cuts "channels in the rocks" (v. 10) and "dams up the streams" (v. 11).

*Job 28:12–19*: After he observed many of humanity's technological advancements that demonstrated their ingenuity and intelligence, Job asked a pointed question: "But where can wisdom be found, and where is understanding located?" (v. 12). Job pointed out that wisdom could not be found in the oceans or the seas. Wisdom could not be bought with gold or silver. Wisdom was much more valuable than any precious stone: gold, silver, onyx, lapis lazuli, coral, quartz, pearl, or topaz.

*Job 28:20–28*: After pointing out the source for many types of precious commodities and emphasizing the value of wisdom over precious stones and valuables, Job again asked, "Where then does wisdom come from and where is understanding located?" (v. 20). Job noted that wisdom was "hidden from the eyes of every living thing" (v. 21); even Abaddon and Death have only heard about the source of wisdom (v. 22).

After carefully listing all the things humanity knows, how much more valuable wisdom is than any other precious commodity, and highlighting the hiddenness of wisdom, Job declared, "God understands the way to wisdom and He knows its location" (v. 23). God established wisdom when He created the world and made limits to natural processes like wind, rain, and lightning. Because God established wisdom, Job concluded, "The fear of the Lord is this: wisdom. And to turn from evil is understanding" (v. 28). Knowing the ways of the Lord is equal to fearing the Lord and is how one obtains wisdom. Understanding, the thing that makes a person turn from evil, is a response to the fear of the Lord.

"He made known to us the mystery of His will, according to His good pleasure that He planned in Him for the administration of the days of fulfillment—to bring everything together in the Messiah, both things in heaven and things on earth in Him" (Ephesians 1:9–10). "The mystery of His will" was what Job, Eliphaz, Bildad, and Zophar had all been trying to figure out.

"The mystery was made known to me by revelation, as I have briefly written above. By reading this you are able to understand my insight about the mystery of the Messiah. This was not made known to people in other generations as it is now revealed to his holy apostles and prophets by the Spirit" (Ephesians 3:3–5). Job and his friends wrestled with an incomplete revelation. They did not have a complete knowledge of Christ because He had not yet come.

"This grace was given to me—the least of all the saints—to proclaim to the Gentiles the incalculable riches of the Messiah, and to shed light for all about the administration of the mystery hidden for ages in God who created all things" (Ephesians 3:8–9). Job understood much about the natural world, but he struggled to understand the intricacies of God, especially regarding God's divine justice.

"For I consider that the sufferings of this present time are not worth comparing with the glory that is going to be revealed to us" (Romans 8:18). This was the perspective Job lacked. Paul understood that in spite of the sufferings he experienced in this life, there would be a final payday in which the glory he received would make the sufferings he experienced pale in comparison.

"We know that all things work together for the good of those who love God: those who are called according to His purpose" (Romans 8:28). Job and his friends struggled with this because it had not been revealed to them yet. They processed Job's experience with human reason and reached a limit to their understanding. They could not reason their way to understanding the kingdom of God and its relationship to earthly humanity.

God will make all things new. He will come back and restore all things. When we are able to see our situations from God's perspective, we will view them in a proper way. When we view our situations from God's perspective, we understand that, even if we die, to be present with Him in glory is gain. When we view our situations from God's perspective, we understand that He has worked all things out for our good and that our future glory will far outweigh our present suffering. But Job didn't fully understand these points.

*Job 29:1–25*: Job expressed a lament for the way things used to be. In the past, he felt God's friendship (vv. 4–5a), he still had his children (v. 5b), he had a position of authority (v. 7), he was thought to have great wisdom (vv. 8–11), and he helped the poor and the oppressed for the sake of justice (vv. 12–17). In the midst of his suffering, Job knew God had a place in his life. He seems to be wondering, "Why does serving God have to be this hard?"

## Closing

When we made the choice to live for the Lord and live according to His Word, we were separated from some things. But that same choice joins us to others who are like-minded in faith and we will find a new place of belonging.

### The Daily Word

Job asked the question, "Where can wisdom be found, and where is understanding located?" It's not found in the ocean depths. It's not exchanged for gold, silver, precious pearls, sapphire, coral, or quartz. Wisdom is beyond all the riches the world offers. Job knew that the source of wisdom was found in the all-seeing, all-knowing God.

Like Job, you may ask yourself, *What is wisdom and where does it come from?* The Word of God says that the fear of the Lord is wisdom and to turn from evil is understanding. You can search through books and online resources or seek your mentor's advice, but ultimate wisdom comes from fearing God. To fear God means to have a reverent respect for all He is capable of, believing He holds all the mysteries of the world together. As you walk in God's ways, resisting evil and temptations, you display understanding. You must believe God is bigger than all of the things of the world. Wisdom is worth more than any precious stone. Wisdom is greater but not unattainable. Today, ask the Lord for wisdom, and He promises it will be given to you!

**But where can wisdom be found, and where is understanding located? . . . He considered wisdom and evaluated it; He established it and examined it. He said to mankind, "The fear of the Lord is this: wisdom. And to turn from evil is understanding." —Job 28:12, 27–28**

Further Scripture: Ephesians 1:7–9; Colossians 2:2–3; James 1:5

## Questions

1. Why do you think Job started chapter 28 by talking about earthly treasure and how one may obtain it? What did he say was more valuable than precious metals or jewels?

2. How does man acquire wisdom (Proverbs 2:6; James 1:5)? What does the Bible say about it (Job 12:12; Proverbs 8:11; James 3:17)?

3. How did God define wisdom in chapter 28? Have you ever asked God for wisdom? If so, how did it help the situation?

4. Read Job 29:7–17. What did this passage teach you about Job's character? His position in society? Is it possible Job held a position of authority?

5. How did Job 29 foreshadow Jesus as Lord and Savior (Isaiah 61:2–3; Matthew 5:4; 11:4–5)?

6. What did the Holy Spirit highlight to you in Job 28—29 through the reading or the teaching?

# Lesson 21: Job 30

*The Promised Redeemer:* Stormy Skies

## Teaching Notes

### Intro

Job hung on to his faith with tenacity. This chapter is about the midway point of Job's final speech in which he expressed a lot of what he was deeply feeling. Because of this, the tone of today's chapter is a little depressing. After Job reflected on the good things he had experienced in his past, he began this part of his speech with a key phrase: "But now" (v. 1). All of the outward calamities Job faced were starting to affect his mental state.

### Teaching

*Job 30:1–15:* Job reflected on his loss of honor. His position in life had changed from being a person of honor to one who sat on an ash heap. McKenna notes,

> No one other than Christ Himself has experienced a greater fall from fame than Job. Symbolically, he fell from the best seat in the city gate (29:7) and the governor's chair (29:25) to the exile of an ash heap outside the city walls (30:19). Young men who had fallen silent before him in reverence (29:8–9) are now replaced by the mocking crowd of the dregs of humanity (30:1). Instead of the aged standing in honor of him, princes falling in silence, and nobles whispering in his presence (29:8–10), Job is the object of ridicule from the rabble.[1]

Job's experience as described in chapter 30 resembles Jesus' experience in the time between the garden of Gethsemane and the cross.

Job went into great detail to describe these dishonorable men who had formerly revered him but now mocked him (vv. 2–8). Formerly, Job had no use of their labor—they were unable to provide for their own needs, they scavenged for their sustenance, they were treated like thieves, they had no permanent homes,

---

[1] David McKenna, *Job*, vol. 12 of The Preacher's Commentary (Nashville: Thomas Nelson, 1986), 180, 208.

they spoke and behaved like donkeys without even having names for themselves, and they were forced to leave society. These were truly the dregs of Job's society, and now they taunted him.

These men were now very bold in the disrespect they showed Job (vv. 9–15). They sang spiteful songs about Job. They stayed far away from him and treated him as an untouchable. They spat in his face.

Job charged God with responsibility for the way the rabble treated him: "Because God has loosened my bowstring and oppressed me, they have cast off restraint in my presence" (v. 11). This thought was debilitating to Job. All of his strength had been taken away. Job used images of captivity and war to describe how the rabble had treated him (v. 12). Job saw terror at every turn. He saw his dignity taken from him as though by a tornado (v. 15). Even in the midst of this kind of trouble, what could be described as "the valley of the shadow of death" (Psalm 23), God was with Job. But his trouble had not yet stopped; his humiliation was not yet complete.

*Job 30:16–19*: Physical suffering took a toll on Job. Job knew pain in every single form. His resources were exhausted. He experienced days and nights of gnawing pain. Job claimed his clothing was "distorted with great force; He chokes me by the neck of my garment" (v. 18). Job may have been referencing his own thrashings in the night from fever, but it is clear Job ultimately held God responsible for his sufferings. Job walked the line between blasphemy and truth in these verses as he remembered the heights from which he had fallen. Job had no explanation for God's perceived change in attitude toward him. Job knew that he had not changed, so he felt God had. Job did not know who his real adversary was.

*Job 30:20–23*: Job set forth several images to describe how he felt God treated him. He felt as though God failed to acknowledge his cries and ignored him as he stood to voice his complaints (v. 20). He felt God turned against him and became his adversary (v. 21). He felt God had scattered him on the wind (v. 22). Ultimately, he felt God was leading him to his own death (v. 23).

*Job 30:24–31*: Job appealed to God's compassion while expressing exactly how he felt. Job pointed out that even people wouldn't condemn "a ruined man . . . because of his distress" (v. 24). How much more should God have compassion on someone like Job? Job pointed out he had shown compassion to those "who have fallen on hard times" and the poor (v. 25). However, everything now felt upside down: "When I hoped for good, evil came" (v. 26). His stomach was so upset he could not rest. His skin was "blackened, but not by the sun" (v. 28). He lived outside the city with wild animals (v. 29). His physical ailments continued to worsen (v. 30).

Job's humiliation was only exceeded by Christ's. Isaiah portrayed Christ's sufferings this way: "He was despised and rejected by men, a man of suffering who knew what sickness was. He was like someone people turned away from; He was despised, and we didn't value Him" (Isaiah 53:3). Job poetically summed up his reversal of fortune by noting his instruments only knew songs of lament and weeping (v. 31).

## Closing

The wind and the ravages of life can change everything. We must hold on to the Lord in order to make it through life. Job's sufferings foreshadowed the sufferings of Christ, but God was bigger than the sufferings of both. "For I am persuaded that not even death or life, angels or rulers, things present or things to come, hostile powers, height or depth, or any other created thing will have the power to separate us from the love of God that is in Christ Jesus our Lord" (Romans 8:38–39).

## The Daily Word

Job persevered in his suffering, but he still expressed his misery, his aching, and the mockery he received from the community. His physical pain never ended—day and night the pain gnawed at him. And yet Job knew the Lord was with him; even if it meant to his deathbed, the Lord would lead him. He found hope in a living Redeemer.

Today, you may need to hear you are not alone in your pain, how someone else has also endured great pain day and night. You may be sick and in such physical pain that words can't even begin to describe it. You may see no end in sight except through death. The days are hard, and the nights are no different. Just as Job knew this pain, your Savior, Jesus Christ, experienced this intense pain as well. People rejected and despised Jesus. People turned away from and devalued Him. The Apostle Paul, in the midst of his own suffering, responded with the hope that no matter what he went through, nothing would separate him from the love of God. So today, in the mist of your pain, understand in your heart that you are not alone, even if it feels like it. Others have endured this pain too. Hold on to the hope that nothing will ever separate you from Christ. Dear friend, *the Lord will see you through.*

**Night pierces my bones, but my gnawing pains never rest. My clothing is distorted with great force; He chokes me by the neck of my garment.**
**—Job 30:17–18**

Further Scripture: Job 19:25–26; Isaiah 53:3; Romans 8:38–39

## Questions

1. Job said, "They do not hesitate to spit in my face" (v. 10). Where else in the Bible did someone experience being spat in the face (Matthew 26:67; Mark 14:65)? What was taking place ?

2. Job was clearly in great anguish over his present state. Job said, "I cry out to You for help, but You do not answer me; when I stand up, You merely look at me" (v. 20). Has there ever been a time in your life when you felt God had turned His back on you when you were in deep distress? Why does it sometimes seem like God has turned His back on us?

3. The physical pain Job experienced was extreme (vv. 16–18; 27–30). How was Job able to endure thinking God had turned His back on him?

4. What did the Holy Spirit highlight to you in Job 30 through the reading or the teaching?

# Lesson 22: Job 31

*The Promised Redeemer:* The Case of Innocence

## Teaching Notes

### Intro

Our phrase for the book of Job is *The Promised Redeemer*, and it reminds us that no matter how bad things seem to get, we just have to hang on and wait on the Lord. Job expected his help to come from God. Job went through every possible thing that could go wrong in his life. Yet Job 19:25–26 says: "But I know my living Redeemer, and He will stand on the dust at last. Even after my skin has been destroyed, yet I will see God in my flesh." In chapter 31, we find Job's final claim of his innocence. "He did so in the form of a negative confession complete with self-imprecations."[1] Job thought "if God remained silent this would be a vindication of his innocence. However, if he had been guilty, God would have to intervene and impose the punishment Job had designated."[2] Wiersbe divides the chapter based on characteristics of Job: *Job the man* (vv. 1–12); *Job the employer* (vv. 13–15); *Job the neighbor* (vv. 16–23, 29–32); *Job the worshipper* (vv. 24–34); and *Job the steward* (vv. 38–40).[3]

### Teaching

*Job 31:1–12: Job the Man:* Job acknowledged he was human, and he acknowledged the power of the sexual appetite. But he emphasized he had made a covenant with God to protect himself against "the sin of lust."[4] Lust had not been an issue in his life. *Nelson's Commentary* states, "Job's sufferings had caused him to make a sweeping inventory of his inner life."[5] James 1:13–15 states lust is the

---

[1] Michael Brennan Dick, "The Legal Metaphor in Job 31," *Catholic Biblical Quarterly* 41 (1979): 42, 47.

[2] Norman C. Habel, *The Book of Job* (New York: Cambridge University Press, 1975), 164.

[3] Warren W. Wiersbe, *The Wiersbe Bible Commentary: Old Testament* (Colorado Springs: David C. Cook, 2007), 855.

[4] Earl D. Radmacher, Ronald B. Allen, and H. Wayne House, eds., *Nelson's New Illustrated Bible Commentary* (Nashville: Thomas Nelson, 1999), 635.

[5] Radmacher et al., 635.

first step toward sin, and when sin is fully grown, it is the first step toward death. *Nelson's Commentary* continues by outlining the steps of lust found in Job 31[6]:

1. *Looking upon a virgin* (v. 1b). Job pointed out that since God sees everything, there would be no way to hide that sin from Him (vv. 2–4). Job suggested God should weigh his actions to see that he had walked in truth and integrity (vv. 5–6) (Leviticus 19:35–37; Proverbs 11:1; Matthew 5:28; Hebrews 4:12–13). As believers, we need to clean up this stuff now before it can cause us to sin. That is where the act of repentance comes in—asking for God's forgiveness for ways we have fallen short in this area.

2. *Allowing one's heart to follow one's eyes* (v. 7). This moves beyond just looking lustfully at someone and allows the heart to begin to think about what acting on that lust could mean. This is one of the things that leads to divorce, even in the church—allowing the heart to begin to desire and act upon what has been seen and looks good.

3. *Allowing oneself to be enticed by a woman and then scheming to have her* (v. 9). Job even moved on to adultery and asked that someone find him guilty if he had ever allowed that to happen (Proverbs 6:27–29; Ephesians 5:3–7; Hebrews 13:4). *Nelson's Commentary* points out this progression is not normal or natural. We think it's unavoidable, but that's not true; it is a serious moral failure.[7] Don't miss that Job was able to stand up against these accusations because he was innocent.

*Job 31:13–15: Job the Employer.* In his examination of himself, Job considered how he treated others, even how he treated his servants. Job found himself without fault in how he treated his servants, both male and female, and one day he would stand before God and be judged for how he had treated them (Ephesians 6:9).

*Job 31:16–23, 29–32: Job the Neighbor.* Job pointed out there was not a time when he had not helped others or shared his food with the fatherless.

*Job 31:24–28: Job the Worshipper.* Job shared he had not placed his trust in wealth or money but in God. He said he hadn't worshipped anything else—idols, the moon, or the sun—but only God. If he had, he would have deserved his punishment. Job's understanding in the one living God was not usual in a culture that worshipped multiple gods, idols, and elements of nature.

---

[6] Radmacher et al., 635.

[7] Radmacher et al., 635.

*Job 31:29–37*: Job continued to point out all he had done so he could be found righteous before God. In verse 35, Job referred to God as "my Opponent." He wanted God to hear his case. We all need a mediator. Wiersbe points out, "Job asked God . . . to give him three things: a hearing, an answer to his charges, and a document to prove his innocence."[8] Job was ready to be found innocent and then vindicated by God. In his confidence to prove his innocence, Job went too far, showing his lack of humility before God.

*Job 31:38–40: Job the Steward*: Job added a last area in which he had evaluated himself—how he had taken care of the land God gave him. Once again, Job explained he had been innocent of any wrongdoing toward the land or the tenants who worked it.

## Closing

Job asked for a mediator, and he will be given one in chapter 32. Sometimes, however, mediators don't just take one side. Jesus is our mediator, and in His language, we must acknowledge we are guilty before Him.

---

### The Daily Word

Job believed he had walked in integrity and righteousness toward others. However, in the event he had done anything wrong in the Lord's eyes, he laid it all on the line. If he had lived an impure life and acted in lustful ways, if he had not given to the poor or not given to a person in need of clothing, if he had placed his confidence in gold and rejoiced in wealth, if his heart had been enticed in any other way, then Job was willing to receive the consequences. He was ready for his indictment. Job understood God saw his ways and numbered his steps. God would surely know if Job walked in falsehood.

Are you able to open all the pages of your life before God? Is there a page or two you'd want to keep secret and covered up? Here's the deal—God sees everything. He knows all. There is nothing you can hide from God, so it's really not worth the effort. Even though God knows everything about your life, you need to understand in your head and believe in your heart that He loves you no matter what. Not only does He love you, but His grace covers your sin, your guilt, and your shame. Christ died for you to be *set free*. You don't have to carry the weight of your sin. It is done. Child of God, the Lord longs for you to walk in freedom. *Receive God's grace and mercy and open all the pages of your life to Him.*

---

[8] Wiersbe, 855.

**Does He not see my ways and number all my steps? —Job 31:4**

Further Scripture: Proverbs 5:21; Romans 6:22; Hebrews 4:13

## Questions

1. Have you ever made a covenant with your eyes like Job did in Job 31:1? If so, what was it and did it help you?

2. After examining your own heart, do you, like Job, ever tell God to punish you with what He feels is just? Or do you instead just ask for mercy and forgiveness?

3. What might Job have been talking about in verses 26–27? Could it have been about worshipping the sun and moon? Have you ever found yourself worshipping false idols in your own life? What are they?

4. What did the Holy Spirit highlight to you in Job 31 through the reading or the teaching?

# Lesson 23: Job 32—33

## *The Promised Redeemer*: Elihu's Angry Response

## Teaching Notes

### Intro

Today, our study of Job will feel as though it's from a different book. There's no Eliphaz or Bildad or Zophar. In fact, in chapter 32, we will be hearing from a new character—Elihu. In two days from now, I'll share with you some perspectives about who Elihu was. Parsons states Elihu seemingly interrupted the argument that had taken place through much of the book of Job.[1] Elihu was setting the stage for Yahweh (the LORD) to speak. It appears Elihu was serving as a mediator (Job 36). Elihu called for Job to repent for self-righteousness and encouraged Job to exalt God's works that were evident in nature. In Job 37, Elihu told Job it was time for him to fear God.

### Teaching

*Job 32:1–5*: Verse 1 states Job's friends had stopped answering Job because he seemed self-righteous to them. But Elihu appeared, and he was angry with Job because Job had justified himself instead of God (v. 2). Four times the text states Elihu was angry—at Job (v. 2) and at Job's friends (vv. 3, 5).

*Job 32:6–22*: These verses contain Elihu's first speech. Elihu acknowledged he was younger and less mature than Job and so had hung back intimidated, without saying anything. Elihu voiced his respect for those who were there and were older than him (vv. 6–7). In verses 8–10, Elihu acknowledged God had divinely inspired his words—his wisdom had come from "the breath of the Almighty" who had given him understanding. Elihu pointed out that wisdom did not only come to the elderly but to anyone God chose. In verse 10, Elihu told his hearers to listen to him—to pay attention to his words. This was the first of ten admonitions to them.

---

[1] Gregory W. Parsons, "The Structure and Purpose of the Book of Job," *Bibliotheca Sacra* 138:550 (April–June 1981): 141.

Elihu had listened to all the speeches of the four men (Job, Eliphaz, Bildad, and Zophar), even though he was not mentioned in the former chapters. Although he paid close attention to their claims, no one convinced him Job was guilty. Elihu emphasized that his wisdom came from God. Could Elihu have been the pre-incarnate Christ? We'll return to this in two days. Elihu evaluated the speeches of the three friends (vv. 11–13). In verses 14–22, Elihu demonstrated his impartiality. Job's friends were dismayed and speechless (v. 15). Elihu was driven to deliver God's message (vv. 16–19), and he again promised his impartiality to all those who had something to say (vv. 20–21). If Elihu was not impartial, God would remove him from speaking for Him (v. 22).

## Closing

Pastor Jack Wellman identifies four reasons why Christians cannot be silent:[2]

1. *Because words are necessary* (Romans 10:14, 17). We cannot live out our calling only through our actions and hope those actions will be enough to introduce Christ to others. Words are necessary because "faith comes by hearing" (v. 17 NKJV) about Christ and what He has done for us.

2. *Because we cannot be ashamed of the gospel of Christ* (Luke 9:26; 12:9; Romans 1:16). Although we can hold back from sharing our faith with others, Paul wrote, "For I am not ashamed of the gospel, for it is the power of God for salvation to everyone who believes, to the Jew first and also to the Greek" (Romans 1:16 ESV).

3. *Because we cannot help but preach* (Jeremiah 20:9; Acts 4:20; 9:15; 1 Corinthians 9:16). Jeremiah shared that if he didn't speak of God, his heart would be "as it were a burning fire shut up in my bones, and I am weary with holding it in, and I cannot" (Jeremiah 20:9 ESV). If we are not willing to put our lives on the line for Him, will He be willing to put His life on the line for us?

4. *Because of Jesus' compassion* (Matthew 28:18–20; Romans 1:14; Revelation 20:12–15). Jesus died on the cross for us with compassion—with passion! Therefore, we should feel compelled to share what Jesus did to rescue those who do not know Him.

If we are too much like Job's friends, we will not share about Christ with others. But when we accept what Christ has done for us, we cannot stay silent about what He has done!

---

[2] Jack Wellman, "Why Christians Can't Be Silent About the Gospel," Patheos, March 15, 2017, https://www.patheos.com/blogs/christiancrier/2017/03/15/why-christians-cant-be-silent-about-the-gospel/.

## The Daily Word

After Job responded to his three friends, a new friend emerged with a message for Job. Elihu witnessed the previous interactions among Job, Bildad, Eliphaz, and Zophar, and a word from the Lord rose within him to the point he could not stay quiet anymore.

If the Lord has given you a message, a verse, or an edifying word for another person, speak those words out. If you wake up every day with the same person and message on your heart or if you think about it several times throughout the day, then that's when you know you have to communicate it! Ask the Lord for the opportunity to talk with that person, trust the Lord will grant clarity for your words, and then, go for it! Yes, it will take courage. Yes, it will take boldness. Yes, it will take faith. But friend, God will be with you. Speak it out. The Lord says you are *His mouthpiece, His vessel, and His ambassador* to proclaim the good news in boldness and in power through the Holy Spirit. Today, rise up and say the message on your heart delivered with love.

**My heart is like unvented wine; it is about to burst like new wineskins. I must speak so that I can find relief; I must open my lips and respond.**
**—Job 32:19–20**

Further Scripture: Exodus 4:11–12; 2 Corinthians 5:20; 2 Timothy 1:7–8

## Questions

1. A man named Elihu began to speak in Job 32. Where did this man come from? When did he enter the picture and who could he be?

2. In Job 32, was Elihu mad at his friends for condemning Job without any proof of wrongdoing, or was he frustrated that they just hadn't found any answers for him?

3. In Job 33:9, was Elihu claiming he was sinless?

4. Do we have the right to accuse God of being unjust, knowing He is greater than us, especially since we do not have all the facts (Job 33:12–14)?

5. What did the Holy Spirit highlight to you in Job 32—33 through the reading or the teaching?

# Lesson 24: Job 34—35

*The Promised Redeemer:* Crying Out

## Teaching Notes

### Intro

Job's three friends had serious issues with Job. In spite of his friends' repeated accusations that Job's own sin must have caused the suffering that he experienced, Job invited his friends to examine every area of his life, to discover he had not sinned, almost to the point of self-righteousness (Job 31). In Job 32, a new character, Elihu, expressed his anger at both Job and his three friends. Chapters 34 and 35 are a continuation of Elihu's speech.

### Teaching

*Job 35:1–2:* Elihu challenged Job on whether or not it was right to question God's judgment by declaring himself to be righteous. Elihu's question was basically, "Who do you think you are to come before the Almighty and say, 'I am righteous'?" Elihu thought Job implied "his ethical standards were higher than God's"[1] and questioned Job's legal status to question God's righteousness in the first place.

*Job 35:3–7:* Elihu summarized the focal point of Job's complaint in verse 3: avoiding sin didn't profit Job. Job had never said these exact words, but they were an implication of the points he had made throughout his speeches. Elihu called out Job's self-righteousness. The *NKJV Study Bible* notes, "God was not under any obligation to Job for any work or deed. Therefore, it was logically inconsistent for Job to demand that God must appear in court."[2]

*Job 35:8–14:* Elihu observed people often cried out to God because they were oppressed by someone mightier than themselves (v. 9), implying Job had not been sincere in his prayers. MacArthur proposes three reasons God had not heard Job's prayers: *pride* (vv. 10, 12), *wrong motives* (v. 13), and *lack of patient trust* (v.

---

[1] NKJV Study Bible (Nashville: Thomas Nelson, 2014), 824.

[2] NKJV Study Bible, 824.

14).[3] Elihu pointed out that no one questioned where God was when He provided the good things people sang about in the day. Charles Spurgeon noted, "It is easy to sing when we can read the notes by daylight, but he is the skillful singer who can sing when there is not a ray of light by which to read."[4]

Elihu contended God did not have to answer a person's prayer when he was full of pride and devoid of pure motives (vv. 12–13). God was not obligated to answer Job because of Job's lack of patient trust in God.

What would it have looked like for Job to cry to God out of humility, the right motives, and with patience? The Institute in Basic Life Principles outlines words and phrases used throughout the Bible to describe crying out to God:[5]

1. *A cry of deep distress*: "zaaq" (Hebrew). "You saw the oppression of our ancestors in Egypt and heard *their cry* [zaaq] at the Red Sea. You performed signs and wonders against Pharaoh, all his officials, and all the people of his land, for You knew how arrogantly they treated our ancestors. You made a name for Yourself that endures to this day. You divided the sea before them, and they crossed through it on dry ground. You hurled their pursuers into the depths like a stone into churning waters" (Nehemiah 9:9–11). In their deep distress, the Israelites realized they had nowhere else to turn but to God.

2. *To cry out for help*: "tsaaq" (Hebrew). "So *he cried out* [tsaaq] to the LORD, and the LORD showed him a tree. When he threw it into the water, the water became drinkable" (Exodus 15:25a). Moses knew there was nothing he could do to find or create water for the Israelites to drink. Out of his desperation, he cried out to God.

3. *To call with a loud sound*: "qara" (Hebrew). "Jabez *called out* [qara] to the God of Israel: 'If only You would bless me, extend my border, let Your hand be with me, and keep me from harm, so that I will not cause any pain.' And God granted his request" (1 Chronicles 4:10).

4. *To shout a war cry*: "ruwa" (Hebrew). "And the men of Judah *raised the battle cry* [ruwa]. When the men of Judah *raised the battle cry* [ruwa], God routed Jeroboam and all Israel before Abijah and Judah" (2 Chronicles 13:15). This cry was done together, as a collective group.

5. *A cry for help*: "shavah" (Hebrew). "He fulfills the desires of those who fear Him; He hears *their cry* [shavah] for help and saves them" (Psalm 145:19).

---

[3] John MacArthur, *The MacArthur Bible Commentary* (Nashville: Thomas Nelson, 2005), 589.

[4] Charles Spurgeon, "Songs in the Night," Spurgeon's Sermons Volume 44: 1898 (Grand Rapids: Christian Classics Ethereal Library), 98, https://ccel.org/ccel/s/spurgeon/sermons44/cache/sermons44.pdf.

[5] "What Does It Mean to Cry Out to God?" Institute in Basic Life Principles, https://iblp.org/questions/what-does-it-mean-cry-out-god.

6. *A cry of deep distress*: "tsaaqah" (Hebrew). "For the One who seeks an accounting for bloodshed remembers them; He does not forget *the cry* [tsaaqah] of the afflicted" (Psalm 9:12).

7. *To cry out*: "krazo" (Greek). "But when he saw the strength of the wind, he was afraid. And beginning to sink *he cried out* [krazo], 'Lord, save me!' Immediately, Jesus reached out His hand, caught hold of him, and said to him, 'You of little faith, why did you doubt?'" (Matthew 14:30–31).

8. *To implore with a strong voice*: "boao" (Greek). "So *he called out* [boao], 'Jesus, Son of David, have mercy on me!' Then those in front told him to keep quiet, but he kept crying out all the more, 'Son of David, have mercy on me!' Jesus stopped and commanded that he be brought to Him. When he drew near, He asked him, 'What do you want Me to do for you?' 'Lord,' he said, 'I want to see!' 'Receive your sight!' Jesus told him. 'Your faith has healed you'" (Luke 18:38–42). This man was not ashamed to admit he needed Jesus' help. He did not allow his pride to keep him from asking for Jesus' help with a loud, strong voice.

The Institute in Basic Life Principles also outlines characteristics of a cry to God:[6]

1. *Genuine humility*: "For the One who seeks an accounting for bloodshed remembers them; He does not forget the cry of the afflicted" (Psalm 9:12).

2. *Unconditional surrender*: "If I had been aware of malice in my heart, the Lord would not have listened" (Psalm 66:18).

3. *A plea for mercy*: " Because of the LORD's faithful love we do not perish, for His mercies never end. They are new every morning; great is Your faithfulness!" (Lamentations 3:22–23).

4. *Personal helplessness*: "I am the vine; you are the branches. The one who remains in Me and I in him produces much fruit, because you can do nothing without Me" (John 15:5).

5. *Faith in God's power and resources*: "So the disciples came and woke Him up, saying, 'Lord, save us! We're going to die!'" (Matthew 8:25).

6. *Desperation*: "I called to the LORD in my distress, and I cried to my God for help. From His temple He heard my voice, and my cry to Him reached His ears" (Psalm 18:6).

## Closing

Elihu called out Job's pride, self-righteousness, and lack of trust in the Lord. How do we make sure we are not praying the same way? Examine yourself: What is

[6] "What Does It Mean to Cry Out to God?"

your motivation in coming before the Lord and asking Him for anything? Are you asking the Lord to save your neighborhood? Do you want to see your marriage restored? Do you want to see your kids walking with the Lord?

## The Daily Word

Elihu continued speaking to Job about the message so heavy on his heart. Elihu spoke from his perspective and gave possible reasons for God's silence through Job's suffering. Elihu confronted the pride he witnessed creep into Job's heart. Because of Job's pride, God did not answer when he cried out.

You may think to yourself, *I need help, but asking for help from the Lord or others—no way.* You may believe asking for help or crying out reveals weakness, or you fear you may have to release control to someone else. You'd rather pretend you have it together than let go of your pride. However, the Lord desires for you to ask Him for help. He already knows you need it. He wants you to ask Him because it's in the asking for help that you finally surrender. In asking, you reveal your humility, your helplessness, your faith in God's power and God's resources, and your trust in God for victory. It is *OK* to cry out. Christ came to earth for you. He sent the Holy Spirit to *help* you. You have the body of Christ to *help* you. The Lord promises to hear your cry for help. He will save you and deliver you from your troubles. Open your heart and cry out for help today. The Lord is with you and will answer your humble cry for help.

**There they cry out, but He does not answer, because of the pride of evil men. —Job 35:12**

Further Scripture: Psalm 34:17; 145:19; John 15:5

## Questions

1. Who did Elihu call "wise men" and those "knowledgeable ones" (Job 34:2)?
2. After reading Job 34, did Elihu speak the truth to Job, or was he arrogant? What did he say to influence your judgment?
3. Throughout Job, did Job's friends speak the truth in love? Did they do nothing more than tear him down and tell him how horrible of a person he was? How does Scripture teach us to treat others (Matthew 7:1–6; Romans 12:10; Galatians 5:14; Ephesians 4:32)?
4. What did the Holy Spirit highlight to you in Job 34—35 through the reading or the teaching?

# Lesson 25: Job 36

*The Promised Redeemer:* The Mediator

## Teaching Notes

### Intro

The goal of reviveSCHOOL has been to point out how all of Scripture points to the Messiah. Sometimes that pointing is a foreshadowing of Christ; sometimes it has been Christ Himself who has shown up; sometimes we have seen a type of Christ figure. Elihu came onto the scene after Job prayed for a mediator. Elihu gives two speeches in today's chapter, his fifth and sixth in total.

### Teaching

*Job 36:1–7:* Elihu asked for patience as he began another speech by asserting that God had "perfect knowledge" (v. 4). MacArthur observes Elihu "began by repeating the thought that though God sends trouble, He is just and merciful."[1] Elihu challenged Job's assertion that the wicked were not punished by God.

*Job 36:8–15:* MacArthur notes the word "affliction," used in verse nine, came from a root word meaning "misery" or "poverty."

> The image evoked by this word is that of a person bowed down under the weight of a heavy burden. Scripture portrays the Lord as seeing the afflictions that bring pain to His people and hearing the anguished cries of those in distress. . . . The Lord urges us to place our burdens on Him, for he is strong enough to bear them and loves us so much that He will assist us in our time of need (1 Peter 5:7). Moreover, since He controls all events, we can be assured that He is accomplishing good out of the temporary difficulties we are now facing (Romans 8:28). The entire story of Job provides vivid example of this fact.[2]

---

[1] John MacArthur, *The MacArthur Bible Commentary* (Nashville: Thomas Nelson, 2005), 590.
[2] MacArthur, 590.

Constable observes two possible outcomes to God's teaching according to Elihu: "hearing (v. 11) and not hearing (v. 12), and each has consequences."[3] Those who have a godless heart, who do not want to hear God's teaching harbor anger, refuse to turn to God for help, live in a life of shame, and eventually die (vv. 13–14). The godly who suffer turn to God, submit to Him, learn from their suffering, and live (v. 15).[4] *Nelson's Commentary* charges, "Do not reject God's message by failing to cry out to him for help."[5]

*Job 36:16–21:* Wiersbe highlights three warnings Elihu gave to Job:[6]

1. *Job might try to buy his way out of his suffering* (vv. 18–19). A writer in *The Wall Street Journal* observed, "Money is an article which may be used as a universal passport to everywhere except heaven, and as a universal provider for everything except happiness."[7]
2. *Job might consider taking his own life* (v. 20).
3. *Job might give up hope and turn to sin* (v. 21).

*Job 36:22–33:* In his final speech, Elihu urged Job to try something new. He painted a picture of the greatness of God and urged Job to praise God.[8]

Elihu was a picture of Christ. He represented a mediator between God and Job. Elihu's name meant "He is my God" or "God, the Lord."[9] His father's name was Barachel, which means "God blesses" or "May God bless."[10] So Elihu was "He is my God," the son of "God blesses."

Elihu suddenly showed up in Job's story similarly to how Jesus suddenly made His first public appearance at His baptism. "After Jesus was baptized, He went up immediately from the water. The heavens suddenly opened for Him,

---

[3] Thomas L. Constable, *Expository Notes of Dr. Thomas Constable: Job*, 121, https://planobiblechapel.org/tcon/notes/pdf/job.pdf.

[4] Constable, 121.

[5] Earl D. Radmacher, Ronald B. Allen, and H. Wayne House, eds., *Nelson's New Illustrated Bible Commentary* (Nashville: Thomas Nelson, 1999), 638.

[6] Warren W. Wiersbe, *The Bible Exposition Commentary: Job–Song of Solomon* (Colorado Springs: David C. Cook, 2004), 74.

[7] *The Wall Street Journal*; cited in Wiersbe, 74.

[8] Wiersbe, 74.

[9] Steve Kline, *Living Room Theology* (podcast), January 4, 2017, iTunes; available at https://itunes.apple.com/us/podcast/living-room-theology/id1195467009?mt=2.

[10] Constable, 110.

and He saw the Spirit of God descending like a dove and coming down on Him. And there came a voice from heaven: 'This is My beloved Son. I take delight in Him!'" (Matthew 3:16–17).

Elihu was a Buzite (Job 32:2). Buzite means "the Despised." So Elihu was "He is my God," the son of "God blesses" of the tribe "The Despised."[11]

> "'Elijah does come first and restores everything,' He replied. 'How then is it written about the Son of Man that He must suffer many things and be treated with contempt?'" (Mark 9:12). All of Elihu's names and his entire family heritage pointed to the coming Christ.

> "Then Herod, with his soldiers, treated Him with contempt, mocked Him, dressed Him in a brilliant robe, and sent Him back to Pilate." (Luke 23:11)

Elihu was also from the family of Ram (Job 32:2), which can mean "high" or "exalted."[12]

Elihu began his speeches by being angry at Job "because he [Job] had justified himself rather than God" (Job 32:2). The self-righteous will always try to justify their lives. It doesn't work. We can see another picture of this in the story of the good Samaritan found in Luke 10, when an expert in the law questions Jesus. "But wanting to justify himself, he asked Jesus, 'And who is my neighbor?'" (Luke 10:29). Jesus responds with the famous parable and shows the man just how impossible it is to live a self-righteous lifestyle.

## Closing

Job asked for a mediator and got one in Elihu. Elihu served as a picture of Christ. Christ serves as our mediator. Christ serves as our ransom. Christ is the light of life, and Elihu showed up in the midst of Job's darkness with a better answer than Job's three friends. Elihu told Job that Job could not justify himself. He needed God to do that, just like we need Christ to justify us before God.

---

[11] "Elihu the Son of Barachel the Buzite," www.thetrueman.org, November 11, 2018; http://www.thetrueman.org/elihu-the-buzite/. Accessed on April 17, 2023, from the Internet Archive, https://web.archive.org/web/20181117132917/http://www.thetrueman.org/elihu-the-buzite/.

[12] Mark Allen Powell, ed., *HarperCollins Bible Dictionary, Revised and Updated* (New York: HarperOne, 2011), 865, s.v. "Ram."

## The Daily Word

Elihu continued speaking into Job's life and even asked Job to be patient with him a little longer. In many ways, Elihu answered Job's plea for a mediator. As one who received knowledge from a distant place, Elihu spoke different truths into Job's life in the midst of his suffering. Elihu warned Job to be careful not to turn to sin in the midst of his affliction.

When you are stuck in a pit of despair, this is not the time in your life to turn to sin. Lord willing, through your affliction, you will be refined and will grow in perseverance, character, and hope. Don't give up on hope and choose sin. When life gets tough, don't turn to alcohol and begin drinking your sorrows away. When life gets tough, don't just go out shopping and accumulate debt. When life gets tough with your marriage, don't turn to other relationships to fill the void. Instead, *turn to the Lord.* Press on in hope through the affliction. *Nothing else but Christ will satisfy your heart.* Nothing. No woman. No man. No drink. No purchase. Nothing but the love of Christ. Keep your eyes fixed on Jesus until He shows up. And He will show up because He is faithful. Don't lose hope.

**Be careful that you do not turn to iniquity, for that is why you have been tested by affliction. —Job 36:21**

Further Scripture: Psalm 37:24; Romans 5:3–5; 2 Corinthians 4:1–2

## Questions

1. Elihu said he had more to speak on God's behalf (Job 36:2). Did God need or want someone to "speak" for Him? Elihu also said "one who has perfect knowledge is with you" (Job 36:4). Did Elihu claim that he was perfect? Has someone in your life spoken like Elihu?

2. Elihu said if you obey and serve God, then all your days will be spent in prosperity and pleasure (Job 36:11). Was this statement accurate? Why or why not (John 16:33; Acts 14:22; 2 Timothy 3:12; Hebrews 12:1–11; 1 Peter 4:12–13)?

3. Elihu said Job chose iniquity instead of affliction from God (Job 36:21). Was that true? Why or why not? Has there been a time when you felt you were being judged by someone who "spoke for God"? Did that alter your perspective of God? Why or why not?

4. What did the Holy Spirit highlight to you in Job 36 through the reading or the teaching?

# Lesson 26: Job 37

*The Promised Redeemer:* Fear Before God

## Teaching Notes

### Intro

The book of Job is difficult to study because it is long and repetitive. Much of the book has been about the three arguments that each of Job's three friends presented to him (that's nine arguments in all). To each argument, Job responded that he had not sinned. Although his friends could not understand, Job put his hope in *The Promised Redeemer* (Job 19:25–26). At the end of Job 31, Job was beginning to focus on himself and had taken his eyes off the Lord. In chapters 32—37, a new character, Elihu, entered representing God. Elihu came to be the mediator between Job and his friends. Elihu became a spokesman for God.

### Teaching

*Job 37:1–9*: Elihu spoke, stating his heart was pounding at what he had to do and pointing out God's thunderous voice (vv. 1–3). He called his hearers to listen to his words that came directly from the Lord. Elihu was beginning to build a case of who God is as he prepared for God to speak directly to Job and his friends. God's voice thundered across the sky with majesty, and He takes actions mankind could not understand (vv. 4–9). *Nelson's Commentary* states, "God uses the winter storms to stop the hand of every man so that he cannot work but instead may recognize the work of God."[1] Further, Elihu's speech "praise[d] the all-powerful God with a series of metaphors" and "describe[d] God as keeping the wind in a chamber just as He does the snow and hail."[2] For example, in verse 9, Elihu mentioned the chamber in which God kept the snow and hail stored. Isn't that an awesome image?

*Job 37:10–12*: In these verses, Elihu described the breath of God, which can form ice and freeze watery areas. God's breath saturates the clouds and scatters lightening through the moisture-laden clouds. *Nelson's Commentary* states that, in verse

---

[1] Earl D. Radmacher, Ronald B. Allen, and H. Wayne House, eds., *Nelson's New Illustrated Bible Commentary* (Nashville: Thomas Nelson, 1999), 638.

[2] Radmacher et al., 638.

12, God is portrayed "as the wise Captain who skillfully charts the course for the clouds, which respond obediently to His hand at the helm."[3]

*Job 37:13–17*: The clouds respond to God's direction and guidance. *Nelson's Commentary* explains God causes storms to take place for three reasons: "(1) for punishment for people's wickedness, (2) for the nourishment of the earth, and (3) for supplying the needs of His people."[4] For example, a farmer tends to be a man of prayer because the success of his crops and his very livelihood depend on how the weather treats his land. Therefore, "God uses storms both to judge the earth and to bring the blessing of rain for His people"[5] (Exodus 15:7–10; Deuteronomy 28:21).

*Job 37:18–21*: "Ancient mirrors were firm and unbreakable because they were made of polished bronze."[6] Only God has the power to spread weather across the earth. Therefore, Elihu told his listeners they should be willing to learn what they should say before God (vv. 18–20). God's power is so much greater than ours that we cannot even look directly at the sun—something God created (v. 21). How much more difficult would it be to approach God face-to-face?

*Job 37:22–24*: Verse 22 states that God would come from the north. *Nelson's Commentary* explains that "in ancient times, north was viewed as the direction of God's abiding place"[7] (Isaiah 14:13). God would appear in gold splendor and majesty (Exodus 34). "Finally, Elihu speaks of the reverential awe and worshipful wonder that all people should have for their omnipotent Creator."[8] Therefore, because of who God is, men fear Him (v. 24) (Job 23:13–16; Psalms 19:9; 33:8; 34:11; 86:11; 111:10; Proverbs 1:7; 9:10; Ecclesiastes 12:13; Jeremiah 5:22).

## Closing

Fear of God means to have terror, dread, respect, reverence, and honor. How do we fear God (Psalms 34:11; 86:11; Ecclesiastes 12:13)? We need to respect and reverence God by considering His creation (the power of nature at His disposal), reading His Word, and staying fast in our faith.

*1 John 4:18*: "There is no fear in love; instead, perfect love drives out fear, because fear involves punishment. So the one who fears has not reached perfection in

---

[3] Radmacher et al., 638.

[4] Radmacher et al., 638–39.

[5] Radmacher et al., 639.

[6] Radmacher et al., 639.

[7] Radmacher et al., 639.

[8] Radmacher et al., 639.

love." We don't have to be afraid of God's judgment or fear Him because Jesus took away our punishment when He died on the cross for us. God does not want us to cower in fear but to enjoy sweet peace in His care.

## The Daily Word

In Elihu's final words to Job, he passionately described the Lord's great and mighty works through the weather and creation. He clearly presented his case for how the Lord can handle control of our lives, and he wanted Job to stop and just listen. In doing so, the final point Elihu spoke into Job's life was to fear God with a pure heart. As Elihu stated, God frowns upon those who carry themselves with superior wisdom. The God of all creation holds all wisdom, so why be prideful about it and think you know better than God?

In just moments, pride can easily creep into your heart. You may think you already know the outcome of a situation or believe you know the reasons why something happened or assume you have it all together. Remember, God is the God of all creation and all wonders—yes, He created you, and He knows your heart. He longs for you to fear Him with all your heart and without any pride. As you walk through any trial or suffering, *focus on God's creation, and read through His Word to know Him more.* As you do these two things, it will help you turn from self-centeredness to *fearing God* with a pure heart. The same God who set the boundary of the sea and gives the rain controls your life. He is more than able. Allow Him to teach you His way.

**Therefore, men fear Him. He does not look favorably on any who are wise in heart. —Job 37:24**

Further Scripture: Psalm 19:9; 86:11; Jeremiah 5:22–24

## Questions

1. What did the drama of a storm remind Elihu about as far as God was concerned (Job 36:32–33; 37:1)?

2. What did Elihu say was a reason God uses winter storms (Job 37:6–7)?

3. Elihu wanted Job to "Stop and consider God's wonders." Take a few minutes and focus on that yourself. Consider all God has done for and through you.

4. In verse 24, what did Elihu finally speak on how we should regard God (Job 28:24–28; Matthew 10:28; 11:25)?

5. What did the Holy Spirit highlight to you in Job 37 through the reading or the teaching?

# Lesson 27: Job 38

*The Promised Redeemer*: Creator of the Universe

## Teaching Notes

### Intro

Yesterday's lesson concluded Elihu's speeches (chapters 32—37). Elihu's central task was to remind Job he was not God and he should stop acting like he was. Dr. Benjamin Jowett was once asked what his opinion of God was. After giving a few sentences of response, Dr. Jowett remarked, "It's really not the question to ask. The question to ask is, 'What is God's opinion of me?'"[1] This switch in perspective is what happened in Job 38. Now we will get God's opinion on what has gone on. MacArthur characterizes God's response to Job as an "interrogation" and notes that "God had his day in court with Job."[2]

### Teaching

*Job 38:1–3*: God answered Job "from the whirlwind." While God answered Job from a whirlwind, others encountered Him in interesting ways:

- *Thunder*—"On the third day, when morning came, there was thunder and lightning, a thick cloud on the mountain, and a loud trumpet sound, so that all the people in the camp shuddered. Then Moses brought the people out of the camp to meet God, and they stood at the foot of the mountain. Mount Sinai was completely enveloped in smoke because the LORD came down on it in fire. Its smoke went up like the smoke of a furnace, and the whole mountain shook violently. As the sound of the trumpet grew louder and louder, Moses spoke, and God answered him in the thunder" (Exodus 19:16–19).

- *A soft whisper*—"Then He said, 'Go out and stand on the mountain in the LORD's presence.' At that moment, the LORD passed by. A great and mighty wind was tearing at the mountains and was shattering cliffs

---

[1] Benjamin Jowett; quoted in Christopher Ash, *Job: The Wisdom of the Cross* (Wheaton: Crossway, 2014), 374.

[2] John MacArthur, *The MacArthur Bible Commentary* (Nashville: Thomas Nelson, 2005), 591.

before the LORD, but the LORD was not in the wind. After the wind there was an earthquake, but the LORD was not in the earthquake. After the earthquake there was a fire, but the LORD was not in the fire. And after the fire, there was a voice, a soft whisper. When Elijah heard it, he wrapped his face in his mantle and went out and stood at the entrance of the cave" (1 Kings 19:11–13a).

- *A storm*—Ezekiel 1:4.[3]

Wiersbe notes that God's questioning of Job "centered on His works in nature and consisted of seventy-seven questions interspersed with divine commentary relating to the questions. The whole purpose of this interrogation was to make Job realize his own inadequacy and inability to meet God as an equal and defend his case."[4] Job asked for this very thing: "Then call, and I will answer, or I will speak, and You can respond to me" (Job 13:22).

Wiersbe groups God's questions to Job over the next few chapters into three sections:

1. "Can you explain My creation?" (Job 38:1–38)
2. "Can you oversee My creation?" (Job 38:39—39:30)
   a. Job's first response (Job 40:1–5)
3. "Can you subdue My creation?" (Job 40:6—41:34)
   a. Job's second response (Job 42:1–6)[5]

Job wanted an audience with God. Now he had it, and God did not hold anything back. It is likely that even after God's first question to Job in verse 2 that Job regretted asking for a day in court with God.

*Job 38:4–7*: Wiersbe observes that God began His string of questions with "the creation of the earth." God "compared Himself to a builder who surveys the site, marks off the dimensions, pours the footings, lays the cornerstone, and erects a structure."[6]

---

[3] Warren W. Wiersbe, *The Bible Exposition Commentary: Job–Song of Solomon* (Nashville: David C. Cook, 2004), 76.

[4] Wiersbe, 76.

[5] Wiersbe, 76.

[6] Wiersbe, 77.

*Job 38:8–11*: God had Job consider the seas. God knit the seas together, and then they "burst forth like a baby emerging from the womb."[7]

*Job 38:12–15*: Here, God had Job consider the sun. "Had Job ever told the sun to rise and dispel the darkness?" God commanded the light as it stretched across the world to reveal the details of the landscape and put an end to evil deeds.[8]

*Job 38:16–24*: Eleven questions highlight the vast dimensions of creation. Humanity has only ever traveled 35,853 feet (6.79 miles) down into the depths of the ocean[9] and 14.8 billion miles into the outer reaches of space.[10] God intimately knows every inch of creation because He made it.

*Job 38:25–30*: God questioned Job about rain (vv. 25–28), hail, and frost.[11]

*Job 38:31–33*: God questioned Job about the stars and constellations.[12] Christopher Ash notes, "The heavenly government of the world is under God's control."[13]

*Job 38:34–38*: God called Job's attention to the clouds.[14]

*Job 38:39–41*: These verses begin the description of six beasts and five birds that continues into chapter 39.

## Closing

This is the first time that God responded to Job and He addressed Job's pride. Wiersbe notes, "God didn't question Job's integrity or sincerity; He only questioned Job's ability to explain the ways of God in the world. Job had spoken the truth about God (42:7), but his speeches lacked humility."[15]

---

[7] Wiersbe, 77.

[8] Wiersbe, 77.

[9] Yasemin Saplakoglu, "Explorer Reaches Bottom of the Mariana Trench, Breaks Record for Deepest Dive Ever," Live Science, May 13, 2019, https://www.livescience.com/65468-explorer-breaks-record-deepest-ocean-dive.html.

[10] Voyager Mission Status, Jet Propulsion Laboratory, accessed May 22, 2023, https://voyager.jpl.nasa.gov/mission/status/.

[11] Wiersbe, 78.

[12] Wiersbe, 78.

[13] Christopher Ash, *Job: The Wisdom of the Cross*, Preaching the Word, ed. R. Kent Hughes (Wheaton, IL: Crossway, 2014), 387.

[14] Wiersbe, 78.

[15] Wiersbe, 77.

## The Daily Word

After Elihu addressed Job's prideful heart and the importance of fearing God, the Lord answered Job from a whirlwind. The Lord gave Job His opinion in the form of several questions about creation, essentially asking Job, *Can you make and control My creation?* Yes, Job may have walked in integrity, but did he fully recognize the full magnitude of God's hand in all of creation? Clearly Job never had a reason to challenge God, even during his suffering.

Although you may have great character and success in life, *God is still God.* There is no one besides the Lord. He is your rock and a refuge, who makes your way perfect. He counts the number of stars and gives names to them all. He is great, vast in power, and His understanding is infinite. Today, realize how much you do not know and how amazing God is. This truth will keep you humble and at a place of dependency before the Lord. Even when you walk through difficulty, remember God, the creator of the universe, also holds your life in His hands. You may know God, but do you really *know* God?

**Who is this who obscures My counsel with ignorant words? Get ready to answer Me like a man; when I question you, you will inform Me. Where were you when I established the earth? Tell Me, if you have understanding. —Job 38:2–4**

Further Scripture: 2 Samuel 22:32–33; Job 38:34–35; Psalm 147:4–5

## Questions

1. What did the Lord mention was Job's biggest mistake in Job's attempt to explain his sufferings (Job 19:6)?

2. Why do you think God spoke directly to Job and not his friends (Job 7:6–21; 30:20)? Why is crying out to God important?

3. How do you think Job felt as he heard question after question from God? What have you questioned God about?

4. About what parts of creation did God question Job?

5. Where else in Scripture was God's presence made known in a whirlwind (2 Kings 2:1–11; Psalm 77:18; Isaiah 66:15; Ezekiel 1:4)?

6. What did the Holy Spirit highlight to you in Job 38 through the reading or the teaching?

# Lesson 28: Job 39—40

*The Promised Redeemer:* Behemoth

## Teaching Notes

### Intro

In yesterday's lesson, Job finally got what he wanted: a conversation with God. Job had been asking for a conversation with God because he felt he was suffering unjustly. Job endured his friends insisting he had sinned and deserved everything that happened to him. Job maintained his innocence but began to feel somewhat self-righteous. Elihu came onto the scene, called Job out for his self-righteousness, and admonished him to start praising God rather than insisting on his own righteousness. God responded to Job by asking him 77 questions from chapters 38—40. In chapter 39, we read how God questions Job about a variety of animals. In chapter 40, God questions Job about an altogether different kind of animal.

### Teaching

*Job 40:1–2:* God concluded his first speech to Job. Constable notes,

> God's first speech began and ended with a challenge to Job (38:2; 40:2). Job had found fault with God for allowing him to suffer when he was godly. He had said he wished he could meet God in court to face Him with His injustice and to hear His response (13:3, 15). Now God asked Job if he still wanted to contend with Him after God had reminded him of his power and wisdom.[1]

*Job 40:3–5:* At the beginning of his trial, Job understood he could not defend himself against God. He was hesitant to address God: "How then can I answer Him or choose my arguments against Him?" (Job 9:14). Job became gradually more confident and demanded an audience with God: "Then call, and I will answer, or I will speak, and You can respond to me" (Job 13:22). Job moved from knowing he could not answer God to demanding an audience with God to then

---

[1] Thomas L. Constable, *Expository Notes of Dr. Thomas Constable: Job,* 132, https://planobiblechapel.org/tcon/notes/pdf/job.pdf.

becoming so arrogant he called himself a prince: "I would give Him an account of all my steps; I would approach Him like a prince" (Job 31:37). Job became arrogant.

Job initially told his friends to cover their mouths at the site of his suffering (Job 21:5), now Job covered his own mouth at God's interrogation of him. Wiersbe summarizes Job's response as, "I am insignificant and unworthy. I have no right to debate with God."[2]

*Job 40:6–8*: These verses begin God's second speech. God continued to answer Job from the whirlwind, challenging him to answer His questions.

*Job 40:9–14*: Wiersbe notes God essentially asked Job, "Do you have the strength and holy wrath it takes to judge sinners?"[3] God challenged Job to get dressed up like a judge and actually execute judgment and justice on the wicked. When Job was able to accomplish these tasks, then God would "confess to you that your own right hand can deliver you" (v. 14).

*Job 40:15–24*: God referenced "Behemoth" (v. 15). "Behemoth" means "beast," but Wiersbe suggests the term could also mean super-beast.[4] Some believe Behemoth could have been some kind of dinosaur.[5] God listed several qualities of Behemoth:

1. He ate grass (v. 15).
2. He was strong and mighty (v. 16).
3. He had a powerful body (v. 16a).
4. He had strong muscles (v. 16b).
5. He had bones like iron rods (v. 18).
6. He lounged in the river (v. 21).
7. He was hidden under water (v. 21).
8. He wasn't afraid of the river (v. 23).
9. He had a massive cedar tail (v. 17).
10. No one could capture him (v. 24).

---

[2] Warren W. Wiersbe, *The Bible Exposition Commentary: Job–Song of Solomon* (Nashville: David C. Cook, 2004), 80.

[3] Wiersbe, 80.

[4] Wiersbe, 80.

[5] John MacArthur, *The MacArthur Bible Commentary* (Nashville: Thomas Nelson, 2005), 592.

Several options could have fit this description:

1. *Elephant*—one major problem. The text described Behemoth as having a massive cedar tail while elephants have a small tail.[6]
2. *Water buffalo*—one major problem. Water buffalos do not have large tails either.[7]
3. *Hippopotamus*—most commentators think Job described a hippopotamus,[8] but the description of a "cedar tail" still would not work for a hippopotamus.

*Answers in Genesis* proposed that "Behemoth" was some sort of dinosaur.[9] God reminded Job that He created Behemoth alongside Job. Wiersbe notes that while Job "ate a variety of fine foods," he was "weak and unable to fight" Behemoth.[10] Behemoth was "the foremost of God's works; only his Maker can draw the sword against him" (v. 19).

## Closing

This animal (Behemoth) was so great that only God could control it. Job, for all of his bluster, stood powerless to master an animal God had created.

## The Daily Word

God gave Job a chance to answer. Job admitted he had no words and covered his hands over his mouth. Then the Lord resumed questioning Job about how he had challenged God's justice. Because the Lord saw his heart, God knew Job had developed an attitude problem that needed to be smoothed out so that his relationship with God could be restored. God went on to describe a Behemoth, possibly a dinosaur-type creation, and questioned if anyone could capture such a super beast apart from Himself. If Job couldn't capture this beast, then how could Job justify himself before God?

God is capable of being in charge. So let go of control in your life and let God's will be done. How do you do that? Pause. Pray. Don't force things to happen. Find security in God. If God puts a burden on your heart and opens the door to something new, even if it doesn't make sense, walk through that door in

---

[6] MacArthur, 592.

[7] B. Coureyer, "Qui Est Behemoth?" *Revue Biblique* 82 (1975):418–43.

[8] MacArthur, 592.

[9] Allan Steel, "Could Behemoth Have Been a Dinosaur?" Answers in Genesis, August 1, 2001, https://answersingenesis.org/dinosaurs/could-behemoth-have-been-a-dinosaur/.

[10] Wiersbe, 80.

obedience to God. If you know God is in it, then let Him be God. God owns the cattle on a thousand hills. If you are praying for a loved one to come back to Christ, wait upon the Lord. If God can turn the heart of a king, then He is also able to turn the heart of a wayward child. Again, *God is capable of being in charge.* Rest in the Lord. Seek the Lord. Then go and follow Him. He is in control!

**Would you really challenge My justice? Would you declare Me guilty to justify yourself? Do you have an arm like God's? Can you thunder with a voice like His? —Job 40:8–9**

Further Scripture: Psalm 50:10; Proverbs 21:1; Revelation 1:17

## Questions

1. After God questioned Job in chapter 39, He called him a faultfinder (Job 40:2). How did Job respond?

2. God said, "Now gird up your loins like a man" (Job 40:7 NASB). What did He mean?

3. Why do you think God chose to speak to Job out of the storm? What other ways has God spoken to people in Scripture? How has He spoken to you?

4. God asked Job, "Would you declare Me guilty to justify yourself?" Did you recognize Job did that in earlier chapters? Have you ever heard others do the same thing? How did you respond to them?

5. What did God challenge Job to do for Him so He could acknowledge that Job could save himself (Job 40:10–14)? What does Scripture teach about people saving themselves?

6. What did the Holy Spirit highlight to you in Job 39—40 through the reading or the teaching?

# Lesson 29: Job 41—42

*The Promised Redeemer:* Knowing God Better

## Teaching Notes

### Intro

I'm so excited this lesson is the *last* lesson from the book of Job. The book of Job can be hard. Job can even make Leviticus seem easy. Remember that in chapters 38—41, the Lord spoke and told Job He'd had enough of him (and his friends) complaining and whining. Job heard God's response, and it made him want to hide. Job 42 gives Job's response to God's words. Despite his whining and complaining, Job stuck it out and kept his eyes on the Lord.

### Teaching

*Job 42:1–6:* In the first six verses, Job passed judgment on himself. MacArthur states, Job "still did not know why he suffered so profoundly, but he quit complaining, questioning, and challenging God's wisdom and justice."[1] Job exclaimed that he knew no plans of God could be thwarted and that he had talked about things he knew nothing about (vv. 1–3) (Job 38:2–3).

Job understood God had rebuked him for his pride (v. 4), and he recognized "God's judicial authority to demand answers from His own accuser, Job."[2] Job realized he had been in the wrong. MacArthur states, "At last, Job said he understood God whom he had seen with the eyes of faith. He had never grasped the greatness, majesty, sovereignty, and independence of God so well as he did at that moment"[3] (v. 5). In verse 6, Job repented of his guilt before God. Job covered himself in ashes, showing that he was broken and repenting.[4] Charles Spurgeon said, "The door of repentance opens into the hall of joy."[5] Remember Job was

---

[1] John MacArthur, *The MacArthur Bible Commentary* (Nashville: Thomas Nelson, 2005), 593.

[2] MacArthur, 593.

[3] MacArthur, 593.

[4] MacArthur, 593.

[5] Charles Spurgeon; quoted in William W. Wiersbe, *The Bible Exposition Commentary: Job–Song of Solomon* (Colorado Springs: David C. Cook, 2004), 81.

still diseased and had still lost everything when he repented. The only thing that changed was Job's heart. Satan had been proved wrong in the charges he brought against Job and in believing he could destroy someone's true faith in God.[6]

*Job 42:7–9*: This begins another section of God speaking. God addressed Eliphaz and the other friends because they too had misspoken about Him, but His servant Job had not (v. 7). MacArthur points out that God rebuked them "for those misrepresentations and arrogance. This does not mean everything they said was incorrect, but they had made wrong statements about the character and works of God, and also had raised erroneous allegations against Job."[7] God then gave them the opportunity to seek forgiveness through Job by sacrificing seven bulls and seven rams (v. 8). This did not include Elihu. They did as they were told, and Job prayed for them (v. 9a). "And the LORD accepted Job's prayer" (v. 9b). Job served as the mediator between his friends and God and is an incredible example of what the gospel calls us to do. This also showed a massive shift in the friends' theology about who God is. God restored them all because of His goodness and mercy.

*Job 42:10–17*: The Lord then restored Job's prosperity by doubling everything Job once had (v. 10). After Job's restoration, all his family and friends who had shunned him before returned to his house with sympathy, money, and gold as a "restoration fund"[8] (v. 11). God blessed Job with 14,000 sheep, 6,000 camels, 1,000 pairs of oxen, and 1,000 female donkeys (v.12). Each of these numbers reflects a doubling of what Job originally possessed. Job was also given the same number of children as he had before (v. 13). The names he gave his daughters show how he responded to this blessing: "Jemimah means 'daylight,' Keziah means 'sweet smelling,' and Keren-happuch describes a beautiful color that women used to paint their eyelids"[9] (v. 14). Job was so pleased with the gift of his daughters that he gave them a share of the inheritance their brothers received, something that by Jewish law only happened when there were no brothers to receive the inheritance (v. 15).

Job was seventy years old when he was first struck down with disease, and he lived another 140 years after his restoration[10] (v. 16). MacArthur explains, "Job died in prosperity, and his days were counted as a blessing"[11] (v. 17).

---

[6] MacArthur, 593.

[7] MacArthur, 593.

[8] Wiersbe, 82.

[9] MacArthur, 594.

[10] Wiersbe, 82.

[11] MacArthur, 594.

# Closing

MacArthur identifies these characteristics of Job as a husband:

1. Job modeled godliness for his wife (1:1).

2. Job was the spiritual leader in his home (1:5).

3. Job lovingly corrected his wife's wrong response to the disasters that befell them (2:10).

4. Job was [his wife's] example in how to suffer righteously by trusting in God (2:10).

5. Job did not hold his wife's wrong response against her—they later started a new family all over again (42:13–14).[12]

Job took on the role as the spiritual leader of his family. He stepped up to the role when there was no one else who could do it. Job became an example of what it meant to trust in God during adversity. In reflecting on the end of the book of Job, Wiersbe wrote: "This chapter assures us that no matter what happens to us, God always writes the last chapter. Therefore, we don't have to be afraid. We can trust God to do what is right, no matter how painful our situation might be."[13]

Wiersbe states that the greatest blessing Job received through this journey was "knowing God better and understanding His working in a deeper way."[14] Constable states that the takeaway from the book of Job is that "we do not need to know why [something happens] if we know God."[15] Job had hope, despite it all.

## The Daily Word

After the Lord spoke to Job about His strength and majesty over creation, He gave Job a chance to respond. At last, Job completely humbled himself, acknowledged God's greatness, and replied to the Lord, "I know that You can do anything and no plan of Yours can be thwarted." Job *repented* of his prideful words when he realized he had spoken about things he did not understand. The Lord accepted Job's prayer of repentance for himself and later on behalf of his three friends as well. After Job prayed, the Lord *restored* his prosperity and *restored*

---

[12] MacArthur, 594.

[13] Wiersbe, 82.

[14] Wiersbe, 82.

[15] Thomas L. Constable, *Expository Notes of Dr. Thomas Constable: Job*, 143, https://planobiblechapel.org/tcon/notes/pdf/job.pdf.

his relationships with his brothers, sisters, and former acquaintances. The Lord blessed the subsequent part of Job's life even more than the first.

*Repent and restore.* It may take a lifetime for a father to repent of wrongdoing toward a son, but when repentance occurs, the Lord promises restoration. A husband and wife may endure an entire weekend without speaking to each other because of a misunderstanding. But the moment they repent before the Lord and one another, restoration begins. Repentance reveals a humbled heart. Humble yourself, repent to God and to others, and you will be restored. The Lord promises this over and over and over. What are you waiting for? Ask the Lord to reveal any areas in your life that need repentance. If He *reveals* an area, *repent* with a broken and contrite heart, ask the Lord for forgiveness, and you will be *restored!* Today, take a minute to seek the Lord and repent. His mercies are new each morning, and He promises healing and restoration.

**Therefore I take back my words and repent in dust and ashes. . . . After Job had prayed for his friends, the LORD restored his prosperity and doubled his previous possessions. —Job 42:6, 10**

Further Scripture: 2 Chronicles 7:14; Hosea 6:1; 1 Peter 5:10

## Questions

1. In Job 41, God talked to Job about Leviathan. From the description given, do you think this could be describing Satan? Why or why not?

2. Do you think Job 41:34 supports the idea of this chapter being about Satan? Pride is a sin and the downfall for many. Where else in Scripture is pride an issue (Genesis 3:4–6; Proverbs 6:16–17; Ezekiel 28:17)?

3. God showed Job's friends mercy through Job's prayers for them. Do you think the friends learned a valuable lesson that day? Have you ever misspoken of the Lord and had to go back and say you were sorry?

4. In your opinion, could Job 42:12–17 be a result of the promise the Lord gave in Joel 2:25–27 to restore? Why or why not?

5. What did the Holy Spirit highlight to you in Job 41—42 through the reading or the teaching?

# Lesson 30: Psalms 1—3

*King of Glory*: Introducing the Psalms

## Teaching Notes

### Intro

This is the beginning of our study in Psalms, and our 393rd lesson so far. I'm a little nervous about teaching Psalms, not because I'm afraid to show my emotions but because the psalmists were willing to put their hearts on the line in these psalms. The challenge for us all is to let our study of the psalms stretch our ability to be vulnerable before God. The book of Psalms was first called Praises, and then The Book of Praises. In the creation of the Septuagint, the name was changed to Psalms from the Greek word that meant "plucking or twanging of strings," indicating each psalm was created to be sung with musical instruments.[1] Many of the psalms have titles and subtitles that "convey various kinds of information such as authorship, dedication, historical occasion, liturgical assignment to a worship director, liturgical instructions, plus other technical instructions of uncertain meaning due to their great antiquity."[2]

The 150 individual psalms have a variety of authors. King David wrote 73, the sons of Korah wrote ten, Asaph wrote 12, Solomon wrote two, and Moses, Heman, and Ethan each wrote one. Fifty psalms were written anonymously, although many scholars suggest the prophet Ezra wrote some of them. The Psalms cover a period of 900 or so years, beginning when Moses wrote Psalm 90 and ending when Psalm 126 was written after the exile had been concluded. MacArthur describes a twofold background for the psalms: "(1) the acts of God in creation and history, and (2) the history of Israel."[3] MacArthur further describes two opposing dimensions that exist in the psalms: "(1) a horizontal or temporal reality, and (2) a vertical or transcendent reality."[4] Simply put, that means the experiences of mankind are seen on the horizontal, while the experiences with God are on the vertical.

---

[1] John MacArthur, *The MacArthur Bible Commentary* (Nashville: Thomas Nelson, 2005), 596.

[2] MacArthur, 595.

[3] MacArthur, 595–96.

[4] MacArthur, 596.

The collection of psalms has a variety of content that includes: psalms of wisdom of how to live; psalms of lament about the problems of life; psalms of penitence or penance; psalms of kingship; psalms of thanksgiving; and messianic psalms. Further, the collection is divided into five books. Each section ends with a verse or verses of doxology: (1) Psalms 1—41; (2) Psalms 42—72; (3) Psalms 73—89; (4) Psalms 90—106; and (5) Psalms 107—150.[5]

Psalm 2 is one of the messianic psalms, and we'll be studying many of the messianic and prophetic psalms as we go. The phrase for the book of Psalms is *King of Glory*, and it's where we'll start out and see how it goes. As we go, keep in mind that prophetic psalms had messages for the people of the time, as well as a future message about the coming of the Messiah.

## Teaching

*Psalm 2:1–6*: This psalm is about human rebellion against God (v. 1). The kings and rulers of the earth had come together in rebellion against God and His Anointed One—His Son, the Messiah (v. 2). In rebellion, the people wanted to be freed from the restraints of God they felt were holding them back (v. 3). They saw the restraints as "yoke-bonds," which God was using to hold them[6] (Jeremiah 5:5; Hosea 11:4). God responded to their rebellion with mocking laughter and then spoke "from His perfectly balanced anger"[7] (vv. 4–5). God explained He had already consecrated His King—His Son—on Zion, His holy mountain who would present His decree to the world (vv. 6–7). Note that this is "the only OT reference to the Father/Son relationship in the Trinity, a relationship decreed in eternity past and demonstrated in the incarnation, thus a major part of the NT."[8] God promised that the nations would be the Anointed One's inheritance (v. 8).

*Psalm 2:9–12*: The rebellious would be broken with a rod of iron, so the kings of the world should listen and receive instruction (vv. 9–10). God gave the rebellious the opportunity for repentance so they could serve Him with awe and rejoicing (v. 11). The rebellious people were given two choices: "They could either love and respect the Lord's Anointed and so experience His great blessing, or they could refuse to submit and incur God's wrath."[9]

---

[5] MacArthur, 596–98.

[6] MacArthur, 598.

[7] MacArthur, 598.

[8] MacArthur, 599.

[9] Earl D. Radmacher, Ronald B. Allen, and H. Wayne House, eds., *Nelson's New Illustrated Bible Commentary* (Nashville: Thomas Nelson, 1999), 649.

# Closing

Psalm 2 is for us as well. We too have been rebellious. We too have a choice to make. We can choose to be redeemed through the saving work of Jesus Christ and be allowed to experience God's great blessing in our lives. Or we can choose to remain rebellious, refuse to submit ourselves to God, and incur God's wrath. The choice is ours and must be made individually.

---

## The Daily Word

The book of Psalms opens with a choice: follow the advice of the wicked, take the path of sinners, and join a group of mockers *or* delight in the Lord's instruction and meditate on it day and night. The Word of God says if you choose the second option you will be happy! Happiness expresses feelings of joy and satisfaction. All those who take refuge in the Lord are happy. Even so, happiness is not based on circumstances or trials. You are to find joy in the Lord in every circumstance, even through trials. You do so by keeping your eyes fixed on Jesus and not on yourself as you go through your day.

So today, try something. Make the choice to open the Word of God and ask the Lord for one verse to focus on all day long. Intentionally listen to music with edifying lyrics. Spend time with people who also delight themselves in Jesus. Then, at the end of your day, ask the Lord to show you how considering His Word and truth all day long had an effect on your day. Try this for a several days in a row as a discipline *to stay connected with the Lord*, and it may just turn your life around!

**How happy is the man who does not follow the advice of the wicked or take the path of sinners or join a group of mockers! Instead, his delight is in the Lord's instruction, and he meditates on it day and night. —Psalm 1:1–2**

Further Scripture: Psalm 2:12; Ecclesiastes 2:26; James 1:2

---

# Questions

1. The writer of Psalm 1 used the words "walk," "stand," and "sit" (NASB). Why do you think he used this verbiage? What is meant by "walk in the counsel of the wicked"? What about "stand in the path of sinners"?

2. Psalm 1:3 uses a simile to describe the man who delights in the law of the Lord. Do you see yourself in this description? Why or why not? What would be significant about a tree that is growing by streams of water?

3. When we read the words, "the way of the wicked leads to ruin," in Psalm 1:6, what should it drive us to do?

4. In Psalm 2:9, the writer said, "You will break them with a rod of iron." If you are a parent, have you ever needed to "rule with a rod of iron" with your children? Explain this verse through the lens of a loving parent.

5. Who does Psalm 2 point to? Which verse in this chapter brings you the greatest satisfaction? Why?

6. Have you experienced the Lord's protection and defense like David described in Psalm 3? If so, in what way?

7. What did the Holy Spirit highlight to you in Psalms 1—3 through the reading or the teaching?

# Lesson 31: Psalms 4—6

*King of Glory*: Praying in the Morning

## Teaching Notes

### Intro

Today, in our second lesson in Psalms, we're in Psalms 4—6. Our phrase for Psalms is *King of Glory*. Today, we're looking at a psalm of lament, so emotions will be all over the place. MacArthur identifies two elements in the lament psalm: "(1) declarations of innocence and (2) confidence and prayers for protection."[1] David's prayer was for God to help him while defeating his enemies.

The exact situation David was facing is not known, but it is possible that the psalm was written before David fled from Jerusalem. In that time, David turned to his Lord in prayer. Wiersbe points out that "no amount of danger or discomfort should keep us from our time of morning fellowship with the Lord."[2] Notice in the title of the psalm it gives directions for the choir director to use flutes as accompaniment.

### Teaching

*Psalm 5:1–3*: David asked God to listen to his words, his sighing, and his cries (vv. 1–2). MacArthur points out, "David may have been the anointed theocratic king on earth, but he fully understood that the ultimate King of all Israel and of the whole earth is God."[3] Verse 3 is a theme verse for prayer: "At daybreak, Lord, You hear my voice; at daybreak I plead my case to You and watch expectantly." Some refer to this as a morning psalm that shows we should create a "habit that helps a person to dedicate all the activities of the day to the glory of God."[4] David had an appointment with God every morning. He guarded that time against all interruptions, and he approached the time of prayer both orderly

---

[1] John MacArthur, *The MacArthur Bible Commentary* (Nashville: Thomas Nelson, 2005), 600.

[2] Warren W. Wiersbe, *The Wiersbe Bible Commentary: Old Testament* (Colorado Springs: David C. Cook, 2007), 878.

[3] MacArthur, 601.

[4] Earl D. Radmacher, Ronald B. Allen, and H. Wayne House, eds., *Nelson's New Illustrated Bible Commentary* (Nashville: Thomas Nelson, 1999), 651.

and systematically. The word translated "direct" in verse 3 (NKJV) was used to describe the placing of the pieces of the animal sacrifices in order on the altar (Leviticus 1:8). It also described the arranging of the wood on an altar (Genesis 22:9), the placing of the loaves of bread on the table in the tabernacle (Leviticus 24:8), and the setting of a meal before guests (Psalm 23:5). David wasn't careless in his praying; he had everything arranged in order. The same word also has a military connotation: a soldier presenting himself to his commander to receive orders[5] (Psalm 55:18; 59:17). David was very specific in his prayers and I believe we should use his approach of being orderly, systematic, and specific, and then wait expectantly for God's answer. The more we model the power of prayer, the more God receives the glory.

*Psalm 5:4–6*: David sought the Lord in prayer. He focused on God's goodness that could not stand evil and hated evildoers (vv. 4–5). David was building a case of what he wanted God to do. The word "boastful" was also used to "describe the praise of God."[6] When praising self, the boast becomes "a twisted, human perversion of true praise."[7] Wiersbe states that we please God when we fear Him (Psalm 147:11), when we praise Him sincerely (Psalm 69:31), when we have faith (Hebrews 11:6), and when we identify with His Son in whom He is well pleased (Matthew 3:17).[8]

*Psalm 5:7–12*: David stated he entered God's house—the temple—so he could bow down before God in awe and reverence (v. 7). David asked God to lead him—to keep him in the path of the Lord (v. 8). Psalm 119:1–5 gives an example of walking uprightly before God. In verse 9, David then asked for justice against his enemies whose speech was untrustworthy, whose actions were destructive, and who were deceitful[9] (Romans 3:10–18). David asked God to crush them because they rebelled against God (v. 10). MacArthur states, "The psalmist prays for the just ends of the wicked according to God's revealed standard of justice."[10] These enemies had rebelled against the Lord and against the Anointed One and had become enemies of the Jews, God's chosen people who had been promised His protection.

---

[5] Wiersbe, 878.

[6] Radmacher et al., 651.

[7] Radmacher et al., 651.

[8] Wiersbe, 878.

[9] Thomas L. Constable, *Expository Notes of Dr. Thomas Constable: Psalms*, 51, https://planobiblechapel.org/tcon/notes/pdf/psalms.pdf.

[10] MacArthur, 601.

David asked that God let those who found refuge in Him rejoice forever and be able to boast about the Lord (v. 11). Finally, David stated that the Lord blesses the righteous one and surrounds the righteous one with favor like a shield (v. 12).

## Closing

If I had one more lesson, I would say don't miss Psalm 5:12: "For You, LORD, bless the righteous one; You surround him with favor like a shield." It ultimately points to Him, the righteous one, Jesus.

---

## The Daily Word

What do you do first when you wake up in the morning? Check your phone? Go make coffee? Care for young kids who need your attention? Today, begin with prayer. While the coffee brews, before you click on the Facebook app, open Instagram, check your email, or even in the midst of watching morning cartoons with your little ones, *pause and pray.* Call upon the name of the Lord. Allow Him to hear your voice as you begin your day. Think of a few of His attributes you are grateful for and give Him praise. Share with Him what's on your heart for the day and ask Him to help you.

He hears your prayers, and He promises to answer when you call upon His name. And because you know He hears you, expect Him to answer. He may answer with a no, a yes, or a not right now, but He will answer, making your paths straight and giving you understanding along the way. Remember, *wake up* and pray with expectation!

**At daybreak, LORD, You hear my voice; at daybreak I plead my case to You and watch expectantly. —Psalm 5:3**

Further Scripture: Psalm 6:9; Jeremiah 29:12; 1 John 5:14

---

## Questions

1. What might the sacrifices of righteousness mentioned in Psalm 4:5 look like (Psalms 51:17; 141:2; Micah 6:8; Romans 6:13; 12:1; Hebrews 13:15–16)?
2. Read Psalm 4:6; John 1:9; and 8:12. How did David point to the Messiah? Or did he?
3. Contrast David's statement in Psalm 5:4 with the serpent's words about God in Genesis 3:4–5. Why must our understanding of God be David's view?
4. Have you ever felt this kind of grief and turmoil that is expressed in Psalm 6? How does reading these words encourage you and give you hope?

5. In Psalm 6:9, David made a confident statement. Why do you think he was so sure God heard and received his prayer? Where else do we see this kind of assurance (John 11:41–42)? Do you have this same confidence?

6. What did the Holy Spirit highlight to you in Psalms 4—6 through the reading or the teaching?

# Lesson 32: Psalms 7—9

*King of Glory*: God Cares for Us

## Teaching Notes

### Intro

This is kind of refreshing—we're not in Job! We're trying to look at the whole context of the book of Psalms in order to get a better understanding of the Messiah. There are at least seven authors in Psalms. Some of the authors include David, Moses, Solomon, and the sons of Korah. At least 50 psalms are anonymous. One of the purposes of the psalms was they were sung during different events of life—songs of praise, ascent, lament, joy, and love. We are going to look at Psalm 8, which starts with directions from David for the choirmaster. The song was to be played on a Gittith, which has been described as a guitar-like harp.[1]

About Psalm 8, commentary writer James Johnston wrote, "Yahweh reveals His majesty in this world by using weak people to do His great work. God reveals His majesty by defeating His enemies through the weakness of children."[2]

### Teaching

*Psalm 8:1–2*: Verses 1–2 focus on God's creation of mankind. Verse 1 references God with two titles—"Yahweh" and "our Lord." "Yahweh" refers to "the covenant keeping God of Israel," while "the Lord" is based on the Hebrew name Adonai and refers to "the sovereign over all His creation, including His people."[3] David was building his case. He was complimenting the Lord.

Jesus also talked about this idea of God working through children in the New Testament (Matthew 21:16). Constable writes, "Even the weakest human beings praise their Creator!"[4] God can use children to silence the enemy! Wiersbe gives examples of children or the weak being used by God, writing, "The cry of

---

[1] John MacArthur, *The MacArthur Bible Commentary* (Nashville: Thomas Nelson, 2005), 603.

[2] James A. Johnston, *The Psalms: Volume 1; Psalms 1–41*, Preaching the Word, ed., R. Kent Hughes (Wheaton: Crossway, 2015), 95.

[3] Thomas L. Constable, *Expository Notes of Dr. Thomas Constable: Psalms*, 61, https://planobiblechapel.org/tcon/notes/pdf/psalms.pdf.

[4] Constable, 62.

baby Moses ultimately brought Egypt to her knees, and the birth of Samuel was used by God to save Israel and bring David to the throne. David himself was but a youth when he silenced Goliath and defeated him (1 Samuel 17:33, 42–43). God has used the weak and helpless to praise Him and help defeat His enemies."[5]

*Psalm 8:3–4*: Verses 3–4 focus on how God cares for us. "If the whole universe is diminutive [extremely small] in the sight of the divine Creator, how much less is the significance of mankind!"[6] Regardless of the size of the universe God cares about mankind. He created us.

*Psalm 8:5–8*: Verses 5–8 focus on how God crowns us in His own image. It is crazy to think that God would even use us, isn't it? He crowns us with glory and honor to do His work (Job 7:17; 25:16; Psalm 144:3–4). Despite our weakness, God thinks about us, uses us, and loves us.

Ron Forseth noticed that throughout Scripture, the people God used were broken and a little dysfunctional. Forseth wrote, "We talk about 'great lives' in the Bible—and there are many of them—but the thing that amazes me is how many of those 'great lives' were actually lived by damaged people with serious family issues."[7] I want us to look at the names Forseth studied.

- Adam (Genesis 3:12)
- Eve (Genesis 3:6)
- Cain (Genesis 4:8)
- Noah (Genesis 9:20–21)
- Abraham (Genesis 12, 20)
- Sarah (Genesis 16)
- Lot (Genesis 18—20)
- Job (Job 2:9)
- Isaac (Genesis 26)
- Rebekah (Genesis 27)
- Jacob (Genesis 25; 27; 30)
- Rachel (Genesis 31:19)
- Reuben (Genesis 35:21)

---

[5] Warren W. Wiersbe, *Be Worshipful: Glorify God for Who He Is* (Colorado Springs: David C. Cook, 2004), 46.

[6] MacArthur, 603.

[7] Ron Forseth, "20+ Messed Up Bible Heroes and What We Can Learn from Them," Sermon Central, October 14, 2019, https://www.sermoncentral.com/pastors-preaching-articles/ron-forseth-20-messed-up-bible-heroes-and-what-we-can-learn-from-them-1613.

- Moses (Exodus 2; 32:19; Numbers 20:11)
- Aaron (Exodus 32)
- Miriam (Numbers 12)
- Samson (Judges 16)
- Eli (1 Samuel 2, 4)
- Saul (1 Samuel 16, 18, 19, 31)
- David (2 Samuel 11)
- Solomon (1 Kings 11)[8]

These were the people that God used to make a difference! We elevate people we've learned about in Scripture but fail to realize that they were messes just like us. Why are we reading this list? Because this was what David had been talking about. God used all of these people, despite their weakness, because God wanted them to be over His land. God uses us despite our weaknesses.

Constable explains, "God made man a little lower than Himself, in His own image that no other created beings bear. . . . God has crowned man with glory and majesty by giving him the authority to rule over creation as His agent. . . . Jesus Christ, last Adam will fulfill mankind's destiny when He returns to earth and brings all creation under His control"[9] (1 Corinthians 15:27–28). Until then, this should be our perspective: we are to be broken pots that allow the light of Christ to shine through us.

*Psalm 8:9*: Even as a broken vessel, when Christ is working in us, anything is possible. Constable pointed out, "Man has tamed, and even domesticated, many kinds of animals, but he finds it impossible to control himself without divine assistance."[10]

## Closing
Wiersbe does a great job of summarizing the work of the Divine Trinity:

- "God the Father created us to be kings, but the disobedience of our first parents robbed us of our crowns."
- "God the Son came to earth and redeemed us to be kings" (Revelation 1:5–6).

---

[8] Forseth.

[9] Constable, 63–64.

[10] Constable, 64.

- God the Holy Spirit "can empower us to 'reign in life by one, Jesus Christ'" (Romans 5:17).[11]

---

## The Daily Word

These days, people host all kinds of celebrations and get special treats for everything—like scoring a goal at soccer, getting promoted at work, losing a tooth, or any calendar holiday. Today, celebrate the work of God's hands! Not only did God make you, but He made the heavens, moon, and stars. He made the sheep, oxen, birds in the sky, and fish in the ocean. All of it was made by His hands. And He made man to rule over it all. He put everything under your feet, all His wonderful works. God describes you as a clay vessel holding all His power to do the work He called you to do.

So when you feel defeated, when you feel knocked down, when you feel you've messed up and don't measure up, it is time to stand up. You are a child of God. You are the work of His hands—and He cares for you. You are able to press on because the creator of the universe, God Almighty's power is at work in your life. *Give thanks to the Lord throughout the earth. Celebrate and have a special treat today* because the Lord has done great things and has given you so many reasons to rejoice, boast, and sing about His name!

**What is man that You remember him, the son of man that You look after him? You made him little less than God and crowned him with glory and honor. You made him lord over the works of Your hands; You put everything under his feet. —Psalm 8:4–6**

Further Scripture: Psalm 8:9; 9:1–2; 2 Corinthians 4:7–9

---

## Questions

1. Does it bring you comfort that God looks deep within our minds and hearts? When is it comforting and when is it not?

2. How can God both love the world and hate the wicked (Psalms 5:5; 7:11; John 3:16)?

3. The psalmist in Psalm 8 began and ended with praising the majestic name of God. Why do you believe he found this to be important? What is the importance of a name to God Himself (Exodus 3:14–15)?

4. How can you continue to have joy and rejoice in the Lord (Psalm 19:8; John 15:9–11; Philippians 4:4–8)?

---

[11] Wiersbe, 48.

5. In Psalm 9:17, what are some reasons people ignore God? Who are the ones God will not ignore forever?

6. What did the Holy Spirit highlight to you in Psalms 7—9 through the reading or the teaching?

# Lesson 33: Psalms 10—12

*King of Glory*: Atheists or God-Followers

## Teaching Notes

### Intro

Today we're reading Psalms 10—12, but we'll be studying Psalm 10. I encourage you, as we read through the book of Psalms, to slow down and read each psalm, even if we don't specifically study it. As we study our selected psalms, we're looking for how the coming Messiah is presented. That won't happen in every psalm, but it will happen in most. Our phrase that we're starting with for our study of Psalms is *King of Glory*. Psalm 10 was originally a part of the ninth psalm.[1] The ninth psalm now presents confidence in "the sure coming of divine justice," while the tenth psalm's concern is "injustice is rampant and God seems disinterested."[2] Psalm 10 carries a sense of urgency, asking for God to deliver them immediately from their enemies.[3]

### Teaching

*Psalm 10:1–11*: Psalm 10 has no title or instructions, and there is no author acknowledged specifically for this psalm. It begins with asking God why He is so far away and why He is hiding when the psalmist is in trouble (vv. 1–3). These are words of lament, and while the author was upset as he wrote, his focus seems to be on the issues with the wicked, not anger at God.[4] His question is why God seems to be apathetic to his needs. In fact, the concern was that the wicked did not believe God existed and as such do not believe in being possibly judged by God (vv. 4–11). *Nelson's Commentary* points out that the wicked "turn reality upside down by praising evil and spurning God."[5] There is arrogance in the belief

---

[1] Earl D. Radmacher, Ronald B. Allen, and H. Wayne House, eds., *Nelson's New Illustrated Bible Commentary* (Nashville: Thomas Nelson, 1999), 654.

[2] John MacArthur, *The MacArthur Bible Commentary* (Nashville: Thomas Nelson, 2005), 604.

[3] Radmacher et al., 654.

[4] MacArthur, 604.

[5] Radmacher et al., 654.

that there is no God. This speaks to atheists who do not believe in God, rather than agnostics who do not care that God exists.

I feel like our society is moving toward atheism. There has been a rise of "nones" who believe in nothing. Researcher Gervais has concluded there are more atheists than surveys have reported. A 2018 survey of 2,000 people found that 26 percent identified as atheists. When the statistical percentages are extended toward the entire American population, there could be as many as 64 million atheists in the United States.[6] Pew Research Center found that atheists tend to be male (68 percent), younger (born after 1980), Caucasian (78 percent), and highly educated (43 percent have college degrees).[7] Recent surveys have found an increase from 36.6 to 55.8 million of those who indicate they are "nones."[8]

Michael Lipka of the Pew Research Center has portrayed ten facts about atheists in America:

1. The number of American atheists has almost doubled over the past few years.
2. American atheists tend to be male and "younger than the overall population."
3. American atheists tend to associate with Democrats and "with political liberalism."
4. Eight percent of American atheists believe in God or in some "universal spirit."
5. Religion is not important to nine out of ten atheists.
6. Few American atheists (9 percent) talk about their atheistic views weekly, and 65 percent seldom or never do.
7. They do not look to religion to answer questions or deal with moral issues.
8. Mainstream Americans like people who are members of major religious groups more than atheists.
9. Over one-half of Americans would not support an atheist becoming president.
10. Over half of Americans say it's possible to be moral without believing in God.[9]

---

[6] Brian Resnick, "How Many American Atheists Are There Really?" Vox, May 17, 2017, https://www.vox.com/science-and-health/2017/4/13/15258496/american-atheists-how-many.

[7] Michael Lipka, "10 Facts About Atheists," Pew Research, June 1, 2016, http://www.pewresearch.org/fact-tank/2016/06/01/10-facts-about-atheists/.

[8] Michael Shermer, "The Number of Americans with No Religious Affiliation Is Rising," *Scientific American*, April 1, 2018, https://www.scientificamerican.com/article/the-number-of-americans-with-no-religious-affiliation-is-rising/.

[9] Michael Lipka, "10 Facts About Atheists," Pew Research, June 1, 2016, http://www.pewresearch.org/fact-tank/2016/06/01/10-facts-about-atheists/. Accessed on July 18, 2023, from the Internet Archive, https://web.archive.org/web/20160603143917/http://www.pewresearch.org/fact-tank/2016/06/01/10-facts-about-atheists/.

Our hearts should be breaking over these numbers. How is this even possible? Because we're not talking about Jesus? Because we're waiting for these atheists to walk into a church? Because we're expecting them to come to us? Regardless of the reasons, we're not reaching those who are proclaimed atheists. And, somewhere along the road, these individuals have been hurt through the church. We can never argue people into the kingdom of God. That's why Jesus came in, and He's got this because He knows we cannot do it. We are all sinners, and sin leads to death (Romans 6:23). God loves us so much He sent His Son to die for us, to take away that sin. It takes just as much faith to believe in God as it does to deny His existence!

*Psalm 10:12–18*: If we do not believe in God, things will not get any better for us (v. 15). But "the Lord is King forever and ever" (v. 16).

## Closing

Former atheist and writer C. S. Lewis wrote:

> I am trying here to prevent anyone saying the really foolish thing that people often say about Him: "I'm ready to accept Jesus as a great moral teacher, but I don't accept His claim to be God." That is the one thing we must not say. A man who was merely a man and said the sort of things Jesus said would not be a great moral teacher. He would either be a lunatic—on a level with the man who says he is a poached egg—or else he would be the Devil of Hell. You must make your choice. Either this man was, and is, the Son of God: or else a madman or something worse. You can shut Him up for a fool, you can spit at Him and kill Him as a demon; or you can fall at His feet and call Him Lord and God. But let us not come with any patronizing nonsense about His being a great human teacher. He has not left that open to us. He did not intend to.[10]

Will you give Jesus a chance? Will you humble yourself today and ask God to show you that this is real? If you will do this, God will show up in your life. He loves you so much that He died for you! Ask for God's forgiveness by saying, "Lord, I was so arrogant that I couldn't see you. Are you real?" I can guarantee you that God will show up in response. When you trust in Jesus, it doesn't mean that you have all the answers, but it means that you have something to hold on to!

---

[10] C. S. Lewis, *Mere Christianity* (New York: HarperOne, 1980), 52.

## The Daily Word

The Lord will guard you and protect you, even in a world full of wicked people wandering everywhere: people boasting in themselves, living with greed, despising the Lord, and believing God doesn't exist. God allows hard things to happen in this fallen world, and you may not understand why. Sometimes His protection comes in the form of peace and strength in the middle of a trial. Sometimes God's protection doesn't look like you thought it would. You endure a car accident or a house fire, a bad word spoken to you, or a sickness. You don't feel protected. Trust that God is in your midst. He sees something you may not see, and He's working on the bigger picture. He is with you.

With faith in Jesus, trust and believe His promises. When you find yourself in a fearful situation, *pray and believe God* is your shield, your horn of salvation, your stronghold, your refuge, and your Savior. When you call to Him, you will be saved. Rest in knowing whatever trial you face today the Lord will protect and guard you.

**You, LORD, will guard us; You will protect us from this generation forever. The wicked wander everywhere, and what is worthless is exalted by the human race. —Psalm 12:7–8**

Further Scripture: 2 Samuel 22:3–4; Psalm 10:3–4; 2 Thessalonians 3:3

## Questions

1. What were the psalmists' feelings about how God handles the wicked? Do you sometimes feel the same way? Where can you go in scripture to combat that lie of God's inactiveness?

2. What is the difference between the pain of a believer who says "God has forgotten" and the sinner who vainly takes comfort in the idea that God has forgotten (Psalm 10:11)?

3. What did David's friends mean when they told him to "escape to the mountain like a bird" (Psalm 11:1)? What was David's reaction to this?

4. David had complete trust in God (Psalms 11—12). How do you know that God is in complete control of your circumstances (Exodus 2:23–25; 3:6–15; Matthew 19:26)?

5. Compare the vain words of man to the words and promises of God (Psalm 12; 2 Corinthians 1:20). What are some promises that you began to doubt but then God proved Himself faithful?

6. What did the Holy Spirit highlight to you in Psalms 10—12 through the reading or the teaching?

# Lesson 34: Psalms 13—15

*King of Glory*: Living Righteously

## Teaching Notes

### Intro

Scripture has regularly contrasted the way of the wicked with the way of the righteous. Jesus said, "How narrow is the gate and difficult the road that leads to life, and few find it" (Matthew 7:14). In today's assigned passages, Psalm 14 describes the way of the wicked while Psalm 15 describes the way of the righteous. MacArthur notes that, in Psalm 15, "The saved sinner is described as exhibiting indications of ethical integrity."[1] Wiersbe observes, "Psalm 15 is not a prescription for being saved but a description of how saved people ought to live if they want to please God and fellowship with Him."[2]

Wiersbe notes, "The rabbis taught that there were 613 commandments for the Jewish people to obey if they wanted to be righteous." Psalm 15 lists 11 commandments to obey. Isaiah 33:15–16 lists six requirements: "The one who lives righteously and speaks rightly, who refuses profit from extortion, whose hand never takes a bribe, who stops his ears from listening to murderous plots and shuts his eyes against evil schemes—he will dwell on the heights; his refuge will be on the rocky fortresses, his food provided, his water assured." Micah 6:8 lists three: "Mankind, he has told each of you what is good and what it is the LORD requires of you: to act justly, to love faithfulness, and to walk humbly with your God." Habakkuk 2:4 simplifies all the lists and brought the requirements down to one: "Look, his ego is inflated, he is without integrity. But the righteous one will live by his faith."[3]

### Teaching

*Psalm 15:1*: Even though David was king, he was not free to come and go in the house of the Lord as he pleased. Only the priests could do that.[4] The "tent" on

---

[1] John MacArthur, *The MacArthur Bible Commentary* (Nashville: Thomas Nelson, 2005), 607.

[2] Warren W. Wiersbe, *The Bible Exposition Commentary: Job–Song of Solomon* (Colorado Springs: David C. Cook, 2004), 116.

[3] Wiersbe, 115.

[4] Wiersbe, 116.

the "holy mountain" was where God's people went to seek the presence of the Lord. David said, "At daybreak, LORD, You hear my voice; at daybreak I plead my case to You and watch expectantly" (Psalm 5:3). What patterns have you established to see the Lord daily?

*Psalm 15:2–5*: Only when our pattern of seeking the Lord has been established can we begin to see the effects of living a righteous life. MacArthur observes these verses almost follow a question and answer format in "triplets of positive and negative descriptions."[5] Wiersbe characterizes these verses as describing how to go about "obeying God's precepts."[6] Eleven precepts are outlined:

1. Live blamelessly (v. 2a).
2. Practice righteousness (v. 2b)—Saved people were charged to be holy, to be characterized by standing rightly before the Lord, by reflecting His attitude in every situation.
3. Acknowledge the truth in your heart (v. 2c).
4. Do not slander with your tongue (v. 3a)—Saved people are not to tear others down in a malicious way.
5. Do not harm your friend (v. 3b)—Saved people should have no desire to bring ill will to people close to them.
6. Do not discredit your neighbor (v.3c)—Saved people should not speak negatively of their neighbors.
7. Despise the one rejected by the Lord, but honor those who fear the Lord (v. 4a).
8. Keep His Word whatever the cost (v. 4b)—Saved people stay consistent in their walk with the Lord regardless of what they may have to give up or lose.
9. Do not lend money at interest (v. 5a).
10. Do not take a bribe against the innocent (v. 5b).
11. The one who does these things will never be shaken (v. 5c)—Wiersbe points out that the Hebrew word translated "shaken" implied "violent shaking."[7]

Righteous people, who have ordered their life according to these precepts, will have security in their faith before the Lord.

---

[5] MacArthur, 607.

[6] Wiersbe, 116.

[7] Wiersbe, 117.

## Closing

As He concluded the Sermon on the Mount, Jesus said, "Therefore, everyone who hears these words of Mine and acts on them will be like a sensible man who built his house on the rock. The rain fell, the rivers rose, and the winds blew and pounded that house. Yet it didn't collapse, because its foundation was on the rock. But everyone who hears these words of Mine and doesn't act on them will be like a foolish man who built his house on the sand. The rain fell, the rivers rose, the winds blew and pounded that house, and it collapsed. And its collapse was great!" (Matthew 7:24–27).

Just as Psalm 15 teaches that those who build their lives on the foundation of spending time with the Lord and living a righteous life will not be shaken, Jesus also taught that living according to His teachings would produce the same results.

## The Daily Word

Where do you intentionally seek the presence of the Lord? Is it in a chair every morning before the sun rises? Is it on the bathroom floor before you hop in the shower? Is it on the commute to work with the radio off? Seeking God's presence may look differently for everyone, *but the key is to be intentional.*

The Lord's strength flows through your life from your time in His presence. In His presence, your will, wants, and desires are emptied. Your walk becomes godly and righteous as you depend on His power and strength. You will live honestly, practice righteousness, and acknowledge God's truth in your heart through your time in His presence. These behaviors happen not because they are forced through your effort but because your love for the Lord increases through His ongoing presence and power within you. Security in Jesus as your rock and your firm foundation are found in His presence. Ultimately, as a follower of Jesus, you will live in the presence of God forever. Until that time comes, *intentionally seek His ongoing presence*, and His love and grace will over-flow from your life.

**LORD, who can dwell in Your tent? Who can live on Your Holy Mountain? . . . the one who does these things will never be moved. —Psalm 15:1, 5**

Further Scripture: Micah 6:8; Matthew 7:24–25; 1 Corinthians 3:16

## Questions

1.  David asked, "How long will You hide Your face from me?" (Psalm 13:1b). Have you ever felt as though God was hiding His face from you? How did this make you feel? Did this make you want to give up on Him or seek Him even more?

2.  David was going through a tough time, but he still praised God through it (Psalm 13:5–6). Have you ever found yourself praising Him through the trials in your life?

3.  What did David call people who did not believe in God (Psalm 14:1)? Do you believe that there are really any true atheists?

4.  Where else does the Bible say there is no one who does good (Psalm 14:3; Romans 3:23)?

5.  David gave ten guidelines for living a righteous or blameless life (Psalm 15). Where else in the Bible are ten guidelines given for living a righteous or blameless life? Can anyone live up to these standards?

6.  What did the Holy Spirit highlight to you in Psalms 13—15 through the reading or the teaching?

# Lesson 35: Psalms 16—17

*King of Glory*: Finding Eternal Joy

## Teaching Notes

### Intro

There's not a day when the book of Psalms doesn't speak into your life. We've already looked at a variety of psalms. Some scholars identify Psalm 16 as a personal psalm of joy of God's goodness, while others identify it as a psalm of lament. As we walk through this psalm, it will feel a little like the suffering servant of Isaiah 53. In Psalm 16 is the language of lament, and in that is the expression of joy. Within the psalm, "my" is used 12 times, such as "my portion," "my future," "my conscience," and "my right hand." David's joy is expressed through his delight, his pleasure, his pleasantry, or just being glad. All of this language demonstrates that God was doing something special in David's life. This is also a messianic psalm and much of the end of the psalm was used by both Paul and Peter to describe Jesus as the Messiah. The subheading for Psalm 16 is "A Davidic Miktam." There are six of these in the book of Psalms. Scholars do not agree on what the word means but suggest it could mean: "engraved in gold, to cover, secret treasure, [or] a poem containing pithy sayings."[1] Wiersbe uses three descriptions to explain the themes within each section: "The Lord of Life" (vv. 1–8); "The Conqueror of Death" (vv. 9–10); and "The Joy of Eternity" (v. 11).[2]

### Teaching

*Psalm 16:1–8*: In verse 1, David asked for protection or preservation, meaning that he asked God "to keep or to watch over" as "a shepherd watched over his sheep."[3] In verse 2, David wanted to enjoy all the good things God had given him (Psalms 21:3; 23:6; 73:25, 28; Matthew 19:17). David knew God is the giver of every good and perfect gift (James 1:17).

---

[1] Warren W. Wiersbe, *The Wiersbe Bible Commentary: Old Testament* (Colorado Springs: David C. Cook, 2007), 891.

[2] Wiersbe, 891–92.

[3] James A. Johnston, *The Psalms: Volume 1; Psalms 1–41*, Preaching the Word, ed., R. Kent Hughes (Wheaton: Crossway, 2015), 175.

David also took delight in the holy people (the believing remnant) who were in the land, trusted God, and obeyed His covenant (v. 3). God calls us to be holy (Exodus 19:6; Leviticus 19:2; 20:7–8, 26; 21:8; Deuteronomy 7:6). Surround yourself with those who are holy. The other group in the land was made up of the unbelieving worshippers of idols. David said he would not speak their names (v. 4). While we should surround ourselves with those who are holy, we're also called to go out into the world (Romans 12:2; James 1:27; 4:4). We have to be in the world to be light and salt for Christ.

In verse 5, David recognized that God was his portion. The phrase "my portion" illustrates the inheritance each of the 11 tribes (all except Levi) received in the Promised Land. For David, God Himself was his portion and his future. Then David recognized the land he had received and his role as steward of it (v. 6) (rules for the land: Deuteronomy 19:14; 27:17; Proverbs 15:25; 22:28). David depended upon God for counsel and spent his nights in "discipline and chastening."[4] He identified that God was the foundation on which he lived his life (v. 8).

*Psalm 16:9–10*: These verses begin the messianic prophecy in this psalm. Wiersbe points out that the phrase "my body will rest secure" was spoken about the Messiah, not about David himself.[5] The identification continues in verse 10: "For You will not abandon me to Sheol; You will not allow Your Faithful One to see decay." Peter's entire message at Pentecost is based on Psalm 16:9–10 (Acts 2:22–31). David prophesied that the coming Messiah would conquer death. Paul also referenced Psalm 16 in Acts 13:35 when he explained that the Messiah's body would not decay (Luke 24:28–31, 36–43). The resurrection of Christ was the theme in both Paul's and Peter's preaching.

*Psalm 16:11*: Verse 11 gives a wonderful picture of the abundant joy in heaven in which there are eternal pleasures. The reality of eternal life is being in the presence of the *King of Glory* forever.

## Closing

David never stopped learning, praying, and listening to God. We have the same opportunity—to learn and listen and experience joy in God.

---

[4] Wiersbe, 891.

[5] Wiersbe, 892.

## The Daily Word

As a follower of Christ, keep the Lord on your mind always. *Always.* When you wake up, make breakfast for your family, walk into that board meeting, play that sports game, walk up the steps to preach that sermon, wait on the doctor's report, tuck your kids to bed at night, or burn the midnight oil writing papers for school . . . keep the Lord on your mind *always!* Why? Because when you do, you won't be shaken or feel defeated in life. You won't be shaken when you lose the game or your kids won't listen to you. You won't feel defeated when you don't have approval from your peers, your coworkers, or your teachers, or when the health test reveals unwanted results.

Keep your mind focused and your eyes fixed on Jesus, the author of your life. He has plans for you, not to harm you but to prosper you for good. He holds your future and will reveal the path of life to you even through the trials. As you keep the Lord in mind and rest in His presence, He promises you will experience *joy.* Try it today. Keep the Lord on your mind *at all times.* Read His Word. Give thanks to Him for His promises. Sit in the quiet and let His Spirit speak to your heart. Rest in Him. Not in yourself. Not in your things or your agenda. Not in strife or in fret. *Rest in Him.* In Him, you won't be shaken.

**I keep the LORD in mind always. Because He is at my right hand, I will not be shaken. Therefore my heart is glad and my spirit rejoices; my body also rests securely. . . . You reveal the path of life to me; in Your presence is abundant joy; in Your right hand are eternal pleasures. —Psalm 16:8–9, 11**

Further Scripture: Psalm 16:5–6; Jeremiah 29:11; Hebrews 12:2

## Questions

1. Psalm 16:8 and 11 both mention the right hand. What is the significance of the right hand in the Bible, and where else in the Bible do you hear of the right hand being mentioned (Genesis 48:13–14; Psalms 110:1; 118:16; Acts 2:33; Romans 8:34; Ephesians 1:20–21; Hebrews 10:12–13)?

2. How does Psalm 16:9–10 point to Jesus' resurrection, as well as our salvation? Who else in the New Testament quotes these verses about the Messiah (Acts 2:25–28)?

3. In Psalm 17, David cried out to the Lord for vindication from his enemies. Do you ever find yourself pleading your case before God or wanting to take vengeance on someone you think has done you wrong? What does the Bible say about this (Deuteronomy 32:35–36; Ezekiel 25:17; Romans 12:17–19; James 1:19–20)?

4. How often do you look for fulfillment in this lifetime instead of looking forward to the day when we meet Jesus face to face in eternity (Psalm 17:14)?

5. What did the Holy Spirit highlight to you in Psalms 16—17 through the reading or the teaching?

# Lesson 36: Psalm 18

*King of Glory*: The Head of the Nations

## Teaching Notes

### Intro

Reading the book of Psalms has been an emotional rollercoaster for me. The emotional extremes are significant. Psalm 18 is emotionally up as a psalm of thanksgiving, and it's one of the royal psalms. "Although the title seems to refer to only one specific occasion (e.g., 'on the day'), it does state that God's deliverance was 'from the hand of all his enemies and from the hand of Saul.' Therefore, it is preferable that the language of this superscription be understood to summarize the testimony of David's entire life in retrospect."[1] This is the second longest superscription (only Psalm 60 is longer) within the psalms.[2] Psalm 18 strongly resembles 2 Samuel 22:1–2.

### Teaching

*Psalm 18:1–18*: Wiersbe explains that the first 18 verses of Psalm 18 are about how "God delivers when we call on Him."[3] The first three verses present David's prelude of praises. David said, "I love You, Lord." MacArthur explains that the Hebrew word for "love" used here was "not the normal word for love that often bears covenant meaning, but is a rare verb form of a word group that expresses tender intimacy."[4] (In John 21:15–17, a similar type of love is expressed.) In verse 2, David used seven metaphors to describe what God was to him: his rock, his fortress, his deliverer, his mountain, his shield, his salvation, and his stronghold (Psalms 84:9; 89:18). The Lord was ALL David needed when he faced life's tough battles. God answered his call and saved him from his enemies (v. 3).

---

[1] John MacArthur, *The MacArthur Bible Commentary* (Nashville: Thomas Nelson, 2005), 609.

[2] James A. Johnston, *The Psalms: Volume 1; Psalms 1–41*, Preaching the Word, ed., R. Kent Hughes (Wheaton: Crossway, 2015), 193.

[3] Warren W. Wiersbe, *Be Worshipful: Glorify God for Who He Is* (Colorado Springs: David C. Cook, 2004), 75.

[4] MacArthur, 609.

David faced death and cried out in desperation and terror (vv. 4–5). David cried out while facing death, and God heard him (v. 6).

In verses 7–15, David presented a "theophany, a vivid, poetic picture of God's presence . . . largely described by various catastrophic responses by all creation."[5] David saw God's power and anger as the earth shook and the mountains trembled (vv. 7–8). The heavens parted, and God came down to earth, riding a cherub and soaring on the winds (vv. 9–10). He thundered from heaven and hurled arrows and lightning bolts (vv. 13–14). The foundations of the world and the depths of the sea could be seen at God's rebuke (v. 15). God rescued David out of the deep waters and from his powerful enemy (vv. 16–17). The Lord delivered David (v. 18). (These scriptures provide examples of love intimacy with the Lord: Psalms 102:13; 103:13; Isaiah 49:15; Hosea 1:7.)

*Psalm 18:19–27*: Wiersbe explains that verses 19–27 are about how God rewards us when we obey.[6]

*Psalm 18:28–45*: Wiersbe points out that these verses are about how God equips us when we submit to Him.[7] David went through so many experiences in life to get to this point and God equipped him to grow in those experiences.

Verse 43 states that God delivered David and appointed him as head of the nations. This also speaks about the coming of the Messiah, who will be over all nations. Matthew 25:31–34 gives a picture of Psalm 18:43 in the prophetic picture of the Messiah who is head of the nations: "When the Son of Man comes in His glory, and all the angels with Him, then He will sit on the throne of His glory. All the nations will be gathered before Him, and He will separate them one from another, just as a shepherd separates the sheep from the goats. He will put the sheep on His right and the goats on the left. Then the King will say to those on His right, 'Come, you who are blessed by My Father, inherit the kingdom prepared for you from the foundation of the world.'" The rest of Matthew 25 explains the sheep nations are those aligned with Israel.

Revelation 7:9–10 supports this picture: "After this I looked, and there was a vast multitude from every nation, tribe, people, and language, which no one could number, standing before the throne and before the Lamb. They were robed in white with palm branches in their hands. And they cried out in a loud voice: Salvation belongs to our God, who is seated on the throne, and to the Lamb!"

---

[5] MacArthur, 609.

[6] Wiersbe, 76–77.

[7] Wiersbe, 77.

# Closing

Wiersbe states, "God is glorified when we worship him."[8] In all of this, God is glorified in our worship. David's psalm closes with these words: "Therefore I will praise You, Yahweh, among the nations; I will sing about Your name. He gives great victories to His king; He shows loyalty to His anointed, to David and his descendants forever." This is a royal messianic prophecy that points to the Davidic Covenant and then points to the Messianic Covenant. In Romans 15:9, Paul brings Psalm 18 into focus.

## The Daily Word

Think of a time when you cried out to the Lord with an emotional, heartfelt prayer. Perhaps you needed healing, an impossible provision, supernatural wisdom, or protection from harm's way. And then God moved—He answered in an "only God" type of way. Did you stop and worship, giving praise and thanksgiving to the Lord? Maybe you didn't have the words to praise the Lord? Maybe you want to enter His gates with thanksgiving and His courts with praise, but you just feel stuck when you try to articulate it. Take a minute and read David's words in Psalm 18 aloud. Seriously, do it. David praised the Lord with such a depth of worship and praise. You can learn from this man who cried out to the Lord through every circumstance and witnessed the Lord move in impossible, "only God" ways to deliver and heal him.

Today, begin praising the Lord with the phrase: "I love You, Lord, my strength." It may seem simple, but repeat the words out loud, over and over, until it comes from a place of real adoration to the Lord. *God is glorified when you worship Him.* Call to the Lord who is worthy of praise, and you will be saved.

**I love You, Lord, my strength. —Psalm 18:1**

Further Scripture: Psalm 18:2–3; Mark 12:30; Revelation 14:7

## Questions

1. Psalm 18 is nearly identical to 2 Samuel 22, but the very first line is not found in 2 Samuel. What is that line? Do you perceive the Lord as your strength? What does (or would that) look like?

2. Look at Psalm 18:20–24; it basically has the same message as Job 23:11–12 and 27:6. How could both men make these claims of righteousness?

---

[8] Wiersbe, 78.

3.  Three to four times in Psalm 18, depending on the translation, David referred to the Lord as his rock (Psalm 18:2, 31, 46). What book did we study with the theme "Rock"? Do you think of God in this way? Why or why not?

4.  Look up Psalm 18:26 in at least three different translations and explain what the second part of this verse means.

5.  What did the Holy Spirit highlight to you in Psalm 18 through the reading or the teaching?

# Lesson 37: Psalms 19—20

*King of Glory*: Words to Pray

## Teaching Notes

### Intro

We are continuing in our study of the Wisdom Books and specifically our study of the book of Psalms. In Psalm 18, we looked at how David praised God in prayer with tender intimacy. This picture of David's prayer life is one I want. I want David's intimacy and relationship with the Lord in prayer. Today, I'll give you eight words that may help you think through how to pray. In Psalm 20 is a prayer given before a battle, and Psalm 21 is a prayer of celebration after the battle. That means we need some information about the battle, but none is specifically given in the psalm or in biblical commentaries. Because of the celebratory words of Psalm 21, we know the battle ended well.

### Teaching

*Psalm 20:1–5*: Wiersbe points out that the first five verses cover the prayers of the people for their king.[1] In verse 1, the people prayed that Yahweh would protect the king in his day of trouble. I mentioned we'd look at eight words we can use in prayer. These come from Jim Erwin and will be italicized throughout these notes.[2] The first is *Answer me* (Psalm 20:1, 9). As we pray, we can express that we need God to answer. The second is also in verse 1, *Protect me*. Asking God for protection is a biblical prayer!

Note that six times in the nine verses of Psalm 20 does the word "may" begin the prayer request. In verse 2, the people said, *Help me*. MacArthur explains that the words "from the sanctuary" and "out of Zion" refer to "the place of God's symbolic presence in the ark David had recaptured and installed in a tabernacle on Mount Zion."[3] This is how we should be praying, because every day we are in a battle. Also in verse 2, the people prayed, *Sustain me*.

---

[1] Warren W. Wiersbe, *The Bible Exposition Commentary: Job–Song of Solomon* (Colorado Springs: David C. Cook, 2004), 131.

[2] Jim Erwin, "Psalm 20:1–9 Trusting God in Prayer," Patheos, April 18, 2016, https://www.patheos.com/blogs/jimerwin/2016/04/18/psalm-201-9-trusting-god-prayer/.

[3] John MacArthur, *The MacArthur Bible Commentary* (Nashville: Thomas Nelson, 2005), 611.

In verse 3, the people prayed, *Remember me.* Of course, God remembers us, but by asking God to remember, we also remember our relationship with Him. "Selah" means to pause and reflect about God.

Then, they prayed, *Give me* (v. 4) and *Fulfill me* (vv. 4–5). Verse 4 can feel like a prosperity prayer in which we demand what we want. We think of the heart as fleshly and deceitful (Jeremiah 17:9; Matthew 15:19; Mark 7:20–23; Romans 7:18–20). But the word "heart" has another understanding (Hebrews 4:11–13). Psalm 37:4 says, "Take delight in the LORD, and He will give you your heart's desires" (Psalm 37:5–7). The Word of God changes our hearts and makes them pure and in tune with God's will (Matthew 5:8; John 15:7).

*Psalm 20:6–9*: The final words are given in verses 5–8: *Lift me.* Pray that God will lift us up to present His will to others. This entire psalm is about trusting that God hears our prayers and wants to respond to our needs.

## Closing

This is such a wonderful picture of how we can pray before the battle.

---

### The Daily Word

You face a spiritual battle every day as you seek first the kingdom of God and His righteousness. The enemy sets out to destroy your heart, your life, and your mind to keep you from fulfilling your whole purpose from the Lord. Nevertheless, you have the Lord on your side as you pray to answer you, protect you, help you, sustain you, and remember you. *Do not fear.*

God asks you to delight in Him with a pure heart. As you do so, your desires will line up with His desires for you. His strength, timing, wisdom, and protection allows you to fulfill your purpose from the Lord. Some people may take pride in chariots and horses, but as a believer, take pride in the Lord your God. As things on this earth collapse and fall apart, guess who stands firm forever? The *King of Glory!* *The Lord who is strong and mighty will give you the victory.* Raise your banner high in the name of the Lord. He is worthy to be praised.

**May He give you what your heart desires and fulfill your whole purpose. Let us shout for joy at your victory and lift the banner in the name of our God. May Yahweh fulfill all your requests. —Psalm 20:4–5**

Further Scripture: Psalm 20:7–9; 37:4; Ephesians 6:12

## Questions

1. In Psalm 19:1, what did David say is declaring the glory of God? How does creation declare the work of His hands and reveal knowledge? Read Romans 1:20. How do these two verses support one another and state a similar truth?

2. How does the law of the Lord restore or renew the soul (Psalms 19:7; 23:3)?

3. David asked the Lord to cleanse him of his hidden faults (Psalm 19:12). What are hidden faults? Compare them with willful sins (Psalm 19:13).

4. How can presumptuous, deliberate, or willful sin have dominion or rule over us (Psalm 19:13; Romans 6:12–14)? Have you ever had a sin you struggled to overcome? How did you get free of it?

5. Read Psalm 19:14. Why did David ask that the words of his mouth and the meditation of his heart be pleasing in the Lord's sight? Have you ever struggled with your words to God not matching your heart? How can you bring them into alignment (Proverbs 4:23; Jeremiah 17:9; Luke 6:45; Hebrews 3:13)?

6. Psalm 20:7 says, "Some take pride in chariots, and others in horses, but we take pride in the name of Yahweh our God." Do you turn to the Lord first in times of trouble or need? Or, do you "trust" in other things or people to help you?

7. What did the Holy Spirit highlight to you in Psalms 19—20 through the reading or the teaching?

# Lesson 38: Psalms 21—22

*King of Glory*: The Fifth Gospel

## Teaching Notes

### Intro

David wrote Psalm 22, but we don't know what occasion led to him writing this psalm.[1] Constable observes that Psalm 22 is similar to Psalm 69.[2] Wiersbe notes that Psalm 22 can be viewed as the first part of a trilogy with Psalms 23 and 24. In Psalm 22, the Good Shepherd died for his sheep. In Psalm 23, the Great Shepherd cared for his sheep.[3] In Psalm 24, the Great Shepherd returned and rewarded his sheep. MacArthur notes that Psalm 22 began with a lament over suffering and moved to praise of God by its conclusion.[4] The first 21 verses describe suffering while the final ten contain praises to God. MacArthur observes that the New Testament "contains 15 messianic quotations of or allusions to this psalm leading some in the early church to label it 'the fifth gospel.'"[5] *Nelson's Commentary* notes, "Although this psalm speaks of David's own distress and the Lord's deliverance of him, it also prophetically describes in remarkable detail Jesus' crucifixion and resurrection."[6]

### Teaching

*Psalm 22:1*: Job 3, Psalm 69, and Jeremiah 23 all contain similar expressions of lament just as the first 21 verses of Psalm 22 do. Jesus quoted Psalm 22 as He hung on the cross: "About three in the afternoon Jesus cried out with a loud voice, 'Elí, Elí, lemá sabachtáni?' that is, 'My God, My God, why have You forsaken

[1] Warren W. Wiersbe, *Be Worshipful: Glorify God for Who He Is* (Colorado Springs: David C. Cook, 2004), 90.

[2] Thomas L. Constable, *Expository Notes of Dr. Thomas Constable: Psalms*, 113, https://planobiblechapel.org/tcon/notes/pdf/psalms.pdf.

[3] Wiersbe, 90.

[4] John MacArthur, *The MacArthur Bible Commentary* (Nashville: Thomas Nelson, 2005), 612.

[5] MacArthur, 612.

[6] Earl D. Radmacher, Ronald B. Allen, and H. Wayne House, eds., *Nelson's New Illustrated Bible Commentary* (Nashville: Thomas Nelson, 1999), 662.

Me?'" (Matthew 27:46). MacArthur notes that the word "forsaken" used in verse 1 meant "a strong expression for personal abandonment, intensely felt by David and supremely experienced by Christ on the cross."[7]

Jesus had told His disciples, "Look: An hour is coming, and has come, when each of you will be scattered to his own home, and you will leave Me alone. Yet I am not alone, because the Father is with Me" (John 16:32), but as He hung on the cross, He cried out that God had forsaken Him. While God was still with Jesus as He hung on the cross, He felt like God had abandoned Him as He took on the sin of the world and, as Wiersbe notes, "In some inexplicable way He experienced what condemned, lost sinners experience 'away from the presence of the Lord.'"[8]

*Psalm 22:2–5*: MacArthur characterizes David's complaint as, "even though You have not responded to me, You remain the Holy One of Israel who had demonstrated His gracious attention time and time again to Your people."[9] *Nelson's Commentary* notes, "Even in the midst of great pain, David confesses his faith in the God of his fathers."[10]

*Psalm 22:6–11*: Wiersbe points out that David's experience of suffering left him abandoned by the people.[11] As he described the Messiah, Isaiah wrote, "Just as many were appalled at You—His appearance was so disfigured that He did not look like a man, and His form did not resemble a human being" (Isaiah 52:14). Just as David was "scorned by men and despised by people" (v. 6), so was Jesus: "The people stood watching, and even the leaders kept scoffing: 'He saved others; let Him save Himself if this is God's Messiah, the Chosen One!'" (Luke 23:35).

In the midst of his suffering, David continued to depend on the Lord; he did not abandon his faith in the Lord. He expressed his dependence on the Lord in verse 11 as a reiteration of verse 1.

*Psalm 22:12–21*: Wiersbe notes David "was condemned by the law."[12] David described his enemies as bulls (v. 12), lions (v. 13), dogs (v. 16), and oxen (v. 21). David said he was "poured out like water . . . my heart is like wax melting within me" (v. 14). *Nelson's Commentary* notes, "David's distress is so profound that he feels as if his life has been drained from him, as one might empty a jug

---

[7] MacArthur, 612.

[8] Wiersbe, 91.

[9] MacArthur, 612.

[10] Radmacher et al., 662.

[11] Wiersbe, 91.

[12] Wiersbe, 91.

of water."[13] As Jesus hung dead on the cross, a soldier pierced his side and blood and water flowed out of Him (John 19:34). David said, "My tongue sticks to the roof of my mouth." "After this, when Jesus knew that everything was now accomplished that the Scripture might be fulfilled, He said, 'I'm thirsty!'" (John 19:28).

David's hands and feet were not literally pierced as he describes in verse 16. This was a figure of speech for his suffering. But as a prophet, David looked ahead to what the Messiah would experience: "Since he was a prophet, he knew that God had sworn an oath to him to seat one of his descendants on his throne" (Acts 2:30). Isaiah 53:5 says, "But He was pierced because of our transgressions, crushed because of our iniquities; punishment for our peace was on Him, and we are healed by His wounds." Zechariah wrote, "Then I will pour out a spirit of grace and prayer on the house of David and the residents of Jerusalem, and they will look at Me whom they pierced. They will mourn for Him as one mourns for an only child and weep bitterly for Him as one weeps for a firstborn" (Zechariah 12:10). Verse 18 was a clear allusion to Jesus: "After crucifying Him they divided His clothes by casting lots" (Matthew 27:35).

*Psalm 22:22–31*: Wiersbe observes David began to describe a great assembly (vv. 22–25).[14] David could not stay quiet. He had gone from suffering to being delivered. MacArthur notes, "His exuberance is meant to be contagious."[15]

Finally, Wiersbe makes note of "the glorious kingdom" (vv. 26–29).[16] "On that day Yahweh will become King over the whole earth—Yahweh alone, and His name alone" (Zechariah 14:9). This glorious kingdom came through suffering that led to praise. This glorious kingdom impacts the generations to come.[17] The gospel message will spread geographically and throughout time.

## Closing

Psalm 22 proclaims the same message as Matthew, Mark, Luke, and John: "When Jesus had received the sour wine, He said, 'It is finished!' Then bowing His head, He gave up His spirit" (John 19:30).

---

[13] Radmacher et al., 663.

[14] Wiersbe, 93.

[15] MacArthur, 612.

[16] Wiersbe, 93.

[17] Wiersbe, 93.

## The Daily Word

Have you ever thought, *No one understands my pain, my misery, my distress. I just feel all alone. Where is God in this?* David prophesied about the Messiah's pain and distress generations before God sent Jesus to the earth. When it came to pass, Jesus cried out to God, His father, just as David had written: "My God, My God, why have You forsaken me?" David first prophesied it, and then, you read the story of Jesus—He indeed suffered pain, but God delivered Jesus from His suffering. Jesus was resurrected, going from death to life. In fact, Psalm 22 is quoted, referenced, or alluded to fifteen times in the New Testament. Some in the early church even refer to it as the "fifth gospel."

And just as Scripture prophesied of Jesus, the same is true for you. God will resurrect your life from the pit and what feels like death. *He will redeem your pain as you trust Him through any circumstance.* One day He will lift you up, and you will praise His name. You will testify to others about His great name. So press on. Just as Jesus held on to the hope in His father, hang on to hope found in Christ's love.

**My God, my God, why have You forsaken me? Why are You so far from my deliverance and from my words of groaning? My God, I cry by day, but You do not answer, by night, yet I have no rest. But You are holy, enthroned on the praises of Israel. Our fathers trusted in You; they trusted, and You rescued them. They cried to You and were set free; they trusted in You and were not disgraced. —Psalm 22:1–5**

Further Scripture: Psalm 22:27–31; Matthew 27:46; Acts 2:29–30

## Questions

1. David said the Lord had "given him his heart's desire" (Psalm 21:2). He repeated this in Psalm 37:4. Do you agree with these verses? How do you balance David's statements with Jeremiah's assertion, "The heart is more deceitful than anything else" (Jeremiah 17:9)? Do our desires have to line up with the Word of God before we receive them? Why or why not?

2. How does each verse in Psalm 21:3–6 individually point to Jesus?

3. Where else and who in Scripture repeated what David said in Psalm 22:1 (Matthew 27:46)?

4. The entirety of Psalm 22 is about the birth, life, burial, and resurrection of Jesus. How do you think David could have written these details generations before Jesus was born? Do you think he knew what he was writing about?

5. What did the Holy Spirit highlight to you in Psalms 21—22 through the reading or the teaching?

# Lesson 39: Psalms 23—25

*King of Glory*: The King of Glory

## Teaching Notes

### Intro

While Psalm 23 is a beloved psalm, Psalm 24 paints a picture of the Messiah that coincides with the larger theme of reviveSCHOOL. Wiersbe notes Psalm 22 can be viewed as the first part of a trilogy with Psalms 23 and 24. In Psalm 22, the Good Shepherd died for His sheep. In Psalm 23, the Great Shepherd cared for His sheep. In Psalm 24, the Great Shepherd returned and rewarded His sheep.[1] F. B. Meyer observes Psalm 23 tells of the cross, Psalm 24 tells of the crook, and Psalm 25 tells of the crown.[2]

Psalm 24 could have been written when the Ark was brought to Jerusalem. The early church designated Psalm 24 as an ascension psalm.[3] Wiersbe notes that the psalm opens with the people speaking in verses 1–2, the leader asking questions in verses 3, 8a, and 10a, and the people answering the leader's questions in verses 4–6, 8b, and 10b. This psalm was sung every Sunday in Herod's temple. The church assigned this psalm to be read on Ascension Day (Acts 1:9), 40 days after Easter. Christians understood Jesus to be "the Lord of Glory" who returned to heaven after the resurrection and who will return to establish His kingdom.[4]

Colossians 2:15 says, "He disarmed the rulers and authorities and disgraced them publicly; He triumphed over them by Him." The ascension carried with it the idea of triumph. Ephesians 4:8–10 says, "For it says: 'When He ascended on high, He took prisoners into captivity; He gave gifts to people.' But what does 'He ascended' mean except that He descended to the lower parts of the earth? The One who descended is also the One who ascended far above all the heavens, that He might fill all things."

---

[1] Warren W. Wiersbe, *The Bible Exposition Commentary: Job–Song of Solomon* (Colorado Springs: David C. Cook, 2004), 132.

[2] F. B. Meyer, "'Through the Bible' Commentary," StudyLight.org, https://www.studylight.org/commentaries/fbm/psalms-24.html.

[3] John MacArthur, *The MacArthur Bible Commentary* (Nashville: Thomas Nelson, 2005), 613.

[4] Wiersbe, 138.

## Teaching

*Psalm 24:1–2*: MacArthur divides Psalm 24 into stages. The first two verses contain stage one: "Worship of the Creator through Contemplation."[5] David knew the Lord owned everything in the world. The Lord had "universal ownership"[6] over all of creation. Exodus 19:5 says, "'Now if you will listen to Me and carefully keep My covenant, you will be My own possession out of all the peoples, although all the earth is mine.'" Psalm 50:12 says, "If I were hungry, I would not tell you, for the world and everything in it is Mine."

*Psalm 24:3–6*: "Worship of the Savior" was MacArthur's second stage of the psalm (vv. 3–6).[7] David outlined two qualifiers for those who would worship God: they must have clean hands and pure hearts (v. 4). *Nelson's Commentary* notes, "Clean hands refer to a person's actions; pure heart refers to inner attitude."[8] Clean hands and a pure heart became a description of David: "He chose David His servant and took him from the sheepfolds; He brought him from tending ewes to be shepherd over His people Jacob—over Israel, His inheritance. He shepherded them with a pure heart and guided them with his skillful hands" (Psalm 78:70–72). MacArthur notes, "These sample qualities do not signify sinless perfection, but rather basic integrity of inward motive and outward manner."[9] David knew that righteousness was received from his Savior (v. 5).

*Psalm 24:7–10*: In stage three of the psalm, which MacArthur titles "Worship of the King,"[10] David instructed the city gates to "lift up your heads" and for doors to "rise up" (v. 7). MacArthur points out, "These are bold personifications indicating that the city gates needed to stretch themselves to make way for the entrance of the great King."[11] Constable notes, "Normally people bowed their heads as majesty passed, but in this figure the gates did the reverse."[12]

The *King of Glory* was victorious over His enemies (v. 8). Constable equates the *King of Glory* with Yahweh and notes, "The Lord is glorious because He is

---

[5] MacArthur, 613.

[6] MacArthur, 613.

[7] MacArthur, 613.

[8] Earl D. Radmacher, Ronald B. Allen, and H. Wayne House, eds., *Nelson's New Illustrated Bible Commentary* (Nashville: Thomas Nelson, 1999), 665.

[9] MacArthur, 614.

[10] MacArthur, 613.

[11] MacArthur, 614.

[12] Thomas L. Constable, *Expository Notes of Dr. Thomas Constable: Psalms*, 135, https://planobiblechapel.org/tcon/notes/pdf/psalms.pdf.

omnipotent, as seen in His victory over His enemies and His provision of salvation. Israel's divine King was fully glorious because He was unconquerable."[13]

Verse 9 repeats verse 7, once again calling the gates to participate in the worship of the King. Similarly, verse 10 repeats the idea of verse 8, identifying the Lord as the *King of Glory*.

Wiersbe proposes that the gates were addressed twice to reference Jesus. When Jesus entered Jerusalem on Palm Sunday, this psalm had probably been sung that morning, but it wasn't applied to Him. Instead, just a few days later Jesus was crucified on Golgotha. However, after His crucifixion and resurrection, He was received into heaven as the conquering *King of Glory*. Later, Jesus will return to earth to fight against the armies of the world, He will win and establish His kingdom on earth.[14] Revelation 19:11 describes this picture: "Then I saw heaven opened, and there was a white horse. Its rider is called Faithful and True, and He judges and makes war in righteousness." Zechariah 14:9 says, "On that day Yahweh will become King over all the earth—Yahweh alone, and His name alone."

## Closing

How do you get ready for the return of the *King of Glory*? Steven Cole outlines three ways to be ready for Jesus' return.[15]

1. To be ready for Jesus' coming, He must be your Master.
   "On that day many will say to Me, 'Lord, Lord, didn't we prophesy in Your name, drive out demons in Your name, and do many miracles in Your name?' Then I will announce to them, 'I never knew you! Depart from Me, you lawbreakers!'" (Matthew 7:22–23)

2. To be ready for Jesus' coming, you must be His servant.

3. To be ready for Jesus' coming, you must live in expectation of His return.
   "Those slaves the master will find alert when he comes will be blessed. . . . You also be ready, because the Son of Man is coming at an hour that you do not expect." (Luke 12:37a, 40)

---

[13] Constable, 135.

[14] Wiersbe, 140.

[15] Steven J. Cole, "Lesson 61: Are You Ready for Christ's Return? (Luke 12:35–48)," Bible. org, June 13, 2013, https://bible.org/seriespage/lesson-61-are-you-ready-christ's-return-luke-1235-48.

# The Daily Word

Have you ever stopped and wondered what the phrase *"King of Glory"* means? The word "glory" is defined as weight. When used to describe a person, it denotes that the person carries power and solemnity, deserving honor. Describing the Lord as the *King of Glory* prompts you to give the Lord the appropriate respect and honor that He deserves as the awesome, almighty, one and only King of your life. "Lift up your heads" and "rise up" direct you to get ready for the coming King.

The psalmist says to have clean hands and a pure heart, not setting your mind on anything false. The Lord doesn't ask you to be perfect but rather to live with actions and an inner attitude honoring God. Rise up and make Jesus the King of your life, serve Him with all your heart, and *expect the King of Glory to appear*. Seek the Lord's face and trust Him. He is worthy of it all.

**Lift up your heads, you gates! Rise up, ancient doors! Then the King of glory will come in. Who is this King of glory? The Lord, strong and mighty, the LORD, mighty in battle. —Psalm 24:7–8**

Further Scripture: Psalm 24:3–4; Matthew 17:5; Revelation 19:1

## Questions

1. Read Psalm 23. Stop at the beginning of each verse and think how that verse pertains to you. Write down your observations.
2. Do you think Psalm 24:4 refers to Jesus? Why or why not?
3. Psalm 25:22 says, "Redeem Israel, O God, out of all his troubles" (ESV). Has God redeemed Israel yet, or is redemption still to come? Why or why not?
4. What did the Holy Spirit highlight to you in Psalms 23—25 through the reading or the teaching?

# Lesson 40: Psalms 26—28

*King of Glory*: This One Thing

## Teaching Notes

### Intro

We have three chapters today, but we'll only cover one in the lecture. So please slow down and take the time to read all three and see how you can see the Messiah in all three. Remember that our phrase for the book of Psalms reflects His presence: the *King of Glory*. Psalm 27 is "characterized by strong contrasts such as both lament and laud; persecution and praise; plus warfare and worship."[1] And, it's a psalm of trust as David affirms "the reality of God in his life . . . a strong desire to live in the presence of God and points to the ongoing need for believers to continue to 'wait' on the Lord."[2] Wiersbe explains that, "According to the title of this psalm as recorded in the Septuagint, David wrote it 'before he was anointed.' This means it was probably written when he was exiled from home and being hunted by King Saul and his men."[3] This would have been before David's second anointing in 2 Samuel 2. To summarize Psalm 27, David was chased by evildoers (v. 2), threatened by false witnesses (v. 12), and they all wanted to kill him (vv. 2, 12). Yet David could write: "Though an army deploys against me, my heart is not afraid; though a war breaks out against me, still I am confident" (v. 3). In this process, six movements take place.

### Teaching

*Psalm 27:1–5*: The first movement is in verses 1–3: "A determination not to fear enemies because of God's presence."[4] David was unafraid of the evildoers who wanted to do him harm because God was his light, salvation, and strength (v. 1). Foes and enemies stumbled before him (v. 2), and he was unafraid and confident

---

[1] John MacArthur, *The MacArthur Bible Commentary* (Nashville: Thomas Nelson, 2005), 615.

[2] Earl D. Radmacher, Ronald B. Allen, and H. Wayne House, eds., *Nelson's New Illustrated Bible Commentary* (Nashville: Thomas Nelson, 1999), 666.

[3] Warren W. Wiersbe, *Be Worshipful: Glorify God for Who He Is* (Colorado Springs: David C. Cook, 2004), 107.

[4] Radmacher et al., 666.

(v. 3). David had only one concern and desire: to live in God's house all the days of his life (v. 4). I have known people in my life who are sold out for the Lord—who want to dwell in God's presence every minute of every day (John 15:1–8). We are going to hang out on verse 4 today.

"I have asked one thing from the Lord" (v. 4a): Camden McAfee points out that there are five times in Scripture in which "one thing" is discussed:[5]

1. *One thing I ask* (v. 4): Knowing God is the heart of prayer.
2. *One thing you lack* (Mark 10:21): Knowing God is the heart of surrender. The young ruler lacked one thing—putting God first to follow Christ.
3. *One thing is necessary* (Luke 10:41–42): Knowing God is the heart of service. Being in the presence of the Lord.
4. *One thing I know* (John 9:25): Knowing God is the heart of a witness: "I once was blind, but now I can see. I am changed!"
5. *One thing I do* (Philippians 3:13–14): Knowing God is the heart of ambition. Paul pressed on toward the goal to which he had been called.

## Closing

When we focus on the *King of Glory*, all the other distractions go away—trying to make everything perfect, trying to do everything we are asked to do, trying to impress others. My prayer is that some of these verses will speak to your heart in a way that models faith to you.

## The Daily Word

If you could ask the Lord for one thing, what would it be? David prayed for fellowship with the Lord all the days of His life. Today, focus your attention on this one thing—to dwell with the Lord. *Dwell means to remain for a time.* Yes, you still have to go through your day, but as you do, rest in Jesus. Abide in the Lord like a branch on a vine. Read His Word. Take the time to know God day after day after day. The more you know God, the more strength you will have to press on.

When you are nervous about an upcoming test, ask the Lord for wisdom and peace. When you carry a heavy burden, admit you can't do it on your own, and ask the Lord for help. When you have a temptation in front of you, pause and ask the Holy Spirit for power to resist the enemy and flee. Focus on Christ, and don't

---

[5] Camden McAfee, "Just One Thing—God Asks of You," *Mind's Seat* (blog), https://marmarthunder.wordpress.com/2015/12/02/just-one-thing-god-asks-of-you/.

be distracted by the things of the world. The world may entice you, but the Lord is enough. Dwell with Him.

**I have asked one thing from the LORD; it is what I desire: to dwell in the house of the LORD all the days of my life, gazing on the beauty of the LORD and seeking Him in His temple. —Psalm 27:4**

Further Scripture: Luke 10:39, 41–42; John 15:4; 1 John 3:6

## Questions

1. In Psalm 26:2, David asked the Lord to examine him, try him, and test him. Have you ever asked God to do this to you? Do you believe it is an easy prayer to pray? Why or why not?

2. Psalm 26:8 says, "Oh LORD, I love the habitation of Your house and the place where Your glory dwells." What do you think it feels and/or looks like to be where God's glory dwells? Have you ever been in the presence of God's glory?

3. Psalm 27 is a psalm of fearless trust in the Lord. Would you say that you have this kind of trust in God? If not, what do you think could help you have this kind of trust in Him?

4. Psalm 27 also talks about seeking God's face. What do you do to seek God's face?

5. Psalm 27:14 says to wait for the Lord. Has the Lord ever made you wait on Him? Has this been easy or hard? Can you think of at least three reasons why sometimes God might make us wait on Him?

6. In Psalm 28, David referred to the Lord as his rock, his strength, his shield, and his shepherd. Do you ever use the different names of God when you pray? What significance do you think this could have on the way you look at God and how you pray?

7. What did the Holy Spirit highlight to you in Psalms 26—28 through the reading or the teaching?

# Lesson 41: Psalms 29—30

*King of Glory*: Dedicating the House to God

## Teaching Notes

### Intro

This is, amazingly, our 405th lesson in reviveSCHOOL. What a wonderful opportunity this has been to embrace the study of the Bible as we identify how the Messiah is presented in each book. Psalm 30 is not about our confidence in ourselves, but about what God has done for us. David confessed this in Psalm 30. David found a way to express his emotions through the psalms he wrote.

### Teaching

*Psalm 30:1–3*: *Nelson's Commentary* points out that "David begins his song with a strong determination to praise God."[1] David's praise was in response to God's protection and healing (vv. 1–2). In our study of Psalm 20, we looked at the eight words that can be prayed: to answer, protect, help, sustain, remember, give, fulfill, and lift up. David used these words repeatedly in his psalms, two (lifted up and healed) in verses 1–2. According to these first verses, David was facing enemies and, according to MacArthur, had recovered from "a near-death experience."[2] David acknowledged he had been guilty, and God had spared him from ultimate punishment (v. 3).

*Psalm 30:4–5*: David called his people to praise God as well (v. 4). David reminded the people that God's anger was short-lived, and they could find joy in Him in the morning (v. 5; Lamentations 3:22–23). David wrote, "His anger lasts only a moment, but His favor, a lifetime" (v. 5a).

*Psalm 30:6–10*: David confessed he once found his security in himself and thought he was invincible (v. 6). MacArthur describes David's attitude as having

---

[1] Earl D. Radmacher, Ronald B. Allen, and H. Wayne House, eds., *Nelson's New Illustrated Bible Commentary* (Nashville: Thomas Nelson, 1999), 668.

[2] John MacArthur, *The MacArthur Bible Commentary* (Nashville: Thomas Nelson, 2005), 617.

an "independent attitude and arrogant talk"[3] (Proverbs 1:32; Jeremiah 22:21). David realized "he was acting like his arrogant adversaries" (Psalm 10:6).[4] Yet, through God's favor, David understood who God was and wanted Him to be his Lord (vv. 7–10).

The title of this psalm is: *A psalm; a dedication song for the house. Davidic.* Let's work through this title. What house was David referring to? Biblical scholars are not sure. Perspectives include:

1. The house was one of David's palaces, meaning David referred to the place in which he lived.

2. The temple of the Lord. Most scholars would side with this possibility. First Chronicles 21:1–21 tells the story of how Satan incited David to take a census of the people of Israel. David's decision was driven by pride, and it was not in response to anything God told him to do. Israel was afflicted because of David's decision. This is the picture David described in Psalm 30:6. In 1 Chronicles 21:9–15, David was given three choices to right the situation before God, one of which would have taken David's life. David couldn't make the choice and asked God to, so God sent a plague on Israel. Psalm 30 is the continuation of David's learning process as he grew from arrogance about his own abilities to have faith in the power of the Lord (2 Samuel 24:10, 14). In 1 Chronicles 21:16, David fell on the ground before God in humility. Psalm 30:11 records, "You turned my lament into dancing; You removed my sackcloth and clothed me with gladness." I cannot say with certainty that Psalm 30 was written after the events of 2 Samuel 24, but it follows the events and the feelings of arrogance and pride, and then sadness and humility, that David spoke of. Because of this, David purchased a plot of land on which he could build a place to worship the Lord (1 Chronicles 22:1).

# Closing

We all have done some sinful things. David's sin caused 77,000 men to die. I don't think any of us can measure up to that. God is a redeeming God, and He wants us to be able to experience what it means to worship anew in Him, just as David did. My hope for you is that you can experience the freedom of releasing the weight of that sin so you can rejoice in the Lord. Psalm 30 ends with these words: "You removed my sackcloth and clothed me with gladness, so that I can sing to You and not be silent. Lord my God, I will praise You forever" (vv. 11b–12). David realized that it was not about him but about how he could glorify

---

[3] MacArthur, 617.

[4] MacArthur, 617.

God. Following Christ is not about what you can get out of it but about how you can glorify God through your bodies (1 Corinthians 6:19–20).

---

## The Daily Word

God never lets you go. He loves you. No matter how far in the pit you have fallen, He loves you. Even at rock bottom, the Lord will pick you up. If you cry out to Him for help, He will heal you. He never stops loving you. You may have sinned. You may feel trapped and caught, not able to see a way out. Your whole life may feel like a blur.

Remember, *with God there is always a way out.* He promises to restore, to reconcile, and to redeem every situation. Begin by crying out for help, let go of any pride or selfishness, and allow the Lord's light to shine into the cracks of your brokenness. You may have cried all night in your sorrow. You may have lost your marriage, your job, your children, or a loved one. The Lord hears every cry. He promises to turn your lament into dancing. He'll remove your sackcloth and clothe you with gladness. As you open your eyes to begin each new day, His mercies never ever end. They are new every morning. Great is His faithfulness each and every day. Give thanks to God for His great faithfulness.

**For His anger lasts only a moment, but His favor, a lifetime. Weeping may spend the night, but there is joy in the morning. . . . You turned my lament into dancing; You removed my sackcloth and clothed me with gladness, so that I can sing to You and not be silent. LORD my God, I will praise You forever. —Psalm 30:5, 11–12**

Further Scripture: Lamentations 3:22–23; Romans 8:28; Ephesians 1:7

---

## Questions

1. God's voice is mentioned several times in Psalm 29. How did the psalmist describe it, and what were some of the things he compared it to? What do you think was happening to David to make him write this psalm?

2. According to Psalm 29:10, the Lord sits as King forever. In 1 Samuel, the Lord was rejected as King by His people, and they asked for an earthly king (1 Samuel 8:7). Did their decision remove God from His throne? Have you ever seen the church "reject God as King"? If so, what is the probable outcome for the church's future?

3. In Psalm 30, what were some of the things God delivered the psalmist from? What are some things you feel God has delivered you from? Do you believe

there is anything God can't or won't deliver you from? If so, what? Why would God choose not to deliver you from certain circumstances?

4. In Psalm 30, verses 5 and 11 explain we have God's favor, which comes with joy and dancing. What does verse 12 say our response/purpose should be? Do you see this in your own life? If not, could it be because you haven't grasped that you have His favor for a lifetime?

5. What did the Holy Spirit highlight to you in Psalms 29—30 through the reading or the teaching?

# Lesson 42: Psalms 31—32

*King of Glory*: Faith, Hope, and Love

## Teaching Notes

### Intro

The Messiah has shown up in almost every chapter of Psalms. The Psalms have been an emotional roller coaster of expressing gratitude for when God works, alternating with the psalmists' thoughts of trying to do things themselves. MacArthur noted that in today's reading, Psalm 31 "contains more of David's problems, prayers, and praises. David will again walk a road that takes him from anguish to assurance."[1]

### Teaching

*Psalm 31:1–5*: Wiersbe noted when others do evil, we can trust God for His strength.[2] David delighted in the Lord, so he was confident nothing could go wrong. As he walked with the Lord, David's purposes became the Lord's, so his confidence could not be shaken. Even if the Lord led him to a difficult place, David was confident God was working His purposes through David. First Peter 4:19 says, "So then, let those who suffer according to God's will entrust themselves to a faithful Creator while doing what is good."

*Psalm 31:6–8*: David expressed his hatred for "worthless idols," especially when they were compared to the true God (v. 6). David rejoiced because God delivered him from his enemies and "set my feet in a spacious place" (v. 8). Wiersbe emphasizes, "When others cause pain, ask God for His mercy."[3] David knew that as he trusted God, God would make His mercies new every morning.

*Psalm 31:9–18*: David described the negative consequences he experienced "because of my iniquity" (v. 10). David was distressed (v. 9), in deep grief (v. 10),

---

[1] John MacArthur, *The MacArthur Bible Commentary* (Nashville: Thomas Nelson, 2005), 617.

[2] Warren W. Wiersbe, *Be Worshipful: Glorify God for Who He Is* (Colorado Springs: David C. Cook, 2004), 118.

[3] Wiersbe, 118.

ridiculed and feared (v. 11), forgotten (v. 12), and conspired against (v. 13). In spite of all of this, David expressed his trust in the Lord (v. 14). Wiersbe observed that "when others see the victory, God gets the glory."[4]

*Psalm 31:19–24*: David expressed that God had never failed to show His love to him, even when it seemed like he was under attack. David ended the psalm by encouraging us to have faith in the Lord because of His faithfulness (vv. 23–24).

Throughout the entire psalm, David expressed faith, hope, and love:

- *Faith*: Verses 1, 6, 14, and 19 all emphasize faith. "LORD, I seek refuge in You; let me never be disgraced. Save me by Your righteousness" (v. 1). "I hate those who are devoted to worthless idols, but I trust in the LORD" (v. 6). "But I trust in You, LORD; I say, 'You are my God'" (v. 14). "How great is Your goodness that You have stored up for those who fear You and accomplished in the sight of everyone for those who take refuge in You" (v. 19). This faith was all under the umbrella of trust in the Lord.
- *Love*: "Love the LORD, all His faithful ones. The LORD protects the loyal, but fully repays the arrogant" (v. 23).
- *Hope*: "Be strong, and let your heart be courageous, all you who put your hope in the LORD" (v. 24).

# Closing

Where are you in the aspects of faith, hope, and love? Jesus said, "'If you have faith the size of a mustard seed,' the Lord said, 'you can say to this mulberry tree, "Be uprooted and planted in the sea," and it will obey you'" (Luke 17:6). Hebrews 11:1 says, "Now faith is the reality of what is hoped for, the proof of what is not seen. For by it our ancestors won God's approval." Kyle Blevins noted, "The purpose of faith is to lead us to know the heart of God."[5] Hebrews 11:6 says, "Now without faith it is impossible to please God, since the one who draws near to Him must believe that He exists and that He rewards those who seek Him."

Blevins elaborated, "Faith is the belief that there is something better to seek, while hope is the expectation, or the certainty, that it is there. Hope is the fuel that keeps faith alive in our quest to find love."[6] Proverbs 24:14 says, "Realize that wisdom is the same for you. If you find it, you will have a future, and your hope will never fade."

---

[4] Wiersbe, 119.

[5] Kyle Blevins, "Why 'Faith, Hope, and Love' Are so Important and Will Last Forever," Crosswalk, March 3, 2021, https://www.crosswalk.com/faith/bible-study/why-faith-hope-and-love-are-so-important-and-will-last-forever.html.

[6] Blevins.

First Corinthians 13:13 says, "Now these three remain: faith, hope, and love—but the greatest of these is love." Love displayed is the clearest picture of God that humanity has. Paul's description of the church at Thessalonica remembered that "your work produced by faith, your labor motivated by love, and your endurance inspired by hope in the Lord Jesus Christ" (1 Thessalonians 1:3). Because of the Thessalonians' faith, hope, and love, they "became an example to all the believers in Macedonia and Achaia. For the word of the Lord rang out from you, not only in Macedonia and Achaia, but in every place that your faith in God has gone out. Therefore, we don't need to say anything, for they themselves report what kind of reception we had from you: how you turned to God from idols to serve the living and true God and to wait for His Son from heaven, whom He raised from the dead—Jesus, who rescues us from the coming wrath" (1 Thessalonians 1:7–10).

## The Daily Word

Have you felt tired of keeping the secret of unconfessed sin? Have you told lies to keep others from knowing the truth? Did hiding sin wear your body down? Friend, life with Christ isn't meant to be like that. Jesus came to forgive you of your sin so you can walk with freedom, joy, and peace. If you acknowledge your sin to Him, no matter how difficult it may feel or what a mess you will find yourself in, *He has promised to forgive you and redeem your life.* He will cleanse you from all unrighteousness and restore the joy of your salvation. The Lord will take away your guilt and groaning. Stop running away from the Lord and begin to take steps toward Him. Humble yourself, acknowledge your sin, release it to the Lord, and trust Him for what will happen next. Pray to the Lord: "But I trust in You, God, You are my God. The course of my life is in Your power, deliver me from the power of my enemies." The Lord will restore your life one step at a time as you *trust* in *Him.* Why don't you begin today? Take that first step. The Lord will be with you.

**When I kept silent, my bones became brittle from my groaning all day long. For day and night Your hand was heavy on me; my strength was drained as in the summer's heat. Then I acknowledged my sin to You and did not conceal my iniquity. I said, "I will confess my transgressions to the LORD," and You took away the guilt of my sin. —Psalm 32:3–5**

Further Scripture: Psalm 31:14–15; Acts 3:19; 1 John 1:9

## Questions

1. Psalm 31 is quoted throughout the Bible. Where can Psalm 31:5 be found in the New Testament, and who spoke these words (Luke 23:46; Acts 7:59)?

2. What does Psalm 31 emphasize (Psalm 31:1, 6, 14, 19)? How well do you completely trust the Lord when everything seems to be against you?

3. What did David say in haste or panic at one point in Psalm 31? What was his fear? What did David do when he felt the Lord's presence was gone? What did he encourage the people and us to do (1 Corinthians 13:13)?

4. What did David recognize God did for not confessing his sin (Psalm 32)? What happened when he finally confessed? Why is God's discipline good (Hebrews 12:1–13)?

5. What did David instruct us not to be like in Psalm 32? What are we to do instead? When are the times that you have been a "senseless horse"? What is the glorious promise of trusting the Lord?

6. What did the Holy Spirit highlight to you in Psalms 31—32 through the reading or the teaching?

# Lesson 43: Psalms 33—34

*King of Glory*: Praising God for His Provision

## Teaching Notes

### Intro

We are continuing to look for where we can see the Messiah in these psalms. About Psalm 34, Constable said, "In this combination individual thanksgiving and wisdom psalm, David glorified God for delivering His people, and he reflected on the Lord's promise to bless the godly with long life."[1] The subtitle of this psalm is long: "Concerning David, when he pretended to be insane in the presence of Abimelech, who drove him out, and he departed." That tells us that Psalm 34 is about the event that is covered in 1 Samuel 21:10–15. According to 1 Samuel 21:10, David fled and ran to King Achish who was over the Philistines. Wiersbe explains the dynastic title of the Philistine kings was Abimelech, so it also refers to King Achish.[2]

### Teaching

*Psalm 34:1–7*: David began in praise of the Lord (v. 1). Wiersbe provides four reasons we should praise the Lord, all of which are supported in Psalm 34: (1) God answers prayer (vv. 4, 15); (2) God provides what we need (vv. 9–10); (3) God delivers us from trouble (v. 17); and (4) God protects us from danger (v. 7).[3] These four are a basic outline of the entire psalm. Our praise is heard by the humble who will hear it (v. 2). Therefore, David asked the people to praise God with him (v. 3). Paul used the language of David: "Rejoice always! Pray constantly. Give thanks in everything, for this is God's will for you in Jesus Christ" (1 Thessalonians 5:16–18). Thomas Watson said, "In prayer we act like men. In praise we act like the angels."

---

[1] Thomas L. Constable, *Expository Notes of Dr. Thomas Constable: Psalms*, 169, https://planobiblechapel.org/tcon/notes/pdf/psalms.pdf.

[2] Warren W. Wiersbe, *The Wiersbe Bible Commentary: Old Testament* (Colorado Springs: David C. Cook, 2007), 915.

[3] Wiersbe, 915.

David praised God for answering his prayer and delivering him from his fears (v. 4). In 1 Samuel 21:12, David became fearful when the Philistine servants told Achish all about him. Here, David praised God for taking those fears from him. David described those who trusted God as being radiant with joy (v. 5) (Exodus 34:29). Through the Holy Spirit transforming our lives, we now reflect the glory of the Lord (2 Corinthians 3:18). David reminded the people that all were poor before the Lord, and He heard them and saved them (v. 6). David then stated that the Angel of the Lord camped around those who feared God and rescued them (v. 7). This is possibly the appearance of the pre-incarnate Christ or an appearance of the Lord Himself.

*Psalm 34:8–10*: Verse 8 provides transition: "Taste and see that the LORD is good." *Nelson's Commentary* says about verse 8: "The center of biblical mission in the Old Testament is found in the words taste and see. The task of Israel was to attract the nations to their God."[4] When the people were involved in worship of idols and other gods who were not sufficient, they saw what the Jews' God was like and they wanted that too. Wiersbe defines the word "taste" as "feeding on the Lord through His Word and experiencing all He has for us. It means knowing Him better and enjoying Him more."[5] When people see what we have in Christ, they wonder if they can have it too. David said those who feared God, or revered God and held Him in awe, would lack nothing (v. 9). Those who seek the Lord will lack nothing (v. 10).

Theologian John Piper explains, "God is always doing 10,000 things in your life, but you may be aware of three of them."[6] That same article gives four truths about how God provides for us: (1) "God may provide differently than we expect" (Psalm 37:25); (2) "God provides more of Himself" (Psalm 37:4; Matthew 7:9–11); (3) "God's ultimate provision has already been given in the gospel" (James 1:17); and (4) "God provides finally in eternity" (1 Peter 2:9).[7]

*Psalm 34:11–22*: David may have called the children together for verse 11 to teach them to fear the Lord. Then David outlined what they needed to do: delight in life, keep their tongues from evil and their lips from deceit, turn from evil and do good, and seek peace (vv. 12–14).

Verses 19–20 prophesies about the Messiah: "Many adversities come to the one who is righteous, but the LORD delivers him from them all. He protects all

---

[4] Earl D. Radmacher, Ronald B. Allen, and H. Wayne House, eds., *Nelson's New Illustrated Bible Commentary* (Nashville: Thomas Nelson, 1999), 670.

[5] Wiersbe, 915.

[6] John Piper quoted in Matt Brown, "Four Truths About God's Provision," Desiring God, December 14, 2015, https://www.desiringgod.org/articles/four-truths-about-gods-provision.

[7] Brown, "Four Truths About God's Provision."

his bones; not one of them is broken." This is a prophetic psalm about Jesus, the *King of Glory*. In John 19:33–36, John recorded:

> When they came to Jesus, they did not break His legs since they saw that He was already dead. But one of the soldiers pierced His side with a spear, and at once blood and water came out. He who saw this has testified so that you also may believe. His testimony is true, and he knows he is telling the truth. For these things happened so that the Scripture would be fulfilled: Not one of His bones will be broken.

John quoted Psalm 34:20 in John 19:36.

## Closing

Psalm 34 truly is about praising the Lord, regardless of what is going on in your life.

---

### The Daily Word

Do you wake up in the morning thinking about a certain situation? Do you continue to wait for the Lord to move in a specific way? Is there something that pains your heart? You can't see the future. You don't know the outcome. All you can do is live one day at a time. You know the truth—to not worry, to cast all your anxieties on the Lord, and to believe He is able to do the impossible. And yet all you can do is wait, hope, trust, and rejoice in the Lord. It doesn't feel like enough, but the situation remains out of your control.

Today, remember God's promise that He is *your help and your shield*. Rejoice in the Lord for strengthening you in weakness and for providing you with wisdom and protection. Even during times of suffering, even during the waiting, even during this trial—*rejoice in His holy name*. As you rejoice through your affliction, the Lord promises to produce endurance and character. Your hope will grow stronger day by day as God pours out His everlasting and consistent love. As you wait, picture God's love covering you like a warm blanket wrapping around you. You must sit and rest long enough to feel His love pouring out over you. Yes, circumstances may remain difficult, but God's love for you is even greater. Hang on to hope, and don't let go.

**We wait for Yahweh; He is our help and shield. For our hearts rejoice in Him because we trust in His holy name. May Your faithful love rest on us, Yahweh, for we put our hope in You. —Psalm 33:20–22**

Further Scripture: Psalm 34:1; Romans 5:3–5; 1 Thessalonians 5:16–18

---

# Questions

1. Psalm 33 begins with praising and worshipping God with different musical instruments. How important do you think praise and worship are to the Lord? What benefits does praise and worship have for you? What are some other ways you can praise and worship the Lord?

2. Psalm 33:6–9 parallels what other part of the Bible (Genesis 1)? Why do you think David mentioned this? Do you believe creation itself proves God's existence?

3. Psalm 34:1 says, "His praise shall continually be in my mouth." How do you think you can praise God continually with your mouth?

4. Psalm 34:8 says, "O taste and see that the LORD is good." What do you think this means? Do you believe it is possible to "taste" the Lord and not see that He is good? Just because we follow the Lord, does that mean we won't ever experience anything bad (Psalm 34:19)?

5. What do you think "fear the Lord" means in the context of Psalm 34? Do you think we serve an angry God? Should nonbelievers fear the Lord (Psalms 1:4–6; 34:16; Revelation 21:8)?

6. Could Psalm 34:20 be prophetic of Jesus' crucifixion (Exodus 12:46; John 19:36)?

7. What did the Holy Spirit highlight to you in Psalms 33—34 through the reading or the teaching?

# Lesson 44: Psalms 35—36

*King of Glory*: Pray for Deliverance

## Teaching Notes

### Intro

We're continuing our study in the book of Psalms as we focus on those that point us to the Messiah, the *King of Glory*. Psalm 35 feels very real as David prayed for victory against his enemies. *Nelson's Commentary* explains, "David places an unusual emphasis on the role of his enemies."[1] Wiersbe explains that this psalm was written while David was being hunted down by Saul and even David's own men. Wiersbe states, "David was championing the right cause, for he was God's chosen king, while Saul was trying to destroy him so that one of his own sons would become king."[2] Not only was Saul's pride on the line with David as the next king, but so was Saul's family lineage. In this psalm, David told God he was tired of being chased by his enemies and asked God to fight them for him. *Nelson's Commentary* states David "appeal[ed] to God the Warrior and Judge to plead [his] cause" and asked God to intercede for him against his enemies.[3]

### Teaching

*Psalm 35:1–3*: David began his psalm by asking God to oppose those who opposed him (v. 1). Then David asked God to use His battle weapons to fight David's battle for him (v. 2). Both images of the Judge and the Warrior are seen in these two verses. The image of the shield in verse 2 is visualized in Ephesians 6:10–18 in Paul's description of the armor of God. David asked God to draw His spear and javelin to use against those who hunted him to assure David of God's deliverance (v. 3). Exhausted by running for his life, David wanted God's assurance that He would give him deliverance.

---

[1] Earl D. Radmacher, Ronald B. Allen, and H. Wayne House, eds., *Nelson's New Illustrated Bible Commentary* (Nashville: Thomas Nelson, 1999), 671.

[2] Warren W. Wiersbe, *The Wiersbe Bible Commentary: Old Testament* (Colorado Springs: David C. Cook, 2007), 916.

[3] Radmacher et al., 671.

A lot of people go through a period in their lives when they feel they haven't heard from God. Many will turn away from their faith. David needed to hear God at that moment, and he asked for it!

*Psalm 35:4–8*: David asked that God disgrace and humiliate those who wanted to kill him so they would turn back in shame (v. 4). David wanted them to be blown away like "chaff in the wind, with the angel of the LORD driving them away" (v. 5). In Psalm 34:7, "The Angel of the LORD encamps around those who fear Him and rescues them." Notice the consistent theme of what the Angel of the Lord takes on. Whether this was the pre-incarnate Christ or not, the Angel of the Lord rescued and provided deliverance to those who feared him. And I believe the presence of God was there. In verse 6, David asked that those who had hunted him become the hunted with the Angel of the Lord pursuing them. Jesus knew who the enemy was against Him, and He pursued the enemy, even to the cross for us.

David pointed out twice in verse 7 that his enemy had attacked him "without cause." This can feel familiar to us because the enemy is constantly trying to crush us as well, and he uses lies and deceit in the process. David asked that his enemy be ruined, falling into the net and the pit that they had placed to ensnare him (v. 8).

*Psalm 35:9–14*: David proclaimed he would be able to rejoice in the Lord and take joy in being delivered (v. 9). Last week (lesson 37), we looked at eight reasons to pray: answers, for help, for sustenance, to be remembered, to be given to, for what we need, and to be fulfilled.[4] David said the Lord was always taking care of Israel, especially the poor (v. 10). *Nelson's Commentary* states the poor are mentioned in the book of Psalms 25 times, usually in terms of how they were being mistreated. The poor "deserve to be high on the agenda for any nation or public servant to honor God and receive divine blessing."[5] Within Psalm 35, emphasis is placed on the results of the work with the poor by those who are on God's side: rescuing the perishing (v. 17), quieting the unjust (v. 19–25), and glorifying the Lord (v. 18, 27–28).[6] *Nelson's Commentary* adds one caveat to these results: "assuming that the spirit behind one's efforts is a genuine concern for justice and righteousness."[7]

[4] Jim Erwin, "Psalm 20:1–9 Trusting God in Prayer," Patheos, April 18, 2016, https://www.patheos.com/blogs/jimerwin/2016/04/18/psalm-201-9-trusting-god-prayer/.

[5] Radmacher et al., 671.

[6] Radmacher et al., 671.

[7] Radmacher et al., 671.

David continued with his complaints. The witnesses against him were malicious and did evil to him, even though he had done good for them (vv. 11–12). David went on to describe how he had been good to them. He had worn sackcloth when they were sick, fasted and prayed for them, and even grieved deeply for them (vv. 13–14).

*Psalm 35:15–28*: Those David had cared for turned on him when he had trouble with Saul (v. 15). They mocked him and gnashed their teeth at him (v. 16) (Job 16:9–10; Psalm 112:10; Lamentations 2:16). David asked how long God would watch this take place. Instead, David requested that God rescue him from them (v. 17). In return, David promised he would exalt God among all people (v. 18). David asked God to rescue him from those who hated him unjustly "without cause" (vv. 19–21). David said he knew God had seen what was happening to him and begged God to stay close to him (vv. 22–23). Finally, David asked God to vindicate him so his enemies could not rejoice over his downfall (vv. 24–26). God does not sleep (Psalm 121:4). David asked that those who wanted David to be vindicated would recognize the Lord was at work and exalt God's actions (v. 27). David would proclaim God's righteousness (v. 28).

Remember Saul lived another seven years and tried to find ways to get rid of David throughout those years. Yet God did vindicate David completely. Vindication doesn't always happen overnight. It takes place in God's timing, not ours.

## Closing

The prophet Elijah ran for his life from Jezebel and hid in a cave feeling totally alone. In 1 Kings 19:17–18, God reminded him that He would leave 7,000 of His followers in Israel. As we go through the times when we are asking God to rescue us from our enemies, there will be others (like the 7,000 left in Israel) who will be there to help and support us.

## The Daily Word

As a believer in the Lord, Scripture says you will face enemies: the world, the flesh, and the devil. You must stay alert, walk in the Spirit, and put on the full armor of God. Remember, the enemy prowls around seeking to destroy you. Even so, trust the Lord will deliver and protect you from these enemies. God will fight for you. The Lord will be your help and your deliverer. He will calm the storm.

No matter what harm goes on around you, no matter how difficult circumstances appear, remember to trust in God's great love. You can't love both the things of this world and the Lord. Choose to love the Lord your God with all your heart, soul, and mind. His faithful love reaches the heavens. His faithfulness reaches the clouds. His righteousness is like the highest mountains and His judgments like the deepest sea. From this great love, *the Lord powerfully fights for you, friend. He desires victory over your life.* He takes pleasure in your well-being. In Christ, you are an overcomer. So do not fear. Instead, delight in the Lord's deliverance as you yield to Him.

**Oppose my opponents, Lord; fight those who fight me. Take Your shields—large and small—and come to my aid. Draw the spear and javelin against my pursuers and assure me: "I am your deliverance." —Psalm 35:1–3**

Further Scripture: Psalm 36:5–6; 1 Peter 5:8; 1 John 2:15–16

## Questions

1. Has anyone ever repaid you evil for good as David said in Psalm 35:12? How did you react? What does the Bible say about this (Matthew 5:44; Luke 6:29; Romans 12:19)?

2. David humbled himself and fasted and prayed for his enemies, according to Psalm 35. Have you ever found yourself doing this for your enemies? What was the result, and how easy was this?

3. What does Psalm 36:5–7 say about God's nature to those He loves and who turn to Him?

4. In Psalm 36:9, David referred to God as "the fountain of life." Do you believe he was talking about life in this world or the next world or both? Why do you think he described it as a fountain? Where else in the Bible can we find this phrase or something similar (Proverbs 10:11; 13:14; Jeremiah 2:13; Revelation 7:17)?

5. What did the Holy Spirit highlight to you in Psalms 35—36 through the reading or the teaching?

# Lesson 45: Psalm 37

*King of Glory*: The Need for Patience in the Lord

## Teaching Notes

### Intro

Psalm 37 is one of my favorite psalms. Our phrase for the book of Psalms is the *King of Glory*, which is a picture of God taking on human flesh and carrying the glory of God here on earth. Psalm 37 is a wisdom psalm and was written as an acrostic.[1] Wiersbe suggests David wrote this psalm while he was preparing Solomon to take his place as king (1 King 2:1–3).[2]

*Nelson's Commentary* says the psalm's "simple message is to maintain patience in the midst of troubles."[3] This fits with the key message of the Psalms of God and Israel and their relationship. If Israel can maintain patience with all that is going on around them, then God can begin to reveal how He wants to show Himself in His covenant with them. Wiersbe explains that since God owns the land they were on, they would be allowed to live on it if they were obedient. "If Israel disobeyed the Lord, He would first chasten them in the land (invasion, drought, famine), but if they continued to rebel, He would then take them out of the land (captivity)."[4] God was asking them to trust Him. This is a powerful picture of God's covenant with Israel. *Nelson's Commentary* outlines the psalm with these divisions: "(1) the need for patience in light of the apparent success of the wicked (vv. 1–11); (2) the need for patience in light of the final judgment of the wicked (vv. 12–22); (3) encouragement for the righteous in view of the role of the wicked (vv. 23–33); and (4) a renewed call for patience in view of the apparent success of the wicked (vv. 34–40)."[5]

---

[1] Earl D. Radmacher, Ronald B. Allen, and H. Wayne House, eds., *Nelson's New Illustrated Bible Commentary* (Nashville: Thomas Nelson, 1999), 672.

[2] Warren W. Wiersbe, *The Bible Exposition Commentary: Job–Song of Solomon* (Colorado Springs: David C. Cook, 2004), 164.

[3] Radmacher et al., 672.

[4] Wiersbe, 164.

[5] Radmacher et al., 672.

# Teaching

*Psalm 37:1–11*: They were not to fret or worry about evildoers who prospered (v. 1). "Do not be agitated" can also be understood as do not fret. "The psalmist calls for patience, a renewed sense of dependence upon the Lord, and a renewed sense of pleasure in knowing Him."[6] The wicked may prosper in the short-term, but they will quickly wither and die (v. 2). Therefore, the psalmist said they were to trust in God, do what was right, and live securely in God's land (v. 3). This is faith in action, not a picture of salvation. They were to delight in the Lord, and then He would give them what was most important (v. 4). *Nelson's Commentary* explains, "When the righteous have desires that spring from the Lord, the Lord will surely fulfill those desires"[7] (1 Thessalonians 5:16–18).

Verse 5 says to "commit" or "to roll it over on" the Lord.[8] That means we give over everything to the Lord to handle (1 Peter 5:7). After commitment comes trust in God. God acts to support our righteousness (v. 6). The psalmist said to be still before Him and to wait expectantly (v. 7). Furthermore, they were to refrain from anger and not fret (v. 8), because the evildoers would be destroyed, and the people of God would inherit the land (v. 9). Think about the context of these verses if David was preparing Solomon to take over his throne in verses 10–11: the wicked will perish, but the humble will inherit the land of God. Jesus quoted this verse (Matthew 5:5).

Wiersbe explains, "'Inherit the land' refers to the security of future generations in the Land of Promise, according to God's covenant, for God had a great work for His righteous remnant to do in that land, culminating in the coming of Messiah"[9] (Genesis 12:1–3; 13:14–18; 15:7–21). Psalm 37 is a prophetic picture of the role of the land when the Messiah returns. The wicked will be cut off (vv. 9, 22, 28, 34, 38).

*Psalm 37:12–21*: The actions of the wicked were so outrageous God laughed at them (vv. 12–13). The wicked used violence against the upright to get what they wanted, and they would perish in the same way when they turned against each other (vv. 14–15). The arms of the wicked would be broken, while God supported the righteous (vv. 16–19). God knows everything and watches over. "(1) God knows our circumstances and provides for us; (2) God knows how long we will live and will sustain us to the end; (3) God knows that our days on earth are

---

[6] Radmacher et al., 672.

[7] Radmacher et al., 672.

[8] Radmacher et al., 672.

[9] Wiersbe, 166.

only the beginning of our days with Him in eternity."[10] The wicked will perish and the righteous will prosper (vv. 20–21).

*Psalm 37:22–23*: Those whom God blessed would inherit the land, and those whom God cursed would be destroyed (v. 22). Verse 23 is the reality of verse 4: Take delight in God, and He will establish our steps.

*Psalm 37:24–40*: God orders our way and keeps us from stumbling (v. 24). Throughout his life, the psalmist had seen God's generous provision for the righteous (vv. 25–26). Therefore, God's people should turn away from evil and dwell in God's land forever (vv. 27–29). They were to hold on to the Word of God (vv. 30–31), and the Lord would judge the wicked (vv. 32–33). They were to wait for the Lord, and He would give them the land (v. 34).

## Closing

If this psalm really was for Solomon, he forgot much of it. In his reign, Solomon split the land by allowing the worship of idols to come into the land through his marriages to pagan women. As we walk out God's teachings, we can be assured that God is preparing us for more, all for His glory.

## The Daily Word

Committing your way to the Lord means to *dedicate, give, or devote* your plans, your time, your heart, and your thoughts to the Lord. *Everything*. It's not a neutral, halfway, only-when-you-feel-like-it sort of thing. It's dedication, and it may mean giving up other things to keep your commitment to the Lord. Commitment isn't negotiable. It's saying, "I'm all in." In this world, commitment seems like a fading character quality. If you don't feel like doing something, the world accepts your lack of commitment. However, that's not how the Lord designed your walk with Him.

Committing to the Lord is how you journey with Him; it's how you have a relationship with Jesus. If you just show up when you feel like it or when you are desperate, you miss out on the beauty and peacefulness of walking with Jesus. He longs for you to commit to walking with Him. God says, "Trust Me with all your heart." As you commit to Him and trust Him . . . the Lord *promises to act*. So today, what is your role? Commit your way to Him and trust Him. Get out of the way. Stop taking control and forcing the action. God is in control. He's got it, and He will act!

---

[10] Radmacher et al., 673.

**Commit your way to the LORD; trust in Him, and He will act. —Psalm 37:5**

Further Scripture: Psalm 37:23–24; Proverbs 3:5–6; Isaiah 40:28–29

## Questions

1.  What are four things David said to do in verses 3 through 7? Do these qualities describe you?

2.  Has there been a time in your life, or maybe even right now, when the Lord asked you to be still and wait for Him to act? Did you wait or act on your own? What did you learn in that process?

3.  What was Jesus doing in Matthew 5:5 when He quoted Psalm 37:11? How many Beatitudes are there? Which number was this particular verse? What was Jesus trying to teach us through Matthew 5:5?

4.  In what ways does the Lord uphold the righteous (Psalm 37:17, 23–24; Isaiah 41:10)?

5.  Why do you think departing from evil or sin is important to the Lord (Psalm 34:14; Matthew 6:13; 2 Peter 3:9–13; 1 John 3:6–7)?

6.  What did the Holy Spirit highlight to you in Psalm 37 through the reading or the teaching?

# Lesson 46: Psalms 38—39

*King of Glory*: Focusing on God Rather Than
Ourselves and Others

## Teaching Notes

### Intro

The message of Psalm 38 is not so encouraging. This psalm is about David admitting he sinned and had already received his discipline. Constable explains, "This discipline came in the form of opposition from enemies that the psalmist asked God to remove."[1] David asked God to remove the enemies but recognized he had to deal with his sin. When we sin, at some point, there will be a consequence. If you don't know Jesus, that consequence will be death. This is a prayer of penitence. *Nelson's Commentary* states, "The psalms of penitence are a model for our own prayers of confession and a warning against the type of behavior that will lead to God's correction."[2]

There are seven penitent psalms: Psalms 6, 32, 38, 51, 102, 130, and 143. Psalm 51 presents David's prayer of repentance: "Create in me a clean heart." Wiersbe points out, "Not all affliction comes from disobedience, but physical troubles can be a consequence of sin" (John 5:14; 9:1–3).[3] In Psalm 38:18, David did not hesitate to confess his sin, and he expected "that the merciful God will forgive and restore him."[4]

### Teaching

*Psalm 38:1–8*: Wiersbe describes the takeaway message of these verses as, "We can focus on ourselves and experience sin's painfulness."[5] David was in anguish

---

[1] Thomas L. Constable, *Expository Notes of Dr. Thomas Constable: Psalms*, 184, https://planobiblechapel.org/tcon/notes/pdf/psalms.pdf.

[2] Earl D. Radmacher, Ronald B. Allen, and H. Wayne House, eds., *Nelson's New Illustrated Bible Commentary* (Nashville: Thomas Nelson, 1999), 674.

[3] Warren W. Wiersbe, *The Bible Exposition Commentary: Job–Song of Solomon* (Colorado Springs: David C. Cook, 2004), 167.

[4] Radmacher et al., 674.

[5] Wiersbe, 168.

over God's discipline and felt "God might be placing His heaving hand on him in wrath, as He does on the wicked."[6] God's discipline felt overwhelming to him, and even his health and strength had been impacted by his sin (vv. 2–3, 7). This does not mean God punishes us all by taking our health. Most sickness is simply the result of living in a fallen, broken, decaying world. David's sin had become too great a burden for him to carry (v. 4). David said he even had body odor from the festering wounds he carried (v. 5). The heavy burden causes him to be bent over in constant mourning (v. 6). Wiersbe describes David's actions as that of someone who "walked about all day like a man at a funeral."[7] Wiersbe concluded, "We are free to disobey the Lord, but we are not free to change the consequences."[8]

*Psalm 38:9–14*: Wiersbe describes the takeaway message of these verses as, "We can focus on others and experience sin's loneliness."[9] David continued to talk about his health issues—his heart, his strength, and his eyesight (vv. 9–10). Even his friends and relatives were staying away from him (v. 11). What David was going through was impacting the others around him (Job 2:9–10). People who were out to get rid of David set traps for him and plotted against him (v. 12). He felt like a deaf and speechless person (v. 13–14). He had no arguments he could verbally make. Some theologians point to this as a foreshadowing of Jesus' silence before those who accused Him[10] (Mark 14:61).

*Psalm 38:15–22*: Wiersbe describes the takeaway message of these verses as, "We can focus on the Lord and experience sin's forgiveness."[11] Constable writes about these verses, "David was remarkable for his ability to wait for God"[12] (v. 15). David acknowledged his hope in his Lord. The word "hope" can mean, "to wait with expectation," and can be expressed with confidence (Job 13:15; Hebrews 10:23).[13] There are other references to hope in the Scriptures (Genesis 8:12; Job 29:21; Ezekiel 13:6). The object of hope is always God—His Word, His judgment, and His mercy. David's "years of suffering at Saul's hands, his critics in the

---

[6] Radmacher et al., 674.

[7] Wiersbe, 168.

[8] Wiersbe, 168.

[9] Wiersbe, 168.

[10] Radmacher et al., 674; John MacArthur, *The MacArthur Bible Commentary* (Nashville: Thomas Nelson, 2005), 623.

[11] Wiersbe, 169.

[12] Constable, 185.

[13] Radmacher et al., 674.

tribe of Benjamin, and his treatment by Absalom taught him to do this."[14] David asked God to not allow his enemies to rejoice over his suffering (v. 16). David acknowledged he was at the end of his rope (v. 17), so he confessed his sin (v. 18). Therefore, David asked God to come near to him and to help him (vv. 19–22). Wiersbe states David made three points here: "Be with me . . . Be near me . . . Be for me and help me."[15] These statements offer David's statement of sin and his request to be restored in God's presence.

## Closing

David needed a savior—to be physically and emotionally saved—and he begged God to intervene in all areas of his life. He asked God to be his Rescue. Constable writes, "Sometimes believers bring physical, emotional, and interpersonal suffering on themselves by sinning. In such cases, God may discipline us with pain so we will learn not to do the same thing again. In the process, we should reaffirm our trust in God and our deliverer from all our woes."[16]

This is what Christ ultimately does for us. Christ wants to give us salvation. The question for now is: Who are you focusing your life on right now? Maybe you need to read the psalms of penitence as you seek joy in Christ.

## The Daily Word

The guilt of sin can rest on your shoulders like a heavy weight. After a season of living in sin, making choices you know are against God's will, even your body can be affected physically. This lifestyle of sin becomes a burden too heavy to bear, leaving you with no physical strength. You feel stuck and hopeless.

Hear this today: *you have hope in Christ*. It begins with repenting before the Lord. He has not left you. He stands near you with wide-open arms like a father welcoming a child home. But you—*you*—need to walk toward the Father's arms and receive His loving embrace. If the steps ahead seem too difficult and healing from all that has been destroyed feels impossible . . . *hang on to the hope in Jesus*. Nothing is impossible with Jesus. He died so you may live. He died so you may be free. Therefore, humble yourself and turn from your sinful ways to receive His love. He will answer you when you walk into His loving arms, wash away your guilt, and cleanse you from your sin. He will help you with the steps ahead as your Savior and your Redeemer. Run into His open arms of love. He is there waiting for you. What are you waiting for?

---

[14] Constable, 185.

[15] Wiersbe, 169.

[16] Constable, 186.

> **For I am about to fall, and my pain is constantly with me. So I confess my guilt; I am anxious because of my sin. . . . Lord, do not abandon me; my God, do not be far from me. Hurry to help me, Lord, my Savior. —Psalm 38:17–18, 21–22**
>
> Further Scripture: Psalm 38:15; 51:1–3; 1 John 1:9

## Questions

1. What was the reason for God's hand to be "pressing down" on David?

2. What are some verses in Psalm 38 that remind you of things Jesus experienced?

3. What is the difference between worldly and godly sorrow (2 Corinthians 7:9–10)? Did David have confidence that God would forgive him? What confidence do you have (1 John 1:9)?

4. Why was David holding his tongue around the wicked? Why is it important to hold your tongue in some situations (James 3:2, 5–12)?

5. How did David move from hopelessness to hope in Psalm 39? What did David do in verses 8–13 of Psalm 39 to bring about the change? Would you say you live with the hope of Christ and with eternity in view, even during tough times (1 John 2:17)?

6. What did the Holy Spirit highlight to you in Psalms 38—39 through the reading or the teaching?

# Lesson 47: Psalms 40—42

*King of Glory*: Thanksgiving and a Cry for Help

## Teaching Notes

### Intro

Each week as we look at all these psalms, we try to highlight one chapter that points to the coming Messiah. Psalm 40 is a messianic psalm. I am going to discuss where we see the Messiah in this psalm. In Psalm 40, David started out with a thankful heart and then immediately went to crying out for help. Over and over, we see this in the psalms. Wiersbe wrote that in Psalm 40, "David praised God for all that He had done."[1] This Davidic psalm begins with instruction to the choir director, which implies this passage was to be sung.

### Teaching

*Psalm 40:1*: Because God answered his prayers, David praised Him. God had provided what David needed and protected him from danger. Wiersbe wrote, "God delivered David from his enemies and from Saul."[2] The Lord heard David's cries and answered him. *Nelson's Commentary* states, "The words 'He inclined to me' presents the image of the Creator of the universe, the King of heaven, stopping from His throne to save the helpless."[3] The crazy thing is God does this for all of us! When we turn to God and wait with confident trust and faith, He will answer our prayers (Psalm 130:5). David is an incredible example of how we should pray to God.

*Psalm 40:2*: David declared that God brought him up from a desolate pit. David had not literally been in a muddy, slimy pit. *Nelson's Commentary* states, "David writes this poem during a period of terrible stress; he feels stuck in a pit or swamp. No matter how hard he tries he cannot get out."[4]

---

[1] Warren W. Wiersbe, *The Bible Exposition Commentary: Job–Song of Solomon* (Colorado Springs: David C. Cook, 2004), 171.

[2] Wiersbe, 171.

[3] Earl D. Radmacher, Ronald B. Allen, and H. Wayne House, eds., *Nelson's New Illustrated Bible Commentary* (Nashville: Thomas Nelson, 1999), 675.

[4] Radmacher et al., 675.

*Psalm 40:3*: David asked for a new song to sing to praise God. What I see here is David saying, "God, instill in me something new." Wiersbe wrote, "A quaint country preacher used verses 2–3 for a sermon text, and his 'points' were: God brought him up, stood him up, and tuned him up!"[5] This tuning up implied David received a new song. Who put the new song in his mouth? How did it get there? God. God gave David a new song. K. Jason French wrote, "The song has been put there by God. God! It has not been 'earned' by the feeble works of man. The psalmist doesn't say, 'I learned a new song! I earned a new song! A song of praise by, and for, my efforts, my wisdom, my riches, my greatness!'"[6] Do you know how refreshing that is? It means God can continue to pour it out to us every single day. Let's look at this new song mentality. These psalms represent praise: Psalms 33:3; 96:1; 98:1; 144:9; 149:1. These verses imply that singing a song and/or playing an instrument is considered as praise.

I am spending so much time on this phrase, "He put a new song in my mouth," because I think it actually points to the gospel. God is the one that radically changes our lives. God gives us the opportunity for salvation. My simple proposal is that the new song is a prophetic picture of the gospel (1 Corinthians 1:18–19; 2 Corinthians 5:17). When we are saved, we are washed by the blood (Ezekiel 36:25–28; John 3:3, 5–8). There is a freshness and a newness in a song that comes from the Lord that will draw people to the Lord. If you allow Christ to change your life from the old to the new, many will see and trust in the Lord. There is a theme of this ongoing new song in Revelation 14:3 and 15:3. Revelation 5:9 shows God is always bringing something new to bring people to Him.

*Psalm 40:4–6*: There are two different views on the phrase "open my ears." *Nelson's Commentary* states, "The Lord not only gives us ears to hear His words, but also grants us understanding so that we can truly obey Him."[7] Constable presents a different view writing, "The clause 'You have opened (lit. dug, or pierced) my ears' may mean that David viewed God as having made him His willing slave by being so gracious to him (cf. Exodus 21:6)."[8] I tend to lean toward the first view.

*Psalm 40:7–8*: There are many arguments for this psalm being a messianic psalm. One of these arguments is found in Luke 24:27. *Nelson's Commentary* states,

---

[5] Wiersbe, 172.

[6] K. Jason French, "God Put a Song in Your Heart," Desiring God, March 15, 2015, https://www.desiringgod.org/articles/god-put-a-song-in-your-heart.

[7] Radmacher et al., 675.

[8] Thomas L. Constable, *Expository Notes of Dr. Thomas Constable: Psalms*, 189, https://planobiblechapel.org/tcon/notes/pdf/psalms.pdf.

"David brings his sacrifice, but his focus is on presenting his own life to the Lord (Romans 12:1–2)."[9] It is amazing to see that many of the psalms are seen throughout the New Testament. In Hebrews 10:4–10, Jesus spoke the words of this psalm to the Father.

*Psalm 40:9–10*: David spoke of the attributes of God: righteousness, faithfulness, salvation, love, and truth.

*Psalm 40:11–17*: Remember earlier, we talked about how David went from thanksgiving to a cry for help. Here is where we see that. It seems like a completely different text—much like the ups and downs of our lives. Despite the troubles, David trusted God. Despite our troubles, we can trust God.

## Closing

As believers in Christ, we know no matter where we are emotionally, our hope lies in God. We have been given hope. That is a cool picture to me! We saw David praising God, giving God all He asked, and trusting Him. This is a great example to follow. This is one of those psalms that points to Christ, the *King of Glory*.

## The Daily Word

Life is full of highs and lows. One moment you find yourself in a pit of despair, and the next moment you feel on top of a mountain. Everyone goes through these emotions and feelings as life continues with unexpected joys and trials. One thing remains certain—Christ came to put a new song in your mouth. Christ came to hear your cry for help and fill you up with His great love. Christ came to lift you out of the pit of muddy clay, set your feet on the firm rock of salvation, and make your steps secure. In Christ, you are a new creation.

So, when you are in the middle of a mess, *cry out to Him and He will hear you.* No matter how many troubles surround you, if your sins have overtaken you or if you are unable to see clearly, the Lord will rescue you. He will deliver you and help you. Friend, the Lord delights in you. You don't need to walk in a place of darkness. Put your hope in God. Praise Him—your Savior and your God. Praise Him through the storm, the fog, the heaviness. Praise the name of the Lord!

**I waited patiently for the LORD, and He turned to me and heard my cry for help. He brought me up from a desolate pit, out of the muddy clay, and set my feet on a rock, making my steps secure. He put a new song in my mouth,**

---

[9] Radmacher et al., 675.

a hymn of praise to our God. Many will see and fear and put their trust in the LORD. —Psalm 40:1–3

Further Scripture: Psalm 40:17; 42:11; 2 Corinthians 5:17

## Questions

1.  In Psalm 40, David said the Lord's "plans for us are too numerous to list." Have you ever thought about the plans the Lord may have for you? Take a few minutes now to consider what plans He may have for your life. What do you think they are?

2.  Meditate on Psalm 42:1. Has your soul ever longed for God? If so, where did you find relief?

3.  In Psalm 42:5–6, David spoke to his own soul. Do you find yourself giving your soul "pep talks"? David placed his hope in God. Are you? Why or why not? How are you doing this?

4.  What did the Holy Spirit highlight to you in Psalms 40—42 through the reading or the teaching?

# Lesson 48: Psalms 43—45

*King of Glory*: A Royal Wedding Song

## Teaching Notes

### Intro

Today we are talking about Psalm 45—a royal wedding psalm. According to *Nelson's Commentary*, a royal wedding song celebrates human marriage in such a manner that the New Testament writer can apply it to Jesus as well. The wedding that takes place in Psalm 45 points to the *King of Glory* who is coming back for His bride. This psalm celebrates human marriage, but it also celebrates the glorious reign of Christ.[1]

To set the tone for the royal wedding psalm, Constable makes several historical observations. "This royal psalm glorified a king as he prepared for his wedding. The writer related the counsel that the bride had received as she anticipated the wedding. He then predicted that people would honor the king forever because of the descendants born to him. The psalmist . . . appears to have spoken prophetically of [the ultimate marriage feast with] Christ."[2] Human marriage is a beautiful picture of Christ and the body of Christ. Man is to lead his wife as Christ leads His church. The sons of Korah wrote this love song for the choir director. When the sons of Korah wrote this song, they may have had Solomon in mind. Solomon married an Egyptian princess. Solomon was also anointed as king. He was also noted for his wealth in gold. He was closely associated with the city of Tyre.

### Teaching

*Psalm 45:1–2*: Wiersbe said there are four ways to describe this king. In the first two verses, Wiersbe described him as the gracious Son of Man (vv. 1–2).[3] Here

---

[1] Earl D. Radmacher, Ronald B. Allen, and H. Wayne House, eds., *Nelson's New Illustrated Bible Commentary* (Nashville: Thomas Nelson, 1999), 678.

[2] Thomas L. Constable, *Expository Notes of Dr. Thomas Constable: Psalms*, 203, https://planobiblechapel.org/tcon/notes/pdf/psalms.pdf.

[3] Warren W. Wiersbe, *The Bible Exposition Commentary: Job–Song of Solomon* (Colorado Springs: David C. Cook, 2004), 179.

the song described the royal groom as one full of joy and inspiration. King Saul was described as "an impressive young man" (1 Samuel 9:2). But King David was also described as handsome (1 Samuel 16:12). Interestingly enough, when Isaiah described the coming Messiah, he said: "He didn't have an impressive form or majesty that we should look at Him" (Isaiah 53:2). But these verses in Isaiah described Jesus during His suffering. The phrase, "grace flows from your lips," means that the king was very well spoken.

*Psalm 45:3–5*: In these verses, Wiersbe described the royal groom as a victorious warrior.[4] The king stood for the causes of truth, humility, and justice (v. 4). It is not often that a warrior walks in truth, humility, and justice.

*Psalm 45:6–7a*: Wiersbe next described the royal groom as a righteous king.[5] Here the psalm switched from talking about a man to talking about God. Constable said the psalmist "did not mean that the king was God but that he stood in the place of God and represented Him."[6] This human king who represented God could describe Jesus. There was clearly a messianic direction in verse 6. The king's scepter was called "a scepter of justice" (v. 6). In Revelation 11:15, voices from heaven said, "The kingdom of the world has become the kingdom of our Lord and of His Messiah, and He will reign forever and ever!" This sure sounds like Psalm 45:6. Hebrews 1:3 describes Jesus as "the radiance of God's glory and the exact expression of His nature." Jesus was God who came here to earth and died for us, then ended up sitting "at the right hand of the Majesty on high." This image goes with Psalm 45:6, where the throne is forever, and the scepter of the kingdom is one of justice.

*Psalm 45:7b–17*: Wiersbe then described the royal groom as the glorious bridegroom.[7] In verse 7b, God is presented as both God as the Father and God as the Son. Some would say the phrase, "more than your companions," means the Son of God is superior to angels.[8] Hebrews 1:5–9 repeats several of the statements made in this psalm, so Psalm 45:6–7 points to Jesus. The sons of Korah wrote about the groom getting ready for his bride.

In verses 8–9, the king was surrounded by radiant women. His bride was prepared with golden garments. In verse 10, the psalm transitions to focus on the bride. Our task, as the church, is to get the bride ready for the return of the

---

[4] Wiersbe, 180.

[5] Wiersbe, 180.

[6] Constable, 204.

[7] Wiersbe, 181.

[8] Constable, 204.

groom. We should put our focus on the groom because He is coming. But so many times, we are consumed with everything else instead of focusing on Christ. We need to work and make our entire being about Him. We need to get beautiful for the groom.

Constable explains the bride was to "make her husband her primary object of affection," which would "make her even more attractive to him."[9] When you have a healthy perspective of human marriage, you will have a healthy perspective of Christ's return. Verse 12 implies that when the bride makes the groom her priority, people will be attracted to her because she is connected to the king. The psalm concludes by describing the bride and her companions being led to the king to enter the palace with gladness and rejoicing (vv. 13–15). The people will praise the king forever and ever (v. 17).

Ross states the Apostle John had Psalm 45 in mind when he wrote Revelation 19:6–21. "As he looked forward to the marriage of Christ, the Lamb, in heaven, he recalled how the bride clothed herself with acts of righteousness in preparation for Him."[10] Revelation 19:6–8 describes the marriage of the Lamb. The bride "was given fine linen to wear, bright and pure. For the fine linen represents the righteous acts of the saints" (Revelation 19:8). Then, in Revelation 19:11–21, John described the royal groom going forth to battle in righteousness.

## Closing

This is a neat picture. It kind of makes you wonder if we are the only reason He hasn't come back yet. As the bride, let us begin to pray through how we begin to get ourselves prepped and ready for the bridegroom. This might mean going through one of the psalms of confession and realizing there is still sin in our lives. It might mean letting go of our parents, our friends, our neighbors, so we can focus on Him. Whatever it is, will you just ask the Holy Spirit to show you how to get ready for His return?

## The Daily Word

Just as a bride prepares to marry her groom, the Church must prepare to reunite with Jesus when He returns. A groom prepares and leaves his father and mother, and a bride leaves her home in order to unite together as one, as husband and wife. The Church, the bride of Christ, must prepare herself to see Christ again—by

---

[9] Constable, 205.

[10] Allen P. Ross, "Psalms," in *The Bible Knowledge Commentary: Old Testament*, ed. John F. Walvoord and Roy B. Zuck (Colorado Springs: David C. Cook, 1985), 828.

being washed clean of sin and walking in righteousness, blameless before the Lord. *Are you ready for Christ to return?*

Are you hanging on to your past? Are you clinging to the comfort of this world, not fully committed to the Lord? To prepare for the return of Christ as a believer, you must leave behind your old ways and hold fast to the hope in Christ. Allow His Spirit to transform you into a new creation. Allow the Lord to come in and create His beauty in you. Trust that He is able. As a believer, the Lord molds you to resemble Christ. Therefore, when Christ returns, you can stand ready and prepared to meet the *King of Glory*. You can be ready for His glory to come. Get ready because Jesus is coming back!

**Listen, daughter, pay attention and consider: forget your people and your father's house, and the king will desire your beauty. Bow down to him, for he is your lord. —Psalm 45:10–11**

Further Scripture: Ephesians 5:25–27; Revelation 19:7–8; 21:1–2

## Questions

1. Psalm 44:6 says, "For I will not trust in my bow, neither shall my sword save me." That verse sounds like victory and salvation comes from outside of ourselves. Where in Scripture might you find these truths (Deuteronomy 20:4; Psalm 44:7; Proverbs 21:31; Romans 10:9–10; 1 Corinthians 15:57; Hebrews 7:25)?

2. When you read Psalm 45:2–8, do you picture these verses being about Jesus? Could the rest of Psalm 45 possibly be painting a picture of Israel after Jesus returns? Why or why not?

3. What did the Holy Spirit highlight to you in Psalms 43—45 through the reading or the teaching?

# Lesson 49: Psalms 46—48

*King of Glory*: God's City of Jerusalem

## Teaching Notes

### Intro

I am excited about the study of Psalm 48 because it is all about Jerusalem. One of the things our team has been able to do is spend time in Jerusalem and pray for the peace of Jerusalem. Many scholars refer to this psalm and others (Psalms 76; 84; 87; 122; and 132) as the "Songs of Zion"[1] because "the emphasis is on the Lord and Mount Zion" (another title for Jerusalem).[2] What we get to see in Psalm 48 is God delivering Jerusalem from its enemies. Israel is about the size of New Jersey, so why are so many countries in the world concerned about what happens in Israel and Jerusalem? There is an ultimate battle for the city of Jerusalem.

### Teaching

*Psalm 48:1–3*: Wiersbe describes these verses as, "God and their city."[3] Verse 1 describes Jerusalem as "the holy city of our God." Someone asked me why I care so much about the city of Jerusalem. The answer is in 1 Kings 14:21: "Jerusalem, the city where Yahweh had chosen from all the tribes of Israel to put His name." Jeremiah 3:17 says the city will be called "Yahweh's Throne, and all the nations will be gathered to it." The nations will not be gathering because the Messiah has returned, but because of the name of Yahweh. It will be a precursor to the second coming of the Messiah. Jerusalem is God's eternal city. The *King of Glory* will reside in Jerusalem. In Canaanite poetry, the king always resided on the north slope of the city. Here the psalmist explained the city of God was tangible and was Jerusalem.

---

[1] Earl D. Radmacher, Ronald B. Allen, and H. Wayne House, eds., *Nelson's New Illustrated Bible Commentary* (Nashville: Thomas Nelson, 1999), 679.

[2] Warren W. Wiersbe, *The Bible Exposition Commentary: Job–Song of Solomon* (Colorado Springs: David C. Cook, 2004), 185.

[3] Wiersbe, 185.

David took Jerusalem from the Jebusites (2 Samuel 5:6–9) and made the city his capital. The city sat 2,500 feet above sea level, making it into a natural fortress, and was located near the place where the north-south and east-west trade routes crossed. This was also the place where the Ark of the Covenant was brought, which made it a holy city. Wiersbe states, "The greatness belongs to the Lord and not to the city, for in His grace, the Lord chose Zion."[4] Isaiah 2:2 states the city of Jerusalem is not only important for its past but for its future as well. The *King of Glory* would reside there. Isaiah 60:1 states the glory of the Lord would shine over Jerusalem.

*Psalm 48:4–7*: Wiersbe describes these verses as, "God and their enemies."[5] The besieging armies could not prevail against God's stronghold on Jerusalem. God's presence terrified them. Look specifically at verse 7, "You wrecked the ships of Tarshish with the east wind" and consider the winds from the east, west, north, and south. The east wind "came from the desert and was notoriously violent."[6] The east wind is probably what flattened the home of one of Job's sons as well as the force that parted the Red Sea (Jeremiah 18:17). Other calamities from the east wind included scorched crops, dried up springs, and a plague of locusts. However, the west wind brought "moisture from the Mediterranean Sea between November and February," blew away the locusts, and ended severe droughts.[7] The north wind brought cold temperatures and could impact the people's health. The south wind was gentle and "quiets the earth," and lasts a single day in the spring.[8] This is a good picture of Jerusalem—because it is surrounded by all kinds of things and nations that impact the city and the nation of Israel. This is a prophetic picture of what Jerusalem has and will experience.

*Psalm 48:8–14*: Wiersbe describes verses 8–11 as, "God and their worship."[9] God would establish the city of Jerusalem as His city forever. God has the power to establish Jerusalem as His city through the natural and/or the supernatural. God can do it through the battles brought upon Israel by its enemies, or He can intervene with His own angels. A simple example is when God sent His angel to a Syrian camp who killed 185,000 men. *Nelson's Commentary* explains that in verse 9, the verb for the phrase "we have thought" "refers to making comparisons and looking for similarities, thinking and considering with discrimination. The point

---

[4] Wiersbe, 185–86.

[5] Wiersbe, 186.

[6] Radmacher et al., 680.

[7] Radmacher et al., 680.

[8] Radmacher et al., 680.

[9] Wiersbe, 186.

is that nothing can be compared to the loyal love of God."[10] Wiersbe describes verses 12–14 as, "God and their future."[11] Their God would always lead them in Jerusalem.

## Closing

What happened between Psalm 48 and today? This outline comes from The History Channel:

- 1,000 BC     David established Jerusalem as his capital.
- 960 BC     King Solomon built the first temple.
- 586 BC     Babylonians destroyed the temple and sent the Jews into exile.
- 536 BC     Persian King Cyrus allowed the Jews to rebuild the temple.
- 332 BC     Alexander the Great captured Jerusalem. For several hundred years, control of the city passed among different groups, such as the Romans, Persians, Arabs, Turks, Crusaders, Egyptians, and Islamists.
- 37 BC     Herod built the second temple.
- AD 30     Jesus was crucified.
- 70     Romans destroyed the second temple.
- 632     Muhammad died. Islamists believe Muhammad ascended to heaven from the Temple Mount in Jerusalem.
- 691     the Dome of the Rock, an Islamic shrine, was built on the Temple Mount at the place where Muhammad is believed to have ascended to heaven.
- 1099–1187     European Christians took pilgrimages to Jerusalem to retake the city and maintain the city as a religious site.
- 1516–1917     Jerusalem and much of the Middle East was ruled by the Ottoman Empire.
- 1917–1948     Great Britain took control of Jerusalem and the surrounding region, which was part of Palestine at that time.
- 1948     Israel declared its independence and took over all the land of Palestine from Great Britain.

---

[10] Radmacher et al., 680.

[11] Wiersbe, 186.

- 1948–1968    During the first 20 years of the establishment of Israel, Jerusalem was divided into four areas: Israel had control of the western part of the city, and Jordan controlled east Jerusalem. After the bloody 1967 Six-Day War between Israel and the Arab States of Egypt, Syria, and Jordan, Israel took control of the majority of Jerusalem.
- 1980    Israel declared the city of Jerusalem its capital.
- Today    The interior compound of the Temple Mount remains in Palestinian control while the exterior is guarded by Israeli forces.[12]

The Temple Mount is the third holiest site in Islam and is currently home to mosques. It is also a holy site for Jews as the historic location of the two temples and the anticipated site of the third temple. For that reason, it is also holy to some Christians who believe that the Messiah will return with the building of the third temple. It's easy to see why there's such conflict over what happens in Jerusalem. Jews are not allowed on the Temple Mount. Consequently, Jewish leader Ariel Sharon's visit led to the second Palestinian uprising against Israel. Despite the conflict, Jerusalem is God's city. We must get the people ready for Jesus' return.

## The Daily Word

Are you in a situation that feels like it's just too much for you to figure out how to get through it? The battle seems hard and hopeless. You just don't know what to do, what to say, whom to turn to. You feel alone. Isolated. Frozen. Stuck.

Here's the good news: *God promises to fight your battles for you.* He goes before you. He goes behind you. He says not to worry. He even says to be still. Stop trying. Stop researching. Stop thinking through "what if" scenarios. Stop trying to be right or make excuses. Stop it. Be at rest. Surrender to the Lord. The same God who is exalted over the nations promises to care, love, and be with you wherever you go. God is able to fight your battle. He is able to make the enemies cease. He is able to cut through chains of iron and break any strongholds and years of bondage. Moment by moment, day by day, trust the Lord. When He gives you direction and guidance, then make the move, say the word, and read the Scripture. But until then, rest in *Him.* He's got you in His loving hands!

---

[12] History.com Editors, "Jerusalem," History.com, March 27, 2023, https://www.history.com/topics/ancient-middle-east/history-of-jerusalem.

"Stop your fighting—and know that I am God, exalted among the nations, exalted on the earth." Yahweh of Hosts is with us; the God of Jacob is our stronghold. —Psalm 46:10–11

Further Scripture: 2 Chronicles 32:7–8a; Psalm 46:1–3; Isaiah 45:2

# Questions

1. After reading Psalm 46:1, can you confidently repeat verses two and three? If not, why do you think that is?

2. Look at Psalms 19:1 and 46:8. How are these verses similar? What are these "works"?

3. Psalm 46:10 says, "Be still and know that I am God." Another translation says instead, "Cease striving." How do you do this?

4. How would you summarize Psalm 47 with two or three sentences? What specifically does this chapter say about God as King?

5. What did the Holy Spirit highlight to you in Psalms 46—48 through the reading or the teaching?

# Lesson 50: Psalms 49—50

*King of Glory*: Misplaced Trust in Wealth

## Teaching Notes

### Intro

Psalm 49 is a wisdom psalm. The sons of Korah wrote it for the choir director for the people to sing. According to *Nelson's Commentary*, Psalm 49 is one of instruction set to music. The psalm "calls for the wise person to realize that there is nothing to fear from the oppressive rich: like animals, they too will die. But the righteous will live forever."[1] The title for Psalm 49 is "Misplaced Trust in Wealth."

The authors were the sons of Korah. Their background is interesting. God told Moses and Aaron to take a census of the Kohathite men between the ages of 30 and 50 years old (Numbers 4:1–5). Aaron and his sons had the responsibility to take care of the most holy objects. These items included the Ark, the table of God's presence, the bowls and pitchers used in the drink offering, the lampstand and the lamps from the tabernacle, and the gold altar (Numbers 4:7–20). Whenever the camp moved, these also had to be packed up and moved. Then the Kohathites would transport the objects, but they could not touch these items themselves or even look at them or they would die (Numbers 4:15, 20). God also told Moses and Aaron to take care of the Kohathite clans so they would not be wiped out by the Levites because the Kohathites had an important function to fulfill (Numbers 4:17–20).

In Numbers 16, Korah and other prominent Israelite men rebelled against Moses and Aaron and told them all the Israelites were holy. They questioned why Moses and Aaron exalted themselves above the Israelite community (vv. 1–3). This was jealousy on their part because they had been carrying these holy things their entire lives but could not touch them, but Moses and Aaron could. Moses responded by saying he did what God called him to do. He said if these who rebelled lived and died like everyone else, there would be no proof he did what God wanted him to do. However, if God did something unprecedented, and the ground opened and swallowed them all, along with everything they had,

---

[1] Earl D. Radmacher, Ronald B. Allen, and H. Wayne House, eds., *Nelson's New Illustrated Bible Commentary* (Nashville: Thomas Nelson, 1999), 680.

the people of Israel would know God was in charge. (vv. 28–30). The ground immediately opened just as Moses had described and swallowed all of Korah's people and all of their possession into Sheol, and then closed back over them (vv. 31–35). While it looks like they were all swallowed up, the census in Numbers 26 showed a small group of Korah's people did not die (vv. 9–11).

## Teaching

*Psalm 49:1–4: Nelson's Commentary* explains verses 1–4 as "a call for understanding" that goes out to all people universally.[2] The Hebrew word for "world" (v. 1) means "the total human scene, the whole sphere of passing life."[3] The phrase "riddle" or "dark saying" means "enigma" and "refers to a perplexing moral problem: how do the righteous come to terms with oppressive rich people who seem to have no thought for God?"[4] The psalmists said they would explain this dilemma using a musical instrument.

*Psalm 49:5–9:* The psalmist acknowledged the sins of his foes but said he had no fear for them. They put their trust in their personal wealth but did not have enough money to redeem themselves before God. The word "pit" (v. 9) referred to "the power of death in its dark aspect."[5] Only God can deliver anyone from the power of death. Wiersbe explains that it is *not* a sin to be wealthy "if we acknowledge God as the Giver and use what He gives to help others and glorify His name."[6] (See Mark 10:24–25; Luke 16:15.)

*Psalm 49:10–12:* The wealthy without God would die and others would receive their wealth. All they had to show for their lives was their eternal resting place— their graves. Humankind, like animals, will die. Having wealth will not prevent that from happening.

*Psalm 49:13–15:* Those who followed this path were arrogant, and they were headed for Sheol. But God has the power to redeem the wealthy and the poor from the power of Sheol. This points to the redemptive work of "the Lord [who] has already ransomed us from sin and the power of the grave."[7]

---

[2] Radmacher et al., 680.

[3] Warren W. Wiersbe, *The Bible Exposition Commentary: Job–Song of Solomon* (Colorado Springs: David C. Cook, 2004), 187.

[4] Radmacher et al., 681.

[5] Radmacher et al., 681.

[6] Wiersbe, 187.

[7] Wiersbe, 188.

*Psalm 49:16–20:* Therefore, they were not to be afraid of those who had wealth, who would take nothing with him when he died, and would never again see the light of day. But, "a man with valuable possessions but without understanding is like the animals that perish" (v. 20).

## Closing

Having the background of the sons of Korah brings this passage to life. You have to wonder if the words of Psalm 49 came from the family experiences outlined in Numbers. The wisdom of this psalm seems to have deep roots in what happened to the people of Korah who wanted what others had and missed the important role they already had. These lyrics came from someone who had learned what was real and what was important.

## The Daily Word

Do you ever find yourself looking at your neighbors and comparing your life to theirs? Perhaps they seem more successful or wealthier from the world's perspective. Whether you have much or little on this earth, *the key is to focus your heart and mind on the Lord*, not on the things of this world. Jesus said it is easier for a camel to enter through the eye of a needle than for a rich man to enter the kingdom of God. So keep your eyes on Jesus and not on others or on accumulating more wealth.

Today, give thanks for the gifts God has given you—both material and spiritual, remembering every good and perfect gift comes from the Lord. Resist the temptation to compare yourself to others or even to judge others and their success. Trust the Lord with a pure heart and live obediently to the things the Lord is calling *you* to do. Whether rich or poor, the Lord desires all people to give up their lives for the sake of the gospel. The more you give up, the richer you become in the Lord. You can never outgive God!

**They trust in their wealth and boast of their abundant riches. Yet these cannot redeem a person or pay his ransom to God. —Psalm 49:6–7**

Further Scripture: Matthew 16:25–26; Mark 10:24–25; Luke 16:14–15

# Questions

1. Who was the intended audience for Psalm 49? What is the overall message the psalmist was trying to get across?

2. What is the problem with trusting in wealth (Mark 10:23–24; 1 Timothy 6:17)? What is the purpose for the wealth God gives us (Matthew 6:33; 2 Corinthians 9:10–12; 1 Timothy 6:18–19)? How can you know if you are trusting in wealth or in God?

3. In Psalm 49, what are some things that money cannot buy or do (Matthew 16:26; Luke 12:20–21; 1 Timothy 6:7)?

4. If God does not hunger for food, what does Scripture say He does "hunger" for (Hosea 14:2; Romans 12:1)?

5. What did the Holy Spirit highlight to you in Psalms 49—50 through the reading or the teaching?

# Lesson 51: Psalms 51—53

*King of Glory*: David's Confession of Sin

## Teaching Notes

### Intro

Psalm 51 is one of the best-known psalms. It is a psalm of repentance and of confession. The context of the psalm is David's sin with Bathsheba and his being confronted by the prophet Nathan (2 Samuel 11:26–29; 12:1–20). David committed adultery with Uriah's wife Bathsheba, and to cover the first sin, David had Uriah killed on the frontline in battle. David thought he got away with his sins. Nathan had the tough job of releasing a word of judgment from God on David with the words, "You are the man! Why then have you despised the command of the Lord by doing what [God] considers evil?" (2 Samuel 12:7–9). David and his entire house suffered consequences from David's sin. This was the context for Psalm 51 (2 Corinthians 7:10). Our question is, Are we coming to God in the right manner? Psalm 51 is a true outline of repentance.

### Teaching

*Psalm 51:1–2*: David cried out to God for mercy, something he did not deserve but was possible through God's faithful and unfailing love. He asked God to pardon, which meant blotting out or removing his sin. Blotting out was the only way to remove writing off papyrus to make the paper clean to use again. David wanted to be made clean again—to have his guilt taken away, forgiven, and removed from him (Psalm 9:5; Isaiah 43:25).

*Psalm 51:3–6*: David then confessed his sin. He took responsibility for his sin (v. 3) and recognized his sin had been against God (v. 4a). David was ready to accept the consequences of his sin (v. 4b). There were direct consequences of David's sin, especially the death of the child who had been conceived during his affair with Bathsheba. In verse 5, David stated he had been sinful since birth—this was not the only time he had sinned (Romans 3:10–12). David summarized God's standard of righteousness (v. 6).

*Psalm 51:7–12*: David wanted to be purified and made clean (v. 7). He prayed for both forgiveness and restoration (Exodus 12:22). In verses 8–9, David took responsibility for his sin. He begged God for restoration (John 1:9). David asked for a clean heart and a renewed spirit (v. 10). He was ready to find his joy in his Lord again. David wanted to be in God's presence (v. 11) and restored in God's salvation (v. 12).

*Psalm 51:13–17*: David made two promises to God. First, he would teach others about the ways of God and bring other sinners to Him (v. 13). Second, he would praise God, because he knew God did not want his sacrifice, but the praise of his broken spirit (vv. 14–17). God wants us to come before Him with a broken and humbled heart.

*Psalm 51:18–19*: Finally, David turned his prayer toward Zion (also called Jerusalem). His prayer became that of intercession for Jerusalem so God would be glorified. God called David to prosper Zion, and he was ready to pick up that call again.

## Closing

The greatest step I ever took was the night that I accepted Christ and was able to let go of the hold sin had on my life. It was a cleansing of my life. There are times when we all need to come before God, accept His merciful forgiveness, and become cleansed before Him.

## The Daily Word

Psalm 51 recounts David's prayer of confession after committing his sins of adultery, murder, and cover-up regarding his relationship with Bathsheba. If you have concealed sin in your life, you will not prosper in your relationship with the Lord. Eventually, others will discover your hidden sin. And the Lord sees all. He knows your heart, and, yes, He sees your sin as well. Nevertheless, the Lord loves you. If you confess your sin to Him, He will show you mercy. He longs for you to turn away from sin and back to Him.

Today, ask the Lord, "*Is there anything I need to confess?*" Pause, close your eyes, and just listen to the Holy Spirit. If He brings anything to mind, release it to Him and ask for forgiveness with a genuine heart. You can't fake repentance. The Lord knows your heart. Then, turn away from your sin and commit your life to the Lord. Ask Him to create in you a clean heart and renew a steadfast spirit within you. Ask Him to restore to you the joy of your salvation and renew a right spirit within you. Remember, Jesus died to prove His love for you, saving you from your sin. He forgives you and loves you so much. Turn to Him today.

**Wash away my guilt and cleanse me from my sin. For I am conscious of my rebellion, and my sin is always before me. Against You—You alone—I have sinned and done this evil in Your sight. —Psalm 51:2–4**

Further Scripture: Psalm 51:10–13; Proverbs 28:13; Romans 5:8

## Questions

1. What was the reason or situation that caused David to write Psalm 51 (2 Samuel 11)? Even though David sinned against multiple people, who did David say he truly sinned against (Genesis 39:9)?

2. What were three major requests David made to God in Psalm 51 (Psalm 51:2, 12, 13)? Has there been a time when you have cried out to the Lord in complete repentance as seen in this psalm?

3. How does Psalm 51 reveal we are a sinner not only by choice but also by nature (Matthew 15:19; 1 John 1:8)? How do we know that our own goodness cannot earn us salvation or entrance into God's family since we are, in fact, born in sin (Ephesians 2:8–9; Titus 3:3–7)?

4. What was David saying when he asked God to create in him a clean heart and to renew a right spirit within him (Jeremiah 24:7; Ezekiel 11:19; 36:25–27)? When did the Lord give David the Holy Spirit (1 Samuel 16:13)? What possibly was David's fear in asking this request (1 Samuel 16:14)?

5. What was David's understanding about sacrifices that would or would not honor the Lord in Psalm 51:17? What does the Lord take pleasure in?

6. Can you spot any differences between Psalms 14 and 53?

7. What did the Holy Spirit highlight to you in Psalms 51—53 through the reading or the teaching?

# Lesson 52: Psalms 54—56

*King of Glory*: Seeking God in Betrayal

## Teaching Notes

### Intro

Psalm 55 is another psalm of lament and was written for a choir with stringed instruments. It is based on David's betrayal by a close friend (Psalm 55:12–14). In 2 Samuel 15, David's son Absalom led a revolt against his father because he wanted to be king. It is possibly against this backdrop of Absalom's rebellion and/ or Ahithophel, David's counselor who sided with Absalom (2 Samuel 15:31) that David wrote Psalm 55 (vv. 20–21).[1] David possibly recited 2 Samuel 15:31 in this psalm.

### Teaching

*Psalm 55:1–8*: MacArthur described verses 1–8 as "the prayer of distress."[2] *Nelson's Commentary* describes these verses as "a call for God to hear in the midst of the distress."[3] The prophet Nathan prophesied that David's family would turn on him (2 Samuel 12:9–12). David begged God not to ignore his plea for help (Psalms 10:2; 13:1; 27:9; 44:24; 69:17; 143:7). David's prayer expressed his distress over those who had become his enemies. *Nelson's Commentary* states, "David's shock is not that he is in distress again or even that he has more enemies. The great shock is that the enemy is his own friend."[4] The weight of betrayal caused David to be unable to sleep, and his heart shuddered in terror (vv. 2–4). He was overwhelmed by fear and horror at the betrayal and wanted to just fly away to safety (vv. 5–8).

Some of you listening to this today feel that desperate—you just want to get away from whatever is making you miserable. MacArthur describes David's

---

[1] John MacArthur, *The MacArthur Bible Commentary* (Nashville: Thomas Nelson, 2005), 636.

[2] MacArthur, 636.

[3] Earl D. Radmacher, Ronald B. Allen, and H. Wayne House, eds., *Nelson's New Illustrated Bible Commentary* (Nashville: Thomas Nelson, 1999), 684.

[4] Radmacher et al., 684.

feelings as "escapist feelings."[5] Can't we all relate to the desire to just get away from it all? Others in the Old Testament felt the same way (1 Kings 19; Jeremiah 9:2–6; 40:1–6). Instead of running, David turned to the Lord. We can too!

*Psalm 55:9–15*: MacArthur described verses 9–15 as "the prayer of justice."[6] David described the situation he faced—one of violence, strife, crime, trouble, destruction, oppression, and deceit in the city (vv. 9–11). Added to that was the betrayal of a friend-turned-enemy, which made what he was facing unbearable (vv. 12–13). Possibly what hurt the most was the friend-turned-enemy, who was the one he had worshipped with (v. 14). David asked for God's justice against those who had come against him (v. 15).

*Psalm 55:16–23*: MacArthur described verses 16–23 as "the prayer of assurance."[7] David called the Lord to save him (v. 16). He knew with assurance that God heard his complaints and his groaning, and despite what he was facing, he knew God would redeem him (vv. 17–19). David pointed out the deceitful actions of his friend (vv. 20–21). Yet David knew he could give that burden to the Lord, and the Lord would sustain Him. God would take care of his enemies. Regardless, David would trust in the Lord (vv. 22–23).

## Closing

As we close today, I want to compare David, the king of Israel, and Jesus, the *King of Glory*.

- David was betrayed by his son, Absalom, and his counselor and friend, Ahithophel (2 Samuel 15:1–2); Jesus was betrayed by His disciple, Judas (Luke 22:47).
- David crossed the Kidron Valley (2 Samuel 15:23); Jesus crossed the Kidron Valley (John 18:1).
- David climbed down the Mount of Olives weeping (2 Samuel 13:30); Jesus wept on the Mount of Olives (Luke 22:39–44).
- David was rejected by his own people (2 Samuel 15); Jesus was rejected by the Jews (Zechariah 14:4).

All this shows how Psalm 55 points to Jesus.

---

[5] MacArthur, 636.

[6] MacArthur, 636.

[7] MacArthur, 636.

## The Daily Word

*God is for you.* The God of the universe, the Almighty Maker of heaven and earth, *He is for you.* The Father God who sent His Son Jesus to earth to die for the sins of the world . . . yes, *He is for you.* He loves you. He holds your life in His hands.

You have nothing to fear. Nothing. Run to Jesus when you are afraid and trust Him. *He is for you.* God is your friend, your protector, and your deliver. He is always with you and will never leave you. *He is for you.* Today, hang on with hope to this one thing: *God is for you.* Repeat this until you believe it deep in your soul: God is for you. *God is for you. God is for you.* Now walk in this promise today—at school, at work, at home, or in your car. Even as you lay under the covers not wanting to get up, do the hard thing, get up, and remember—*God is for you.* Amen and amen.

**This I know: God is for me. —Psalm 56:9**

Further Scripture: Psalm 56:3–4, 13; Romans 8:31

## Questions

1. Do you think we have the right to ask God to destroy our enemies as David did in many of his psalms (Psalm 54:5)?

2. David said in Psalm 54:7, "For He has delivered me from all trouble." Can you say the same thing about your life? What's the difference between being delivered from trouble and not having any trouble in your life?

3. In Psalm 55:9–11, David talked about a city that was supposed to be holy being plagued by violence, strife, iniquity, mischief, destruction, oppression, and deceit. How often do we, as Christians, look for help from a sinful world when our trouble lies within our own church walls?

4. In Psalm 55:12–14, David talked about how it was not the enemy who was causing him disappointment and hurt but rather the betrayal of his friends. This points to the Messiah and Judas. How much harder is it for you to forgive someone who is your friend as opposed to your enemy when they hurt you?

5. What does Psalm 56:8 say about God's love for you?

6. What did the Holy Spirit highlight to you in Psalms 54—56 through the reading or the teaching?

# Lesson 53: Psalms 57—59

*King of Glory*: Mercy, Trust, and Praise

## Teaching Notes

### Intro

The psalms depict real stuff from David's life, not just stories. Psalm 57 is one of four that was set to the tune "Do Not Destroy," along with chapters 58, 59, and 75 (by Asaph). In Psalm 57, David was fleeing and in despair. Philip Yancy wrote, "David wrote and sang the psalms as therapy for himself. Somehow, telling himself the truth enabled him to rise above his fear and see a transcendent God who remained in control."[1] In all of this, we will see Jesus as the *King of Glory*.

The backdrop for this psalm is recorded in 1 Samuel 20—24. We are going to see where David came from and how he ended up in the predicament discussed in these psalms.

- Jonathan showed his loyalty to David. He shot an arrow as a sign David should run from Saul.

- David went to Nob where he ate showbread with the priest Ahimelech and obtained Goliath's sword.

- In Nob, Doeg the Edomite (Saul's chief herdsman) saw David's actions and reported them to Saul. Saul responded in anger by killing Ahimelech, 85 priests, and Nob men, women, children, oxen, donkey, and sheep. Saul was God's chosen one, but his heart had hardened to a point he did things beyond what he could have imagined. There are choices you and I make daily that could harden our hearts. The *King of Glory* is always waiting to restore us back. Unfortunately, Saul never came to that point.

- David fled to Gath (Philistine). He went to the King Achish, pretending to be insane in order to remain safe.

- David left and escaped at first to a cave of Adullam with his 400 men.

---

[1] John C. Maxwell, *The Maxwell Leadership Study Bible* (Nashville: Thomas Nelson, 2007), 503.

- During this time, Saul continued to pursue David. Saul was closing in on the other side of the mountain from David. The Philistines attacked, so Saul left.
- David then hid in a second cave in the wilderness of En-gedi.
- Saul again pursued David with 3,000 choice soldiers. Saul actually went into David's cave unintentionally. David chose to spare Saul's life and cut off the corner of his robe.

I wanted to review all that because it is important to understand what David was feeling. He was fleeing for his life! This was what was happening in his life. David was chosen to be in the palace, but he was in the wilderness. It is possible God was preparing David. Wiersbe wrote, "Better to be in the will of God in a cave than out of His will in a king's palace."[2]

The structure of chapter 57 is:

1. A call for mercy in the midst of calamities (vv. 1–3)
2. A confession of trust in the midst of trouble (vv. 5–6)
3. A determination to praise God in the midst of the people (vv. 7–11)

## Teaching

*Psalm 57:1*: David begged for mercy. I love where it says, "In the shadow of your wings." It gives the picture of a mother bird whose baby comes up underneath her wings to take refuge and to find safety.

*Psalm 57:2–3*: David continued to cry out to, "God who performs His purpose in me." The word "performs" is translated "will perfect." The point is that God acts on behalf of His servant. Gamar (which translates to "perform") means "to end, finish, perfect; to come to an end, fulfill." This refers to the completing, finishing, and perfecting of God's work in one's life. The idea is God begins to work out His purpose in the lives of His servants and continues His work until it is absolutely and completely done.

*Psalm 57:4–6*: David compared his foes to lions prowling around for prey. In the midst of his distress, David exalted God, shouting his praise to the Lord. David declared his enemies were "preparing a net." Though his enemies expected David to be easily caught like a bird, through God's mercy, they fell into their own pit.

---

[2] Warren W Wiersbe, *Be Worshipful: Glorify God for Who He Is* (Colorado Springs: David C. Cook, 2004), 195.

*Psalm 57:7*: When David declared his "heart was steadfast," he needed to hear that truth out loud. It makes me think of Paul near the end of his life (2 Timothy 4:6–7). David assured God that he had remained faithful to God who had provided for him from the beginning (1 Corinthians 15:58).

I encourage you to be steadfast! A steadfast heart is one fixed on the Lord's promise and not wavering between doubt and faith. Looking at ourselves and situations, the natural will cause doubt and lead us down a road that leads to unbelief.

*Psalm 57:8–11*: These verses contain the refrain (a line or phrase that repeats at the end of a verse and reinforces the song's main point) (vv. 5, 11). "Be exalted, O God, above the heavens, let Your glory be above all the earth." David called upon the Lord to manifest His greatness in such a way that people had to say, "This is the Lord's doing; it is marvelous in our eyes."

*Psalm 58*: This psalm is subtitled The Just Judgment of the Wicked (NKJV). David lamented how wicked Saul and his men were.

*Psalm 59*: This psalm is subtitled The Assured Judgment of the Wicked (NKJV). David moved from lament to singing and praising God.

## Closing

Speak truth over yourself continually! Feelings and emotions are terrible leaders. Feelings can easily cause doubt, which leads to unbelief. Be led by truth (Job 13:15)!

The Hebrew word for trust is *yachal*. "Yachal means to wait, hope, trust, expect, be patient; remain in anticipation. Yachal is often translated to 'hope.'"[3] Also, read Hebrews 13:5–6 and Romans 8:28.

John Piper once said, "Not only is all your affliction *momentary*, not only is all your *affliction* light in comparison to eternity and the glory there, but all of it is *totally meaningful. . . . Every millisecond of your pain from fallen nature or fallen man—every millisecond of your misery in the path of obedience—is producing a peculiar glory you will get because of that.*"[4] Piper also said, "Do not lose heart, but take these truths . . . and day by day, focus on them. Preach them to yourself every morning. Get alone with God and preach his word into your mind until your heart sings with confidence that you are new and cared for."[5]

[3] *New Spirit-Filled Life Bible: NIV* (Nashville: Thomas Nelson, 2014), 1145.

[4] John Piper, "Your Suffering Is Working for You," December 2, 2015, in *Ask Pastor John*, episode 741, https://www.desiringgod.org/interviews/your-suffering-is-working-for-you.

[5] John Piper, "None of Our Misery Is Meaningless," Desiring God, July 9, 2018, https://www.desiringgod.org/messages/the-glory-of-god-in-the-sight-of-eternity/excerpts/none-of-our-misery-is-meaningless.

## The Daily Word

Today, *choose to find your confidence in the Lord.* Choose to sing praises to the Lord. Choose to proclaim His promises about His far-reaching, faithful love. No one is too far away for His love to reach. His love is as high as the heavens, and His faithfulness reaches the clouds.

You may feel as though you are in a pit today. Still, lift up your head and begin to muster praises to the Lord. Your praises will bring Him glory and exalt Him. What the enemy may have wanted for evil, you can turn to praise. Therefore remain steadfast and immovable, keeping your eyes on the Lord. Remain faithful to proclaim His praises in the midst of heartache, and He will give you eyes to see what He sees. It's a choice. Ask yourself: *Am I going to complain and dwell on negative thoughts or am I going to rise up and praise God for His faithful love?* Today, choose to rise up, friend! Rise up and find your confidence in the Lord one day at a time!

**My heart is confident, God, my heart is confident. I will sing; I will sing praises. . . . For Your faithful love is as high as the heavens; Your faithfulness reaches the clouds. God, be exalted above the heavens; let Your glory be over the whole earth. —Psalm 57:7, 10–11**

Further Scripture: Genesis 50:19–20; 1 Corinthians 15:58; 2 Timothy 4:6–7

## Questions

1. Do you ever find yourself praising God in a similar way like David did in Psalm 57:7–11? If so, what was the reason for it? Do you think we need a specific reason to praise Him in this extravagant way?

2. Psalm 57:7 says, "My heart is steadfast, O God, my heart is steadfast; I will sing and give praise." Do you remain steadfast in the Lord in times of both good and bad? If not, what steps can you take to change this?

3. Psalm 58 is called an imprecatory (a spoken curse) psalm. It is such an intense cry for justice that it seems to be a call for revenge. What's the difference between justice and revenge? Is it ever OK for us to seek revenge on someone (Deuteronomy 32:35; Romans 12:19; Hebrews 10:30)?

4. The psalmist referred to God as his stronghold several times in Psalm 59. What is a stronghold? Is it always a good thing?

5. What did the Holy Spirit highlight to you in Psalms 57—59 through the reading or the teaching?

# Lesson 54: Psalms 60—62

*King of Glory*: Trust in God Alone

## Teaching Notes

### Intro

Lesson 54 will cover Psalms 60, 61, and 62. As we go through each one of these psalms, let's slow down and let the Lord speak to us—to grow us in our emotions in the Lord. Today, we'll talk about how Psalm 62 can carry us through whatever challenges we face.

### Teaching

*Psalm 62:1–2*: The phrase, "I rest in God alone," means silently waiting for God. Whatever we face, we can be confident God is in it and has it under control. By depending on God, we can find rest. So, let's walk through the process of how we can get to the place where we rest and trust in God. David wrote Psalm 62 for the choir director, Jeduthun. More than likely, Jeduthun was the designated worship director. According to Constable, the theme is, "My soul finds rest in God alone."[1] In 1 Chronicles 9:16, Obadiah is listed as the great-grandson of Jeduthun. In 1 Chronicles 16:37–42, David left Asaph and his relatives before the Ark of the Covenant. Among them were Heman and Jeduthun who played musical instruments before God. Clearly, Jeduthun was a worship director; he played instruments and his sons were also very involved. First Chronicles 25:1–3 describes Jeduthun's huge history in music. Jeduthun was an incredible worship leader, an incredible man of God, and an incredible prophet who was passing those traits down to his sons.

Some say David wrote this psalm while his son Absalom was ruling over Judah in Hebron. Others say he wrote it while facing treason from someone else.[2] The point is that amid all of this opposition, David had silent confidence that victory was coming. David said, "I will never be shaken" (vv. 2, 6).

---

[1] Thomas L. Constable, *Expository Notes of Dr. Thomas Constable: Psalms*, 256, https://planobiblechapel.org/tcon/notes/pdf/psalms.pdf.

[2] John MacArthur, *The MacArthur Bible Commentary* (Nashville: Thomas Nelson, 2005), 640.

*Psalm 62:3–4*: David's questions in verse 3 are a metaphor describing an imminent collapse.[3] David's opponents planned to take him down from his high position, and they took pleasure in lying (v. 4). The language, "blessing with their mouths but cursing inwardly," brings to mind the religious people who looked good on the outside but were traitors inside. This traitor mentality was demonstrated when Ahithophel said one thing to David and another thing to Absalom (2 Samuel 15). It was also demonstrated when Judas said one thing to Jesus while setting up with the soldiers to come and arrest Jesus.

*Psalm 62:5–6*: Again, David stated his intent to rest in God alone, to wait silently and confidently in God (a repetition of v. 1). Then in verse 6, David repeated verse 2, stating God was his rock, his salvation, and his stronghold. He would not be shaken.

*Psalm 62:7–8*: David said his refuge was in God (v. 7). He called people to trust God at all times and to pour out their hearts before Him (v. 8). In other words . . . pray, pray, pray, pray, pray.

*Psalm 62:9–12*: "Men are only a vapor; exalted men, an illusion" (v. 9). This reminds us of the wealthy who we were talking about a couple of days ago. These guys for whom we have such high respect—well, they come and go. "They are less than a vapor" (v. 9).

*How do you rest in God alone?* Hebrews 4:11 says, "Let us then make every effort to enter that rest, so that no one will fall into the same pattern of disobedience." *How can we enter into that rest?* We have to make an effort to be still and to listen to God. It takes a diligent effort on our part. For many of us, it is so hard to sit and rest.

John Piper did an incredible job of describing how to do this.[4]

1. Pay close attention to what you've heard so you won't drift away (Hebrews 2:1).
2. Don't neglect your great salvation (Hebrews 2:3).
3. Consider Jesus (Hebrews 3:1). When you're finding rest, the only focus should be your great salvation—on Jesus, Himself.
4. Don't harden your heart (Hebrews 3:8). How do Christians harden their hearts? By losing focus on Jesus to allow the world, the flesh, and Satan to become distractions.

---

[3] MacArthur, 640.

[4] John Piper, "The Danger of Dull Hearing," Desiring God, April 10, 1988, https://www.desiringgod.org/messages/the-danger-of-dull-hearing.

5. Take care against an evil, unbelieving heart (Hebrews 3:12). When you don't pay attention, then you slowly, slowly, slowly become hardened. Your hardened heart becomes skeptical about the things of God. Even believers begin to doubt God can do incredible stuff.

6. Exhort one another every day against the deceitfulness of sin (Hebrews 3:14). Holding fast to God allows us to encourage each other.

7. Fear the unbelief that will keep you from your promised rest (Hebrews 4:1). God has guaranteed us eternal rest. Focus on Jesus so you can experience this rest.

When David wrote this psalm, he encouraged Jeduthun to sing, "I'm finding my rest in Him. And when I find my rest in Him, nothing else matters."

## Closing

Lord, we say thanks for this word and thank You for David encouraging us to find and wait in You silently. To trust in You, to know You're going to deliver us from these situations. I praise You for allowing us to have quiet confidence that the victory is coming. We know ultimate rest is coming through You, whether or not we experience it here. We know we will experience it through eternity. For that reason alone, Lord, we can be confident in You. May we never be shaken because our hope comes from You.

## The Daily Word

You will face moments in life, such as sickness, failure, consequences of sin, and fear. There may be times you simply want to run away and hide. However, God has more for you than avoiding the hard times in life. You have to wake up and face reality. You have to face the diagnosis. You have to face the consequence. You have to face your fear. *With God by your side, you can do this.*

To *rest in God alone* means to have a silent confidence in the Lord. Believe in your heart and live with confidence knowing that no matter what happens, the Lord is with you and has control. And that is enough. Consider Jesus through everything. He is more than enough, and He is more than able to help you. Trust in the Lord *at all times*. And just talk to Him—pray, pray, pray, and then pray some more. The Lord never grows weary of hearing the heart of His people. You won't be shaken as you set your mind on God, your rock, your salvation, your stronghold, and your refuge. It will be OK. Rest in the Lord.

**Rest in God alone, my soul, for my hope comes from Him. He alone is my rock my salvation, my stronghold; I will not be shaken. My salvation and**

glory depend on God, my strong rock. My refuge is in God. Trust in Him at all times, you people; pour out your hearts before Him. God is our refuge.
—Psalm 62:5–8

Further Scripture: Psalm 118:6–8; Isaiah 43:1–2; John 14:1

## Questions

1. In Psalm 60:1 and 10, David stated, "God has rejected us." Who is "us"? In verses 11–12, how did David say they would be delivered? Who treads down our adversaries today?

2. In Psalm 62:2 and 6, David said, "He is my rock and my salvation." Could the use of the word "rock" be an indirect reference to the Messiah? Why would we connect "rock" to the Messiah? By calling God his rock, what did David infer?

3. According to Psalm 62:10, what did David say not to trust in?

4. Explain what you think the end of Psalm 62:12 means. Read verses 10–12 to keep it in its context.

5. What could "let me take refuge in the shelter of your wings" mean? How would you explain this to someone who has not been "churched"?

6. What did the Holy Spirit highlight to you in Psalms 60—62 through the reading or the teaching?

# Lesson 55: Psalms 63—65

*King of Glory*: Knowing God

## Teaching Notes

### Intro

Psalm 63 is a psalm of David that was written when he was in the wilderness in Judah. If you remember the history of David from 1 and 2 Samuel, you know David was in the wilderness of Judah often. While most scholars agree this psalm was written when David was fleeing, they disagree on which of two occurrences of David fleeing this was written. Some have argued this psalm was written when David fled from Saul (1 Samuel 23). Others have argued it was written when David fled Absalom (2 Samuel 15).[1]

### Teaching

*Psalm 63:1–2*: David found himself in "a land that is dry" and "without water" (v. 1). But David's response was different from the way most people would have responded. David knew God personally. He started this psalm by declaring, "You are my God." David learned how to meet with God all the way back when he was a shepherd. Before he fought Goliath, David told Saul, "Your servant has been tending his father's sheep. Whenever a lion or a bear came and carried off a lamb from the flock, I went after it, struck it down, and rescued the lamb from its mouth. If it reared up against me, I would grab it by its fur, strike it down, and kill it. Your servant has killed lions and bears; this uncircumcised Philistine will be like one of them, for he has defied the armies of the living God" (1 Samuel 17:34–36).

David started with a declaration of his relationship with God, then stated his intention to seek God. The New King James Version translates part of verse 1 as "early will I seek you." David disciplined himself to be like God. First Corinthians 9:24–27 says, "Don't you know that the runners in a stadium all race, but only one receives the prize? Run in such a way to win the prize. Now everyone who competes exercises self-control in everything. They do it to receive a perishable crown, but we, an imperishable crown. So, I do not run like one who

---

[1] John MacArthur, *The MacArthur Bible Commentary* (Nashville, Thomas Nelson, 2005), 640.

runs aimlessly or box like one beating the air. Instead, I discipline my body and bring it under strict control, so that after preaching to others, I myself will not be disqualified."

When David disciplined himself to meet with God, he became devoted to God. David's soul yearned and longed for God. His devotion became desire: "My body faints for you" (v. 2).

*Psalm 63:3–5*: God's presence transformed David. David learned God's love in His presence and was transformed. David's love for God turned into worship of God. David's worship turned into satisfaction of God. The more of God's goodness David understood, the more satisfied He was just simply in His presence. When David wrote this, he was on the run in the desert away from all the comforts of the palace, yet he was still satisfied with God's goodness in God's presence.

*Psalm 63:6–8*: David meditated on God's goodness and His promises. This was intentional behavior. Before David went to bed, he set his mind on God's promises and goodness. David found shelter in his relationship with God as he clung to God. David's faith was not in his own hands. David's faith was in God's promises to sustain him. In the midst of a difficult season, David believed God would sustain him and had not forsaken him.

*Psalm 63:9–11*: David had confidence in God's deliverance. David did not take this vengeance for himself. He trusted God to do it for him in the same way he did not take vengeance on Saul himself.

## Closing

God used David to lead His people and do amazing things, but that was through David's discipline of seeking God and reminding himself of God's promises. As we discipline ourselves, our desires are changed. As our desires change, we are transformed and worship God. As we worship God, we find satisfaction in Him.

## The Daily Word

Walking with Jesus is a two-way street. It takes discipline and devotion. If you are thirsty, the Lord will satisfy you. When you gaze upon the Lord in His presence, you will see His strength and His glory. As you think of your need for the Lord, He will be your helper. When He hides you in the shadow of His wings in protection, rejoice in Him. Follow closely to the Lord, and He will hold your hand.

As you spend intentional time with Him, your life will be transformed. Remain in Him, and He will remain with you. Seek the Lord, and you will find

Him when you search with all your heart. Don't just know the Word, *know the God of the Word.* Today, seek to know the God of your salvation.

**I will follow close to You; Your right hand holds on to me. —Psalm 63:8**

Further Scripture: Psalm 63:1–2; Jeremiah 29:13; James 4:8

## Questions

1.  What New Testament passage points to thirst and water (Matthew 5:6; John 4:10–14; 7:37)? What words in Psalm 63:1 indicate this is not an ordinary thirst? Have you ever experienced this kind of earnest longing for God?

2.  Why do you think David said in Psalm 63:3 (KJV), "Your lovingkindness is better than life"? Is there anything in your life you would describe as better than life?

3.  Much of Psalm 65 is describing God. Read verse 7. What story of Jesus does this verse bring to mind (Mark 4:39)? Is there anything else in chapter 65 that points to the Messiah?

4.  What did the Holy Spirit highlight to you in Psalms 63—65 through the reading or the teaching?

# Lesson 56: Psalms 66—67

*King of Glory*: Seven Words of Praise

## Teaching Notes

### Intro

Today as we study Psalm 66—67, we will learn some things that will apply to our lives, and we will see tangible changes in our lives. We will walk differently because we will see from Scripture how David walked and the things he did as a man after God's own heart. The psalms show much of David's struggles, victories, and triumphs. Today, we want to look at the importance of praise: the idea of praising the Lord.

### Teaching

Psalm 66:1–4: Praise is expressed adoration toward God. These are not good feelings about God that we are to hold in our hearts. Praise is actually an expression that comes out. David understood the power of praise. Praise demonstrates trust in the Word of God. The more we learn about the way God operates, the more we learn about His promises and His truths that He gives to us through Scripture. The more we walk through life, through any situation, the more we can declare praise over every situation in our lives—both currently and calling it out in advance. Praise is not just an expression of who God is. It is also like a weapon in our arsenal that allows us to call things out and set things in motion so we can walk in victory. Psalm 150 commands us to praise the Lord. Biblically, we know we will face challenges in life—it is going to happen. But it is not scriptural that the believer should be defeated. Praise actually sets the stage so we can walk in victory.

Today we are going to look at seven Hebrew words for praise found throughout Scripture, and especially in the book of Psalms. Psalm 22:3 tells us God is "enthroned on the praises of Israel." This verse conveys the idea that when praise happens, God enters the room. When we see that God inhabits praise, then something needs to shift in our lives so that we give forth praise and see God move on our behalf. We need to be people of prayer who are constantly praying to God knowing His ear is attentive to our prayers. In Daniel 6:10, we are told Daniel prayed three times a day to God. In Psalm 119:164–165, we are told David praised God seven times a day. When we compare the two, for every ten minutes we spend praying, maybe we should spend 20–25 minutes praising the Lord.

In 1 Thessalonians 5:16–18, Paul encouraged both praying and praising God. David modeled this practice when he was in the midst of some really tough situations. Even when Saul brought as many as 3,000 men with him in his efforts to kill David, David made the choice to praise the Lord. When Paul and Silas were put in jail, they praised God in the midst of solitary confinement, and God moved on their behalf. Praise takes our eyes off what is happening in the natural realm and sets us in a different place, a supernatural realm where God works in our lives and our situations. The psalms are a literature of worship. The prominent feature throughout is praise—singing, shouting, dancing, rejoicing, adoring. These following seven Hebrew words describe ways to praise God.

The following information is taken from a book written by Chris Tomlin and Darren Whitehead titled *Holy Roar*.[1]

*Yadah*: Found in Psalm 67:3. The word "yadah" means to revere or to worship with extended hands. It is called the hands of praise. In the Hebrew, this is not only with the hands straight out, but it's almost like the throwing of a stone or the shooting of an arrow. This word is found 111 times in Scripture, describing the moments when the Hebrew people were so overcome by the glory of the Lord their hands would shoot straight up.

*Halal*: This word, probably the most common one, is called the fools of praise. It means to boast, to rave, to shine, to celebrate, to be clamorously foolish. Psalm 149:3 used this word: "Let them *praise* His name with dancing" (emphasis added). This is where we get the word "hallelujah." David dancing when the Ark of the Covenant was brought into the city is a demonstration of this word (2 Samuel 6:13–16). True halal lays aside inhibitions and ignores self-consciousness. Psalm 150:6 (the last verse of the psalms) says, "Let everything that has breath *praise* the Lord" (emphasis added). This word is used 165 times in the Bible.

*Zamar*: This word means the music of praise. We actually use instruments to make music, to celebrate in song and music, literally to touch the strings or parts of an instrument. Psalm 144:9 used this word: "I will sing a new song to You; I will play on a ten-stringed harp for You." This word is used 41 times in Scripture. Even if you do not play, you are using music to take you to a place where you

---

[1] Chris Tomlin and Darren Whitehead, *Holy Roar: 7 Words That Will Change the Way You Worship* (Nashville: Thomas Nelson, 2017), n.p.

adore and praise God. It is allowing music to be the vehicle that carries your praise to the throne room of God.

*Towdah*: This word means the expectation of praise. We can actually praise the Lord in expectation of what He is about to do or the promise He made in my life that I may not be currently seeing, but I will in expectation praise Him. We see this in Psalm 56:11–12. This word is also an extension of the hand in thanksgiving and confession, but it is for things not yet received. This one is used 32 times in Scripture. Romans 4:20 says Abraham "gave glory" to God for the promise of a son to be born to him by Sarah.

*Barak*: This word signifies the posture of praise. This word is used 289 times in the Psalms. This word means to kneel or to bless God as an act of adoration, to praise, to salute, to thank. It gives the idea of kneeling before God. Psalm 72:11 and 15 says kings and nations will bow before God to kneel and serve Him. In humility, we will actually get down on our knees with our faces on the ground/ floor before the Lord. While in this position of humility, we are actually fixing our eyes on God, the *King of Glory*. There is something about humility that God honors. David used this word for praise repeatedly in Psalm 103.

*Tehillah*: This word means the songs of praise. This is simply a song flowing out of my heart—it is singing from a melody in my heart and adding words to it. It is normally unprepared and unrehearsed. The tehillah is all of psalms, and it comes from this word which means to sing forth to the Lord.

*Shabach*: This word means the shout of praise. This is literally, just as it sounds, to shout out loud to the Lord. It is used 11 times, and it means to literally make a holy roar.

## Closing

David, as a man after God's own heart, knew these things. He had expressions of praise. Throughout Psalms 66 and 67, David used these words to praise the Lord. I encourage you to press into some of these expressions of praise, to go deeper with the Lord, to give Him the honor and praise He deserves.

## The Daily Word

Have you seen the Lord at work in your life today? *Praise the Lord!* Are you having a difficult day and struggling? *Praise the Lord!* Let His praise always be on your lips. *Praise the Lord* as a weapon in the battle! *Praise the Lord* in expectation for fulfillment of His promises.

Today, spend time praising the Lord through different ways of expression: raise your hands, kneel, dance, shout aloud, or sing a new song! Let praise arise from your heart! Fear God and testify of His love in your life. Let all the people and all the nations praise the name of the Lord so the whole world will know the great and mighty Lord of your salvation!

**Come and listen, all who fear God, and I will tell what He has done for me. I cried out to Him with my mouth, and praise was on my tongue. —Psalm 66:16–17**

Further Scripture: 2 Samuel 6:14–15; Psalm 67:3–4; Daniel 2:19–20

## Questions

1. Psalm 66 begins, "Make a joyful noise unto God." Where else does Scripture tell us to make this type of noise (Psalms 98:4; 100:1)? In your own words, what does this look like in your life?

2. In Psalm 66:18, the Scripture reads, "If I regard iniquity in my heart, the Lord will not hear me." Do you agree with this verse? Why or why not? Spend a few minutes with the Lord and search your heart for any iniquity. Repent if something comes to mind.

3. "Let the people praise you" is spoken several times throughout Psalm 67. Why do you think this was important enough for the author to repeat this phrase? Do you praise God? If so, how?

4. What did the Holy Spirit highlight to you in Psalms 66—67 through the reading or the teaching?

# Lesson 57: Psalm 68

*King of Glory*: God's Majestic Power

## Teaching Notes

### Intro

Psalm 68 is a messianic psalm of "prayer, praise, thanksgiving, historical reminder, and imprecation,"[1] and it points to the *King of Glory*. This psalm is one of David's and was written for the choir director, to be sung. This psalm was probably written out of David's excitement about the restoration of the Ark to Jerusalem.[2]

### Teaching

*Psalm 68:1–6*: Wiersbe outlines this psalm and writes that verses 1–6 show "our God is coming to us."[3] In verse 1, God's power causes His enemies to scatter and flee (Numbers 10:33–35). The coming presence of the Lord referred to the Ark. God's enemies will disappear before God (v. 2) while the righteous rejoice before the Lord (v. 3). God's people would sing praises to Him, exalting His name and remembering who He is and who is important to Him: the fatherless, the widows, the deserted, and the prisoners (vv. 4–6). God is in the business of setting people free and watching over them. Constable describes how God is presented as "a majestic warrior riding His chariot through the desert wilderness."[4]

This psalm uses a variety of names and descriptors for God:

- Verse 1: "Yahweh" can be translated as "The Lord" (Exodus 3:15).
- Verse 1: "God" can be translated as "Elohim."
- Verse 11: "Adonai" is translated as "The Lord."
- Verse 14: God is the "Almighty."

---

[1] John MacArthur, *The MacArthur Bible Commentary* (Nashville: Thomas Nelson, 2005), 642.

[2] MacArthur, 643.

[3] Warren W. Wiersbe, *The Wiersbe Bible Commentary: Old Testament* (Colorado Springs: David C. Cook, 2007), 948.

[4] Thomas L. Constable, *Expository Notes of Dr. Thomas Constable: Psalms*, 270, https://planobiblechapel.org/tcon/notes/pdf/psalms.pdf.

- Verse 18: Refers to the "Lord God."
- Verse 20: Describes God as the "God of Salvation."
- Verse 24: Describes God as the "King."

*Psalm 68:7–18*: Wiersbe writes that verses 7–18 show "our God is marching before us."[5] David referred back to the exodus when God led the Israelites through the desert (v. 7). They were given abundant rain, and even manna, in God's blessing (vv. 8–9). God has taken us all through the deserts in our lives. He has gone before us and provided us with sustenance (Judges 5:4–5)! God provided for their needs (v. 10). Verses 11–12 refers back to the exodus, women singing praises about the promises of God (Exodus 15:20–21; 1 Samuel 18:6). Verse 13 refers to sitting in the presence of God.

In verse 14, Zalmon means Black Mountain and, while it could have been "a figurative description of God's blessings, David may have been referring to Abimelech's victory on Mount Zalmon near Shechem (Judges 9:48)."[6] In verses 15–16, David wrote that even the towering mountain of Bashan was jealous of where God chose to dwell (Jeremiah 22:20–21). David described God as being surrounded by thousands of chariots (v. 17). God ascended the heights, taking captives, so the Lord God could live in Jerusalem (v. 18). This is the messianic reference in this psalm. Jesus ascended the heights in His resurrection/ascension and provided freedom to the captives. Paul quoted this as God gave gifts to people, rather than received gifts from people (Ephesians 4:8).

*Psalm 68:19–35*: Wiersbe writes that verses 9–35 show that "our God is dwelling with us."[7] David praised God for daily bearing his burdens and being his salvation (vv. 19–20). Through His power, God crushed His enemies (v. 21). In verses 22–23, MacArthur states, "Whether the enemy tries to escape by land (Bashan) or by sea, God will bring them back to be destroyed by His people (Amos 9:2–4)."[8] God's presence was known in the sanctuary, and singers led His procession while musicians followed (vv. 24–26). The tribes listed in verse 27 all reference the Christ. God will receive universal tributes from all nations (vv. 28–29). When the *King of Glory* returns, everyone will recognize who He is. Verses 29–35 provide another clear messianic prophecy!

---

[5] Wiersbe, 949.

[6] Constable, 271.

[7] Wiersbe, 949.

[8] MacArthur, 643.

## Closing

Wiersbe concludes his commentary on Psalm 68 with "our God receives universal tribute."[9] May we continue to focus on the *King of Glory*!

---

### The Daily Word

Do you feel surrounded by the enemy? Are you hearing lies from the enemy, tempting you to fall into his traps or luring you to seek comfort in anything but the Lord? Perhaps you feel heaviness all around you, almost as though you are paralyzed and unable to do anything.

Rise up, friend, rise up. Allow God's majestic power to arise within you. Abide in Him. Hold every thought captive and remind yourself of God's truth. The Lord promises He will always be with you. His presence goes where you go just as the Ark of the Covenant went with David when he traveled. And David's enemies were scattered by the presence of God. Remember, submit to God, resist the devil, and he will flee from you by the power of Jesus Christ's presence in you. *Rise up*. You are not defeated. Victory belongs to the Lord. May the Lord arise within you. Rise up!

**God arises. His enemies scatter, and those who hate Him flee from His presence. —Psalm 68:1**

Further Scripture: Numbers 10:35; Matthew 28:20; James 4:7

---

## Questions

1. What time in the Bible does Psalm 68:7 refer to (Exodus 13:21–22; 14:19; Nehemiah 9:19)? How do we know today that God is with us?

2. In Psalm 68:13, David referred to the wings of a dove. Where are some of the other places in Scripture that doves are mentioned, and what do they represent (Genesis 8:9–12; 15:9; Leviticus 5:7; Mark 1:10; John 1:32)?

3. The mountains of Bashan are mentioned in Psalm 68:15. What are these mountains known for, and why do you suppose David referred to them as God's abode or dwelling place (Numbers 21:33–35; Joshua 21:27; Ezekiel 27:6; 39:18)?

4. Psalm 68:29 says, "Because of Your temple at Jerusalem, kings will bring presents to You." Is it possible this verse may be a foreshadowing of Jesus' birth (Matthew 2:11)?

5. What did the Holy Spirit highlight to you in Psalm 68 through the reading or the teaching?

---

[9] Wiersbe, 949.

# Lesson 58: Psalm 69

*King of Glory*: David's Request to Be Saved

## Teaching Notes

### Intro

After Psalms 22 and 110, Psalm 69 is the third most-recited psalm in the Bible. That doesn't mean Psalm 69 is more important than other psalms, but it does mean it speaks strongly to what we feel and face. Psalm 69 is a prayer of desperation and is a messianic psalm. *Nelson's Commentary* explains that both Psalms 22 and 69 "begin with the sufferings of David but have their full meaning in the sufferings of Jesus."[1] Both psalms were written 1,000 years before Christ's birth, death, and resurrection. However, while Psalm 22 focuses on Jesus' physical sufferings, Psalm 69 "focuses more on His emotional and spiritual suffering."[2]

At the end of this lesson, we'll look at all of the messianic psalms throughout the book of Psalms. In a messianic psalm, David would describe his own experiences and sufferings, but these would also foretell of what Jesus the Messiah would experience. In Acts 2:30–31 is a description of how David did this: "Since [David] was a prophet, he knew that God had sworn an oath to him to seat one of his descendants on his throne. Seeing this in advance, he spoke concerning the resurrection of the Messiah." David understood that he would speak prophetically (2 Samuel 7:12–16) and that the Messiah would come through his own house.

The subtitle states the psalm was to be sung to the tune of "The Lilies." Four times, David asked to be saved, beginning in verse 1 as well as in verses 14, 16–17, and 18. MacArthur divides the psalm into two sections: "(1) The Prayer of Desperation (vv. 1–28), and (2) The Promise of Salvation (vv. 29–36)."[3]

---

[1] Earl D. Radmacher, Ronald B. Allen, and H. Wayne House, eds., *Nelson's New Illustrated Bible Commentary* (Nashville: Thomas Nelson, 1999), 693.

[2] Radmacher et al., 693.

[3] John MacArthur, *The MacArthur Bible Commentary* (Nashville: Thomas Nelson, 2005), 643.

## Teaching

*Psalm 69:1–3*: MacArthur describes verses 1–3 as "the description of [David's] situation."[4] David asked God to save him because he felt like he was drowning (v. 1). He felt mired in deep mud and stranded in flood waters (v. 2). David was physically exhausted from crying and looking for God (v. 3).

*Psalm 69:4–12*: MacArthur describes verses 4–12 as "the reason for [David's] situation."[5] David stated the people who hated him without cause numbered more than the hairs on his head (v. 4). Jesus quoted David in John 15:25 as the fulfillment of what David said would take place (Matthew 5:17). David knew God understood he was not guilty in this case (v. 5). MacArthur points out David "fears that his dismal situation may be a stumbling block to other believers," and that David worried they could become ashamed of what he was going through (v. 6).[6] David had already been shamed by the reproach or insults of others to the point he was a stranger to his brothers (vv. 7–8). This is another messianic reference. Jesus experienced that as well (Matthew 12:46–50; John 7:3–5). For verse 9, Constable explains, "It was David's preoccupation with building the temple that had turned popular opinion against him."[7] Jesus had the same mentality with God's house when He cleansed the temple of the money changers (Matthew 21:12–13; Mark 11:15–18). Both John 2:17 and Romans 15:3 speak to the truth in Psalm 69 that foretold what Christ would experience. Paul reminded believers that the insults fell on the Lord, not on us. No matter what David did in his worship, people mocked him (vv. 10–12).

*Psalm 69:13–18*: MacArthur describes verses 13–18 as "the hope for [David's] situation."[8] David asked God for His favor, His salvation, and His abundant and faithful love (v. 13). He asked for rescue from the mud, the deep waters that could sweep him away, and from those who hated him (v. 14). He begged God not to let the pit (death) close over him (v. 15). David asked God to answer him because he was in great distress and needed to be ransomed from his enemies (vv. 16–18).

---

[4] MacArthur, 643.

[5] MacArthur, 643.

[6] MacArthur, 643.

[7] Thomas L. Constable, *Expository Notes of Dr. Thomas Constable: Psalms*, 276, https://planobiblechapel.org/tcon/notes/pdf/psalms.pdf.

[8] MacArthur, 643.

*Psalm 69:19–21*: MacArthur describes verses 19–21 as "the reproach of [David's] situation."[9] David knew God was already aware of all he was facing (vv. 19–20). In Matthew 26:37, Jesus experienced the loneliness and sorrow in the garden of Gethsemane that was like what David described in these verses. In verse 21, David was given gall to eat and vinegar to drink—a strong messianic reference, just as Jesus was given on the cross (Matthew 27:34).

*Psalm 69:22–28*: MacArthur describes verses 22–28 as "the revenge for [David's] situation."[10] David asked that his enemies be trapped, and God's rage poured out on them (vv. 22–24). David asked that their fortification be made desolate and no one be allowed to live in their tents (v. 25). Verse 25 is quoted in Acts 1:20 referring to Judas, showing another messianic reference.[11] The suffering of the Messiah was clearly a part of God's plan (Isaiah 53:10). David asked God to cut the lives short of those who had attacked him (vv. 26–28).

*Psalm 69:29–36*: Wiersbe suggests, "David's original psalm ended at verse 29 and the Holy Spirit directed the prophet Jeremiah to add verses 30–36 after the fall of Judah and Jerusalem to the Babylonians."[12] The question about these verses is how did David know what was happening in those verses? Verses 30–36 speak to praising God with thanksgiving because the Lord heard them and did not despise them when they were captives. Wiersbe states David "saw a day coming when the land would be united and healed and the cities populated again."[13]

## Closing

MacArthur provides an outline of messianic psalms and their fulfillment. His outline includes 20 psalms. Psalm 69:8 states David became a stranger to his own family because of his passion for building the temple for the Lord (v. 9). The more we become consumed with passion to be in the presence of the Lord, more people will question what you're doing, throw insults at you, and even disown you. When that happens, you'll be in good company! You'll be looking more like David and a whole lot more like Christ.

---

[9] MacArthur, 643.

[10] MacArthur, 643.

[11] MacArthur, 643.

[12] Warren W. Wiersbe, *The Bible Exposition Commentary: Job–Song of Solomon* (Colorado Springs: David C. Cook, 2004), 215.

[13] Wiersbe, 217.

## The Daily Word

David endured persecution. Christ endured persecution. They both endured lies, insults, and even felt like strangers around their brothers and sisters—all because of their zeal and devotion to God Almighty. As you follow Christ, He promises that you, too, will endure hardship and persecution. When you cry out for help, you may receive silence in return. When you cry out for help, you may receive sour-tasting advice that doesn't satisfy, just as Christ received vinegar and gall. Even so, endurance will come as you find hope in Christ and through His Scriptures. He gives power and strength to His people.

If you are enduring hardship or persecution today, remember you are not alone. The world, your enemies, and the devil do not like the sovereign, mighty, majestic God of your salvation. However, when you draw near to the Lord, He will redeem your life. He will rescue you. Do not fear. The Lord is near to those who love His name. Allow praise and worship to rise up within you and praise His name—Yahweh, Elohim, Adonai, Lord God, God of our Salvation. Praise His holy name!

**You know the insults I endure—my shame and disgrace. You are aware of all my adversaries. Insults have broken my heart, and I am in despair. I waited for sympathy, but there was none; for comforters, but found no one. Instead, they gave me gall for my food, and for my thirst they gave me vinegar to drink. —Psalm 69:19–21**

Further Scripture: Psalm 69:9; Matthew 27:33–34; Romans 15:3–4

## Questions

1. Psalm 69:3 talks about how weary the psalmist was, how parched his throat was, and how blurry his eyes were from crying out to God. Was there ever a time in your life when you cried out to God so desperately as David did here? If so, what was the outcome? Did it take away the situation? Was it easier to get through because of your cries?

2. What do you think David was referring to when he said in Psalm 69:21, "And for my thirst they gave me vinegar to drink"? Do you believe he was, at some time, given vinegar to drink? Where else in Scripture is vinegar mentioned (Ruth 2:14; Matthew 27:34), and who drank it?

3. Where else is the book of life (v. 28) mentioned in Scripture (Philippians 4:3; Revelation 3:5; 13:8; 20:15; 21:27)? What is "the book of life"? How can you be sure your name is in it?

4. According to Psalm 69:30–31, what does the Lord desire from you more than sacrifices?

5. What did the Holy Spirit highlight to you in Psalm 69 through the reading or the teaching?

# Lesson 59: Psalms 70—71

*King of Glory*: God's Help in Old Age

## Teaching Notes

### Intro

We decided to teach on Psalm 71, which was written by an unnamed old man, rather than Psalm 70, since it was another Davidic psalm. I'm intrigued by Psalm 71. The psalm carries the title "God's Help in Old Age." MacArthur explains, "At a time in his life when [the psalmist] thinks he should be exempt from certain kinds of troubles, he once again is personally attacked. Though his enemies conclude that God has abandoned him, the psalmist is confident that God will remain faithful."[1] The psalm has two bookends (vv. 1 and 24) in which the psalmist asked to not be disgraced for trusting in God (Psalm 119:31).

### Teaching

*Psalm 71:1–4*: Wiersbe describes this section as "the Lord helps me now."[2] The psalmist asked that he never be disgraced but that he would be rescued by the Lord (vv. 1–2). *Nelson's Commentary* points out, "The psalmist is concerned not only with his own plight but with the character of God."[3] The psalmist described God as his refuge, rock, and fortress (v. 3). The "rock of refuge" was the place the psalmist could always go to feel safe in God's presence. No matter what we face, we can ALWAYS go to God as our refuge! The psalmist asked God to "deliver him" from the wicked (Psalms 17:13; 37:40; 144:2). "Deliver him" can be understood as "to cause to escape."[4] Wiersbe suggests the psalmist may have been a retired Levite who was being pressured to worship "idols along with the worship of Jehovah."[5]

---

[1] John MacArthur, *The MacArthur Bible Commentary* (Nashville: Thomas Nelson, 2005), 644.

[2] Warren W. Wiersbe, *The Bible Exposition Commentary: Job–Song of Solomon* (Colorado Springs: David C. Cook, 2004), 217.

[3] Earl D. Radmacher, Ronald B. Allen, and H. Wayne House, eds., *Nelson's New Illustrated Bible Commentary* (Nashville: Thomas Nelson, 1999), 694.

[4] Radmacher et al., 694.

[5] Wiersbe, 217.

*Psalm 71:5–13*: Wiersbe describes this section as "the Lord helped me in the past."[6] In verses 5–6, the psalmist began to review his life, recognizing how God helped him at each stage—during his youth, from birth, and while in his mother's womb (1 Samuel 7:12). MacArthur says of the phrase "ominous sign" or "wonder" in verse 7, "People [were] amazed at this person's life, some interpreting his trials as God's care, and others as God's punishment."[7] Wiersbe explains, "Sometimes the Lord selected special people to be signs to the nation"[8] (Isaiah 8:18; Zechariah 3:8). The psalmist praised God all day and asked he not be discarded in his old age (vv. 8–9). *Nelson's Commentary* states, "The psalmist has trusted in God his entire life; it would be sad if he were dismissed by the Lord late in life."[9] The psalmist stated his enemies say God had already abandoned him and he no longer had protection (vv. 10–12). He begged God to disgrace and destroy his enemies (v. 13).

*Psalm 71:14–21*: Wiersbe describes this section as "the Lord will help me in the future."[10] The psalmist promised that he would continue to praise God more and more (vv. 14–16). The psalmist again remembered how God had been with him in his youth and begged God not to abandon him in his old age while he still continued to proclaim God's power to other generations (vv. 17–18). This is the picture of the Shema (Deuteronomy 6:4–9). He told God that His righteousness reaches heaven because of His good things (v. 19). The psalmist acknowledged he had experienced trials, but God would revive him again (v. 20). God would continue to increase his honor and give him comfort (v. 21).

*Psalm 71:22–24*: Wiersbe describes this section as "the Lord be praised for His help."[11] Therefore, the psalmist would continue to praise the Lord, the Holy One of Israel.

## Closing

This is a great picture. Whether you're 30, 50, or 70, we all have a lot to learn about God.

---

[6] Wiersbe, 218.

[7] MacArthur, 644.

[8] Wiersbe, 218.

[9] Radmacher et al., 694.

[10] Wiersbe, 218.

[11] Wiersbe, 218.

## The Daily Word

Everyone knows someone younger to whom they can proclaim and bear witness of God's power to. Think about it for a minute: each generation can offer something to the next because, in reality, everyone is "older" than someone. You are never too old or too young to begin to pour into the generation behind you. There is no excuse.

As the Lord continues giving you hope, take time to proclaim His power to others. Share about the Lord's mighty acts of faithfulness as you stand upon Him, your firm foundation, rock, and refuge. As you received forgiveness and redemption from the Lord, share the story of God's amazing grace. There's no retirement from walking with Jesus. So even when you think no one cares, *remember the Lord gave you the responsibility to proclaim His name to another generation.* Today, open your eyes and ears to someone you can share God's love with. Impact another generation even if it means putting on your glasses or turning up your hearing aids! As you walk in obedience, watch God move in your life!

**God, You have taught me from my youth, and I still proclaim Your wonderful works. Even when I am old and gray, God, do not abandon me. Then I will proclaim Your power to another generation, Your strength to all who are to come. —Psalm 71:17–18**

Further Scripture: Psalm 71:6–8; 119:90; 2 Timothy 2:2

## Questions

1. David, in these psalms, repeatedly asked the Lord to deliver/rescue him. Do you believe this represents the Scripture where we are told to continually knock, seek, and ask (Matthew 7:7–8)? Why or why not?

2. David continually said he put his trust in the Lord. Where does your trust lie? With God, self, or man?

3. In Psalm 71:20b, David said, "And shall bring me up again from the depths of the earth." Do you think this could be speaking of when we will rise and meet Him in the sky (1 Thessalonians 4:14–17)?

4. What did the Holy Spirit highlight to you in Psalms 70—71 through the reading or the teaching?

# Lesson 60: Psalms 72—73

*King of Glory*: A Prayer for the King

## Teaching Notes

### Intro

Psalm 72 is a psalm written for a coronation for a sovereign (1 Kings 2). It can also be called a royal psalm. MacArthur explains that the psalm was "dedicated to the prosperity of Solomon at the beginning of his reign."[1] Solomon is not only connected to the psalm through his coronation, but it is possible "he was the author and wrote of himself in the third person . . . a prayer for God's help as he sought to rule over the people of Israel."[2] Constable says the psalm "describes Solomon's reign but anticipates the rule of his successor, Jesus Christ, on earth in the future."[3]

### Teaching

*Psalm 72:1–4*: MacArthur describes these verses as "a just reign."[4] Remember that in this context, the psalm is about Solomon, but it also points to the *King of Glory*. Verse 1's conflicting language has created debate about who wrote this psalm. The verse points to the father/son relationship and anticipates the relationship between God the Father and Jesus the Son (2 Samuel 7:12–13; Psalm 2:1–12). Verse 1 offers "a prayer that the king would faithfully mediate God's justice on the nation (Deuteronomy 17:18–20)."[5] God would also judge the king on his righteousness (v. 2). Constable suggests that "the psalmist's references to the mountains and hills are probably metaphorical allusions to the king's government"[6] (v. 3). The author asked that Solomon lead by helping the poor and the afflicted (v.4).

---

[1] John MacArthur, *The MacArthur Bible Commentary* (Nashville: Thomas Nelson, 2005), 644.

[2] Warren W. Wiersbe, *The Bible Exposition Commentary: Job–Song of Solomon* (Colorado Springs: David C. Cook, 2004), 218.

[3] Thomas L. Constable, *Expository Notes of Dr. Thomas Constable: Psalms*, 284, https://planobiblechapel.org/tcon/notes/pdf/psalms.pdf.

[4] MacArthur, 645.

[5] MacArthur, 645.

[6] Constable, 285.

*Psalm 72:5–11*: MacArthur describes these verses as "a universal reign."[7] Verse 5 emphasizes that the king's reign would continue from local to an endless reign— long live the king (Psalm 72:5, 15). The rain represents God's blessings on the king and will lead to peace (v. 6).[8] The king's presence would be welcomed. The phrase "the moon is no more" refers "to the length of the Davidic dynasty and, possibly, also to the messianic reign"[9] (2 Samuel 7:16; Psalm 89:3, 4, 29, 36, 37; Luke 1:30–33). His kingdom would expand past the Euphrates River to include the entire earth (v. 8).[10] Sadly, Solomon did not live up to this prayer, and the nation of Israel became divided, but the kingdom of the Messiah will. Verses 9–10 show that "no one will escape the power of His reign, not even those in the wilderness."[11] Verse 11 is very prophetic as it states that even the kings of the earth will bow before Him—a specific messianic picture.

*Psalm 72:12–14*: MacArthur describes these verses as "a compassionate reign."[12] Verse 12 is almost a repeat of verse 4 about the poor and the afflicted. He will redeem them from oppression and violence, "for their lives are precious in his sight." 1 Peter 1:19 echoes that the lives are "precious in His sight." This points to Christ who finds them precious because they had to go through what He had to endure (vv. 13–14).

*Psalm 72:15–17*: MacArthur describes these verses as "a prosperous reign."[13] The prayer for a long reign and a prosperous reign continues (vv. 15–16). Read 1 Kings 10:1–10 for Solomon's meeting with the Queen of Sheba and the gold Solomon received from her. Sheba was also mentioned in verse 10 and points to Solomon's prosperous reign and the reign of the Messiah. Verse 17 begins several verses of the King's name enduring forever (v. 17–19).

*Psalm 72:18–20*: MacArthur describes these verses as "a glorious reign."[14]

---

[7] MacArthur, 645.

[8] Earl D. Radmacher, Ronald B. Allen, and H. Wayne House, eds., *Nelson's New Illustrated Bible Commentary* (Nashville: Thomas Nelson, 1999), 695.

[9] MacArthur, 645.

[10] MacArthur, 645

[11] Radmacher et al., 695.

[12] MacArthur, 645.

[13] MacArthur, 645.

[14] MacArthur, 645.

# Closing

The ultimate reign of prosperity is that we will receive eternal life through Jesus Christ. The whole earth will be filled with His glory (v. 19). *Nelson's Commentary* states, "The name of the great King will be regarded as the greatest name in the universe" and is reminiscent of Paul's writing in Philippians 2:9–11[15]: "For this reason, God highly exalted Him and gave Him the name that is above every name, so that at the name of Jesus every knee will bow—of those who are in heaven and on earth and under the earth—and every tongue should confess that Jesus Christ is Lord, to the glory of God the Father." Everybody. Every tongue. Every tribe. Every nation will bow down. The prayers, the songs of David, son of Jesse is concluded. This closes out the second of the three books that make up Psalms.

---

## The Daily Word

Jesus is the name above every other name. He sends you out with joy and guides you with peace. He rescues the poor and helps the afflicted. He acknowledges the helpless. He redeems the oppressed and ceases the violent. He sees each person as perfectly and wonderfully made. You, child of God, are precious in His sight. No other god on earth offers the unconditional love of the Lord God Almighty, who was, who is, and who is coming. He is the author and the perfecter of your faith, and He is worthy to be praised. His glory will fill the entire earth.

Today, intentionally pray for the day every knee *will* bow and every tongue *will* confess Jesus Christ is Lord. Pray all nations *will* bow down and serve the one true living God! Come, Lord Jesus, come. May you believe in faith it will come to pass. As you pray, ask Jesus to make a way for all people over all the earth to know the name of the Lord our God and bow down to Him. Amen and amen!

**Let all kings bow down to him, all nations serve him. —Psalm 72:11**

Further Scripture: Psalm 72:18–19; Isaiah 55:12; Philippians 2:9–11

---

## Questions

1. When you read Psalm 72, read it as though Jesus is speaking instead of Solomon. How does this chapter now speak to you?

2. Has there been a time in your life when you may have felt like Asaph, envious of the supposed prosperity of the wicked, as he was in Psalm 73:3?

---

[15] Radmacher et al., 695.

3.  In Psalm 73:1–16, Asaph had his eyes on the world, but in verse 17 we see a change in how he viewed things. What do you think caused this change and what are some of the revelations he had? Write about a time when your eyes were opened to the ways of the world versus the ways of God.

4.  What did the Holy Spirit highlight to you in Psalms 72—73 through the reading or the teaching?

# Lesson 61: Psalm 74

*King of Glory*: Feeling Abandoned by God

## Teaching Notes

### Intro

Psalm 74 is another psalm of lament. This psalm was written by Asaph. "Asaph, Heman, and Ethan were Levites who served as a musicians and worship leaders at the sanctuary during David's reign."[1] These three had created "guilds" so their sons and other generations would be trained to continue to lead worship after they were gone. Some scholars have suggested the author of Psalm 74 may not have been Asaph the worship leader but a namesake of his.[2] MacArthur explains the psalm's lament focuses on the issue that "it was bad enough that Israel's enemies had destroyed the temple; but even worse, it seemed to the psalmist that God had abandoned them."[3]

### Teaching

*Psalm 74:1–11*: Wiersbe uses three word pictures to outline this psalm. Verses 1–11 point to "The Sanctuary: 'The Lord Has Rejected Us!'"[4] Verses 1–2 express the feeling of being abandoned by God. God had promised not to abandon His people (Deuteronomy 4:29–31; 26:18–19), but they were feeling that He had (Lamentations 5:20–22). The statement "remember your people" doesn't mean God had forgotten them, but rather it was a request for God to work for them.[5] They requested that God restore the ruins left after the temple was desecrated in Jerusalem (vv. 3–4). "Make your way" asked that God walk around Jerusalem to see the damage that was still taking place in Jerusalem (1 Kings 6:18–22). The damage is described as men cutting trees and smashing carvings with axes,

---

[1] Warren W. Wiersbe, *The Bible Exposition Commentary: Job–Song of Solomon* (Colorado Springs: David C. Cook, 2004), 221.

[2] Wiersbe, 221.

[3] John MacArthur, *The MacArthur Bible Commentary* (Nashville: Thomas Nelson, 2005), 646.

[4] Wiersbe, 224.

[5] Wiersbe, 224.

hatchets, and picks (vv. 5–6). Not only was the temple destroyed, but every meeting place and synagogue were burned down as well (vv. 7–8).[6] In verses 9–11, and 19, God had not raised up new prophets for them, and they questioned how much longer they would be in the situation (Jeremiah 29:10; Lamentations 2:9). As they appealed to God, they also blamed God and questioned if He would even show up.

*Psalm 74:12–17*: Verses 12–17 point to "The Throne: 'The Lord Reigns!'"[7] *Nelson's Commentary* explains, "The Lord is King by virtue of His creation of the earth (Psalm 93)."[8] Asaph stated God had divided the sea and smashed the sea monsters (vv. 12–14). Constable explains, "In Canaanite mythology, the sea and its serpents joined together as enemies of Baal. Supposedly Baal was victorious over these enemies and subsequently became king. The poets of the Bible used the language of Canaanite myth to describe the victories of God in the formation of the earth, in the deliverance of His people from Egypt, and in future battles."[9] In some places in the Old Testament, the Leviathan is equated with Satan (v. 14)[10] (Isaiah 27:1). God had given the Hebrews springs of water and dried up rivers when the people needed to cross over (v. 15). Asaph outlined God's dominion over the earth—the day and night was His because He had created the moon and the sun (v. 16). God created the seasons and established the boundaries of the earth (v. 17).

*Psalm 74:18–23*: Verses 18–23 point to "The Covenant: 'The Lord Remembers Us!'"[11] Wiersbe explains, "Since righteousness and justice are the foundation of His throne, it was logical for Asaph to move in his thoughts from God's throne to God's covenant with Israel (Leviticus 26; Deuteronomy 28—30)."[12] Asaph emphasized the enemy had mocked Yahweh and insulted His name (v. 18). He begged the Lord not to give the life of His dove (Israel) over to the beasts (their enemies) (v. 19). Asaph asked God to remember His covenant with them and not let the oppressed be shamed (vv. 20–21). Asaph called on God to defend His cause and His people instead of allowing the insults against Him to continue (vv. 22–23). These are the same requests made in verse 3. Wiersbe states, "The

---

[6] Wiersbe, 224.

[7] Wiersbe, 224.

[8] Earl D. Radmacher, Ronald B. Allen, and H. Wayne House, eds., *Nelson's New Illustrated Bible Commentary* (Nashville: Thomas Nelson, 1999), 696.

[9] Wiersbe, 186.

[10] Constable, 296.

[11] Wiersbe, 225.

[12] Wiersbe, 225.

nation had been ravaged, the city of Jerusalem had been wrecked, and the temple had been destroyed and burned—but the essentials had not been touched by the enemy! The nation still had Jehovah God as their God, His Word and His covenant had not been changed, and Jehovah was at work in the world!"[13]

Think about the history of the temple:

- The tabernacle was built (Exodus 27:8).
- For 440 years, the tabernacle was in Israel (Leviticus 26:1).
- For 369 years, the tabernacle was in Shilo (1 Samuel 1:3).
- David conquered Jerusalem in 1004 BC (2 Samuel 5), established an altar, and moved the Ark of the Covenant to Mount Moriah (1 Samuel 6).
- David planned to build a house for God (1 Kings 28:19).
- King Solomon built the first temple in 950 BC (1 Kings 7:46–51) and dedicated it (1 Kings 9:3).
- Temple worship took place for 426 years.
- Babylonians destroyed the first temple in 586 BC (Jeremiah 34), and the Jews were taken into exile (Jeremiah 31).
- Daniel prayed toward Jerusalem (Daniel 6:11).
- The altar was rebuilt (Ezra 1:2).
- The prophet Haggai exhorted the people to rebuilt God's temple (Haggai 1:2–4).
- Ahasuerus held a feast with stolen temple treasures in 365 BC (Esther 1:7).
- The temple cornerstone was placed, and the people wept and rejoiced (Ezra 2:13).
- Ezra taught the people with the public reading of the Torah (Ezra 3:12).
- The temple was purified in 165 BC
- Work was completed on Herod's temple (the second temple) (Psalm 48:2) and became the center of Jewish national life.
- The second temple was destroyed by the Romans in AD 70. Jesus stated that the temple would be destroyed (Matthew 24:1–2).
- We are waiting for the third temple to be built. Somehow, peace will come to Israel and the temple will be rebuilt on the Temple Mount (Matthew 24:15; 2 Thessalonians 2:3–4; Revelation 11:1–2).

---

[13] Wiersbe, 225.

## Closing

God is still at work in our world today. He has not forgotten us, and He has not abandoned us. He never will! When the third temple is built, will you be crying out for the Lord? Will you be ready?

---

### The Daily Word

Do you ever wonder why God doesn't just stretch out His hand and cure the sick, destroy the evil in the world, or make the pain go away? By faith, you believe He can. By faith, you trust He will. By faith, you believe He has a plan. You have seen the work of His hands in the past, you have witnessed miracles, and you know the power of the Lord God Almighty. But in this moment, in this circumstance, He doesn't seem to be moving like you know He can, and you begin to feel abandoned by God.

And yet you wait. You wait and you remember the works of His hands and give thanks for the times in your life you witnessed Him perform saving acts on the earth. And you surrender your will to the Lord. You say: "*Not my will, but Your will be done.*" Because even when you don't see Him moving, the Lord God is in your midst, working in ways you cannot see. Today, hold on to the hope, be on watch, and expect the Lord's power to reign in your life for His glory.

**Why do You hold back Your hand? Stretch out Your right hand and destroy them! God my King is from ancient times, performing saving acts on the earth. —Psalm 74:11–12**

Further Scripture: Isaiah 65:24; Luke 22:42; John 5:17

---

## Questions

1. In Asaph's appeal to God in the first two verses, what series of endearing terms did he use to describe the people of God? What actions of God toward His people did Asaph ask God to remember? What did he mean by asking God to remember (Leviticus 26:42)?

2. What did the people of Judah believe about the presence of the temple despite how they lived (Jeremiah 7:4–11)?

3. In what ways can the Lord be described as King (Psalms 44:4; 93; 96:13; 97:1–6; 98:6–9; 99:1–3)?

4. What were the salvation works of the Lord from the past that Asaph was describing in verses 12–17? Are there times when you recall what God did in the past to help you through a tough situation or circumstance?

5. What are some promises in Scripture given to God's people to remind us that He will never fail us?

6. What did the Holy Spirit highlight to you in Psalm 74 through the reading or the teaching?

# Lesson 62: Psalms 75—76

*King of Glory*: It Begins and Ends in Jerusalem

## Teaching Notes

### Intro

The book of Psalms is about connecting emotionally to God and what was happening in the psalmists' lives. Psalm 76 was probably composed to "celebrate the destruction of Sennacherib's Assyrian army in 701 BC, as well as the subsequent assassination of Sennacherib himself"[1] (2 Kings 19:6–7, 36–37). MacArthur also brings to our attention that Psalm 76 points to the end times "when Jehovah will defeat His enemies and bring them into judgment."[2] Wiersbe summarizes the progress of Psalm 76 as, "The psalm begins at Jerusalem and its environs (vv. 1–6), then moves to the entire land of Israel (vv. 7–9), and now it reaches the whole earth (v. 12)."[3]

### Teaching

*Psalm 76:1–3*: Wiersbe outlines the theme of these verses as, "God Wants Us to Know Him."[4] Verses 1–2 state God is known in Jerusalem (Judah, Salem, Zion). In Jerusalem, God wiped out the enemies' weapons (v. 3). Verse 3 is the opposite of the feelings of abandonment from Psalm 74 in yesterday's lesson. In Psalm 76, God is present.

*Psalm 76:4–6*: Wiersbe outlines these verses as, "God Wants Us to Trust Him."[5] God is described as resplendent, which means to give light or be revived in Hebrew, coming down from the "mountains of prey," or from the attackers (v. 4). The enemy had been totally defeated, unable to lift a hand against God (vv. 5–6).

---

[1] John MacArthur, *The MacArthur Bible Commentary* (Nashville: Thomas Nelson, 2005), 647.

[2] MacArthur, 647.

[3] Warren W. Wiersbe, *The Bible Exposition Commentary: Job–Song of Solomon* (Colorado Springs: David C. Cook, 2004), 229.

[4] Wiersbe, 227.

[5] Wiersbe, 228.

*Psalm 76:7–9*: Wiersbe outlines these verses as, "God Wants Us to Fear Him."[6] The psalmist reflected on the victorious power of God and wrote, "You are to be feared. When You are angry, who can stand before You?" This is the theme of Psalm 76 (vv. 7, 8, 11, 12). Wiersbe summarizes verses 8–9 as, "From His throne in heaven, the Lord announced the verdict and the trial was over. There could be no appeal because God's court is the very highest and His judgment leaves the defendants speechless."[7] From Jerusalem and Israel, God's power is feared throughout the earth.

*Psalm 76:10–12*: Wiersbe outlines these verses as, "God Wants Us to Obey Him."[8] Everything will praise God, even "human wrath" (v. 10). Therefore, God's people are to keep their vows before Him and bring their tributes to Him (v. 11). Before God, even the leaders and the earthly kings were humbled (v. 12).

## Closing

In Psalm 76, the enemy has been defeated and God did all the work. The progression of Psalm 76 to cover the whole world is also seen in Acts 1:8 and Matthew 28:18–20. In the psalms, God speaks in different ways. Sometimes He speaks what is obvious, and sometimes He speaks in what is not clear.

> But you will receive power when the Holy Spirit has come on you, and you will be My witnesses in Jerusalem, in all Judea and Samaria, and to the ends of the earth. (Acts 1:8)

The command of Acts 1:8 was also the command to the Israelites—they were supposed to reflect the light of the Lord.

> Then Jesus came near and said to them, "All authority has been given to Me in heaven and on earth. Go, therefore, and make disciples of all nations, baptizing them in the name of the Father and of the Son and of the Holy Spirit, teaching them to observe everything I have commanded you. And remember, I am with you always, to the end of the age." (Matthew 28:18–20)

We are commanded to "go," "make disciples," "baptizing," and "teaching." Look at the progression of Acts 1:8 by reading through these Scriptures:

---

[6] Wiersbe, 228.

[7] Wiersbe, 228.

[8] Wiersbe, 228.

- Romans 1:16—Gospel was intended for both the Jews and the Greeks.
- John 1:11—Jesus came to the Jews who didn't receive Him.
- John 1:14—The Jews rejected Him.
- Romans 10:14–20—Presence of God started in Jerusalem and went throughout Israel, and Jesus followed the same model.
- Romans 11:25—The Jews would have their hearts hardened against Jesus until the fullness of Gentiles have come in.

I believe the Lord has a heart for the city of Jerusalem. My goal is to share the gospel wherever I go, because eventually the Jewish people will see the truth of what God's plan is for their lives. Our job is to love the Jews and minister to them in the process (Romans 15:25–27).

Ultimately, it all started in Jerusalem, it will all come back to Jerusalem, and end in Jerusalem (Zechariah 14:1–4). God will return.

## The Daily Word

Allow God's name to be known: His identity, His reputation, and His character. As a believer, the Lord entrusts you to make His name known and to love others with the same love you receive through Jesus. But first, ask yourself, *Do I really know God? Do I know God in a way that I trust Him, fear Him, and obey Him?*

Press on to *know* God, not in a scholarly way, but in an intimate-relationship way. God has given you the Holy Spirit. God deliverers you from battles, fighting off the enemy as a mighty warrior. He shatters the schemes of the enemy. His strength surpasses your knowledge. God offers grace and mercy each day through His unconditional love. Love people as Christ loves you and share His truth with others. They will even be jealous of the love you receive from the Lord as you walk through life in joy, peace, and love. The day will come when all will praise the name of the Lord, and He will be feared by the kings of the earth. Until then, press on to know God and make His name known.

**God is known in Judah; His name is great in Israel. His tent is in Salem, His dwelling place in Zion. There He shatters the bow's flaming arrows, the shield, the sword, and the weapons of war. —Psalm 76:1–3**

Further Scripture: John 13:34; Acts 1:8; Romans 10:16b–19

# Questions

1.  Many places in Scripture talk about God's name (2 Samuel 7:13). What do you think the psalmist meant by the statement in Psalm 75:1, "For Your name is near"?

2.  Read Psalm 75:7 and Romans 9:11–28. Do you think the passage in Romans is a good explanation for Psalm 75:7? Why or why not?

3.  What does the cup of wine in Psalm 75:8 represent? Where else in Scripture can you find a similar context?

4.  Do you think Psalm 76:1, "God is known in Judah," could be a messianic statement? Why or why not?

5.  The NASB version of the Bible uses the word "feared" four times in Psalm 76 in conjunction with fearing God (Psalm 76:7, 8, 11, and 12). Do you fear God? If so, in what way?

6.  What did the Holy Spirit highlight to you in Psalms 75—76 through the reading or the teaching?

# Lesson 63: Psalms 77—78

*King of Glory*: Remembering the Past, Present, and Future

## Teaching Notes

### Intro

Psalm 78 is long—72 verses long. It's a challenge to cover that much material in 30 minutes, but this is the psalm God told me to teach. And, we have to get to the end of this psalm today! The text walks through the history of Israel—a historical psalm "written to teach the children how gracious God had been in the past in spite of their ancestors' rebellion and ingratitude."[1] The point was to teach the children their past so they would not repeat the same mistakes (v. 8). However, as German philosopher Georg Hegel wrote that the one thing we learned from history is that we don't learn from history.[2] Wiersbe shares that when the writer Asaph reviewed Israel's history, he "saw a sad record of forgetfulness, faithlessness, foolishness, and failure, and he sought to understand what it all meant."[3]

### Teaching

*Psalm 78:1–8*: Wiersbe describes these verses as, "Protecting the Future."[4] Asaph told his readers to listen to these lessons (vv. 1–8). Making sure the children understood what had happened in the past was vital, so the history of their people could be passed down through the generations. We protect the future by knowing and understanding the past.

*Psalm 78:9–64*: Wiersbe describes these verses as, "Understanding the Past."[5] Verses 9–11 cover Ephraim's apostasy when they turned away from battle and did not keep God's covenant. Verses 12–39 recount Israel's sins while they were

---

[1] John MacArthur, *The MacArthur Bible Commentary* (Nashville: Thomas Nelson, 2005), 648.

[2] Warren W. Wiersbe, *The Bible Exposition Commentary: Job–Song of Solomon* (Colorado Springs: David C. Cook, 2004), 231.

[3] Wiersbe, 231.

[4] Wiersbe, 231.

[5] Wiersbe, 231.

in the wilderness. For example, the people were ungrateful for God's provision of manna in the wilderness—they wanted more from God than just manna. This pattern was reflected throughout the entire psalm. God gave the people what they needed and deserved, but they were not satisfied by His provision.

Verses 40–53 recount what happened while the Hebrews were in Egypt and the lessons they were taught there. Asaph listed the plagues God called down on Egypt so His people could be freed. Verses 54–64 recount the more recent sins of the people while they were in the Promised Land. Throughout the psalm, God's punishment was recorded against His people who kept turning away from Him in disobedience. Wiersbe points out that "sometimes God's greatest judgment is to give us what we want (vv. 21, 31, 49–50, 58–59, 62)."[6]

*Psalm 78:65–72*: Wiersbe describes these verses as, "Appreciating the Present."[7] Asaph recounted how God had shown up for Israel—He had beaten back their enemies in shame, He chose the tribe of Judah to be the lineage for the Messiah, He chose David as king (1 Samuel 17:34), and He established His sanctuary forever in Jerusalem. King David shepherded God's chosen people, Israel, with a pure heart and guided them with skillful hands (v. 72).

# Closing

There are two really unique things found in David. His loyalty and pure heart to serve the Lord is one and found in 1 Samuel 13:14, "The LORD has found a man [David] loyal to Him, and the LORD has appointed him as ruler over His people, because you [Saul] have not done what the LORD commanded." The second is when David went to fight Goliath, he put on man's idea of equipping to fight (uniform of Saul), but then David realized that God gave him the skill to be who he is as he functions with a pure heart. The "Goliaths" are going to die. God will give us the skillful hands and a pure heart if we keep our eyes on Him and remember what God has done in the past in order to protect the future.

## The Daily Word

The Israelites shared stories of God's faithfulness from one generation to the next. They shared how the Lord split the sea, led the Israelites with a cloud by day and a fiery light by night, and how He provided streams of water out of stone. These were spiritual markers in their lives, and they signified God's faithfulness. They also shared stories of their own unfaithfulness and sin toward God. And yet, the Lord was compassionate and forgiving and did not destroy them.

---

[6] Wiersbe, 232.

[7] Wiersbe, 233.

Each generation must remember and learn from the past in order to protect the future and appreciate the present. Like the Israelites, you have spiritual markers in your life. Today, what story would you share with this generation to convey God's faithfulness? Don't waste another day—share with your kids around the dinner table tonight, send an email to your grandchildren, or share a video with your extended family about God's faithfulness in your life. It may feel raw and vulnerable, but it's in those intimate, weak, tender moments of life that you receive the Lord clearly and powerfully. Do not be ashamed of your need for Him to move. God is a God who provides and redeems. The next generation will need to stand on these promises just as much as you did! Go and share your story so it won't be forgotten!

**I will declare wise sayings; I will speak mysteries from the past—things we have heard and known and that our fathers have passed down to us. We must not hide them from their children, but must tell a future generation the praises of the LORD, His might, and the wonderful works He has performed. —Psalm 78:2–4**

Further Scripture: Deuteronomy 6:5–7; Psalm 78:6–7; 1 Corinthians 10:11–12

## Questions

1. In Psalm 77:9 Asaph questioned whether God had forgotten to be gracious or had withdrawn His compassion in anger. Would that be consistent with His character? When has the enemy caused you to question the character or actions of God due to fear or other lies?

2. Psalm 77 is about remembering the deeds of the Lord. Why would it be important to remember what He has done in our past?

3. What happened when the sons of Ephraim forgot God's deeds and the miracles that He showed them (Psalm 78:9b–10)?

4. Psalm 78 recounts many of God's mighty deeds and wondrous works. What did Asaph recount about the Israelites? Where can you see the principle in 2 Timothy 2:13 throughout this chapter? How about in your own life? When have you been faithless and yet seen the faithfulness of God?

5. What did the Holy Spirit highlight to you in Psalms 77—78 through the reading or the teaching?

# Lesson 64: Psalms 79—80

*King of Glory*: Revival with the God of Israel

## Teaching Notes

### Intro

Psalm 80 is another lament psalm. The people had been removed because of apostasy—they turned away from God and looked to false idols. Therefore, this psalm is a prayer request for restoration to God. MacArthur explains, "This psalm was probably written from Jerusalem in astonishment at the captivity of the ten northern tribes in 722 B.C."[1] This is another psalm by Asaph and was meant to be sung.

### Teaching

*Psalm 80:1–3*: Wiersbe outlines these verses as, "Save Your Flock."[2] Asaph called for God, the Shepherd of Israel, to rise up to save His flock (v. 1). Asaph described God as sitting on a cherub in the Holy of Holies. This is a psalm of revival. God's presence was there, and Asaph wanted Him to make His presence known before the tribes of Ephraim, Benjamin, and Manasseh (v. 2). Asaph repeated his request that God save them by looking on them with favor (v. 3). "Look on them with favor" can also be translated as "face to shine" and referred to a king smiling on one who came before him with a request, showing the petitioner his request would be well received.[3] God is the Shepherd, He will take care of us and lack nothing (Psalm 23) and as God gathers His sheep, calling them forth, they will respond (John 10).

*Psalm 80:4–7*: Wiersbe outlines these verses as, "Pity Your People."[4] In verse 4, Asaph questioned how long God would remain angry because their prayers seem unanswered. Instead, they had received only manna of tears to eat and

---

[1] John MacArthur, *The MacArthur Bible Commentary* (Nashville: Thomas Nelson, 2005), 649.

[2] Warren W. Wiersbe, *The Bible Exposition Commentary: Job–Song of Solomon* (Colorado Springs: David C. Cook, 2004), 236.

[3] MacArthur, 642.

[4] Wiersbe, 236.

water of tears to drink (v. 5). They were quarreling with their neighbors and being mocked by their enemies (v. 6). Asaph asked again for God to save them (v. 7). The repetition of asking God to save is important to notice (vv. 3, 7) (Numbers 6:24).

*Psalm 80:8–19*: Wiersbe outlines these verses as, "Revive Your Vine."[5] Asaph moved from the image of a shepherd to a vine dresser. MacArthur explains, "The vine is a metaphor for Israel whom God delivered out of Egypt and nurtured into a powerful nation"[6] (Isaiah 5:1–7). The boundaries of Israel had been "the hill country in the south to the mighty cedars of Lebanon in the north, from the Mediterranean Sea on the west to the Euphrates on the east—and beyond."[7] These boundaries are outlined in verses 10–11. However, the walls of Israel had been broken down (v. 12). They were being taken over by the beasts and the creatures of the field (their enemies) (v. 13). Asaph asked God again to take care of the vine God had planted (vv. 14–15). Asaph cried out in desperation because of the destruction that had taken place (v. 16). Psalm 80 is a last-ditch effort of seeking God's help. MacArthur explains the phrase, "with the man at Your right hand," as "a reference to Israel. In a secondary sense, the 'son of man' may allude to the Davidic dynasty and even extend to the Messiah, since He is so frequently called by that title in the New Testament"[8] (Matthew 2:15). Asaph stated they would not turn away from God again and asked God again to revive them (v. 18). For a third time, Asaph asked that God would save them (v. 19). *Nelson's Commentary* explains, "In response to God's work of deliverance, the poet promises renewed praise centered on the name of God."[9] Verse 18 is based on verse 17. When that happens, revival takes place.

## Closing

Revival can take place when we look to Him as the God of Israel who brought forth revival. If we don't see God as the God of Israel, I question whether true revival can take place because there's a lack of a complete picture of who God is.

---

[5] Wiersbe, 237.

[6] MacArthur, 650.

[7] Wiersbe, 237.

[8] MacArthur, 650.

[9] Earl D. Radmacher, Ronald B. Allen, and H. Wayne House, eds., *Nelson's New Illustrated Bible Commentary* (Nashville: Thomas Nelson, 1999), 702.

## The Daily Word

Have you chosen to turn away from the Lord? Have you given in to temptation? Do you try and live life in your flesh by your own strength? Do you believe in God but don't really include Him in your everyday life? Have you slipped further and further away from God? Do you realize you are in desperate need for the Lord to save you and restore you?

*You are never too far gone.* God is able to restore. He is able to save. God is all-powerful and loves you unconditionally. However, you must be willing to repent and turn back to Him. You are the only one who can make this decision. If you are ready, say, "*Yes, Lord, I'm willing to turn to You.*" Then, in faith, turn away from your sin and turn toward God. Receive His grace and mercy. Find refreshment and revival for your soul in His presence. Take steps by faith and believe He will bring you restoration and strength. Make that choice today as you trust God's great love.

**Rally your power and come to save us. Restore us, God; look on us with favor, and we will be saved. —Psalm 80:2–3**

Further Scripture: Numbers 6:24–26; Amos 9:14; Acts 3:19

## Questions

1. When you read Psalm 79:5–6, do you think this could be a current cry from Israel today? Why?
2. In Psalm 80, the phrase, "Turn us again, O God, and cause Your face to shine, and we shall be saved," is repeated three times. Why do you think the psalmist did this? Should this be a cry for today? Why or why not?
3. Meditate on Psalm 80:17. Was this speaking of Jesus the Messiah? Why or why not?
4. What did the Holy Spirit highlight to you in Psalms 79—80 through the reading or the teaching?

# Lesson 65: Psalms 81—82

*King of Glory*: Remember What God Has Overcome!

## Teaching Notes

### Intro

Psalms 81—82 are very different. They are set apart from each other, but both psalms are from Asaph. I believe these psalms are a cry for a revival. I think we are all crying out for revival. I would love to see a people—a nation—turn back to God! We are experiencing a time of extreme divisiveness, yet God can orchestrate things we haven't imagined. Read 1 Chronicles 16:1–5 as a qualifier and backdrop for Asaph.

One thing we see pointed out in Scripture is that there are certain people who are gifted with certain things. I would call Asaph a worship leader—a wonderful worship leader who was recognized to have a gift. There are people today similarly gifted with the gift of worship. I consider worship the *satisfier* of the soul. People who are gifted with worship tend to be the first to understand soul trouble. Asaph recognized there was trouble, and he lamented with a cry for revival. He went from lamenting in chapter 81 to being hopeful God would do great things in chapter 82.

Sometimes our separation from God is a soul entrenchment of the enemy when we get our eyes fixed on other things. God knows remedies for how to get our souls back into a place where we are looking with expectation to the things of God. Worship can be a remedy for lament and discouragement.

### Teaching

*Psalm 81:1–7*: Throughout this psalm, Asaph says he remembered and knew God was their strength, redeemer, and lifter. Verse 6, "I removed his shoulder from the burden" refers to the deliverance of Israel from slavery. Many believe the pots from which they were delivered were the brick laying pots in Egypt. Asaph then referred to "the secret place of thunder." Many times, when you read about thunder and lightning in the Bible, it is followed by the voice of God.

The waters of Meribah were where Moses struck a rock and water flowed from it. God gets offended when He delivers us from our bondages and we complain about the circumstances. Asaph reminds the Israelites what God had saved them from and how God provided for them. Asaph is saying, "Remember!"

When we remember God, our tears will dry because we know He answers our prayers and brings life. At the end of these verses, we see the word "Selah." When I see this word, I always stop and think about what I've just read. This time of reflection is where healing begins, and God calls us back to worship.

*Psalm 81:8–16*: You can hear the lament in these verses. I believe the key verse is verse 13, where Asaph wrote, "Oh that my people had harkened unto me, and Israel had walked in my ways!" The Israelites thought the comfort in their life was going to bring pleasure instead of relying on God as provider and strength.

The book of Psalms often becomes a comfort creature that we just read through, but it is important to stop and remember how God had overcome. This should encourage us to remember how God has overcome when we're despairingly hopeless. When I stop and think about what God has overcome in my life, it might not change my circumstance, but it dries my tears and brings hope. When I start to remember what God has done in my life, my soul begins to stir with refreshment, and I get excited about the future. It feels like strength that has returned after sickness.

In verse 14, you can really see the Lord lamenting not being able to show Himself strong because the people had turned off course. I don't think the Israelites despised God. I think they forgot what God had done for them. I love that verse 16 shows God had greater plans for the Israelites. Who is our rock today? Our rock is Christ. Asaph pointed out that it's not the rock that satisfies but what comes from the rock! I want us to pay attention to the movement here. It took a worship leader to say, "I recognize where we are, but follow me, and let's set a new tone so we may worship God. Remember where we've come from." I love what worship leaders can do. They can take us to where we were, remind us what God has done, and lead us to praise.

*Psalm 82:1–2*: This psalm is not connected to the previous one. It came from another situation—a psalm from Asaph from different circumstances. God will judge the powerful people, those who rule over anything (Job 12:16–23).

God operates in a realm of truth. God doesn't meddle with our lives. Our disobedience sets us on a different path than the one God originally intended. When we walk in our comfort, it takes us out of the path of righteousness. There is a nature to God that makes truth supreme. He doesn't play favorites. He guards His truth, defending those who love His truth, punishing them who disregard it.

*Psalm 82:3–8*: I don't believe God has to get up every day and keeps the universe going. God has ordered the universe to continue, and it follows that instruction until it gets a new one. We were ordered in the same way, but have a filter, our mind, which takes us to the places where we see what God wants to do. God has a big-picture purpose and understanding. God was saying the problem is that things are out of order—it was not His plan to have poor, needy, oppressed, and destitute peoples. We, as Christ followers, are supposed to reorder the light bringing things back into the context of what God had originally planned. God, though Asaph, began the process of worship.

## Closing

In the final verse, Asaph said, "God don't let our falling apart be Your falling apart. I know you can do great things. God, do Your work. Don't let us be a hindrance." When we worship, God can change our laments into dancing. I'm trusting our cry is the same as verse 8. We want to see God's kingdom come, but let it begin in my life.

---

## The Daily Word

The Lord promises His people He will provide. He says, "I am Yahweh." He is the Lord God. The Lord God delivered you from wherever you were before accepting Jesus. The Israelites were in slavery in Egypt, and the Lord brought them back to Israel. He said, "Remember I am your God, and I delivered you and will provide for you. You need to *open your mouth*, and then I will fill it." God promises the same deliverance and provision for you.

To fix your eyes on Jesus, you must face Him. As you do, naturally, your mouth will face Him. Open your mouth. Surrender. Acknowledge your weakness and expect Him to give you strength. The Lord promises to *fill you up*. He promises to *provide for you*. He provides because He cares, He knows, and He has the power to do so. Today, turn to the Lord your God, seeking Him first. In humility, open your mouth. And as you do, you will walk in His promises for your life beyond anything you can imagine.

**I am Yahweh your God, who brought you up from the land of Egypt. Open your mouth wide, and I will fill it. —Psalm 81:10**

Further Scripture: Psalm 81:11–13; Matthew 6:31–33; 2 Peter 1:3

---

## Questions

1.  Psalm 81:7 states, "I proved you at the waters of Meribah." What is meant by God having proved them? Where else in Scripture is Meribah mentioned and in what context (Exodus 17:7)?

2.  Do you think Psalm 81:11–12 is a picture of the modern church's spiritual condition? Why or why not?

3.  In your own words, what does "all the foundations of the earth are out of course" in Psalm 82:5 mean? Is this true for today?

4.  What did the Holy Spirit highlight to you in Psalms 81—82 through the reading or the teaching?

# Lesson 66: Psalm 83

*King of Glory*: I Have to Hear God's Voice

## Teaching Notes

### Intro

Someone said if you read five psalms a day, you'll read the book of Psalms in a month. Fred calls the Psalms the "mental health" book of the Bible. Further, if you want to learn to love God with all your heart, soul, strength, and mind, you need the Psalms. When we break down Psalm 83, we'll see we've probably experienced everything mentioned in this psalm.

### Teaching

*Psalm 83:1–4*: In verse 1, the psalmist gave a command (request) to God by expressing what he needed. He begged God not to remain silent but to speak to him. He needed God to listen to him. He asked God not to remain aloof from him. Is there anything more practical than these requests? When you look back over your life, were there times when you felt God was distant? That He wasn't listening to you? That He wasn't speaking to you? Maybe the psalmist felt God was distant and not hearing him because he was so tuned in to what people said about him—their plots and their growling against him. Isn't that like the human spirit? Doesn't it bother us a lot when people talk against us?

Second Chronicles 20 listed the nations that plotted together against Judah. When the Moabites, Ammonites, and Meunites waged war against Jehoshaphat, he proclaimed a fast and led the people to seek the Lord. This is a very important step for us. The moment we get alarmed, we need to calm down and seek the Lord. Psalm 83 encourages us to decide whom we will listen to. Will we be focused on the enemy or will we be focused on the Lord? In 2 Chronicles 20:14, when the fast ended, the spirit of the Lord came upon Jahaziel, a descendant of Asaph, the writer of this psalm. This is the connection between 2 Chronicles 20 and Psalm 83. After Jehoshaphat had prayed and consulted the people, he "appointed men to sing to the Lord and to praise him" as they led the army into battle (2 Chronicles 20:21). In Psalm 83, they were remembering that praise won the battle.

*Psalm 83:5–10*: The Edomites, Philistines, and Assyrians formed an alliance against them. The psalmist asked God to "do to them as you did to Midian" (v. 9). His request called to mind the days of the judges—of Gideon (Judges 7) and Deborah (Judges 4). This psalm emphasizes that God can do so much with so little. We don't need a vast army or strong fighters. God can use the weak, the unexpected, the choir to praise, and God can use the 300 over the 32,000 (Gideon's small army of 300 from the 32,000 who originally responded to his call). The psalmist prayed for God to speak, to do something. I wonder if we would have the same presence of mind to demand the voice of God. We don't need a vast army because we have a God who speaks. In Genesis 1, God spoke and all of creation came into being. As you move on, there would be no Abraham without the voice of God. There would be no Moses without the voice of God in a burning bush. There would be no Joseph without the voice of God through an angel in a dream. There would be no Mary without the voice of God. You'll never experience the purpose of your life without the voice of God. When God is working, through His voice, anything can happen.

How can you and I, today, hear the voice of God? The list could be endless, but here are a few ways:

*God speaks through prayer.* God's voice is particularly strong and clear in the morning. Are you committed to prayer, to spending time with God listening to Him?

*God speaks through Scripture.* If God ever says anything that violates His Scripture, then it's not God. Everything He says has to go back to Scripture, which is God-breathed and useful (2 Timothy 3:16–17). Scripture will help you figure out God's voice.

*God speaks through His Holy Spirit.* In the book of Acts, in the moment when a person was filled with the Holy Spirit, their ability to communicate was completely changed. Invite the Holy Spirit into your life to speak to you.

*God speaks through the church.* Hebrews 10:25 instructs believers not to forsake assembling together. We can't give up meeting with one another "all the more as you see the day approaching." We've got to be together.

*God speaks through important people in our lives.* We should pick out five people in our lives who love us and whom we trust so we can turn to them. We need to find mentors—people who can speak to us before we make major decisions.

*God speaks through creation.* Many people say God speaks to them when they are out on the water, so they don't go to church. Of course, God is speaking to them on the water—He is constantly speaking. We can't be out looking at the stars or the sunset or noticing the things around us without hearing God speak. When you see the stars, you begin to see that God is infinite. There's no other place to see the tremendous order of God but through His creation.

*God speaks through our talents and the talents of others.* As you begin to serve, to love, to use your gifts, God will begin to direct you into other places. Remember, it's easier to steer a moving car than one that is sitting still. When we're moving, God can begin to steer us in certain directions. It's easier to hear His voice. When you wonder if you're hearing from Him, God will continue to tell you. God will repeat Himself.

*God speaks through worship.* Worship is surrender. Every time we worship, we say to God, "I'm not in charge, You are." When we begin to worship, God speaks in a big way into our lives.

*God speaks through circumstances.* If you got quiet, you could think of a number of ways God speaks. Do you have a longing for His voice, to be in His presence, to be directed by God?

*Psalm 83:16–18*: After a long list of ways the psalmist wanted God to act, he said: "Cover their faces with shame, Lord, so that they will seek your name" (v. 16). Then psalmist then concluded: "Let them know that you, whose name is the Lord—that you alone are the Most High over all the earth (v. 18). Even as the psalmist called God to act against the enemy, he was calling for God to change their hearts—to help them to know Him and turn toward Him.

## Closing

Asaph was a man who knew his history, who knew what God had done in his life, and he wasn't ashamed to tell the story of what God had done not only in his life but in the life of history. Have you shared the stories of what God has done in your life with your kids and grandkids? They need to hear it over and over again.

## The Daily Word

As a follower of Christ, the Holy Spirit dwells in you and speaks to you. As a believer, you hear God's voice in various ways—through prayer, Scripture, dreams, visions, other believers, and creation. But here's the deal . . . you must be intentional to hear God's voice. The concept is similar to your inability to steer a car while it's sitting idle. The car won't steer until you have the key turned on, the car in gear, and begin to move forward. *To hear the Lord's voice in your life, you need to walk with Him.* Trust in Him with all your heart and intentionally acknowledge the Lord in your life. Then He will answer you and direct your steps.

But remember the enemy has a voice as well. It can be loud—telling you lies and luring you into disbelief. Be on guard and intentionally ask the Lord to not be silent. When you call upon Him, He promises He will answer you. God has victory over the voice of the enemy, and you have the power to tell the voice of the enemy to stop in Jesus' name. Today, may you hear the voice of the Lord guiding you in truth.

**God, do not keep silent. Do not be deaf, God; do not be idle. See how Your enemies make an uproar; those who hate You have acted arrogantly. —Psalm 83:1–2**

Further Scripture: Proverbs 3:5–6; Isaiah 30:21; John 14:16–17

## Questions

1. According to Psalm 83:2–4, the enemies of God made plans against His people, to wipe them out as a nation. When in recent history have you seen this same mindset? If possible, research how many times in history people have conspired against the Jews in an attempt to remove or annihilate them (http://www.eretzyisroel.org/~jkatz/expulsions.html). Does this prejudice and hatred still exist today?

2. What were the motivations of those who conspired against the Jews in Psalm 83 (Psalm 83:4, 5, 12)?

3. Psalm 83:12–13 says people who seek to possess the pastures of God will be like what (Psalm 1:4)? Who else will suffer the same outcome? Why do you think that is?

4. Compare Psalms 83:2 and 83:18. Who is exalted in these two verses? How can we exalt the Lord in our lives?

5. What did the Holy Spirit highlight to you in Psalm 83 through the reading or the teaching?

# Lesson 67: Psalm 84

*King of Glory*: Celebrating the Journey

## Teaching Notes

### Intro

I've enjoyed studying the book of Psalms, possibly more than any of the books we've studied so far. I think the reason I've personally enjoyed it is because so much of it focuses on Jerusalem—the earthly city of the Lord and the heavenly city of the Lord. Psalm 84 is considered a Psalm of Ascent and seems a little out of character from the other psalms it's placed with. The other Psalms of Ascent are Psalms 120—134.[1] However, Psalm 84 does not carry the subtitle of ascension that Psalms 120—134 do. MacArthur states this psalm, like the other ascent psalms, "expresses the joy of a pilgrim traveling up to Jerusalem, then up into the temple to celebrate one of the feasts . . . being in the very presence of the Lord God."[2]

Male Jews were required to go to the temple during three holy festivals (Exodus 23:17; 34:23), which reminded "them that they were still pilgrims on this earth" who were returning home.[3] The connection of Psalm 84 with the other Psalms of Ascent is found in verse 7: "They go from strength to strength; each appears before God in Zion." Zion is another title for Jerusalem.

Wiersbe explains, "The phrase 'appears before God in Zion' suggests that this psalm was penned by a Jewish man who could not go to Jerusalem to celebrate one of the three annual feasts."[4]

### Teaching

*Psalm 84:1–4*: Wiersbe describes these four verses as, "My Delight Is in the Lord."[5] The psalmist remembered God's temple and described it as lovely (Psalm

---

[1] John MacArthur, *The MacArthur Bible Commentary* (Nashville: Thomas Nelson, 2005), 652.

[2] MacArthur, 652.

[3] Warren W. Wiersbe, *The Bible Exposition Commentary: Job–Song of Solomon* (Colorado Springs: David C. Cook, 2004), 242.

[4] Wiersbe, 242.

[5] Wiersbe, 242.

26:8). This writer was one of the sons of Korah, who were the gatekeepers for the temple. While the Jews understood that God's presence was only in the temple, God does not reside in a box or a building, and His presence is everywhere (Acts 7:47–50). The psalmist longed for God (v. 2). As we grow in the Lord and experience His presence, the more we will long to go to a different spiritual level with Him. MacArthur points out, "The psalmist admires these birds who were able to build their nests in the temple courtyards, near the altars of God" (v. 3).[6] How happy are those who praise God continually (v. 4).

*Psalm 84:5–8*: Wiersbe describes verses 5–8 as, "My Strength Is in the Lord."[7] The psalmist then began to reflect on the practical issues of going up to Jerusalem. The psalmist pointed out those on the journey drew their strength from God (v. 5). During the journey, even in the valleys or the low points, God would provide spring water and autumn rains for them (v. 6), moving from one of God's provisions (strength) to another. About verse 7, MacArthur writes, "The anticipation of joyously worshipping God in Jerusalem overcame the pilgrims' natural weariness in their difficult journey."[8] This is a cool picture of finding strength from the Lord during the journey.

revive SCHOOL has been a tough journey for us. For two years, we've been in this little room, hammering out the Word of God—doing something that is not our norm, communicating and editing it in ways we've never done before, and this is just what you see. Outside of what is seen is the prep work. If I do not have strength in Him, this journey could not even have been started, much less continue on as it has. But even though the journey is hard, we know God is refining us for the end. This will be a weird image, but I study a ton on the bathroom floor in my bedroom. I sit on the floor with my back against the wall, my highlighters on the floor next to me, with my iPad and papers all around me, and I study the Word. It's hard at 4 a.m. or 12:30 a.m. to do that. This is my reality of going through this journey, and I know God is preparing me for Jerusalem whether here in the earthly state of preparing for the coming days or in the heavenly state of Jerusalem. My eyes are always on the pilgrimage of experience more of the Lord. While I was studying, I asked the Lord to show me Psalm 84 in the New Testament. The Lord gave me multiple illustrations and told me to talk about Jesus.

In Luke 9, Jesus knew His time on earth was coming to an end. Verse 51 states the time was coming for Jesus to be taken up to heaven, so Jesus journeyed to Jerusalem. On the journey, Jesus sent messengers ahead to get things ready

---

[6] MacArthur, 652.

[7] Wiersbe, 243.

[8] MacArthur, 652.

for Him in Samaria, but they did not welcome Him because He was going to Jerusalem (v. 53). When the Samaritans didn't welcome Him, James and John were ready to destroy the village, but Jesus rebuked them and went on to another village (vv. 54–56). Sometimes during the journey, pilgrims are rejected, routes are changed, and the journey isn't easy.

*Psalm 84:9–12*: Wiersbe describes verses 9–12 as, "My Trust Is in the Lord."[9]

# Closing

On Jesus' final journey to Jerusalem, He met blind Bartimaeus whom He healed (Luke 18:35–43). Then Jesus met Zacchaeus the tax collector and saved him, passed Herod's palace in Jericho, and climbed up a difficult 18-mile ascent in the Judean wilderness to Jerusalem. We always want the journey to be smooth and easy, but Jesus' journey was neither. Experiencing God's presence happens in the journey. Jesus' journey continued by the inn of the good Samaritan, of which Jesus told the parable of the man who was beaten up by thieves (Luke 10:30). Jesus' parable told of the Samaritan man who stopped and helped the Jewish man, even putting the man on his own horse, taking him to the inn, and paying for his care. No matter what happens on the journey, God is there to pick us up and provide our care. Our journey with God may be much harder than we anticipate. But, according to Psalm 84:7, we can journey from strength to strength to get through it and flourish. We survive the journey when we depend upon the Holy Spirit.

## The Daily Word

Happiness. How do you find it? The world seems to have all the answers to finding happiness. But in reality, happiness by the world's standards will fade away. Those who spend time in the Lord's presence, praising Him continually, are truly happy. You find happiness when you find your strength in the Lord along your journey. You are happy when you trust in God alone. Relationships on earth will wither, disappoint, and fade away. Things on this earth will rust and get destroyed. The Lord provides many good gifts for you to enjoy, but they are not meant to fulfill your happiness. Therefore, set your mind on the Lord, set your mind on His kingdom, and spend time in His presence.

If you make decisions based on what makes you the happiest, stop. Happiness will not be found in that one thing for very long. Make your decision with the Lord's guidance, His Word, and His truth. Call to Him, and He will answer

---

[9] Wiersbe, 243.

you. He is your helper. Today, do not search out for happiness. Instead, seek the Lord's will for your life.

**How happy are those who reside in Your house, who praise You continually. Happy are the people whose strength is in You, whose hearts are set on pilgrimage. —Psalm 84:4–5**

Further Scripture: Psalm 32:8; 84:11–12; 1 Peter 1:24–25a

## Questions

1. Why do you think the house of God was so dear to the psalmist (Psalm 26:8)? What was the language he used to describe the house of God in Psalm 84:1–2?

2. Three times in this Psalm, the psalmist mentioned being happy or blessed. What was he describing using these specific words? Do these three things describe you?

3. What was the motivation of the people whose "hearts are set on pilgrimage" (Psalm 84:5) to the temple? Are you joyful when you are going to church or about to fellowship with other believers?

4. After asking God to hear his prayer in verse eight, what petition did the psalmist make? Why do you think he was asking for prayer for the king/anointed one (2 Samuel 7)? How often do you pray for those in authority, not just those you agree with but also those you don't (1 Timothy 2:1–4)?

5. Compare Psalm 84:10 with Matthew 6:33 and Philippians 1:21. Where is the emphasis on all these verses?

6. What did the Holy Spirit highlight to you in Psalm 84 through the reading or the teaching?

# Lesson 68: Psalm 85

*King of Glory*: Prayer for Revival

## Teaching Notes

### Intro

I am excited to teach this psalm because verse 6 is *the* verse about revival. We are reviveSCHOOL—it's just exciting! This psalm is written by the sons of Korah. The sons of Korah were entrusted with the holy objects, the best of the best. They eventually turned against the Lord. Those writing these psalms were the remnants who still obeyed the Lord. Who better to write about a need for revival? Who better to understand the need for family redemption?

This psalm was probably written after the Jewish people returned to their land after the 70 years of captivity in Babylon (Jeremiah 29). They had experienced captivity and now they were experiencing freedom.

### Teaching

*Psalm 85:1–3*: The first thing the psalmist did was give thanks to the Lord. This is key to the area of revival. Once you have been set free you have to thank the Lord for it. Thankfulness helps you to overcome the mentality of staying in bondage. When you have a heart of gratitude it keeps you from going back to the captive mentality. When you thank the Lord, it helps to fight all the things of the past.

God was giving the Promised Land back to the Israelites. The people were given their land and their identity back. Their guilt had been taken away. The crazy thing was that all of this was predicted in Isaiah 40:1–2. Obviously, these words were intended for the Israelites, but when was the last time you thanked God for your salvation or your house. If you want to understand true revival, it's a heart of thankfulness.

*Psalm 85:4–7*: Wiersbe stated that in these verses, the psalmist asked for renewed life.[1] Even though the Israelites were now free they still needed restoration and revival. *Nelson's Commentary* states, "God's anger had turned away from the people. Yet until the restoration is complete, the people still feel the effects of God's wrath .

---

[1] John MacArthur, *The MacArthur Bible Commentary* (Nashville: Thomas Nelson, 2005), 648.

. . the people's troubles were due to their own sin disciplined by God."[2] The psalmist asked, "Will you not revive us again so that Your people may rejoice in you?" Revive means to live again, to be renewed in life. Charles G. Finny wrote, "Revival is a renewed conviction of sin and repentance, followed by an intense desire to live in obedience to God. It is giving up one's will to God in deep humility."[3]

We all need to be revived again continually. It is a constant cycle. This is why Paul would go to the same cities over and over again. There are a lot of believers who claim to be Christians in the United States who say "we used to do that" or "we used to read this." My calling is to fan that flame so Christians will fall in love again with the gospel.

> Be alert and strengthen what remains, which is about to die, for I have not found your works complete before My God. Remember, therefore, what you have received and heard; keep it, and repent. But if you are not alert, I will come like a thief, and you have no idea at what hour I will come against you. (Revelation 3:2–3)

Revival happens when you realize God's given you something but you're not doing anything with it. I think this an incredible picture of the church.

*Psalm 85:8–13*: The psalmist vowed to listen for God's words. Once you've been renewed, you ask God for direction and listen to His message.

## Closing

Kyle's closing prayer:

> Lord, I want to pray that You would just allow us to see what we've been given. Open our eyes and our ears to the truth. Thank You for salvation of me, my family, and my team. Thank You for Jesus dying on the cross! Going through the death, burial, and resurrection. We would not be here today without You. Because of who I am in Christ I need to be renewed and revived every day. God, may I not become stagnant or worldly. May I not give into the ways of Satan. May I truly be revived by You. That is what I am asking for, for all those listening, or reading this now. May we realize what we've been given, and that time is too short. I ask that You awaken the spirit and the soul of man. I ask please renew us, so we can reflect You! Revive

---

[2] Earl D. Radmacher, Ronald B. Allen, and H. Wayne House, eds., *Nelson's New Illustrated Bible Commentary* (Nashville: Thomas Nelson, 1999), 704.

[3] Duke Taber, "10 Fantastic Charles Finney Quotes," Viral Believer, https://www.viralbeliever.com/charles-finney-quotes/.

the students of reviveSCHOOL! May we have a spirit of thankfulness. Take away the barriers and the wall and speak to us.

True revival is when the church listens to the Holy Spirit. When we listen to the Holy Spirit, I truly believe we will do what You've asked us to do. Father God, forgive us for not doing the things You've told us to do. Forgive us for holding onto the gospel. Forgive us for holding on to Jesus. We know that You have clearly asked us to share the truth. I ask for forgiveness for the church. Awaken us to the truth of the gospel. May we be people who share what we've been given. Holy Spirit, speak to any one of us and show us what You want us to do. Father, please direct us. May we be like the sons of Korah, learning from the past and not giving into the ways of the world. Father, we need help and direction.

Oh God, revive us again! Our nation needs a revival. I don't know what it is going to take, but I am asking for a national move of Your Spirit. May it start with me, my team, and those listening. I long to see a third great awakening. If there is any way any of us can see or experience that, I ask it would happen. Not for selfish motives but for the harvest. God revive this country and start with the church. In Jesus name we pray, Amen.

## The Daily Word

"Will You not revive us *again*, Lord?" Do you ever wonder if the Lord thinks to Himself: *Seriously, how many times do I need to revive you? I'm tired of you continuing to turn away from Me to other gods and the things of this world. And then you turn back to Me and I revive you again. And the cycle continues.*

The crazy thing is, the Lord doesn't think like that. That's our human perspective—not feeling worthy to receive His redemptive love. Your heavenly Father stands with open arms and a heart full of love and compassion saying, "Welcome back, child of Mine. I love you. Welcome back, child."

The Lord will revive you again. He forgives you. No matter where you are today, turn back to the Lord. Thank Him for His amazing grace and faithful love. Ask Him to forgive you, and then listen to His message for you and follow His ways. It's time to wake up to the truth. Stop living for yourself. Turn back to the Lord and allow Him to renew your mind and revive your life. Today, pray for the church to wake up.

**Will You not revive us again so that Your people may rejoice in You?**
**—Psalm 85:6**

Further Scripture: 2 Chronicles 7:14; James 4:8; 1 John 3:1

# Questions

1. If you have been through a time of failure or maybe even discipline from the Lord, what are some instructions given in this Psalm you can follow?

2. How did the psalmist show his thankfulness to God in Psalm 85:2 (Psalm 32:1–11)? How has this powerful truth affected your walk with the Lord? Are there still sins you are holding on to you know the Lord is asking you to repent from?

3. What was the meaning behind what the psalmist pleas to the Lord in Psalm 85:6? Where does new life come from (Ezekiel 36:25–27; Zechariah 4:6; John 6:63)? When should we pray for revival (Psalm 85:1–5)? Who should we be praying for?

4. How did the psalmist describe the salvation God brings to His people (John 1:14, 17)?

5. What did the Holy Spirit highlight to you in Psalm 85 through the reading or the teaching?

# Lesson 69: Psalms 86—87

## *King of Glory*: God Is in the Highs and Lows

## Teaching Notes

### Intro

The psalms were either written while the writer was experiencing the height of joy or a pit or valleys of sadness and despair. There are psalms that are confident and others that make you say, "Oh, my." Just reading through and teaching the book of Psalms has been fun because the psalms are so real.

In my life, I've had some really high highs and some really low lows. If I had written down my thoughts, I might not have had the flowery words, but I think the sentiment would be the same. As I read through the psalms, I realize I think the same way. We are going to start in Psalm 86. I realize some are coming to this study experiencing highs while others are experiencing lows. The word of God will speak to both.

### Teaching

*Psalm 86:1–7*: David was crying out to the Lord, asking for provision and mercy. How many of you can relate to these first seven verses? Have you been in a situation where you are miserable or in pain? I have! Pain brings an emotional response. The psalms to me are soul expressions written out of emotion. While I know God is good, I have to bring my own understanding of God, my own reasoning, and stay faithful.

God is never closer than when He is necessary! This isn't a prayer of contentment; this is a cry of anguish. I love the idea of bringing my humanity to the Lord and Him coming back asking, "Do you trust me? Do you believe me? Do you think I am here? Do you think I listen?" All of these things tend to build a relationship between the Spirit of God and my soul. I think David was an excellent writer.

*Psalm 86:8–11*: David wanted God's attention, but he didn't want God to think he did not trust the Lord. The part that speaks to me is when David wrote, "Unite my heart to fear thy name." When I hear words like these, I hear David asking, "Please come through this with me. I don't want to mess up my trust here, but I don't understand. Teach me thy way. Help me to see how it looks for You. Take away the things that would say God doesn't care or has abandoned you. Bring my reasoning together with what I know of who You are. If You're satisfied, I am satisfied."

In the midst of my personal pain, I had to focus on others who had it worse than me. That was how I could compensate. If I know God delivers me, and I am satisfied He hears me, because He says He does, I am going to stop agonizing and ask for healing. So, I look at these things thinking about what it would have been like for David. I can't imagine what he went through, but when I see a psalm like this one, I see David's heart for the Lord.

*Psalm 86:12–13*: David praised the Lord and glorified His name. I regard this as David saying, "I look and remember what You have done for me. Thank You!" There is a thankfulness here, yet David still made his case to God. He was struggling. I don't think he was in pain, but he had a sorrow of heart as enemies were pursuing him.

*Psalm 86:14–17*: The proud and the assemblies of violent men were after David. David prayed, "Give me strength and hope. Show me that something is happening for my good." I know there are those listening who are crying out to God, do you hear? Understand? or care? I pray that God would be of help and that God will care for those of you who are listening and need to hear from God right now. I've been so blessed, and yet I deal with hard and painful things.

These psalms help me to be more honest in my prayers. Psalms are very personal, which is why they are so relatable. Pain and suffering are a part of our story. You don't see David doubting God's goodness. I believe that today someone needs to hear this: You can call on God and tell Him anything you like. He is not going to be overwhelmed with your situation. His Holy Spirit that can visit and comfort you, bringing wisdom and understanding. I encourage you today to let God speak to you. Cry out. He hears your prayers.

*Psalm 87:1–3*: I can't leave out Psalm 87 because Israel and Jerusalem are a central part of this ministry. This is a psalm from the sons of Korah and is a beautiful stand-alone psalm. Verse 2 states, "The LORD loveth the gates of Zion more than all the dwellings of Jacob." Zion represents Jerusalem. It seems to say that God has a central city, He loves all Israel, but there is a city He holds in an especially high regard. What does Jerusalem mean? Teacher of Peace. Teacher of peace means standard, or emblem. God loves Jerusalem more than all the rest of Israel.

It says in Psalm 76:1–2, "In Judah God is known; His name is great in Israel. In Salem also is His tabernacle, and His dwelling place in Zion" (KJV). Salem is Jerusalem.

*Psalm 87:4–6*: God started out with a covenant with Israel that has expanded to other believers. From the surrounding nations, those who know God will be counted citizens of Jerusalem. They will be considered birthright citizens. God Himself will secure and provide for Jerusalem.

*Psalm 87:7*: This verse shows how God set Israel apart. Israel still plays a major role in the prophetic part of the last days. They're going to get their Messiah. Everything hinges and springs out of Zion, because Christ is the representation of Zion.

The first place Salem (Zion) is mentioned is in Genesis 14:18–20. "And Melchizedek king of Salem brought forth bread and wine: and he was the priest of the most high God. And he blessed him, and said, Blessed be Abram of the most high God, possessor of heaven and earth: And blessed be the most high God, which hath delivered thine enemies into thy hand. And he gave him tithes of all" (KJV).

Hebrews 7:1–3 is another place that talks about Melchizedek:

> For this Melchisedec, king of Salem, priest of the most high God, who met Abraham returning from the slaughter of the kings, and blessed him; to whom also Abraham gave a tenth part of all; first being by interpretation King of righteousness, and after that also King of Salem, which is, King of peace; Without father, without mother, without descent, having neither beginning of days, nor end of life; but made like unto the Son of God; abideth a priest continually.

I don't see any humans who could fit this description. This psalm has clues that tie into the plans of God. God is going to play everything out thought this tiny nation of Jerusalem, which no one can destroy.

## Closing

Understand these two chapters do not go together. I have spoken on two chapters that are very different, and yet the Holy Spirit has revealed a connection between the two. The God who has written Psalm 87 is the same God who sees me in Psalm 86. The same God who put a plan in place for thousands of years is the same God who knows my name. That is the beauty of these chapters. Even in pain and suffering, God is glorious! He is the strength that lifts us up!

## The Daily Word

Ask yourself: *Is my whole source of joy in the Lord?* Rather than living dry and weary, let the living water of the Lord be your whole source for joy. He alone can satisfy your heart.

May all things in life funnel and filter their way through the Lord. May He deliver you from the pit and pull you out with His compassion and graciousness. The Lord will be slow to anger, rich in truth, and faithful to love. That's who God is. Let the river of His great love and the streams of His grace and mercy flow together as the one true source of joy. Stop looking elsewhere. Stop looking for some joy from the things of this world, some joy from temporary pleasures, some joy from earthly relationships, and then some joy from Jesus. Instead, let the Lord be the source of joy through everything. And once you discover the Lord as your whole source for joy, it will make you want to dance!

**Singers and dancers alike will say, "My whole source of joy is in you."**
**—Psalm 87:7**

Further Scripture: Psalm 86:13; Isaiah 58:11; 2 Corinthians 3:5

## Questions

1. In Psalm 86:11, David wrote, "Teach me thy way, O LORD; I will walk in thy truth: unite my heart to fear thy name" (KJV). Have you ever prayed a prayer like this? Are God's ways always our ways?

2. How is God's truth different from our truth? Are we supposed to be afraid of God and, if so, in what sense?

3. David asked for a sign in Psalm 86:17. Have you ever asked God for a sign? Do you think it's OK to ask God for specific signs under the New Testament (Judges 6:36–40; Matthew 12:39; Romans 8:14; 1 Corinthians 1:22; 2 Corinthians 5:7)?

4. What or where is Psalm 87 talking about when it refers to Zion (Hebrews 11:9–10; Revelation 21:10–27)?

5. What did the Holy Spirit highlight to you in Psalms 86—87 through the reading or the teaching?

# Lesson 70: Psalm 88

*King of Glory*: A Cry of Desperation

## Teaching Notes

### Intro

We can interact with Scripture in a number of different ways: we can study Scripture; we can sing Scripture (which is commanded in Scripture); we can meditate on Scripture; we can simply read Scripture; we can pray Scripture back to God; we can hear Scripture when others read it. Originally, more people would listen to the Word of God rather than reading it. We can memorize Scripture. This one is often missed—we're commanded to write out Scripture in Deuteronomy 17:18. Another way we can interact with Scripture is speed reading in order to get volume in. Varying the way that we interact with Scripture can help us grow spiritually.

### Teaching

*Psalm 88:1–9*: This psalm is universally known as the dark psalm—the saddest in Scripture. Verse 1 contains the most positive statement in the psalm: "You are the God who saves me." The psalmist asked God to listen to his cries (v. 2). He could have asked God to save him or to speak to him, but he simply asked God to listen to him. The great thing about God is that when He's not speaking, He's listening.

The psalmist was overwhelmed to the point that he felt like he was dying (v. 3). His reference to the pit was a reference to Sheol or the grave (v. 4). He was without strength (v. 4). He felt forgotten and cut off from God (v. 5). He felt God had placed him in the lowest pit (v. 6), and felt the heaviness of God's wrath (v. 7). Grief often comes in waves, sometimes minute by minute, to overwhelm us. He was lonely (v. 8). He could not escape his grief (v. 9a). But he called out to God every day (v. 9b) to tell Him how he felt.

*Psalm 88:10–14*: The psalmist wanted to know if God's wonders could be known by someone who was dead (v. 10). Could someone facing such despair and darkness know God's love and faithfulness (vv. 11–12). Despite his grief, the psalmist cried out to God for help through his prayers each morning (v. 13). He wanted to know why God had rejected him by hiding His face (v. 14). Now the psalmist is asking, "Why?"

*Psalm 88:15–18*: Not only did this person declare his despair, he stated this had been his lot in life—since he was a young man, he had suffered and been close to death (v. 15). He had lived in terror so long that he felt destroyed by it (vv. 15–16).

This psalm sounds so different from the other psalms. While other psalms talk about going through difficulties, almost every psalm has a "but you, God" moment when the psalmist turned and started to praise God in the midst of those difficulties. But this psalm never does that. This is a very real experience for many, many Christians. Most every Christian goes through moments like this at some time in his/her life. It may last a few minutes or a few hours or a few days, but for some, it lasts for an awfully long time. Sometimes they experience times of utter hopelessness.

We may be familiar with prayer patterns such as ACTS (Adoration, Confession, Thanksgiving, Supplication) and PRAY (Praise, Repent, Act/Ask, Yield), but we'll never see this as a prayer pattern. Even when all hope was gone, when he was in the depth of despair, this psalmist cried out to God every single day. The one crucial thing in this psalm is this psalmist was committed to keeping on praying and talking to God in the depths of his despair.

Let's compare Psalm 88 with Psalm 22. As you read Psalm 22:1–15, it is so obvious that this psalm describes the Crucifixion. It describes everything Jesus went through, from His thirst to His bones being out of joint on the cross, to being forsaken by God. One of the encouragements from this is that no matter what we go through in this life, Jesus has experienced it. He's experienced every weakness, every bit of hopelessness, especially the suffering on the cross. When we go through these times, there's a fellowship of sharing in His sufferings. There's a closeness we have to God, having gone through the suffering, that we could never have experienced before.

## Closing

If you're going through a time of hopelessness, cry out to God—it will not be the end. Keep crying out to God. Get someone around you who can pray for you. Psalm 88 is so useful to us because it's such a good example of what is available to us today.

## The Daily Word

No matter how difficult, dark, sad, painful, overwhelming, or depressing your life may be, can you still muster the words: *You are the God of my salvation?* If you have walked through a season of desperation, you know salvation in God may be the only thing you have to hang on to, the one, single glimmer of light. This hope in Christ, trusting that He is the author and perfecter of your faith, allows you to press on and cry out in desperation during the long nights and the never-ending days.

No matter how far down in the pit you are, no matter how weary you feel, you are not alone. The Lord is with you. He hears you. He is your salvation. Cry out to Him in desperation. He will set your feet on a rock and make your steps secure. He will raise up your life. Cry out to Him, and He will lift you up.

LORD, **God of my salvation, I cry out before You day and night. May my prayer reach Your presence; listen to my cry. —Psalm 88:1–2**

Further Scripture: Psalm 30:1; 40:2; Jonah 2:6

## Questions

1. This Psalm was written by the sons of Korah. Who were they and what significant event happened to their father (Exodus 6:24; Numbers 4:37; Deuteronomy 11:6; 1 Chronicles 9:19)?

2. What do you think was going on in the psalmist's life to make him cry out so desperately and hopelessly? Does it sound like they are putting the blame on God? Have you ever felt like this?

3. Where else in Scripture can we find such desperate cries for help (Job 19:19–30; Lamentations 3:55)?

4. What did the Holy Spirit highlight to you in Psalm 88 through the reading or the teaching?

# Lesson 71: Psalm 89

*King of Glory*: God's Promises

## Teaching Notes

### Intro

MacArthur explains that Psalm 89 is

> the author's attempt to reconcile the seeming contradictions between his theology and the reality of his nation's conditions. Through the initial 37 verses, he rehearses what he knows to be theologically accurate: God has sovereignly chosen Israel to be His nation, and David's descendants to rule. The last third of the psalm reflects the psalmist's chagrin that the nation had been ravaged and the Davidic monarchy had apparently come to a disgraceful end.[1] [Genesis 12:1–3]

The psalmist Ethan knew the Lord had a promise for the Jewish people, but at the same time the nation of Israel had been destroyed.

I believe there are many who are struggling with hearing God's promise in their lives but not seeing the fruition of that promise. If that is you I encourage you to hold fast. Keep your hand to the plow, and don't give up. That will help you get through tough times.

### Teaching

*Psalm 89:1–2*: The first part of this psalm praises God for His love and faithfulness. MacArthur wrote, "The psalmist exults that the Lord Himself will guarantee the eternality of the Davidic dynasty."[2] In other words, God is not done. God is faithful.

*Psalm 89:3*: We ultimately know God will keep His promises. The *King of Glory* is still going to come back (2 Samuel 7:10–13). When we go through tough times, we can hold onto His promise. I can't say this enough! What I see today in the

---

[1] John MacArthur, *The MacArthur Bible Commentary* (Nashville: Thomas Nelson, 2005), 655.

[2] MacArthur, 656.

American church is that people are quitting before they should. When thing get difficult or results aren't what was expected, people walk away.

*Psalm 89:4*: Without verses 1–4, the rest of the chapter gets really difficult to read. Later the psalmist lamented the hardship the Israelites were experiencing. Psalm 89:29–36 has the same language. Wiersbe states, "God is faithful in His character—praise Him."[3]

*Psalm 89:5–18*: The heavens, the earth, and the people of Israel praised God (Numbers 10:35; Psalm 87:4). The Israelites praised God because they knew His promises.

*Psalm 89:19*: The psalmist described God's covenant with David. Then he recounted the times God spoke to His "loyal ones" or prophets (1 Samuel 13:13–15; 2 Samuel 7:4).

*Psalm 89:20–23*: These verses are similar to Psalm 91.

*Psalm 89:24–25*: The psalmist described the land the Lord promised to the Israelites.

*Psalm 89:26–27*: The Lord promised to make David his firstborn and greatest of the kings on earth. I want to discuss the idea of the firstborn and how it relates to Christ. David was the greatest of the kings of earth then, he was the "king of kings." MacArthur wrote,

> The first-born child was given a place of special honor and a double portion of inheritance (Genesis 27; 2 Kings 2:9). However, in a royal grant covenant, a chosen person could be elevated to the level of firstborn sonship and, thus, have title to a perpetual gift involving dynastic succession (Psalm 2:7). Though not actually the first, Israel was considered the firstborn among nations (Exodus 4:22); Ephraim, the younger, was treated as firstborn (Genesis 48:13–20); and David was the firstborn among kings. Christ can be called the firstborn over all creation (Colossians 1:15), in that He is given the preeminence over all created beings.[4] [Romans 8:29; Revelation 1:5]

---

[3] Warren W. Wiersbe, *The Wiersbe Bible Commentary: Old Testament* (Colorado Springs: David C. Cook, 2007), 971.

[4] MacArthur, 656.

*Psalm 89:28–37*: God will discipline disobedience, but God will not withdraw his love. MacArthur wrote, "God's covenant with David regarding his descendants was as certain as establishment of the sun and the moon in the heavens."[5]

*Psalm 89:38–52*: The psalmist seems to have asked, "How long will You hold Your anger against us? Have You created everyone for nothing? Where is the former act of Your daily love?" Just because you can't see God doesn't mean God has forgotten His promises. This had not been a fun time for the Israelites. After the psalmist finished venting, he went back to praising the Lord.

## Closing

Isn't this us? Isn't this our lives? We can praise, lament, and vent, but we choose to praise Him because we know He keeps His promises. My hope and prayers are that despite your hard times in life, you can hold onto the promises of God. I encourage us to continue to praise him especially when you feel as though you can't see or hear Him.

---

### The Daily Word

Has there ever been a time in your life when you knew the Lord was calling you to something or was raising you up for something specific? Perhaps, years ago, someone gave you a prophetic word, but you have yet to see the Lord fulfill it in your life. God anointed David and made a covenant to establish generations forever. And yet David questioned God's call on his life. He believed in the Lord's faithfulness. He praised Yahweh and knew God's hand would strengthen him always. Even so, David walked through difficult times when his faith was tested.

You may question, doubt, or wonder: *Did I really hear from the Lord? Is He really a faithful God?* Remember to seek first His kingdom. Delight yourself in the Lord. Cultivate and pour into the place the Lord has you in today. Don't look too far ahead, only living for that one golden moment you think is coming. Keep your hands to the plow. Press on, fixing your eyes on the author and perfecter of your faith, Jesus Christ. The Lord will lead you and guide you in His timing. He hasn't left you. Hold on and keep your eyes on Jesus.

**But You have spurned and rejected him; You have become enraged with Your anointed. You have repudiated the covenant with Your servant; You have completely dishonored his crown. —Psalm 89:38–39**

Further Scripture: Psalm 37:3–4; 89:20–21; Proverbs 4:25

---

[5] MacArthur, 657.

## Questions

1.  How could the psalmist make God's faithfulness known to all generations (Psalm 89:1)? How can you communicate God's faithfulness to those around you?

2.  Psalm 89:11 declares, "The heavens are Yours, the earth also is Yours; the world and all it contains, You have founded them." To whom did God give dominion to (Genesis 1:29)? Who is ruling over the works of His hands now (1 Corinthians 15:27; Ephesians 1:22)? How would you explain that everything is in subjection to Him at the present (Colossians 1:15–20)?

3.  How would you explain Psalm 89:14 to someone who doesn't understand the kingdom or character of God?

4.  There is a shift in Psalm 89:38. Do you see any contradictions with the first 37 verses? If so, how would you explain this?

5.  What did the Holy Spirit highlight to you in Psalm 89 through the reading or the teaching?

# Lesson 72: Psalm 90

*King of Glory*: God's Purpose for the Israelites

## Teaching Notes

### Intro

There are a lot of fun facts about this psalm! Psalm 90 is the oldest psalm, and it was written by Moses. I want to paint a picture. Yesterday, we dealt with the perplexity of not seeing God and yet praising Him at the same time. This psalm has a same feel. Moses was asking God for mercy for his people. MacArthur wrote that the psalmist of Psalm 90 "begins with the reflection of God's eternality, then expresses his somber thoughts about the sorrows and brevity of life in their relationship to God's anger and concludes with a plea that God would enable His people to live a significant life."[1]

Even though the Israelites messed up, they asked God for purpose in their lives. Things seemed to fall apart after the incident at Kadesh-barnea. Both Moses' sister Miriam and his brother Aaron died (Numbers 20:1, 22–29), and Moses struck the rock looking for water in disobedience to God.[2] This is the backdrop for Psalm 90. The Israelites had a lot of mistakes but still had a desire for purpose. Today, many people feel as though they have messed up, and God cannot restore or redeem them. Praise God that our salvation is not based on works. We are justified in Him. God knows we are not going to achieve perfection.

### Teaching

*Psalm 90:1–2*: Moses identified himself as "the man of God" (Deuteronomy 33:1; Joshua 14:6). Wiersbe outlines these verses as, "We are travelers and God is our home."[3] I love this image of God as our home, our dwelling place. MacArthur wrote, "God was Israel's sanctuary for protection, substance, and stability."[4] And I love this idea of God as refuge.

---

[1] John MacArthur, *The MacArthur Bible Commentary* (Nashville: Thomas Nelson, 2005), 657.

[2] Warren W. Wiersbe, *Be Exultant: Praising God for His Mighty Works* (Colorado Springs: David C. Cook, 2004), 21.

[3] Wiersbe, 21.

[4] MacArthur, 657.

Wiersbe wrote, "For all mortals, life is a pilgrimage from birth to death, and for believers, it is a journey from earth to heaven, but the road is not an easy one."[5] As evidence, Wiersbe pointed out Jacob's long pilgrimage that was "few and hard" (Genesis 47:9). Then there was Moses' 40 years of wandering in the wilderness, which included the 42 different places the Israelites camped during those 40 years (Numbers 33). Wiersbe also says, "*But no matter where Moses lived, God was always his home.* He 'lived in the Lord.' He knew how to 'abide in the Lord' and find strength, comfort, encouragement, and help for each day's demands."[6] Where is our focus amid the traveling? Moses camped out with the Lord. Even as travelers, God is our home.

In verse 2, Moses referenced time with the words "eternity to eternity." MacArthur wrote, "God's nature is without beginning or end, free from all succession of time, and contains in itself the cause of time."[7]

*Psalm 90:3–6:* Wiersbe outlined verses 3–12 as, "We are learners, and life is our school."[8] Moses painted a picture of man's frailty in verses 3–12 and God's eternality in verses 1–2. God is so big, and our lives are so quick and fast (Genesis 3:19; Isaiah 40:6–7).

*Psalm 90:7–9:* Moses was essentially saying, "We know we messed up." There is no secret sin. MacArthur wrote, "After struggling through his life of afflictions and trouble, a person's life ends with a moan of woe and weariness."[9] Welcome to humanity! So far this has not been super encouraging.

*Psalm 90:10–12:* According to this verse, the average lifespan was 70 years or if you were strong, 80 years. Moses lived 120 years. Wiersbe wrote, "In the school of life we need to learn two important lessons: life is brief and passes swiftly, so make the most of it; and life is difficult and at times seems futile."[10]

We want God's guidance in life so that our lives are a fruitful ministry to the Lord. Moses asked the Lord to "teach the Israelites to number their days carefully." What does it mean to number your days? It means to make the best of every opportunity. Are we numbering our days carefully in ways where God always receives the glory? You hear people say, "If I could just go back, and re-do everything . . ." Psalm 90 shows that even though we are frail, we don't want to

---

[5] Wiersbe, 21.

[6] Wiersbe, 22.

[7] MacArthur, 658.

[8] Wiersbe, 22.

[9] MacArthur, 658.

[10] Wiersbe, 22.

waste our lives. reviveSCHOOL is a great way to number your days for God by learning the mysteries of what He wants to reveal to you.

*Psalm 90:13–17*: Wiersbe outlines these verses as, "We are believers and the future is our friend."[11] We see Moses' plea for mercy and compassion. Moses wanted to find satisfaction in God's love, like manna from heaven (Matthew 5:6). Our satisfaction comes from Christ; He is clearly the bread of life. We should be shouting for joy every day! Moses wanted to rejoice in all the days of his life, even those of adversity (Romans 8:18).

# Closing

May we understand that we have value, significance, and meaning. God pours into us even when that feels as though it is impossible. God will establish, strengthen, and support you, and if you are not compensated here, you will be in heaven (1 Peter 5:10). This is how we can have hope. Wiersbe wrote, "Life is brief, so Moses prayed, 'Teach us.' Life is difficult, and he prayed, 'satisfy us.' His work at times seemed futile, 'Establish the work of our hands.' God answered those prayers for Moses, and He will answer them for us. The future is your friend when Jesus is your Savior and Lord."[12] Moses is saying that even though we mess up, God is a big God. We know life is short, but in the process, God gives us purpose until we are with Him forever!

## The Daily Word

Life can be difficult and trying, but as you press on with hope, even through the pain, begin to seek the Lord in the morning. He alone satisfies you and fills you up with His faithful love. You may even bring your questions to the Lord: what you should do, where you should go, how to spend your time in this quickly fleeting life. Remember, the Lord will teach you and give you wisdom on how to number your days when you seek Him.

Today, you don't need to wander aimlessly or without hope. Pray and ask for the favor of the Lord to be upon you. Ask the Lord to establish the work of your hands. *God's timing is not always your timing*, but that doesn't mean it's a closed door. Sometimes He simply wants you to wait. Your heavenly Father may be saying to you: *"I'm preparing you for something. Just wait, My child!"* May the Lord confirm and establish the work of your hands today. He has a plan for you. Above all, remember you are established *in Christ*. You are

---

[11] Wiersbe, 24.

[12] Wiersbe, 25.

rooted and grounded in Him. You are His, and He will establish the work He has for you.

**Let the favor of the Lord our God be on us; establish for us the work of our hands—establish the work of our hands! —Psalm 90:17**

Further Scripture: Psalm 90:12; Colossians 2:6–7; 1 Peter 5:10

## Questions

1.  Read Psalm 90:1–2. Do you ever struggle with the truth that God has always existed? If so, how do you respond to this struggle?
2.  In Psalm 90:4 Moses said that with the Lord 1,000 years are as yesterday, and Peter repeated this thought in 2 Peter 3:8. How could this truth help you when you're going through difficult times?
3.  Read Psalm 90:12. How does "numbering our days" lead us to have a heart of wisdom?
4.  When you are struggling, have you cried out to God like Psalm 90:13? What do you think God's pity would look like, and how would it be different from His grace?
5.  What did the Holy Spirit highlight to you in Psalm 90 through the reading or the teaching?

# Lesson 73: Psalm 91

*King of Glory*: Protection Through Intimacy

## Teaching Notes

### Intro

The author of Psalm 91 is unknown. MacArthur observed, "This psalm describes God's on-going sovereign protection of His people from the ever-present dangers and terrors which surround humanity" and proposed it was written for an army before they went to battle.[1] We all want God's sovereign protection in our lives. Scripture testifies to the many ways God preserved and protected people like Moses, David, Peter, and Paul. MacArthur noted this Psalm declares, "Nothing can harm a child of God unless the Lord permits it."[2]

### Teaching

*Psalm 91:1–2*: God is called "the Most High" in verses 1 and 9. Because Israel was a place where the sun could be very hot and dangerous to one's health, a shadow was a metaphor for care and protection.[3] Wiersbe noted the description of God as "the Almighty" described "the all-sufficient God who is adequate for every situation."[4] The psalmist declared confidence in the Lord and not in himself. As he referred to God as "my refuge and my fortress" (v. 2), he acknowledged he could not be these things for himself and expressed trust in God to be both on his behalf. This is the sort of confidence the Lord commanded Abram to have in Genesis 17:1: "When Abram was 99 years old, the Lord appeared to him, saying, 'I am God Almighty. Live in My presence and be blameless.'"

*Psalm 91:3–6*: These verses described the very real troubles of life with which followers of the Lord still have to deal. "The hunter's net" in v. 3 represented the net a fowler, a person who trapped birds, used to catch his prey. The image served

---

[1] John MacArthur, *The MacArthur Bible Commentary* (Nashville: Thomas Nelson, 2005), 658.

[2] MacArthur, 659.

[3] MacArthur, 659.

[4] Warren W. Wiersbe, *The Bible Exposition Commentary: Job–Song of Solomon* (Colorado Springs: David C. Cook, 2004), 257.

as a metaphor representing God's deliverance from any plan to endanger the life of one who follows Him.[5]

"The destructive plague" (v. 3) references diseases and epidemics that might arise. The Lord promised to keep His followers from all of it. The psalmist described God as covering His followers "with His feathers," meaning God was near and looking over them. This image was reinforced with a description of taking "refuge under His wings," which implies intimacy with the Lord. Jesus described the type of protection He longed to offer Jerusalem in a similar way: "Jerusalem! Jerusalem! She who kills the prophets and stones those who are sent to her. How often I wanted to gather your children together, as a hen gathers her chicks under her wings, yet you were not willing" (Matthew 23:37)!

The psalmist listed more common situations that would face followers of the Lord: the terror of the night, the arrow, and plagues and pestilence (vv. 5–6). Intimacy with the Lord will protect His followers from all of these as well.

*Psalm 91:7–9*: The psalmist referenced thousands of people falling to pestilence, but it does not cause followers of the Lord to be fearful. This could be a reference to the plagues that came upon Egypt as part of God's deliverance of Israel. God also promised He would multiply the efforts of His people when they encountered enemies: "Five of you will pursue 100, and 100 of you will pursue 10,000; your enemies will fall before you by the sword" (Leviticus 26:8). "How could one man pursue a thousand, or two put ten thousand to flight, unless their Rock had sold them, unless the Lord had given them up?" (Deuteronomy 32:30).

The psalmist promised that those who followed the Lord would see all these things take place because of their intimacy with Him (vv. 8–9). The psalmist specifically referenced "the Most High" in verse 9, God's personal name, to demonstrate the level of intimacy His people have with Him.

*Psalm 91:10–13*: The psalmist used more images to reinforce the idea of the Lord's protection. Another promise for protection from plague was made (v. 10), and angels are described as being ordered to protect the Lord's people (v. 11) to the point the people would not hurt their feet on stones (v. 12). God's people would even be able to withstand lions and poisonous snakes (v. 13).

Interestingly, Satan used verses 11 and 12 in his temptation of Jesus: "Then the Devil took Him to the holy city, had Him stand on the pinnacle of the temple, and said to Him, 'If you are the Son of God, throw Yourself down. For it is written: 'He will give His angels orders concerning you, and they will support you with their hands so that you will not strike your foot against a stone'" (Matthew 4:5–6). Satan misquoted this passage in order to frame his temptation

---

[5] MacArthur, 659–60.

of Jesus, but Jesus' response, "It is also written: Do not test the Lord your God" (Matthew 4:7). This helps us understand we are not to put the Lord's promise of protection to the test by intentionally creating dangerous situations for the Lord to deliver us.

*Psalm 91:14–16:* The speaker switches from the psalmist to the Lord in these verses. The Lord Himself promised protection to the psalmist because of his loving devotion. The Lord promised protection because the psalmist "knows My name" (v. 14). The Lord promised to answer the psalmist, be near in times of trouble, "rescue him and give him honor" (v. 15). Finally, the psalmist would receive "long life" and the Lord Himself would "show him My salvation" (v. 16).

MacArthur noted that while the promises of this psalm could be true of believers in every age of history, the clear references to a messianic king point to this psalm being fulfilled in the life of Jesus.[6]

## Closing

How do we develop intimacy with God that gives us this level of relationship with God? The *Authentic Intimacy* blog prescribed five steps to cultivate intimacy with God[7]:

1. *Desire* intimacy with God—David wrote of his desire "to dwell in the house of the LORD all the days of my life" (Psalm 27:4).
2. Know God's love language—God wants us to love Him with our obedience (Psalm 51:16–17).
3. Love God affectionately.
4. Don't give up!
5. Share in His work.

The word "protection" is throughout Psalm 91. Embrace it so you can start walking out your calling without fear.

## The Daily Word

Trusting in God's protection doesn't mean you will have a perfect, trial-free, healthy, never-get-hurt kind of life. Yes, God watches over you. Yes, He is your refuge. Yes, He is your deliverer. Yes, you can trust Him. His faithfulness will be

[6] MacArthur, 658.

[7] "5 Secrets to Intimacy with God," Authentic Intimacy (blog), June 4, 2015, https://www.authenticintimacy.com/resources/1409/5-secrets-to-intimacy-with-god.

your protective shield, and He will cover you under His wings. *But what does that look like as you walk it out in faith?*

Keep in mind you live in a fallen world with fallen people, and God works in mysterious ways. His ways are higher than our ways. God says you may be pressured in every way, but He promises you will not be crushed. You may be perplexed, but you will not despair. You may be persecuted, but you are never abandoned. You may even be struck down, but you won't be destroyed. You may be weak, but you are strong in Christ. You may have nothing, but you will have peace that passes all understanding. You may be in the midst of trials and tribulation, but even so, consider it joyful because God promises He will never leave you nor forsake you. He will protect you and provide. He will be your refuge. *The key is to never stop trusting Him.* Say out loud: *"You are my refuge and my fortress, my God, in Whom I trust."* Make that your battle cry and open your eyes to see the Lord's protection in your life as you trust Him.

**The one who lives under the protection of the Most High dwells in the shadow of the Almighty. I will say to the LORD, "My refuge and my fortress, my God, in whom I trust." —Psalm 91:1–2**

Further Scripture: Psalm 91:3–4; 2 Corinthians 4:8–9; 2 Thessalonians 3:3

## Questions

1. What feelings are you left with after you meditated on Psalm 91? Do these verses fill you with peace, comfort, and love? Why or why not?

2. Psalm 91:2 mentions that my Lord alone is my refuge, my place of safety, he is my God and I trust him. Do you see God as your safe place and refuge? Do you believe you can trust God? Spend a few minutes with God asking Him these questions.

3. Praises are lifted to God all throughout Psalms. Then, in Psalm 91:9–10, God said "if" (in some versions), which means some action is needed on our part. Where else do we read that God's children need to "do" something in an if/then construction (Exodus 23:22; Deuteronomy 4:29; 1 Chronicles 28:9; 2 Chronicles 7:14; Revelation 3:20)?

4. Psalm 91 is full of promises from God. After you read Psalm 91, look at John 14:23–24. What similarities do you see? How does this speak to you?

5. What did the Holy Spirit highlight to you in Psalm 91 through the reading or the teaching?

# Lesson 74: Psalms 92—93

*King of Glory*: God's Love and Faithfulness

## Teaching Notes

### Intro

Today, we are looking at Psalm 92. Yesterday, Psalm 91 was all about God sending His angels to protect those who were in trouble. Every day, we are looking at pages from the journals of at least seven different authors, so we encounter a multitude of emotions and concerns. Psalm 92 was written anonymously, and it has no instructions for the choir director. The only description given is that it was written for the Sabbath. Some psalms were sung throughout the week; others were sung during the Sabbath period from sundown Friday evening until sundown Saturday evening. This psalm was special because it was written to be a part of the Sabbath worship.

During the week, a lamb would have been sacrificed both during the morning and the evening. On the Sabbath, the sacrifices would have doubled.[1] The Sabbath was a sign between God and the people (Exodus 20:8–11; 31:12–17; Nehemiah 9:13–15). The Sabbath reminded them that God had delivered them from Egypt (Deuteronomy 5:12–15), and worship on the Sabbath brought joy!

### Teaching

*Psalm 92:1–5*: Wiersbe describes these verses as "A Worshiping People."[2] The people were giving thanks and praises in worship. Constable points out that it is appropriate to give praise publicly.[3] They were to praise God in faithfulness, both in the morning and at night, with a harp and a lyre (vv. 1–3). They were praising God throughout the day. The people rejoiced in the Lord for what He had done for them—they shouted with joy (v. 4)! The psalmist described God as

---

[1] Warren W. Wiersbe, *The Bible Exposition Commentary: Job–Song of Solomon* (Colorado Springs: David C. Cook, 2004), 259.

[2] Wiersbe, 259.

[3] Thomas L. Constable, *Expository Notes of Dr. Thomas Constable: Psalms*, 344, https://planobiblechapel.org/tcon/notes/pdf/psalms.pdf.

magnificent and profound (v. 5). The focus was on how good God is. Sometimes, I wonder where our joy is!

*Psalm 92:6–11*: Wiersbe describes these verses as "An Overcoming People."[4] The psalmist described those who had "a shallow nature" and did not know God— they would be eternally destroyed (vv. 6–7).[5] But God would be exalted forever (v. 8). Because of who God is, His enemies would perish (v. 9). God lifted up the psalmist's horn. The horn symbolized strength and majesty, so the psalmist was stating his strength came from God (v. 10a). The psalmist had even been anointed with oil (v. 10b). According to MacArthur, anointing with oil was "based on the practice of making an animal's horns gleam by rubbing oil on them."[6] Some say verse 10 is a messianic reference. *Nelson's Commentary* explains this was "not just a general statement of God's interest in the poet, but a prediction of the coming One—the Lord's Anointed."[7] God gives His people power to overcome their foes (1 Samuel 2:1, 10; Psalms 75:4–5, 10; 89:17, 24; Luke 1:69).

Consider the anointings that took place in the Old Testament. God's anointing came to kings and priests to set people apart for a specific purpose. God used this anointing to call people to specific tasks. In Exodus 29:7, the anointing of Aaron as priest took place. In Exodus 40:15, the Levitical priests were anointed to serve God. Other anointing examples include Samuel in 1 Samuel 10:1 and David in 1 Samuel 16:12–13. The Spirit of the Lord left Saul, even though he had been God's anointed one (1 Samuel 16:14). In 1 Kings 1:39, God anointed Solomon.

The New Testament also includes times of anointing: Luke 4:18–19; 2 Corinthians 1:21; 1 John 2:20, 27. In the New Testament, we are all anointed because we are in Christ. Jared Laskey wrote, "The anointing does not point to the believer; the anointing points to God who empowers the believer."[8] Therefore, we become "a conduit for His power."[9] When we keep our eyes on Christ, we can walk out our anointing.

---

[4] Wiersbe, 259.

[5] Earl D. Radmacher, Ronald B. Allen, and H. Wayne House, eds., *Nelson's New Illustrated Bible Commentary* (Nashville: Thomas Nelson, 1999), 711.

[6] John MacArthur, *The MacArthur Bible Commentary* (Nashville: Thomas Nelson, 2005), 659.

[7] Radmacher et al., 710.

[8] Jared Laskey, "5 Ways to Grow in the Anointing of the Holy Spirit," Charisma News, August 14, 2016, https://www.charismanews.com/opinion/59255-5-ways-to-grow-in-the-anointing-of-the- holy-spirit.

[9] Laskey.

*Psalm 92:12–15*: Wiersbe describes these verses as "A Flourishing People."[10] When we overcome what life throws at us, we thrive in Christ.

## Closing

When we find joy and strength in the Lord, we will grow and flourish.

---

### The Daily Word

As you wake up today, declare the Lord's faithful love over your life. Declare the praises of God. Before you head to bed tonight, declare the Lord's faithfulness in your life. No matter what you may be facing, the burdens you carry, or the battle you are in, declare God's faithfulness. He is faithful yesterday, today, and tomorrow. God is faithful in your life—something powerful happens as you proclaim this truth out loud! Give a voice to the truth resounding in your head. Shout the word "Joy" out loud. Look at someone near you and say, *"Joy!"* Perhaps you aren't feeling joyful, so just begin by whispering, *"Joy."* Then say it in a louder whisper, *"Joy."* Then say it with a regular voice, *"Joy."* Now a little bit louder, *"Joy."* Now shout, *"Joy!"* Are you smiling yet? Smiling itself doesn't mean you have joy. However, smiling sure does make your situation feel less burdensome for the moment as you remember God's great love and faithfulness for you! Release this joyful sound to the Lord in praise! The Lord loves you, and He is working for you! *Joy!*

**It is good to praise Yahweh, to sing praise to Your name, Most High, to declare Your faithful love in the morning and Your faithfulness at night. — Psalm 92:1–2**

Further Scripture: Psalm 92:4; 100:4; James 1:12

## Questions

1. What does it look like for you to give thanks to the Lord and to give praises to His name like the psalmist did in Psalm 92?
2. This Psalm was written for the Sabbath day. Are you intentional about setting aside time on the Sabbath to praise and worship God? How important do you think it is to observe the Sabbath today?
3. Psalm 92:4 says, "I will shout for joy because of the works of Your hands." Meditate on this phrase. Do you find yourself doing this or do you tend to

---

[10] Wiersbe, 260.

take God's creation for granted? Do you think the work of God's hands consists only of what is physically seen?

4. Compare God's majesty (Psalm 93:1) to the people we call majesty or royalty here on earth. What are some similarities? Differences? What is one way that God sees us (1 Peter 2:9)?

5. What did the Holy Spirit highlight to you in Psalms 92—93 through the reading or the teaching?

# Lesson 75: Psalms 94—95

*King of Glory*: Worship and Warning

## Teaching Notes

### Intro

Our phrase for how the book of Psalms points to the Messiah is *King of Glory*. Remember also that every psalm was meant to be sung, either by the choir or the people in worship. MacArthur proposes that Psalm 95, "with its references to the wilderness wanderings, may have been composed by David (Hebrews 4:7) for the Feast of the Tabernacles (Psalm 81)."[1] During the Feast of the Tabernacles, worshippers built temporary booths to stay in to remind them of how God provided for them while they journeyed in the wilderness. MacArthur explains, "After a call to worship (vv. 1–7a), a prophecy in the voice of the Holy Spirit breaks in and reminds the people of the dangers of rebellion and tempting God."[2] This presents both the worship of God and the warnings of God not to do as their ancestors had.

*Nelson's Commentary* points out there are three emotional moods of the worshippers in this psalm: "(1) the worship of God in a mood of celebration (vv. 1–5); (2) the worship of God in a contemplative mood (vv. 6–7); (3) the worship of God in obedience (vv. 8–10)."[3]

### Teaching

*Psalm 95:1–5*: Wiersbe describes verses 1–5 as "come and praise the Lord."[4] Verse 1 tells the worshippers to shout aloud to God, the rock of their salvation (1 Corinthians 10:4). Verse 2 describes the excitement present in worship because God is "above all gods" (v. 3), and over all things (vv. 4–5). This description of how to worship points to the *King of Glory*.

---

[1] John MacArthur, *The MacArthur Bible Commentary* (Nashville: Thomas Nelson, 2005), 661.

[2] MacArthur, 661.

[3] Earl D. Radmacher, Ronald B. Allen, and H. Wayne House, eds., *Nelson's New Illustrated Bible Commentary* (Nashville: Thomas Nelson, 1999), 712.

[4] Warren W. Wiersbe, *The Wiersbe Bible Commentary: Old Testament* (Colorado Springs: David C. Cook, 2007), 978.

As we look back on these verses, focus on these phrases:

- *The rock of our salvation*—God provided the spiritual substance to get through the journey; Jesus is also described as *The Rock* (reviveSCHOOL word for Numbers).
- *A great God, a great King above all gods*—In Acts 2:33, Jesus is described as being above all others at the right hand of God (Philippians 9:2–11).
- *Nothing can separate us from God*—Romans 8:37–39; Paul stated that nothing can separate us from Jesus.

So, how are we to worship Christ? Through shouts of joy and praise; by coming into His presence to worship Him.

*Psalm 95:6–7a*: The posture of worship is described—bowing down to and kneeling before the Lord. Jesus is also Creator/ Maker (Hebrews 1:2). The psalmist described the worshippers as the people of His pasture, the sheep under the care of the Great Shepherd. Here, Jesus was described as the Good Shepherd (John 10:11).

*Psalm 95:7b–11*: Verse 7 ends with a command: if they heard His voice, they were not to harden their hearts against God! Their ancestors had tested and tried God to the point that God became "disgusted" with them (vv. 8–10). Therefore, God would not give them rest and kept them in the wilderness. Jesus, as the Shepherd, called out and the sheep followed because they knew His voice (John 10:4, 16). The Israelites clearly heard His voice, but the question became how they would respond to it.

The event in Meribah was a rebellion in the first generation at Kadesh against God's instructions (Numbers 20:1–13). They did not trust God to provide the water they needed because they had forgotten what He had done. God described them saying, "They are a people whose hearts go astray; they do not know My ways" (v. 10).

## Closing

Hearing God's voice is not difficult. As sheep of the Good Shepherd, the first thing we hear is the voice of Jesus (Romans 8:14). Then, we hear our own voice and question if we really heard God's voice. Finally, we hear the enemy's voice, which attempts to discount God's voice. All of this leads to hard hearts (Romans 8:14). Many of us are wandering in wilderness because we cannot hear the Shepherd's voice. Hebrews 3:7–11 references Psalm 95.

Kyle prays: "God, would you start taking care of my heart and refining it? I really want you to lead it, and I don't want to do this myself (Psalm 139:23–24). I recognize the effect that a hard heart can have on my decisions, my thoughts, my words. I ask for forgiveness for having such a hard heart. Lord, anyone that has a hard heart and doesn't know how they got to this point, if they can't trust Your voice but only their own, would you test, examine, and break the hard heart, creating a soft heart like clay. Make our hearts soft so that we are moldable to look like You. God, we just want to be led by you, listening to Your voice as the sheep being led by the Shepherd. We praise You and we worship You that we can come to you and ask for help. Break us of these things that harden our hearts, Lord, in your name we pray. Amen."

## The Daily Word

Jesus described Himself as the Good Shepherd. As a believer in Christ, you are His sheep. Like any good shepherd who learns the bleats of his flock, the sheep learn to hear and follow the shepherd's voice. And because they follow the voice, the sheep avoid trouble and live a fuller life. In the same way, you are to listen and follow the voice of God. As a believer, you have the Holy Spirit guiding you and counseling you in the way you should go. But sometimes, even though you know the truth and the Scripture, you still don't follow the Lord's voice.

*What if you just followed God's voice in faith without any hesitation*—without a hardened heart, rebellious spirit, or hanging on to hurts of the past, without being distracted with the busyness of life? What if you truly listened and *followed God's voice with a pure, uninhibited heart?* Ask the Lord to create in you a heart willing to listen, willing to follow, and willing to walk in truth. Walk as you hear His voice. Take that step you don't want to but feel nudged to take. Do that thing you are questioning. You don't know what is on the other side of obedience. Chose to listen, be obedient, and walk out God's caring faithfulness in your life. There's an indescribable grace on the other side of obedience.

**Today, if you hear His voice: Do not harden your hearts as at Meribah, as on that day at Massah in the wilderness. —Psalm 95:7–8**

Further Scripture: Psalm 95:6–7a; 139:23–24; John 10:4

## Questions

1. Psalm 94:1 says vengeance belongs to God. Has there ever been a time when you tried to take vengeance into your own hands? What happened?

2. Have you ever gotten away with wrongdoing without anyone knowing about it? What does Psalm 94:8–11 say about this? Why does God discipline those He loves (Psalm 94:13–14; Proverbs 3:11; 19:20; Hebrews 12:7; Revelation 3:19)?

3. Psalm 95:8 says, "Do not harden your heart." What can happen when you harden your heart to God too often (Psalms 81:11–12; 95:9–11; Romans 1:22–32; Mark 8:17; John 12:40; Hebrews 3:8–11)?

4. What did the Holy Spirit highlight to you in Psalms 94—95 through the reading or the teaching?

# Lesson 76: Psalms 96—97

*King of Glory*: King of the Earth

## Teaching Notes

### Intro

Psalm 96 is a royal psalm, which means the focus is on royalty. The subtitle for this psalm is "King of the Earth." When we focus on Him—the *King of Glory*—it's a game-changer. When we take our eyes off ourselves and focus on the King of the Earth, everything changes. John MacArthur said Psalm 96 "anticipates kingdom praise for the Lord from all of the nations of the world."[1]

### Teaching

*Psalm 96:1–3*: The psalmist began with the phrase, "Sing a new song to the LORD . . . all the earth." This brings to mind the image of all the nations coming together to sing a new song to the Lord. The psalmist also urged, "Declare His glory among the nations . . . for the LORD is great and is highly praised" (vv. 3–4). All of us should continue to praise Him. Isaiah 2:2–4 described a kingdom-praise mentality. Isaiah's words are possibly a picture of the nations coming together to sing a new song to the Lord.

　　Wiersbe titled the first three verses, "Sing! The News Is Good!"[2] In verse 2, the phrase, "Proclaim His salvation from day to day," is a picture of genuine praise that includes a testimony to others of God's plan of redemption. In other words, we are going to be preaching the good news through song. In John 4:22, Jesus proclaimed the salvation that we are supposed to proclaim and sing about—the salvation that comes through the Jews. Jesus was not American; He was not Gentile; He was not evangelical; He was Jewish. So, salvation comes from the Jews. In John 14:6, Jesus confirmed this when He said, "I am the way, the truth, and the life. No one comes to the Father except through Me." In Acts 4:12, Peter boldly stated, "There is salvation in no one else, for there is no other name under heaven given to people, and we must be saved by it." Jesus is God. Because God sent His

---

[1] John MacArthur, *The MacArthur Bible Commentary* (Nashville: Thomas Nelson, 2005), 661.

[2] Warren W. Wiersbe, *The Wiersbe Bible Commentary: Old Testament* (Colorado Springs: David C. Cook, 2007), 979.

Son, Jesus, to earth as a Jewish person, then salvation comes from Jesus. This is the message that we need to be sharing. This news is so good that at some point, all the nations will be singing about this. Jesus is King!

Psalm 67 repeats the same message—the nations will rejoice and declare His glory. One day the message of God's mercy will be made known. Psalm 96:2 commands us to "proclaim His salvation from day to day." All of the nations will come to Jerusalem to worship Him. This singing is a prophetic picture, a messianic psalm, a royal psalm of the King coming the second time when all of the nations will bow down and worship Him. When we truly experience God's salvation, then we want to sing, or at least tell about it.

People may hesitate to share the gospel for several reasons. They may be nervous about sharing and/or fear rejection because people won't like what they say. We can listen to those fears or we can listen to the Spirit of God. Before we can share the good news, we have to acknowledge that everybody has sinned and fallen short of the glory of God (Romans 3:23). In order to sing the good news, we have to know what we are singing; we have to know the lyrics. The promise that all nations will come together means someone has articulated the gospel and delivered the message. Romans 6:23 tells us, "The wages of sin is death, but the gift of God is eternal life in Christ Jesus our Lord." Since we all sin, then we earn death; sin leads to death. But God demonstrates or proves His love for us: while we were sinners Christ died for us (Romans 5:8). Now we're starting to sing about the good news—God's love. Ephesians 2:8–9 says, "we are saved by grace through faith." Our salvation has nothing to do with being good; our salvation is based on faith in what Jesus did for us. This leads to confessing with our mouths our belief that Jesus is Lord and God raised Him from the dead (Romans 10:9–10).

*Psalm 96:4–6:* Wiersbe said that in addition to singing because the news is good, we praise because our God is great.[3] "For all the gods of the peoples are idols" means they are worthless and weak. When you do a study on this, they actually paint a picture of God's glory residing and resting in Jerusalem in His sanctuary. Now all the nations are praising God because His name is great in His sanctuary.

*Psalm 96:7–9:* In addition to singing and praising, Wiersbe said we worship because the Lord is worthy. Don't you love this constant imagery of all the nations, all of the earth, worshipping Him as the King of the earth?

---

[3] Wiersbe, 980.

*Psalm 96:10–13*: Wiersbe said we rejoice because the King is coming.[4] What an awesome picture! Psalm 96 prophesies the King is coming, and we have got good news to sing about. John MacArthur said, "The rule of the Lord described in this psalm is not the present universal kingdom (Psalm 93), but one which will be established when Christ returns to earth."[5]

## Closing

The simple question is, are we ready for the King who is coming? How do we get ready? We sing, we praise Him, we worship Him, and we rejoice because we know He's coming! In Revelation 3:11, Jesus said He's coming quickly and to hold on to what we have so no one can take our crown. If we hold on to this understanding that the news is good, that our God is great, that the Lord is worthy, and that the King is coming; then we will live as though He is going to be here today. Jesus said in Revelation 22:12, "Look! I am coming quickly, and My reward is with Me to repay each person according to what he has done." Jesus is watching and at any given moment, He is coming back. Let's get ready!

---

## The Daily Word

The world is firmly established because *the Lord reigns as King over the earth*. Let that sink in for a minute. All the nations proclaim: "The Lord reigns." Not only is the Lord the creator of the heavens and earth, but He is also the King. And because the Lord God Almighty reigns as King, the world will not be shaken. Put your hope in the One who reigns over all . . . the *King of Glory*.

Today, sing a new song. Declare God's glory, proclaim His salvation, and praise Him for His wondrous works to all people in every nation. Find a moment while you are at home alone, or in your car, or out for a run, and begin to sing a song of praise and proclamation to the Lord. Ready? Open your mouth and let the words flow out as a melody! God is so worthy to be praised!

**Say among the nations: "The LORD reigns. The world is firmly established; it cannot be shaken. He judges the peoples fairly." —Psalm 96:10**

Further Scripture: Nehemiah 9:6; Psalm 47:8; 96:1–3

---

[4] Wiersbe, 980.

[5] MacArthur, 662.

## Questions

1.  How was God's promise to Abraham seen in verse three of Psalm 96 (Genesis 12:1–3)? How do you also see Jesus' command to the disciples to spread the good news to a lost world (Psalm 67; Matthew 28:18–20)?

2.  In Psalm 96, how did the psalmist describe all other gods compared to the one true God?

3.  Psalm 96 is found in another version in 1 Chronicles 16:23–33. What happened in those verses so that David proclaimed such worship and praise to the Lord?

4.  Where in Psalm 96 did the psalmist look ahead to the coming Messiah's reign?

5.  What did Psalm 97 proclaim as the foundation of God's throne? Where else in Scripture can you find a description of Psalm 97:2–3 describing the Lord (Exodus 19:16–20)?

6.  What did the Holy Spirit highlight to you in Psalms 96—97 through the reading or the teaching?

# Lesson 77: Psalms 98—99

*King of Glory*: Praise the King

## Teaching Notes

### Intro

According to Warren Wiersbe, Isaac Watts had Psalm 98 in mind when he wrote the famous hymn, "Joy to the World." Wiersbe said the song wasn't about the manger but instead was about the messianic kingdom.[1]

### Teaching

*Psalm 98:1–3*: In the first three verses, *Nelson's Commentary* said there was a call to praise God as Savior (vv. 1–3). These verses feel much like a repeat of Psalm 96. The psalmist praised God for He had performed wonders, or miracles, and won victory (v. 1). According to *Nelson's Commentary*, "The right hand of the Lord is a way of referring to His great salvation of Israel from Egypt."[2] So, it was a way of singing about how God has saved us out of the land we didn't want to be in; how He saves us from all the stuff we've come from.

In verse 2, the psalmist said God revealed Himself to the nations—meaning the Gentiles. God's salvation was designed to spread to the nations. It is clear that God designed Israel to be a light to the nations. Isaiah 42:6 says God appointed His covenant people to be a light to the nations. Isaiah 49:6 also says God would make Israel "a light for the nations, to be My salvation to the ends of the earth." Isaiah 60:3 says, "Nations will come to your light, and kings to the brightness of your radiance." Because of God's movement in their lives, nations would be drawn to the Messiah. These verses are a call to praise God as our Savior. In verse 3, God remembered His love and faithfulness to Israel, and all the nations have seen God's victory. Everybody in all lands will see God's hand on the nation of

---

[1] Warren W. Wiersbe, *The Wiersbe Bible Commentary: Old Testament* (Colorado Springs: David C. Cook, 2007), 981.

[2] Earl D. Radmacher, Ronald B. Allen, and H. Wayne House, eds., *Nelson's New Illustrated Bible Commentary* (Nashville: Thomas Nelson, 1999), 714.

Israel. According to John MacArthur, "These words are a metaphor for the Lord's establishment of His righteous kingdom on earth."[3]

*Psalm 98:4–6*: *Nelson's Commentary* says these verses focus on the call to praise God as King.[4]

*Psalm 98:7–9*: *Nelson's Commentary* says these verses focus on the call to praise God as the coming Judge.[5] Again, this psalm feels so much like Psalm 96. Psalm 96:1 called for "all the earth" to "sing a new song to the Lord." Compare this command to Psalm 98:1. Next, compare Psalm 96:12 with Psalm 98:8. Both psalms have the same ending. Psalm 96:13 says God is coming to judge the world with righteousness. Psalm 98:9 says God will judge the world righteously and the peoples fairly.

Cooper P. Abrams III wrote about the second coming of the Messiah based on Psalm 98. He offers another perspective, which may be good to see. Remember, our phrase for the book of Psalms is the *King of Glory*. The emphasis of Psalm 98 is that we need to get ready because Christ is coming back. Abrams says this psalm is about Christ's return and that the earth is singing a new song because of His return (v. 1). He proposes verse 2 is about Christ returning here on earth; while others suppose "His victory" could refer to Israel's victory over the Medes and the Persians and the Babylonians when the Jewish exiles returned to the land. But Armstrong proposes this is about Christ and the victory He has already given us. Armstrong goes on to say God fulfills His promises through Christ in verse 3. So, in verse 4, all the earth is singing because of Christ. He goes on to say that in verse 7, because of Christ's return, all of the earth comes together.[6]

So, what do we do with the fact Christ is coming to judge the earth? MacArthur says Psalms 96:13 and 98:9 are talking about the time when Christ will return to the earth.[7] Acts 1:11 says Christ will return to earth in the exact way He was taken to heaven. The second time He comes, He is coming to judge us. Why would there be a reason for joy if there's judgment coming? Because Jesus will put an end to the cruelty, the evil, and all of this stuff that we have to deal with. So, let's look at what's going to happen.

In Revelation 16:16–21, Armageddon begins to take place. In Revelation 17:10, seven kings come together and go against each other; but when Christ comes, they stop fighting each other and fight Christ. When Christ comes to

---

[3] John MacArthur, *The MacArthur Bible Commentary* (Nashville: Thomas Nelson, 2005), 662.

[4] Radmacher et al., 714.

[5] Radmacher et al., 714.

[6] Cooper P. Abrams III, "2nd Coming of the Messiah," audio available at https://www.bible-truth.org/1Au-Sermon7.mp3.

[7] MacArthur, 662–63.

judge the earth, this is the stuff that He's going to experience. Christ is going to come and He is going to have to battle. Revelation 18 describes the fall of Babylon and the wiping out of the wicked people. In Revelation 19, there is a lot that happens after the end of seven years. This seven-year period begins with about three-and-a-half years of peace, then the Antichrist reveals himself and things get really bad for three-and-a-half years. In the first three-and-a-half years, the temple is rebuilt and there is some measure of peace. Then, the Antichrist puts himself in the Holy of Holies, in the temple, to equate himself with God. For the next three-and-a-half years, all hell breaks out. Some (pre-tribulation) believe they will be raptured and therefore won't be here for these events. But, I want to get you ready just in case you are here. When Christ comes and cleans house at the end of the seven years, the Antichrist, the beast, and the false prophet will be judged and cast down into a lake of fire. Then, there will be two little groups of remnants left: the Antichrist remnant and a godly remnant. In all of this, there is a 1,000-year reign. In Revelation 20:1–6, the devil is cast into the pit, where he will be held for 1,000 years until he is released for a short time. So, in Psalm 98:9, when we are talking about Christ coming to judge the earth, this is the process we are talking about. During the 1,000 years when the devil has been cast into the pit, Christ is going to reign on earth.

So when we get excited about the coming Judge, it is because we know we are getting that much closer to the *King of Glory* actually showing up in our lifetimes. But if He shows up in our lifetimes, we have to realize it could be a really hard, really tough season. Yes, He will come to judge all the wickedness, but there is a lot of stuff that comes with that. When we praise God as the Savior, as the King, and as the coming Judge, He is coming to clean house. After all this process, Revelation 20:11–15 talks about the judgment of the unsaved. Everyone who has died will be judged according to their works. There is a second death is to be cast into the lake of fire for those who are not found written in the book of life. When we are talking about the coming Judge and praising Him for what is to come, we need to understand what is really coming.

## Closing

When you think about the coming Judge, the best way you can prepare people is to tell them the good news. If you don't want to tell it, then you sing it. Joy to the world, for He is coming! We want everyone to be ready for the return of Christ by delivering the good news.

## The Daily Word

All the nations will gather with shouts of joy and singing from the tops of the mountains to the depths of the sea. During this time, the Word of God declares a time of judgment for all people. The Bible calls the Lord a judge for a reason. It's not a warm, cozy message, and sometimes it's difficult to hear as truth. But yes, *all people will be judged.* The all-knowing and all-seeing God knows if a person believes in Jesus as the way, the truth, and the life or not. Those who believe will have eternal life with Jesus, and those who do not will be thrown into the lake of fire.

If you haven't surrendered your life to Christ, *what are you waiting for?* You don't know the day or the time, but Jesus is coming back. That means the time of judgment is coming. Give your life to the Lord, and you will have security of eternal salvation on the Day of Judgment. No fear. No wonder. No questioning. Just peace. If you surrender your life to the Lord, you will be with Him for eternity. To God be the glory great things He has done.

**Let the rivers clap their hands; let the mountains shout together for joy before the LORD, for He is coming to judge the earth. He will judge the world righteously and the peoples fairly. —Psalm 98:8–9**

Further Scripture: Isaiah 44:23; John 3:16; Revelation 20:11–12, 15

## Questions

1. In Psalm 98:2, what was intended when the psalmist said God had revealed His righteousness in the sight of the nations (Deuteronomy 4:5–6)?

2. When was the last time you shouted for joy and sang to the Lord because of who He is and the works He has done? What has caused you to stop doing this consistently? If it's been awhile, praise Him now!

3. How has the Lord made known His victory/salvation (John 3:16; Romans 5:8)?

4. How many times did the psalmist describe God as holy in Psalm 99 (Isaiah 6:3)? What does holy mean?

5. What did the Holy Spirit highlight to you in Psalms 98—99 through the reading or the teaching?

# Lesson 78: Psalms 100—102

*King of Glory*: Affliction in Light of Eternity

## Teaching Notes

### Intro

Psalm 102 has been described as a psalm of lament, but the end of the psalm has also been described as a messianic psalm. Our phrase for Psalms is *King of Glory*, so the end of this study will help point us to the coming Messiah—our *King of Glory*. Wiersbe suggests Psalm 102 could have been written after the destruction of Jerusalem.[8] The description attached to the psalm is one we have not heard before: "A prayer of an afflicted person who is weak and pours out his lament before the Lord." We do not know the name of the author, but he described himself in this opening description. Verses 8, 14, and 16 seem to outline those areas of affliction. After 70 years of destruction and affliction, the prayer asked God to bring them back into His fold and His presence (Jeremiah 25:11–12; 29:10).

### Teaching

*Psalm 102:1–5*: The psalmist begged God to listen to him, not hide from Him, to listen to him carefully, and to answer him quickly (vv. 1–2). In verse 3, his days vanished like smoke—they seem to be fleeting away (Psalms 31:10; 144:4). In verse 4, the psalmist described the emotional and physical toll he was experiencing—his bones burned, his heart was afflicted, he withered like grass, and he ate little (Psalm 90:4–6; Lamentations 4:8). Even his flesh is barely surviving (v. 5). His entire body was becoming sick from all he was facing—he was physically grieving all the loss.

*Psalm 102:6–11*: The psalmist next describes himself as a desert owl, and then as a solitary bird left to watch over the area (vv. 6–7). His enemies taunted and made fun of him all day long (v. 8). He had nothing to eat but ashes and drank his own tears with his water because he had been put aside from the presence of

---

[8] Warren W. Wiersbe, *Be Exultant: Praising God for His Mighty Works* (Colorado Springs: David C. Cook, 2004), 51.

God (v. 9–10). This is another picture of possibly crying over the destruction of Jerusalem (Psalm 51:11). The word "shadow" usually referred to the idea that life would end shortly. The psalmist withered like the dying grass and recognized his time on earth would not be long (v. 11).

*Psalm 102:12–14*: Beginning in verse 12, the psalmist moves from listing his complaints to focusing on God. This is one of the best transitions you'll see in the psalms of moving out of the depths of problems by looking to the Lord. God wants to walk with us. He is "enthroned forever" as our Lord and God. MacArthur describes this movement as "from earth to heaven—from his dilemma to God."[9] The psalmist knew that one day, God would rise up and show favor to Jerusalem because "the appointed time has come" (vv. 13–14). I believe we are walking into that appointed time for Jerusalem now, and I believe God can be moving in your life right now as well! We have to embrace that moment God gives us.

*Psalm 102:15–22*: These verses are the messianic portion of this psalm. Wiersbe explains, "The throne of David was gone and would not be claimed until the Son of David came to earth, but the throne of God in heaven was secure."[10] When the *King of Glory* returns, He will rule over all the nations (v. 15). This is a beautiful picture of what is to come. This psalmist knew the messianic word and understood God is bigger than anything he or his nation had experienced. Jesus is the Word in flesh and we can find hope in Him and His Word. The restoration of Zion is coming in "a later generation" (v. 18). Alexander Maclaren said, "Zion cannot die while Zion's God lives."[11] Jerusalem cannot disappear because God lives forever.

God will look down from heaven to hear the groaning and to set free those who have been condemned to die (vv. 19–20). All those whom God saves will praise the name of God and serve Him (vv. 21–22; Isaiah 2:1–4).

*Psalm 102:23–28*: The psalmist stated he wanted to live long enough to see God's redemption of Jerusalem. He emphasized that God will reign forever and his own offspring would be established before God. Verse 27 describes the coming Messiah: "But You are the same, and Your years will never end" Hebrews 1:10–12). God is the Alpha and the Omega. The psalm confirms the eternality and the deity of Christ.

---

[9] John MacArthur, *The MacArthur Bible Commentary* (Nashville: Thomas Nelson, 2005), 665.

[10] Wiersbe, 53.

[11] Alexander Maclaren; quoted in Warren W. Wiersbe, *The Bible Exposition Commentary: Job–Song of Solomon* (Colorado Springs: David C. Cook, 2004), 276.

# Closing

So how do we fight the good fight when things seem overwhelming? Consider these statements and scripture verses we can embrace:

1.  Fight the good fight for the faith. (1 Timothy 6:12)
2.  Our breakthrough in Christ has already been fulfilled. (Romans 6:10–11; 2 Corinthians 5:17; Ephesians 1:3—2:14)
3.  Jesus' wholeness and oneness with God has been fulfilled, so there will never be any distance or separation between them and us. (Romans 5:1–2; Ephesians 2:13–18)
4.  God's grace works within us for our benefit as we grow in Him. (Romans 8:28, 32; Philippians 2:13)
5.  We are satisfied in Christ. (Philippians 1:6; Hebrews 12:2)

Because of Christ in your life, you can fight the good fight. It's a lot simpler teaching this than living this, but when you hold on to Christ in your life, anything is possible.

## The Daily Word

Integrity is a big deal to the Lord. It includes being honest—allowing your actions to match your words and your heart. It means no hidden secrets but instead being real, authentic, and pure. The Lord says, *"Let your word 'yes' be 'yes,' and your 'no' be 'no.'"* The enemy gains ground when you live your life deceitfully. The enemy lures you into building upon your lies, making you believe it'd be easier to keep being dishonest. But in truth, you are quenching the Holy Spirit as you continue to sin.

The Holy Spirit came to give you a clean heart, to remove your heart of stone, and to replace it with a heart of flesh. Therefore, if you are stuck in a lie or a place of deceitfulness, surrender your heart to the Lord. Jesus told His disciples, "Blessed are the pure in heart, for they will see God." Today, walk away from the lies through the power of the Holy Spirit. Be honest with the Lord, with yourself, and with others. *Honesty brings freedom*, allowing you to serve the Lord more fully.

**My eyes favor the faithful of the land so that they may sit down with me. The one who follows the way of integrity may serve me. No one who acts deceitfully will live in my palace; no one who tells lies will remain in my presence. —Psalm 101:6–7**

Further Scripture: Proverbs 6:16–19; Ezekiel 36:26–27; Matthew 5:37

## Questions

1. In Psalm 100, how are we admonished to serve the Lord? What is the evidence that we as believers are filled with the Spirit of God (Ephesians 5:18–21)? What are some other things that will fill us with joy in the Lord (Colossians 3:16–25)?

2. What does it say we should do in Psalm 100:3 (1 Kings 18:39)? The HCSB says to acknowledge He is God. Are there times when you have trouble doing this? How can you overcome your fear of acknowledging the Lord to others (Deuteronomy 31:6)?

3. What does it mean to live with a heart of integrity (Psalm 101:2; 1 John 1:6–7)? Do you walk with integrity or can this be a struggle for you?

4. How did the psalmist keep his perspective despite being overwhelmed with his afflictions? What happens to our problems in light of having this perspective of the Lord? What do they say about the deity of Christ?

5. The writer of Hebrews applied Psalm 102:25–27 to Jesus in Hebrews 1:10–12. How is Jesus superior to the angels according to these verses?

6. What did the Holy Spirit highlight to you in Psalms 100—102 through the reading or the teaching?

# Lesson 79: Psalms 103—104

*King of Glory*: God's Benefits to Us

## Teaching Notes

### Intro

Today, I feel the Lord's leading as I teach Psalm 103. There's some pretty cool stuff in this psalm about remembrance we'll be looking at.

### Teaching

*Psalm 103:1–19*: Verses 1–2 begin with the statement, "Bless the Lord" (NASB). The word "bless" actually means "to bend the knee."

The phrase, "O my soul: and all that is within me," shows the psalmist was yearning with his entire being to bless God for all His promises and all He had done. You've probably sung these words in a praise hymn, actually expressing the words of the psalm as they were meant—as a song. Verse 2 adds an important statement: "and forget not all his benefits." It's those benefits I want us to consider. The psalmist listed at least 30 benefits that come from God in this psalm. All these benefits come from God's character.

1. God forgives all our sin (v. 3).
2. God heals diseases (v. 3; Isaiah 53:4–5).
3. God redeems us from all destruction (v. 4; Psalm 18:16–17).
4. God crowns us with lovingkindness (v. 4); Joseph redeemed from the pit (Genesis 37; 41:38–45).
5. God crowns us with tender mercies (v. 4).
6. God satisfies us with good things to eat (v. 5; James 1:16–17).
7. God renews our youth like an eagle's (v. 5; Isaiah 40:31).
8. God performs righteous deeds and judges for all who are oppressed (v. 6).
9. God makes His ways known to us (v. 7).
10. God makes His acts known to us (v. 7).
11. God is merciful and gracious toward us (v. 8; Ephesians 2:8).
12. God is patient and slow to anger (v. 8).

13. God abounds in mercy and lovingkindness (v. 8; Exodus 34:6–9).

14. God gives a temporary reproof for our iniquities (v. 9; Micah 7:18).

15. God's anger doesn't last forever (v. 9).

16. God does not deal with us according to our sin (v. 10; Titus 3:5–7).

17. God has now rewarded us with what we are due for our sins (v. 10).

18. God shows infinite mercy to those who fear Him (v. 11).

19. God removes our sins far away (v. 12; 2 Samuel 12:13).

20. God has fatherly pity on His children (v. 13).

21. God knows our frame, our created being (v. 14).

22. God remembers our frailty (dust) (v. 14; Ecclesiastes 12:7).

23. Man's days are brief, but we still flourish (vv. 15–16; Isaiah 40:6–8).

24. God's mercy is everlasting to everlasting (v. 17).

25. God's righteousness extends eternally (v. 17).

26. God's righteousness is given to those who keep His covenant (v. 18).

27. God's righteousness is given to the obedient (v. 18; Deuteronomy 7:9).

28. God has established His eternal throne in heaven forever (v. 19).

29. God's sovereign hand rules over all (v. 19).

*Psalm 103:20–22*: In verse 20, the psalmist shifts to the angels, God's creation. He asked God to bless the angels who excel in strength, serve as His messengers and ministers, and do God's pleasure (vv. 20–21). The psalmist pointed to the angels as another benefit—they stand charge over us. Finally, the psalmist blessed the Lord and everything about the Lord—His dominion over His creation, His angels, and His people.

## Closing

How has the Lord blessed you? What benefits have you received from God? Have you forgotten the benefits of the Lord today? Sometimes we need to stop and "forget not His benefits." Praise Him with your soul as you remember all He has done for you.

## The Daily Word

Can you recall all the Lord's benefits in your life? You are called to give thanks to the Lord and praise His name. But perhaps there are days when you wonder, *What do I praise the Lord for? I am in a pit. I am feeling blah. Does He even know what's going on with me?* Open your Bible right now and turn to Psalm 103. The psalmist recounted more than thirty *benefits* of the Lord. You can read verse after verse of God's great blessings for you.

So even if you don't feel like praising the Lord right now, *your soul can praise and bless the holy name of the Lord.* As you proclaim and release these words of thanks from your mouth, the enemy's grasp and lies will be undone in the face of truth! Give thanks for His great love that satisfies you with goodness and renews your youth. For as high as the heavens are above the earth, so great is His faithful love toward those who fear Him. Be reminded of this great love and the Lord's many benefits just for you today.

**My soul, praise Yahweh, and all that is within me, praise His holy name. My soul, praise the LORD, and do not forget all His benefits. —Psalm 103:1–2**

Further Scripture: Psalm 103:8; 2 Corinthians 4:6–7; Galatians 2:20

## Questions

1.  In Psalm 103:3, the psalmist wrote God heals all our diseases. Do you believe this? Why do you think people don't get healed sometimes when we pray for them (Deuteronomy 32:39)?
2.  Psalm 103:7 says, "He made known His ways to Moses." God walked with Moses for 40 years in the desert. Do you feel we are able to know His ways the way Moses did? If so, how?
3.  Psalm 103:12 states God removes our transgressions from us "as far as the east is from the west." How far is that? What do you think it means when He says He removes our sins from us (Jeremiah 31:34)?
4.  Psalm 103:13 states, "So the LORD has compassion on those who fear Him." Do you think this means He doesn't have compassion on nonbelievers?
5.  According to Psalm 104:1–2, what does God wear? Describe and meditate on some of the attributes of God mentioned in Psalm 104.
6.  What did the Holy Spirit highlight to you in Psalms 103—104 through the reading or the teaching?

# Lesson 80: Psalms 105—106

*King of Glory*: God's Faithfulness

## Teaching Notes

### Intro

Psalm 105 points us to the truth that because God has been faithful in the past, we can trust Him to be faithful now and in the future. When things seem difficult or confusing, we can hold on to the moments of God's faithfulness in our lives. My mom would always say we need to celebrate these moments. The theme of Psalm 105 is found in verses 1–2; we are to make known God's deeds through praising Him. MacArthur suggests this psalm "possibly originated by command of David to Asaph on the occasion when the ark of the covenant was first brought to Jerusalem."[1] MacArthur goes on to state there are ten imperatives[2] listed in Psalm 105:1–4, which are listed below.

### Teaching

*Psalm 105:1–4*: In verse 1, the psalmist wrote: (1) give thanks, (2) call on His name, and (3) proclaim His deeds. In verse 2–3, the imperatives continue: (4) sing to Him, (5) sing praise to Him, (6) tell about His works, (7) honor His holy name, and (8) let the hearts of those who seek Yahweh rejoice. The imperatives are completed in verse 4: (9) search for the Lord and for His strength, and (10) seek His face always.

*Psalm 105:5–23*: In verses 5–6, the psalmist moved from these imperatives to listing the things God did for His people—His works, His wonders, His judgments, and His chosen ones (Abraham, Jacob, and their descendants). Then, the psalmist recounted their past with God—His covenant with them, their time in the wilderness, and the Promised Land He had given them (vv. 7–23). God had been with Abraham when he wandered among the nations and "were few in number." God protected "His anointed ones" from the kings of those nations (vv. 14–15). God sent Joseph ahead of his people into Egypt to prepare for the famine and for the coming of the Hebrews.

---

[1] John MacArthur, *The MacArthur Bible Commentary* (Nashville: Thomas Nelson, 2005), 667.

[2] MacArthur, 668.

*Psalm 105:24–45*: God blessed the people and made them fruitful; they were more numerous than their foes. God chose Moses and Aaron to lead the people and gave them the power to perform miraculous signs among them. The psalmist reminded his readers of the plagues in Egypt. In every situation, God delivered what He had promised.

## Closing

About Psalm 105, Warren Wiersbe wrote:

> God's people live on promises, not explanations, and it is "through faith and patience" that we see these promises fulfilled (Hebrews 6:12). But God keeping His promise meant much more for Israel than victory over the enemy and the acquisition of riches. It meant accepting the responsibility of obeying the God who had been so faithful to them . . . When we consider all that the Lord has done for us, we find we have the same obligation.[3]

We, too, want to thank the Lord—for getting us to 11 years at Time to Revive (est. 2007). He has walked with us every step of the way and in every place we have gone. Let us continue giving thanks, let us continue calling on His name, let us continue proclaiming His deeds as we walk in obedience to Him!

## The Daily Word

Think about a moment when you experienced God's undeniable faithfulness—a moment you want to remember and never forget throughout generations to come, such as a healing from a serious health issue, a timely provision, a moment of conviction followed by redemption, or a time the Lord miraculously showed up! Take time today to give thanks to the Lord and proclaim His deeds to the people around you.

As you remember the wonderful works of the Lord, perhaps you want to organize a celebration for His faithfulness. Why not have a piece of cake to celebrate the memory of God's faithfulness in your life? Maybe you'd like to give a special gift to someone as a way to celebrate the time in your life God provided for you. However the Lord may lead you as you look back and remember, the key is to press on walking with Jesus while you *remember His faithfulness* and sing hallelujah!

---

[3] Warren W. Wiersbe, *The Bible Exposition Commentary: Job–Song of Solomon* (Colorado Springs: David C. Cook, 2004), 283–84.

Give thanks to Yahweh, call on His name; proclaim His deeds among the peoples. Sing to Him, sing praise to Him; tell about all His wonderful works! —Psalm 105:1–2

Further Scripture: Deuteronomy 8:2; Psalm 105:3–5; 1 Corinthians 11:26

## Questions

1. What does it mean in Psalm 105:4 to "Seek His face continually"? What would this look like for you?

2. In Psalm 105, David gave an account of God's wonderful works on behalf of Israel. Have you ever reflected on all the things God has done for you? Does this encourage you, as it did David, to trust Him in everything?

3. In Psalm 106, the psalmist went back and forth between God saving and delivering His people to punishing them. Why do you think sometimes God seems merciful and at other times He pours out His wrath on His people?

4. How do some of the sins of God's people mentioned in Psalm 106 compare to the sins of God's people today? Do you think we as a nation are walking on shaky ground? Should we be afraid of God's wrath because of our sins today or do you think He will choose to be merciful?

5. What did the Holy Spirit highlight to you in Psalms 105—106 through the reading or the teaching?

# Lesson 81: Psalms 107—109

*King of Glory*: Godly Character Through Opposition

## Teaching Notes

### Intro

Psalm 109 is categorized as an imprecatory psalm, meaning it invokes God's judgment or calamity on one's enemies.[1] While the book of Psalms contains several of these psalms, possibly this psalm pronounced the worst judgments of them all.

### Teaching

*Psalm 109:1–5*: David reflected on his opposition. David's lifestyle was a life-style of praise (v. 1). Similarly, we who are in Christ ought to be characterized by a lifestyle of praise to God: "Therefore, as you have received Christ Jesus the Lord, walk in Him, rooted and built up in Him and established in the faith, just as you were taught, overflowing with gratitude." (Colossians 2:6–7). Though David's life was characterized by praise, he had to live in relationship with others who did not love God in the same way he did. As a result, others treated David poorly (vv. 2–5).

David's character was established in this first section of the psalm:

1. *David praised God* (v. 1). "Then David praised the Lord in the sight of all the assembly. David said, 'May You be praised, Lord God of our father Israel, from eternity to eternity'" (1 Chronicles 29:10).
2. *David prayed to God.* "In return for my love they accuse me, but I continue to pray" (v. 4).
3. *David loved others.* "In return for my love" (v. 4a). David loved his enemies.

*Psalm 109:6–15*: David reacted to his opposition. David suddenly turned from declaring his dependence on God and his love for his enemies to asking God to

---

[1] John MacArthur, *The MacArthur Bible Commentary* (Nashville: Thomas Nelson, 2005), 600.

work against his enemies. David asked God to "set a wicked person" over his enemy (v. 6), for his enemy's prayer to "be counted as sin" (v. 7), and for God to make "his days be few" (v. 8) among other judgments. In Acts 1:20, Peter quoted verse 8 as the apostles sought someone to take Judas' place.

Though David was characterized by his love for others, he asked God to pronounce harsh judgments on the family of his enemy. David asked God to "Let his children be fatherless and his wife a widow" (v. 9), for his enemy's "creditor to seize all he has" (v. 11), and for no one to be gracious "to his fatherless children" (v. 12). David also asked God for his enemy's descendants to "be cut off; let their name be blotted out in the next generation" (v. 13), and for the family of his enemy's "guilt be remembered before the LORD . . . Let their sins always remain before the LORD" (vv. 13–15).

*Psalm 109:16–20*: These verses outline some of the reasons David asked such harsh things of God toward his enemy. His enemy did not care for "the afflicted, poor, and brokenhearted" but instead sought to "put them to death" (v. 16). David's enemy "loved cursing" and "took no delight in blessing," so David asked God to allow him to be cursed and to keep blessings far from him (v. 17). David asked God for this curse to penetrate his enemy's body, to be wrapped around him like a robe or a belt (vv. 18–19).

David's requests can be understood in three ways. First, David could have been venting his frustration to God, bringing all his complaints and bitterness to God. Second, David could have been praying, asking God to do these things to his enemies while not personally taking action. Third, David could have been prophesying, predicting that the things will happen to his enemies because Scripture declared these judgments on people who have done similar things (Deuteronomy 27:15–26).

*Psalm 109:21–31*: David requested help. After David reacted to the opposition he experienced, he asked the Lord to deal with him and his heart kindly (v. 21). This was a dramatic shift in his attitude. Praising God changed David's attitude and brought him back to the man of character we saw earlier in Psalm 109. This man knew he was completely dependent on God to "save me according to Your faithful love" (v. 26). Now, David desired for his enemy to know God's love in the same way he did (v. 27). The behavior of his enemy might not change (vv. 28–29), but David resolved to continue to praise God (v. 30).

## Closing

Because we are redeemed in Christ, we are people of character similar to David's. Like David, there will be times when we experience opposition. The enemy will try to deceive us into getting angry. But if we remain in a prayerful posture, the Lord will take that burden from us, humble our hearts, and return us to the character He intended for us in the beginning.

How do we bring glory to God in the midst of opposition?

1. *Reflect on opposition.* Take time to consider what the enemy is up to, then you can respond appropriately. You can choose to react in a positive way by giving it to the Lord. Even if you choose to react negatively, God can bring you out of it.
2. *Request God's help.* God can change your heart and help you to live out the character of Christ through you.

God will give you the peace, the strength, the wisdom, and the humility to go through the process of whatever is opposing you at the time. When you request God's help, it returns you to the character that David began with. Remember the opposition is lurking, but you have the power of God in you to overcome.

## The Daily Word

Even in the moment of accusation, let the words of your mouth praise the Lord. Thank the Lord even as opposition arises. You may be tired, you may doubt your strength, and even then, praise the Lord.

The psalmist described thanking the Lord "fervently," which means, "passionately or enthusiastically." Imagine passionately cheering for a sports team or enthusiastically singing during a concert. Now imagine turning your passion and enthusiasm to the Lord. In *all of it—even in the midst of opposition*, give thanks and praise. Even if you don't feel it from the depth of your soul, begin to praise and give thanks to the Lord. Eventually, you will begin to unleash that passion and enthusiasm from within. The Lord sees your need. He is your provider. He sees your hopelessness. He is your hope. He sees your weakness. He is your strength. He sees your brokenness. He is your healer. He covers you with His love. Praise the Lord and give thanks for His great name.

**I will fervently thank the LORD with my mouth; I will praise Him in the presence of many. For He stands at the right hand of the needy to save him from those who would condemn him. —Psalm 109:30–31**

Further Scripture: John 16:33; 1 Peter 2:9, 12

## Questions

1.  Psalm 107:2 says to "let the redeemed of the Lord proclaim that He has redeemed them." Has God redeemed you from your enemies? Have you told someone? If not, how could you tell someone? Will you take a step of faith and tell someone of God's redeeming power?

2.  One verse was repeated four different times in Psalm 107. What was the verse? Has God done wonderful things for you? Did you praise Him? Take a few minutes and praise the Lord for something specific that has happened this week.

3.  David said his "heart is confident in God" (Psalm 108:1). Is your heart confident in God? Why or why not?

4.  What did the Holy Spirit highlight to you in Psalms 107—109 through the reading or the teaching?

# Lesson 82: Psalms 110—112

*King of Glory*: The Priestly King

## Teaching Notes

### Intro

Psalms 118 and 110 are the most quoted psalms in the New Testament. That means it was probably quoted in reference to the Messiah. Wiersbe points out verse 1 of Psalm 110 was quoted 25 times, verse 4 was quoted five times, and the psalm was referenced ten times in the book of Hebrews.[1] It is a royal psalm written by David, and it presents one of the most prophetic pictures of Christ as King and as Priest. We have been using the phrase *King of Glory* for the book of Psalms, but for Psalm 110, we could use King and Priest of Glory. Both Jesus and Peter verified David was the author (Matthew 22:43–44; Acts 2:33–35).

### Teaching

*Psalm 110:1–3: Christ the King*: Verse 1 refers to "the Lord" (God the Father) who made a declaration to "my Lord" (God the Son), the root and offspring of David (Mark 12:36; Revelation 5:5; 22:16). Christ sat at God's right hand until He came to earth (v. 1b). Jesus sat at the place of honor at the right hand (Hebrews 10:10–12) until God made His enemies Christ's footstool. MacArthur explains, "The footstool was an ancient Near Eastern picture of absolute victory portraying the idea that one's enemy was now underfoot"[2] (Psalms 8:6–7; 47:3). David was writing a picture of the second coming of Christ, not in reference to the first coming of Jesus (Revelation 19:11–21). Christ is waiting for His enemies to be defeated before He comes back (Hebrews 10:13).

David wrote of the blessings of what God would do. First, the Lord would give Christ His mighty scepter to rule over His kingdom that would extend from Zion (Jerusalem) (v. 2a). This referred to an earthly Zion, not a heavenly Zion. This is the Father allowing the Son to do His work. Second, God would defeat His enemies (v. 2b). Christ's people would volunteer to go to battle in "holy

---

[1] Warren W. Wiersbe, *The Bible Exposition Commentary: Job–Song of Solomon* (Colorado Springs: David C. Cook, 2004), 291.

[2] John MacArthur, *The MacArthur Bible Commentary* (Nashville: Thomas Nelson, 2005), 674.

splendor" for Christ (v. 3a). The army rode pure white horses and wore white garments like priests (Revelation 19:14). MacArthur describes this volunteer army: "The redeemed inhabitants of earth will willingly serve the King of kings and Lord of lords."[3] The phrase, "from the womb of the dawn, the dew of Your youth belongs to You" (v. 3b), describes Christ.

*Psalm 110:4–7: Christ the Priest.* The final four verses point to Christ's priesthood. God had sworn an oath that Christ would be a priest like Melchizedek. Melchizedek was the only person in the Old Testament who served as both king and priest (Genesis 14:17–20) and foreshadowed the coming Messiah (v. 4). We picture the king as one on a horse who came to do battle, while the priest served as a mediator between God and His people. Christ is the ultimate, final King/Priest.

Now the Lord is at the right hand of the Messiah, and He will crush kings on the day of His anger (v. 5). The roles would be reversed—the Father will stand at the right hand of the Son and supply all the Son's needs. "The day of His anger" will be the "Day of the Lord." MacArthur explains "the day of His anger/wrath" refers to the Day of the Lord and will find "its global expression at the end of Daniel's seventieth week (Daniel 9:24–27)."[4] The Day of the Lord is coming to make way for His Son's return.

Further, God would judge the nations, pile up corpses, and crush leaders all over the world (v. 6). There are multiple references throughout scripture to the Day of the Lord (Psalms 2:8–9; 50:1–6; Isaiah 2:4; 9:6–7; Daniel 2:44–45; 7:21–27; Matthew 25:32; Revelation 6:15–17; 14:20; 16:17; 18:19–21). Then, Christ will drink from the brook as the victor and will lift His head in victory (v. 7). David was truly functioning as a prophet of God who released a prophetic word (Acts 2:30).

## Closing

David was inspired by the Holy Spirit to write these verses—to record this word of prophecy. David wrote about the *King and Priest of Glory.* God will bring forth the Day of the Lord to make way for the King and the Priest Jesus.

## The Daily Word

God reigns as the King and the Priest of glory. God will defeat His enemies. God will extend His kingdom. A great army is coming with Jesus' return. But until then, Jesus sits at the right hand of God. The time will come when God will defeat all enemies and crush kings, bringing forth His anger.

---

[3] MacArthur, 674.

[4] MacArthur, 674.

*Are you ready?* What does it mean to be ready? Acknowledge God's power. Acknowledge who He is. *You have no need to live in fear of the world.* So stop fearing the things in this world. Rather, live in fear of the Lord for that is the beginning of wisdom. Fear the Lord for His mightiness and power. Praise His name because *great* is the name of the Lord. Call upon the name of the Lord to subdue your enemies and proclaim His victory so others will know Jesus Christ is the King and Priest of glory. Yes, proclaim victory in Jesus so others will know Jesus Christ. Amen.

**The Lord is at Your right hand; He will crush kings on the day of His anger. He will judge the nations, heaping up corpses; He will crush leaders over the entire world. —Psalm 110:5–6**

Further Scripture: Psalm 47:3; Acts 7:55–56; 15:17–18

## Questions

1.  When you read Psalm 110:1, what does it mean to you? Have you ever been witness to this action?
2.  In Psalm 111:10, what does "fear of the Lord" mean? Where else in Scripture is this kind of fear shown (2 Chronicles 19:7; Job 28:28; Proverbs 2:5; 8:13; 9:10; 15:33; 16:6)?
3.  Psalm 112 is full of the great things in store for God's people. How do these things come from fear of the Lord? Do you fear the Lord? What does that look like in your life?
4.  What did the Holy Spirit highlight to you in Psalms 110—112 through the reading or the teaching?

# Lesson 83: Psalms 113—115

*King of Glory*: God Reaches the Poor,
Needy, and Barren

## Teaching Notes

### Intro

Most people say David wrote this psalm even though Scripture doesn't specifically identify him as the writer. Psalms 113 and 114 are part of the "hallel" psalms and are typically read—or sung—during Passover.

### Teaching

*Psalm 113:1–2*: The psalm begins by calling the servants of the Lord to praise the name of the Lord. The psalmist's word brings to mind a worship song by Chris Tomlin, "Blessed Be Your Name." David urged the people to bless the Lord "forevermore" (v. 2)!

*Psalm 113:3–6*: David continues to praise God for who He is, recognizing He is above all nations and His glory is above the heavens (v. 4). In verse 6, David asked, "Who humbles Himself to behold the things that are in the heavens and in the earth?" (NKJV). The English Standard Version (ESV) translates this verse, "Who looks far down on the heavens and the earth?" In either translation, David praises God's greatness because He is high above heaven and earth, looking down on His creation.

*Psalm 113:7–9*: David next described what God saw as He looked down on the earth. God makes the poor and needy to sit with the princes of His people (vv. 7–8). God grants to barren women both a home and children (v. 9). David's words in verses 7–8 closely resemble Hannah's words found in 1 Samuel 2:8. Hannah actually sang these words in her song of praise after she gave birth to her son Samuel. With these words, Hannah talked about what God does.

One thing the Bible says about Jesus is that He came to set people free, and God has a heart for the downtrodden. If God looks down on earth and has the heart to raise poor people from the dust, the needy from the ash heap (v. 7), and to speak to barren women (v. 9), then what does that say about how He reaches out to us? Sometimes we miss out on God's heart. God has been on a mission since Genesis when Adam and Eve sinned in the Garden of Eden to reconcile mankind back to Himself. That is not just people of wealth or people of poverty—He wishes all people would come to Him, that none would perish.

What does Scripture say about the needy and poor? What does Scripture say about our role? If we are going to praise God for who He is and talk about how He helps people, then we need to know where we fit into that situation. One example to consider is Mephibosheth, the son of Jonathan and grandson of King Saul. He was five years old when his nurse fled with him after hearing of the deaths of King Saul and Jonathan. As she fled, she dropped Mephibosheth, who was injured and whose feet were crippled (2 Samuel 4:4).

When David became king, he remembered he had made a covenant with Jonathan. In 2 Samuel 9, David sought anyone from Jonathan's house to whom he could show kindness. He was told about Mephibosheth, so David had him brought from the city Lo-debar, which means "no word." David showed kindness to Mephibosheth by restoring to him all the land that had belonged to his grandfather Saul. Mephibosheth then lived in Jerusalem and ate from the king's table for the rest of his life. Here was a guy who had lost his inheritance, was crippled in an accident, his family had been killed, and he lived in a place of "no word." But David found him and delivered him by bringing him to the king's table. At that time, it was unheard of for the lame to eat from the king's table. But when Mephibosheth sat at the king's table, you couldn't tell he was lame because you couldn't see his feet. God wants us to find the "Mephibosheths" in our lives, speak truth into them, and help them get to where God wants them to be.

God's heart is for the needy and the oppressed; the church should be at the front of the line to help them. We need to see the story behind each person and then be ready to give to them the love of Jesus that we have received. In Isaiah 58, God told Isaiah to declare to His people their transgressions and sins (Isaiah 58:1). However, the people were asking God why He wasn't listening to them as they fasted and humbled themselves to seek Him (Isaiah 58:2–3). God rebuked them saying that even in their fasting, they continued to please themselves and oppress their workers (Isaiah 58:4–5). God pointed out the kind of fasting to which He called them: "to loose the bonds of wickedness, to undo the straps of the yoke, to let the oppressed go free" (Isaiah 58:6). Jesus came to set the captives free and heal the brokenhearted (Luke 4:18). The only way people can be set free is to be free from sin in Jesus. Isaiah continued God's message calling them to share food with the hungry, bring the homeless into their homes, and cover the naked (Isaiah 58:7). Then, their light would break forth like the dawn, healing would spring up, righteousness would go before them, and God's glory would be their rear guard (Isaiah 58:8). God promised to hear and answer their prayers (Isaiah 58:9). When they poured out themselves for the hungry and afflicted, God promised to guide them, satisfy them, and make them strong (Isaiah 58:10–11).

What are the breaches and divides we see? Where are the holes in our unity? Where are the holes in the body of Christ? God has called us to be repairers of the breaches and restorers of the streets (Isaiah 58:12). Just like Jesus stepped into our lives and repaired and restored us, we can reach out to restore and repair others. Go back to Psalm 113:7 again. Who comes to mind as the poor and needy in your life? Who is God putting on your heart? What would it be like if we started looking in the ash heap for the needy? What would it be like if we looked for barrenness? Yes, it could be barren wombs, but there are other kinds of barrenness.

## Closing

Sometimes we can be caught up in the mission of God and miss the people of God. Be the demonstration of Christ's love (Romans 5:8). Start with just one. Next time you see someone in need, think about whether or not they could be your Mephibosheth. Could God be asking you to take them to the King's table?

---

### The Daily Word

The Spirit of the Lord is upon you. In order to demonstrate His love for you, God the Father sent His Son Jesus to earth to endure the cross so you could be saved. Now you have the love of God within you. His love flows through you. And it is your responsibility to *love* others out of God's great love within you. *How do you demonstrate love to others?* Love those in need of a hand to lift them up and out of the ashes. Help them to set their feet on the one true solid ground.

Who do you know that needs to fill the void in their life with Jesus? They may be empty and unsatisfied with the things of this world and are ready for the Lord to quench their thirst and fill their emptiness. *Will you be love to them? Will you fill them up with the Father's love?* The Lord will equip you as you walk in His ways, listening to His voice, and loving even the least of these. Not for your own glory but for His glory alone. Today, ask the Lord to lead you to someone to love in Jesus' name.

**He raises the poor from the dust and lifts the needy from the garbage pile in order to seat them with nobles—with the nobles of His people. He gives the childless woman a household, making her the joyful mother of children. Hallelujah! —Psalm 113:7—9**

Further Scripture: Psalm 115:1; Romans 5:8; 1 John 4:7–8

---

# Questions

1.  Imagine the *King of Glory* choosing to lay aside His privileges in heaven in order to come to earth and become a man. Meditate on Psalm 113:5–6 and Philippians 2:7–8. Write a prayer or psalm to the Lord telling Him of your thankfulness.

2.  Read Psalm 113:7–8. Does this sound like a fairy tale (think Cinderella)? How do these two verses tell every believer's story?

3.  When reading the description of idols in Psalm 115:4–7, what are your thoughts about those who put their trust in idols? Have you ever found yourself putting your trust in something other than God? Explain what you think Psalm 115:8 means.

4.  Why would Psalm 115:3, "He does whatever He pleases," sound disturbing and fearful if you didn't have complete confidence that God is good?

5.  Psalm 115:16 says, "The heavens are the heavens of the LORD but the earth He has given to the sons of men." Where in Genesis 1 can you find God giving authority of the earth to man? Read Psalm 8:6 and Hebrews 2:8. Who now has rule over the earth?

6.  Psalm 115:17 states, "The dead do not praise the Lord." Is this referring to physical death or could it be spiritual death (John 5:25)? How can someone go from death to life? (John 3:16; 5:21; Romans 10:9, 10)

7.  What did the Holy Spirit highlight to you in Psalms 113—115 through the reading or the teaching?

# Lesson 84: Psalms 116—118

*King of Glory*: Affection for the Lord

## Teaching Notes

### Intro

Today, we are going to dive into Psalm 116. Before we get started, just a couple of tidbits about the other two psalms. Psalm 117 is only two verses and is the shortest chapter of the Bible. Psalm 118 comes right after the shortest psalm and just before the longest, Psalm 119. Something unique about Psalm 116 is the affection for the Lord that comes out of it. Sometimes we encounter people who have a love for the Lord that goes beyond just knowledge. They really have a heart connection with God.

### Teaching

*Psalm 116:1–2*: The psalmist said he loved the Lord because the Lord heard his pleas for mercy (v. 1). This is a covenantal love. We like it when people of influence want to hear what we have to say—just as the psalmist described here. Amazing! The Creator of the universe hears our voice every time we call out to Him. God inclines His ear to us—He wants to hear from us and enjoys listening to us.

In John 10:27, Jesus said, "My sheep hear My voice and follow Me." But don't forget, in this verse, Jesus also said, "I know them." Think about how well God knows your voice—He knows exactly what you sound like. Because He knows the sound of our voice, He has an affection for us. In 1 John 5:14, the Apostle John assured us, "Whenever we ask anything according to His will, He hears us." In Psalm 116:1–2, we see the concept that praise is rooted in love.

*Psalm 116:3–11*: We see we are delivered from death. Could there be a connection between how much some people deeply love God and what they have been delivered from? In verse 3, the snare is something used to trap an animal, something that entangles you. The psalmist said death encompassed him or wrapped around him. "The pangs" describe the sudden or sharp emotional pain the psalmist felt when "Sheol" or death "laid hold" on him (v. 3). In the midst of this suffering, the psalmist called on the Lord (v. 4).

The psalmist described God's graciousness and mercy (v. 5) because He meets us where we are in our suffering. God does not discriminate or look to see how much work you've done—He simply meets you in your need. He hears your distress, and He will respond (v. 6). The psalmist praised God's generosity (v. 7) in delivering him from death (v. 8), so he could walk with God in the land of the living (v. 9). Remember in the earlier verses, the psalmist was so close to death the snares of death encompassed him. But God pulled him from death into the land of the living. We get to walk with Jesus in the land of the living. We will get to walk with Him in heaven. This brings to mind the words of Romans 6:23: "For the wages of sin is death, but the gift of God is eternal life through Jesus Christ our Lord." Not only have we been rescued from death, but we will walk with God and Jesus in heaven. Thinking about living in heaven with God changes our response toward God.

When we have an intimate relationship with God, He hears our distress and delivers us from what afflicts us (v. 10). He hears everything we have to say to Him, and He hears it with an inclined ear. Because of His affection for us, He wants to do for us what we ask of Him.

*Psalm 116:12–19*: As a result of all this, we are dedicated to praise. The psalmist wondered what He could "render" to the Lord "for all his benefits" (v. 12). What are our benefits? He has taken away our sins and lifted us from the pit. We get to live with God in heaven when we leave this earth. But we also get to walk with a resurrection power—the presence of the Holy Spirit inside us. This allows us to strengthen our walk and minister to other people. We get to talk with God anytime we want because He knows our voice and inclines His ear toward us. The psalmist then said he would "pay his vows to the Lord in the presence of His people" (v. 14). We can share with others what God has done in our lives in hopes they will also experience His love for themselves.

Why would God consider the death of His saints as precious (v. 15)? The New King James Bible study notes say, "Those in service to the Lord who are threatened with death are precious to God and are thus saved. Though they may not escape physical death, they will experience eternal life." Once we are saved, we are doing the work of God—whether we are doing a little or doing a lot—so we are precious in His sight. One of the other things we can read into this is the concept of dying to self. When we die to self, we allow God to work through us. As they continue to deny themselves, allowing God to refine them and grow them, they grow closer and closer to the Lord.

The servant professed himself as God's servant, whom God had "loosed" from his bonds (v. 16). God had set the psalmist free from death and from the things that kept him in bondage. Jesus demonstrated this in the upper room with His disciples when He washed their feet. The concept of servanthood was one of the last things Jesus demonstrated for them. As believers, we serve Jesus and we serve others.

The psalmist said he would offer God "the sacrifice of thanksgiving" (v. 17) and repeated his intention to fulfill his vows to God (v. 18). What greater testimony than to tell someone else exactly what God has done for us? The psalmist then concluded with a final call to praise the Lord (v. 19). We should incline our ear to the Lord because God has a lot to say to us; He has a lot of truth to speak into our lives. God has a lot of action He wants us to partake in and a lot of people that He wants us to minister to. When we take the time to incline our ear to Him, we will see Him move in our lives.

## Closing

We have an intimate relationship with the Lord (1) because we are in a covenant relationship with Him, (2) because He hears us, and (3) because we hear Him. So how do we bring more affection into our relationship with God? It's rooted in our love for Him and His love for us. Keep an account of what He has done in your life. What has He delivered you from—not just from death but from what other things? Then be dedicated to praising Him and giving testimony among His people because He is anxiously awaiting our return to Him in heaven.

### The Daily Word

Today is the day the Lord has made; *choose to rejoice and be glad in it.* You have a choice today. Give the Lord praise and honor for the day. Recognize the day is His and walk into it with Him. Rejoice, praise, honor, and give thanks to the Lord. You have breath, you have life, you have salvation in Him. Choose to be glad. Be positive. *What do you have to lose?*

Some people may wake up on the "wrong side of the bed." Others may see the cup half-empty rather than half-full. But either way, child of God, today is a gift. Look up! Fix your eyes on Jesus and give thanks! Let the first words out of your mouth be pleasing to the Lord and edifying to someone else. Look at someone you care about or someone sitting next to you right now and say: "This is the day the Lord has made, *let us rejoice and be glad in it!*" Just do it! It may turn your whole day around because *you* have chosen to focus on the Lord and not on yourself! He's right there with you no matter what the day may hold. Now, get after it! Cheers to a new day!

This is the day the LORD has made; let us rejoice and be glad in it! —Psalm 118:24

Further Scripture: Deuteronomy 28:13; Psalm 19:14; Isaiah 50:4

# Questions

1.  The opening and closing verses in Psalm 118 are also found in 1 Chronicles 16:34; 2 Chronicles 5:13; 7:3; and Psalms 106:1; 107:1; and 136:1. Do you think these verses held significant meaning for the Israelites? Is your foundational belief that the Lord is good? Why or why not?

2.  The psalmist stated, "The Lord is for me" (or "The Lord is on my side" or "The Lord is with me"). Look at the rest of Psalm 118:6. How should the first part of the verse effect your response to the rest of the verse? Do you feel a deep agreement with this verse?

3.  Multiple verses in Psalm 118 point to the *King of Glory*, who is Jesus. Psalm 118:19–20 speaks of a gate of righteousness. Look at John 10:7–9. Do you think this gate in Psalm 118 could be a reference to Christ? Explain your answer.

4.  What did the Holy Spirit highlight to you in Psalms 116—118 through the reading or the teaching?

# Lesson 85: Psalm 119

*King of Glory*: Delight in God's Word

## Teaching Notes

### Intro

Psalm 119 is a fun psalm. Whenever I reference a psalm out on the streets, it's always Psalm 119. With 176 verses, it is the longest psalm. Psalm 119:105 is one of my favorite verses: "Your word is a lamp for my feet and a light on my path." This is the answer for going through life. Studying the Word gives you the next step—a light for your path. Verse 105 is the summary of the entire psalm. The author is unknown, but it is known that the psalm was written under duress (vv. 42, 134, 153). There are many verses within the psalm that point to this duress.

### Teaching

*Psalm 119:1–176*: The psalm was written as an acrostic. It has 22 sections with eight lines each. All eight lines of the first section begin with the first letter of the Hebrew alphabet.[1] Each section then follows throughout the Hebrew alphabet. Thomas Constable breaks these sections down as follows:

1.  The blessing of obeying God's Word (vv. 1–8)
2.  The cleansing power of God's Word (vv. 9–16)
3.  An appreciation for God's Word (vv. 17–24)
4.  A prayer for greater understanding (vv. 25–32)
5.  Loyal commitment to God's Word (vv. 33–40)
6.  God's Word and salvation (vv. 41–48)
7.  God's Word as a source of hope (vv. 49–56)
8.  Strong commitment to God's Word (vv. 57–64)
9.  Confidence in the Word of God (vv. 65–72)
10. God's Word as an object of hope (vv. 73–80)
11. The reliability of God's Word (vv. 81–88)

---

[1] John MacArthur, *The MacArthur Bible Commentary* (Nashville: Thomas Nelson, 2005), 680.

12. The permanence of God's Word (vv. 89–96)
13. The sweetness of God's Word (vv. 97–104)
14. The illumination God's Word provides (vv. 105–112)
15. The reverence God's Word inspires (vv. 113–120)
16. The vindication of those who keep God's Word (vv. 121–128)
17. The wonder of God's Word (vv. 129–136)
18. The righteous character of God's Word (vv. 137–144)
19. The truth of God's Word (vv. 145–152)
20. Love for God's Word (vv. 153–160)
21. Joy in God's Word (vv. 161–168)
22. Salvation in God's Word (vv. 169–176)[2]

Scripture says the "Word became flesh," so all this points to Christ, the ultimate *King of Glory* (John 1:1, 14).

Within the psalm, eight words are used as synonyms for God's Word: The Law (used five times); testimonies (used 23 times); precepts (used 21 times); statutes (used 21 times); commandments (used 22 times); judgments (used 19 times); Word (used 39 times); and ordinances (used 23 times).[3]

Wiersbe points out three kinds of people who reject God's Word: "To unsaved sinners, the law is an *enemy* because it announces their condemnation and cannot save them. To legalistic believers, the law is a *master* that robs them of their freedom. But to spiritually minded believers, the law is a *servant* that helps them see the character of God and the work of Christ."[4]

## Closing

What does the Word of God do for us? Wiersbe points out:

> The Word of God performs many wonderful ministries in the life of the devoted believer. It keeps us clean, gives us joy, guides us, and establishes our values. The Word helps us to pray effectively and gives us hope and peace and freedom. Loving the Word will bring the best friends into our life, help us find and fulfill God's purposes, and

[2] Thomas L. Constable, *Expository Notes of Dr. Thomas Constable: Psalms*, 422–42, https://planobiblechapel.org/tcon/notes/pdf/psalms.pdf.

[3] Constable, 418–19.

[4] Warren W. Wiersbe, *The Bible Exposition Commentary: Job–Song of Solomon* (Colorado Springs: David C. Cook, 2004), 310.

strengthen us to witness. When we think we are "down and out," the Word will revive us and get us back on our feet.[5]

When we go to the Word of God, it breathes new life into us. However, the psalmist ended Psalm 119 with this: "I wander like a lost sheep; seek Your servant, for I do not forget Your commands" (v. 176). In spite of all he knew about God's Word and his desire to follow it, the psalmist acknowledged he still sinned. We need God as the lamp for our feet and a light on our paths!

## The Daily Word

Take a minute to picture yourself on a journey walking along an unknown path. You don't know when or where you will turn left or right or when you will stop for a bit. It's dark outside, but thankfully, you have a lamp to light the path in front of you and guide your feet. However, it only illuminates far enough for the next step, *requiring you to take one step at a time.*

That lamp represents the Word of God. The Word of God brings light into the darkness. The Word reveals your path of life. It may not reveal a five-year plan or even a detailed step-by-step outline, but it will reveal your next step. The Word will instruct you, help you, and shield you. The Word is sweeter than honey on your mouth and brings you hope and understanding. So what do you do with the Word of God? Do you just read it on a Sunday morning and think that time alone will guide your steps for the week? That's not how the Lord intended it. Open the Word every day. Yes, every day. It will light your path daily on your journey. Today, open your Bible and read the Word.

**Your word is a lamp for my feet and a light on my path. —Psalm 119:105**

Further Scripture: Psalm 16:11; 119:103–104; John 1:1, 14

## Questions

1. Psalm 119:11 says, "Your word I have treasured in my heart, that I may not sin against You." Some versions say "hidden" instead of "treasured." How do you treasure/hide something in your heart (Deuteronomy 6:4–8)? How could treasuring/hiding God's Word in your heart keep you from sinning against Him?

---

[5] Wiersbe, 311.

2. How easy is it for you to do what it says to do in Psalm 119:37? How can vanity or worthless things take away from your reliance on God? How about your relationship with Him (Proverbs 11:2; 16:18; 29:23; James 4:1–4)?

3. How can we walk in liberty, or in freedom, by seeking God's precepts, as it says in Psalm 119:45 (John 1:14; 8:36)? How does God's law compare to man's law (Psalm 19:7)?

4. What does the world teach today that is different from what is stated in Psalm 119:73: "Your hands made me and fashioned me" (Genesis 1:26–27; Jeremiah 1:5)? How can the world's view be dangerous?

5. A well-known Scripture verse is Psalm 119:105: "Your word is a lamp to my feet and a light to my path." What do you think this means? Can you think of a specific time/situation in your life when this verse has really stood out?

6. Psalm 119:130 says, "The unfolding of Your words gives light; it gives understanding to the simple." Who are the simple? Why do you think it's sometimes easier for the simple to understand God's Word (Isaiah 55:9; Luke 18:16–17)?

7. According to Psalm 119:165, people who love God's law have great peace. Have you found this to be true in your own life? In other people's lives? What part of God's law do you struggle with the most? Would surrendering that to God give you more peace?

8. What did the Holy Spirit highlight to you in Psalm 119 through the reading or the teaching?

# Lesson 86: Psalms 120—121

*King of Glory*: Delight in the Journey

## Teaching Notes

### Intro

Psalms 120—134 contain the Psalms of Ascent. These were similar to road-trip songs Jewish people sang on their way up the mountain to Jerusalem. David wrote four Psalms of Ascent (122; 124; 131; 133), Solomon wrote one (127), and the remaining ten were written anonymously. Psalm 121 was written anonymously.[1] Psalm 120:5 suggests this group of travelers might have had to go a long way to reach Jerusalem.

Any references in the Psalms of Ascent to "looking up" should be understood as an expression of expectation to see the temple (Psalm 134:1–2). The Israelites were required to go to Jerusalem three times a year for festivals: "Celebrate a festival in My honor three times a year. Observe· the Festival of Unleavened Bread. As I commanded you, you are to eat unleavened bread for seven days at the appointed time in the month of Abib because you came out of Egypt in that month. No one is to appear before Me empty-handed. Also observe the Festival of the Harvest with the firstfruits of your produce from what you sow in the field and observe the Festival of Ingathering at the end of the year, when you gather your produce from the field. Three times a year all your males are to appear before the Lord God" (Exodus 23:14–17). This psalm conveys a sense of assurance that God will keep both individual worshippers and Israel, as a whole, safe.

### Teaching

*Psalm 121:1–2*: MacArthur notes that these verses described *God as helper*.[2] The psalmist had absolute confidence that God would help them should any need arise on their long journey to Jerusalem to worship the Lord. God had all power to help them regardless of their circumstances because they knew Him to be the Maker of the heavens and the earth. Psalm 89:11–13 says, "The heavens are Yours; the earth also is Yours. The world and everything in it—You founded

---

[1] John MacArthur, *The MacArthur Bible Commentary* (Nashville: Thomas Nelson, 2005), 682.

[2] MacArthur, 682.

them. North and south—You created them. Tabor and Hermon shout for joy at Your name. You have a mighty arm; Your hand is powerful; Your right hand is lifted high."

*Psalm 121:3–4*: MacArthur observes that the psalmist viewed *God as His keeper*.[3] Psalm 91:11–13 expressed a similar idea: "For He will give His angels orders concerning you, to protect you in all your ways. They will support you with their hands so that you will not strike your foot against a stone. You will tread on the lion and the cobra; you will trample the young lion and the serpent." Psalm 31:8b says, "You have set my feet in a spacious place."

*Psalm 121:5–6*: MacArthur sees *God described as protector*.[4] Isaiah 25:4 says, "For You have been a stronghold for the poor, a stronghold for the needy person in his distress, a refuge from the rain, a shade from the heat. When the breath of the violent is like rain against a wall." Isaiah 49:2 says, "He made my words like a sharp sword; He hid me like a sharpened arrow; He hid me in His quiver." The Lord will protect His people all day, in all climates. He will never take a day off. He will protect you.

*Psalm 121:7–8*: MacArthur describes *God as our preserver*.[5] The Lord would be with His people on their journey to Jerusalem, but He also promised to be with them all the time in their "coming and going, both now and forever" (v. 8). Houses in Jerusalem have mezuzahs, little scrolls of Scripture, attached to the doorposts of homes in obedience to Deuteronomy 6:9–12: "Write them on the doorposts of your house and on your gates. When the Lord your God brings you into the land He swore to your fathers Abraham, Isaac, and Jacob that He would give you—a land with large and beautiful cities that you did not build, houses full of every good thing that you did not fill them with, wells dug that you did not dig, and vineyards and olive groves that you did not plant—and when you eat and are satisfied, be careful not to forget the Lord who brought you out of the land of Egypt, out of the place of slavery." God would sustain Israel, but they were to intentionally remind themselves of all God had done for them. Deuteronomy 11:20 says, "Write them on the doorposts of your house and on your gates so that as long as the heavens are above the earth, your days and those of your children may be many in the land the Lord swore to give to your fathers." The Word of God was everything His people needed.

---

[3] MacArthur, 682.

[4] MacArthur, 682.

[5] MacArthur, 682.

## Closing

Steven Cole outlines four practical realities of God's protective hand.[6]

1. *If we have a clear conscience, then we can know that God is for us in spite of the slander or opposition of others.* "What then are we to say about these things? If God is for us, who is against us? He did not even spare His own Son but offered Him up for us all; how will He not also with Him grant us everything? Who can bring an accusation against God's elect? God is the One who justifies. Who is the one who condemns? Christ Jesus is the One who died, but even more, has been raised; He also is at the right hand of God and intercedes for us" (Romans 8:31–34). To understand God's protection, we have to come to God with a clean slate.

2. *If we know the sovereign God, then we can trust Him to defend and protect us according to His purpose.*

3. *If we have personally received mercy at the cross, then we should view every circumstance, no matter how frustrating, as an opportunity to proclaim God's mercy to others.* "Consider it great joy, my brothers, whenever you experience various trials, knowing that the testing of your faith produces endurance. But endurance must do its complete work, so that you may be mature and complete, lacking nothing" (James 1:2–4). When we know God's protecting us, we understand God allows us to experience things to make us look more like Him.

4. *If we follow the Savior who laid down His life for us, then we should be ready and willing to pay the price of our commitment to Him.*

I need to come to the table with a clean conscience, a pure mind realizing that God is sovereign; God is in control. Even if the situation isn't the greatest, everything is an opportunity to make me look more like Him. Am I willing to sacrifice my life so that others will see Him? It's a road trip, sing along the way realizing God has got your back no matter what.

## The Daily Word

Think of a time when you were on a journey: a road trip, a hike up a mountain, or a mission trip overseas. Perhaps you've been on a journey through a specific season of life: a sickness, junior high years, unemployment, healing from a difficult relationship, or grieving the loss of a loved one. Whatever comes to mind

---

[6] Steven J. Cole, "Lesson 65: God's Protective Hand (Acts 25:1–12)," Bible.org, August 14, 2013, https://bible.org/seriespage/lesson-65-god-s-protective-hand-acts-251-12.

when you hear the word "journey," picture the Lord with you just as He was with the Israelites on their journey up to Jerusalem.

The Lord is your helper. The Lord is your protector. The Lord is your shelter. The Maker of heaven and earth knows you. He walks with you. No matter what journey you face today, lift your eyes up to Jesus. You are not alone. Day and night the Lord is with you because the Lord God, your protector, doesn't sleep! He will protect your coming and going forever. Lift your eyes up, dear child of God. The Lord is with you on your journey today!

**I lift my eyes toward the mountains. Where will my help come from? My help comes from the LORD, the Maker of heaven and earth. —Psalm 121:1–2**

Further Scripture: Psalm 121:3–4; Isaiah 41:10; Jeremiah 29:11

## Questions

1. Read Psalm 120:1. Do you usually wait until you are in trouble to cry out to the Lord and listen for His answer? Or do you regularly take time to listen for His voice? What does that look like?

2. Have you ever, like the psalmist in Psalm 120:7, felt like you wanted peace, but those around you were not in agreement? What do you think is the best way to handle that situation?

3. How can you find comfort in knowing the Lord neither sleeps nor slumbers (Psalm 121:3–4)?

4. What do you think is meant by "The Lord is your shade at your right hand" (NIV) (Psalms 91:1–2; 121:5)?

5. The writer of Psalm 121 says, "The Lord will keep you from all evil (harm)." How do you explain why evil or tragic things happen to believers (Psalm 34:17–19)?

6. What did the Holy Spirit highlight to you in Psalms 120—121 through the reading or the teaching?

# Lesson 87: Psalms 122—123

*King of Glory*: A Prayer for Jerusalem

## Teaching Notes

### Intro

This is the third Psalm of Ascent. People are coming from all over the country and ascending to Jerusalem; they had to do this three times a year (Exodus 23:13–17). Why Jerusalem (Zion)? Psalm 132:13–14 says because the Lord has chosen it and desired it for His home.

### Teaching

*Psalm 122:1–2*: Wiersbe summarizes the first two verses as having "a heart for God."[1] Constable wrote that these verses show David's "joyful anticipation of worship."[2] "The house of the Lord" referred to the tabernacle of the Lord that had been permanently placed there. It was David's habit to go into God's presence to worship (see 2 Samuel 12:20). David was aware there were some people who could not go to God's house because of physical reasons and because of national exile (see Psalms 42:1–3; 137:2–3). From personal experience, I can tell you that, as you arrive in Israel and approach Jerusalem, it feels like God's presence is stronger. David rejoiced because he could worship God in His dwelling place—he could stand within the gates of Jerusalem (v. 2). *Nelson's Commentary* points out, "There is an almost childlike enthusiasm in these words; a sense of near unreality pervades the mood."[3]

If you do not have a heart for Israel, ask the Lord to give you one. We are the Gentiles whom Paul referred to in Romans 15:27: "Yes, they were pleased, and indeed are indebted to them. For if the Gentiles have shared in their spiritual benefits, then they are obligated to minister to Jews in material needs." We are

---

[1] Warren W. Wiersbe, *The Bible Exposition Commentary: Job–Song of Solomon* (Colorado Springs: David C. Cook, 2004), 338.

[2] Thomas L. Constable, *Expository Notes of Dr. Thomas Constable: Psalms*, 448, https://planobiblechapel.org/tcon/notes/pdf/psalms.pdf.

[3] Earl D. Radmacher, Ronald B. Allen, and H. Wayne House, eds., *Nelson's New Illustrated Bible Commentary* (Nashville: Thomas Nelson, 1999), 730.

obligated to take care of the Jews because we have received salvation through Jesus Christ, who was a Jew.

*Psalm 122:3–5*: Wiersbe summarizes verses 3–5 as having "a heart for praise."[4] Verse 3 describes Jerusalem as a city "solidly joined together." David captured the city of Jebu from the Jebusites in battle, took possession, and strengthened the walls and the defenses. David then renamed it Jerusalem (see 2 Samuel 5:6–10). The city became the place where the twelve tribes were commanded to go and make a public declaration of thanks to God three times a year (v. 4). *Nelson's Commentary* describes these times as, "The people of God would praise God for His goodness in their own lives. Their vocal praises would accompany their offerings of animals, grain, wine, and oil."[5] Jerusalem was the hub of the people for worship and where "civil judgments and decisions were made" that "closely intertwines in the Law of God"[6] (v. 5). Today, nations battle for Jerusalem and the land of Israel.

*Psalm 122:6–9*: Wiersbe summarizes verses 6–9 as having "a heart for prayer."[7] Verses 6–7 record David's prayer for Jerusalem: "Pray for the peace of Jerusalem: 'May those who love you prosper; may there be peace within your walls, prosperity within your fortresses.'" That prayer still stands today, as the world's nations want control over the city and the Temple Mount.

David's prayer for peace was prophetic, as battle after battle took place in Jerusalem—the battle between Saul and David and his mighty men (2 Samuel 8), the Ammonite rebellion (2 Samuel 12:26–31), Absalom's rebellion (2 Samuel 18), Sheba's rebellion (2 Samuel 20), and when David avenged the Gibeonites. These were not all in Jerusalem but were around Jerusalem and were fought for control of Jerusalem. These battles were followed up by the battles between the divided Kingdom of Israel and Judah. The battle today is for Jerusalem; the battle between good and evil will be settled in Jerusalem.

Ironically, the name Jerusalem means "the city of peace," but it has been fought over more than any other city in the world. Today, the fight goes on.

- 1947–49   Israel's fight for independence took place, and in 1948, they proclaimed their status as an independent nation.
- June 1967   The Six-Day War between Israel and Egypt, Jordan, and Syria took place. As a result, Israel took over Gaza and tripled their land holdings.

---

[4] Wiersbe, 338.

[5] Radmacher et al., 730.

[6] Radmacher et al., 730.

[7] Wiersbe, 339.

- 1967–70    Israel was at war with Egypt over the Suez Canal.
- 1973       Egypt and Syria attacked Israel in the Yom Kippur War.
             Other Arab countries supported Egypt and Syria with
             money, weapons, and troops.
- 1978       Israel was attacked by the PLO (Palestine Liberation
             Organization); Israel responded by invading Lebanon.
- 1981–82    Israel attacked the PLO headquarters in Lebanon and
             invaded Lebanon after an assassination attempt on Israel's
             ambassador to Britain.
- 1987       Palestinian uprising against Israel took place.
- 2000       A second Palestinian uprising against Israel took place.
- 2006       Israel battled militants in Lebanon and Gaza.
- 2008–9     Israel fought against Hamas.
- 2012       Israel fought against Hamas.

## Closing

David prayed for the peace of Jerusalem. It's like Genesis 12:3 where God said:
"I will bless those who bless you." Our phrase for the book of Psalms is *King of
Glory*. We believe that, throughout the psalms, the words point to the coming
Messiah. The Prince of Peace will come to Jerusalem (Isaiah 9:6). How do we
know we can trust Jesus as the Prince of Peace?

> "Peace I leave with you. My peace I give to you. I do not give to you as the
> world gives. Your heart must not be troubled or fearful" (John 14:27).

> "And the peace of God, which surpasses every thought, will guard your
> hearts and minds in Christ Jesus" (Philippians 4:7).

> "And let the peace of the Messiah, to which you were also called in one body,
> control your hearts. Be thankful" (Colossians 3:15).

> "Therefore, since we have been declared righteous by faith, we have peace
> with God through our Lord Jesus Christ" (Romans 5:1).

May God give you a heart for the city of Jerusalem!

## The Daily Word

Peace is the opposite of anxiety and turmoil. During days of war, people will say, "Peace not war." The same remains true for your life. You'd rather have peace, not anxiety. Your heart longs to feel settled, secure, and serene. The world doesn't bring or offer lasting peace. David and Isaiah prophesied and prayed for peace in Jerusalem. And then Jesus came as the Prince of Peace. The peace of Jesus controls your heart and guards your mind.

As you let go of control, trouble, fear, and unknowns, receiving the peace of Christ into your life, *you will have peace that passes all understanding.* Release to the Lord your anxious thoughts about a relationship, a tryout, a surgery, or a bill. Say it out loud: *"I release this to You, Lord."* As you let it go, receive and replace that anxiety with peace from the Lord, trusting the Lord to go before you. Christ Jesus is your peace as you allow Him to control your heart and your mind. Rest in Him and not in your own strength or control. And as you prepare for Jesus to return one day, pray for His peace in Jerusalem.

**Pray for the peace of Jerusalem: "May those who love you prosper; may there be peace within your walls, prosperity within your fortresses." Because of my brothers and friends, I will say, "Peace be with you." —Psalm 122:6–8**

Further Scripture: Isaiah 9:6; Philippians 4:7; Colossians 3:15

## Questions

1. In Psalm 122:1, David said he was glad when they said to him, "Let us go to the house of the Lord." Do you feel this way about entering the Lord' presence? For you, is the "house of the Lord" a building, a special place where you feel His presence, or something else?

2. Do you feel compelled to pray for the peace of Jerusalem (Psalm 122:6)? Why or why not?

3. The singers looked to the Lord until He was gracious (shows mercy or favor) to them (Psalm 123:2). Has there ever been a time when the Lord was not gracious or merciful to us? Explain your answer.

4. What did the Holy Spirit highlight to you in Psalms 122—123 through the reading or the teaching?

# Lesson 88: Psalms 124—125

*King of Glory*: The Lord Is on Our Side

## Teaching Notes

### Intro

Psalm 124 is in the section known as Psalms of Ascent. The people sang these psalms when they were on their way to Jerusalem. By singing about what they had been through, the people were in the right frame of mind when they came into Jerusalem. Songs seem to have the ability to create a heart connection for us, so the intent of a hymn or song is to create an emotional connection. Psalm 124 contains a pattern of conditional statements—a set of If/Then statements. It simply means that *if* a certain condition is true, *then* this is the outcome.

Psalm 124 can be broken into two sections or themes. Verses 1–5 talk about deliverance. This is a Davidic psalm, so David wrote about a time when he experienced deliverance. Verses 6–8 express thankfulness for deliverance. The two themes can be connected with a conditional statement: If you are delivered, thankfulness should be your response.

### Teaching

*Psalm 124:1–2*: The word "if" appears as the very first word in the psalm. "If it had not been the Lord who was on our side" was the first condition. Verse 2 added the setting—"when people rose up against us" (NKJV). Since this is a psalm of David, many people connect it with 2 Samuel 5:17–19 when the Philistines attacked Israel. When we go through issues and face challenges and we need to be delivered and protected, when we need God to show up, we can know He is always with us. David invited God into his battle. Sometimes we forget to invite God into our battles—big or small. When God is invited into our battles, He can show up in big ways.

*Psalm 124:3–5*: David explained what would have happened if God hadn't been with them: "Then they would have swallowed us up alive . . . the flood would have swept us away" (vv. 3–5). The flood and torrent would have swept over them if the Lord had not been on their side. But 2 Samuel 5:20–25 states David won that battle because God intervened against the Philistines: "The Lord has burst out against my enemies before me" (2 Samuel 5:20). If we invite the Lord into our battles, we have a better chance of winning. Remember, this is a metaphor, so do we always win the battles if we invite the Lord into them? Not always. Romans 5:3–4 states God might keep us in a battle for a period of time so we can grow. James 1:12 explains God might keep us in the battle to refine us by asking us to remain steadfast under trial. If we've invited God into the battle and think He's not showing up, we might need to stop and ask ourselves what God might be trying to teach us in the battle. Whether God delivers us or keeps us there, we can know that He is with us.

Remember the people were singing this hymn on the way to Jerusalem so they would remember what God had done for them (vv. 1–5). The remaining verses described their thankfulness to God (vv. 6–8).

*Psalm 124:6*: David praised the Lord for their deliverance: "Blessed be the Lord." When you hear "bless the Lord," how do you reconcile that with the understanding that God doesn't need your blessing? Deuteronomy 8:10 says, "And you shall eat and be full, and you shall bless the Lord your God for the good land he has given you" (ESV). In this context, blessing the Lord means giving thanks to Him.

*Psalm 124:7*: David painted a word picture of a predator and prey with the idea of escaping a snare. To catch small prey, you set up some kind of rigging with a thin rope or fish line as a tripwire. When the animal tripped the wire, the rigging would capture the animal. Snares are set up to blend in as part of the environment. When we think of our lives and the enemy that tries to ensnare us, the traps are set up all along our path to blend into our environment. When we get too close to them, they capture us. In this context, maybe the snare captured the bird, but the bird was able to escape. If the snare was broken, then maybe God delivered the creature from that snare. When we think about this attitude of thankfulness, how thankful should we be when we're able to escape from something the enemy has planted or set to capture us?

*Psalm 124:8*: David recognized their help was found in the Lord who made heaven and earth. When we invite the Lord into our battles, we have to remember who we're inviting into battle with us. This is the God who can do everything. He is so big He can help us. When we remember who God is, then we will want to invite Him into every single battle and trial and snare we face in our lives. When we do that, it makes us thankful—it gives us a heart of thankfulness. There are times when God will leave us there because He wants to see us grow. But there are also times when God loves us so much that He wants to see us delivered from whatever we're facing.

This explains why this Psalm of ascent was added to the collection of songs they would sing on the way to Jerusalem. Remembering what God did for them was a reminder that God was on their side. David also demonstrated his thankfulness through this song, which he then shared with everybody else so they could celebrate together.

God is the *King of Glory*, and we have the ability to put the *King of Glory* on display. Look back at verses 1 and 2. David asked everyone else to recall and remember what God did for David specifically and what God did for the people. He wanted everyone to remember to instill an attitude of thankfulness because, at the end of the day, we are all God's people who are reflecting His glory. When we remember all the ways God has delivered us, rescued us, been on our side, then we can share that with everyone around us. David also asked everyone to say it out loud. There is power when we speak out loud that we are going to call the Lord into our battles. There's power when we remember out loud who God is.

Romans 10:9 says, "If you confess with your mouth that Jesus is Lord and believe in your heart that God raised Him from the dead, you will be saved." We all know God can deliver us. We all know God created the world. We all know God can do whatever He wants—He can come and fight my battles for me. But there is a power that comes when we speak that out loud. God asks us to speak out loud that Jesus is our Lord. That is how He enters into a relationship with us. When you speak out loud that Jesus is Lord, you're declaring that you believe in your heart that God raised Him from the dead. When you say out loud, "Jesus, you are the Lord of my life," feel the peace and power that comes over you.

Our job as believers is to reflect the glory of God. We can reflect the glory of God through our actions. But when we have a heart of thankfulness that we speak out loud, there's a different power to that when people are listening to us. When you have been delivered, then express out loud the ways you are thankful. Even if you've gone through a trial or God has you in a place where He seems to be refining you, if you express this heart of thankfulness, then you're doing two things. First, you're declaring to the enemy that the Lord is on your side and you're staying strong in the Lord. Second, you're also saying to the people who see you going through that trial that you're thankful. That makes people curious about the God in your life that you're actually thankful when you're going through a trial.

## Closing

When you are in a battle, invite the Lord into it. When you're delivered, reflect a heart of thankfulness. When you speak out loud how thankful you are to the Lord who delivered you, then you're bringing glory to God. Be emboldened to use the power of your words of thankfulness as a weapon against the enemy and as a testimony to the *King of Glory*.

## The Daily Word

The Lord is with you all the time. He is on your side. Yes, the Maker of heaven and earth promises to be your helper. He is for you. He is with you in battle. He is with you through the storm and through the fire. He is with you today. Have you paused and acknowledged Him in your day? Recognize the Lord is mighty to save and able to offer counsel and guidance.

From the moment you wake up, the Lord is with you. Talk to Him. Invite Him into the day. *Pause and say: "Yes, the Lord is with me."* The Lord fights the battle for you. Cease striving and trying to figure things out on your own. Ask the Lord for His wisdom, power, and strength to flow through you. He can move the enemy. He can heal the sick. He can cause the spirit of doubt and fear to flee. Today, humble yourself and invite the Lord into your day.

**If the Lord had not been on our side when men attacked us, then they would have swallowed us alive in their burning anger against us. —Psalm 124:2–3**

Further Scripture: 2 Samuel 5:19; 1 Chronicles 10:13–14; Romans 8:31

## Questions

1. Psalm 124 begins with a question, "What if the Lord had not been on our side?" (NLT). Meditate on that phrase for a few minutes. What in your life might have been different if the Lord had not been on your side?

2. In the second half of Psalm 124:7, David said: "The trap is broken, and we are free" (NLT). Have you ever stopped to wonder about what 'free' means in your own life? What freedoms have you found in Jesus?

3. David called the ones who trust in the Lord "secure as Mount Zion" (Psalm 125:1 NLT). How can a mountain be moved? What did Jesus say about that (Matthew 17:20)? Would your faith be as a mountain? Why or why not?

4. What did the Holy Spirit highlight to you in Psalms 124—125 through the reading or the teaching?

# Lesson 89: Psalms 126—127

*King of Glory*: Zion's Restoration

## Teaching Notes

### Intro

This week we've talked about Psalm 119, the longest psalm, which focuses on how the Word of the Lord carries us through the daily activities of life. From Psalm 120 through Psalm 134 are the Songs of Ascent, which the people of Israel sang as they went up to Jerusalem to praise God for all He had done. Psalm 126 is the seventh Psalm of Ascent. While we don't know the author, *Nelson's Commentary* says the psalm "comes from the time of the restoration of Jerusalem following the Babylonian captivity," most likely during the time of Ezra and Nehemiah.[1] Ezra 2:1; Nehemiah 7:6; and Isaiah 10:22 describe times when small groups of Jews returned to Jerusalem.

Scripture describes three specific returns.[2] The first, found in Ezra 1—6, was led by Zerubbabel, roughly around 538 BC. The second, described in Ezra 7—10, was led by Ezra in 458 BC. Another wave of returning Jews came with Nehemiah around 445 BC, as described in Nehemiah 1—2. After 70 years of captivity, the Jews were coming home! This psalm tells of their joy in returning home to Jerusalem—home to where they believed God to be.

### Teaching

*Psalm 126:1–3*: What the Israelites experienced was so unexpected it felt more like a dream than a reality. They were back in the land God had said He would give them. Warren Wiersbe described these verses: "Within us is the joy of freedom."[3] Psalm 126 also describes what people experience today through salvation. When you've been in bondage, and then you're set free, you experience the joy of the Lord. When you encounter the *King of Glory*, Jesus Christ, who sets

---

[1] Earl D. Radmacher, Ronald B. Allen, and H. Wayne House, eds., *Nelson's New Illustrated Bible Commentary* (Nashville: Thomas Nelson, 1999), 732.

[2] John MacArthur, *The MacArthur Bible Commentary* (Nashville: Thomas Nelson, 2005), 684.

[3] Warren W. Wiersbe, *The Bible Exposition Commentary: Job–Song of Solomon* (Colorado Springs: David C. Cook, 2004), 344.

you free from whatever it is that binds you (pride, addictions, lust, eating habits, anything), you no longer have that pain or weight. You finally experience freedom and wonder if it's really a dream.

As Israel began to shout with joy, other nations began to realize what God had done for them. Yes, God had kicked them out 70 years before, but now He had brought them back. God truly received the glory of bringing them out from bondage and setting them free. Isn't it great to be filled with laughter? When you're in the middle of God's will, and you know it, it's so refreshing.

Where else have we seen believers wanting something, talking to God about it, and then when it happens, wondering if it was really from God? Acts 12:6–11 describes the time when believers prayed that Herod would release Peter even though he'd just put James to death. An angel set Peter free from his chains and captors, but even as it happened, Peter thought he was seeing a vision. Any obstacle that was in Peter's way, God took care of it. When Peter realized what had happened, "he went to the house of Mary, the mother of John Mark, where many were praying" (Acts 12:12). Even though they were praying for Peter's release, they couldn't believe he stood at the door (Acts 12:13–17).

In Psalm 126, the Israelites had longed for their release, and even though it felt like a dream when it happened, they rejoiced, and the nations recognized that Israel was filled with the joy of the Lord. Do you live a life of joy? Verse 3 says they told others God had done great things for them. When you actually believe God has set you free, then you walk with the joy of the Lord.

*Psalm 126:4–6*: According to Wiersbe, these verses convey, "Around us is the promise of life."[4] The people of Israel prayed for God to restore their fortunes (v. 4). "Watercourses in the Negev" referred to streams in the southern part of Israel. It was an "arid region south of Beersheba called the Negev which is utterly dry in the summer, but whose streams quickly fill and flood with the rains of spring. In this manner, the psalmist prays that Israel's fortunes would rapidly change from nothing to everything."[5] In verse 4, there was this mentality about what the highways from Babylon could become with God's further blessings. As the people returned to Jerusalem, they could become like the flood—travelers moving back into the land as the first people to occupy Jerusalem again. They were asking God to flood this community with His people again, to restore them back into His place. With remnant mentality, they started off small but asked God to restore them as He wanted them to be. *Nelson's Commentary* said: "Ultimately,

---

[4] Wiersbe, 345.

[5] MacArthur, 684.

this is a prayer for the coming of Jesus, who will complete God's work among His people."[6]

Three waves of people returned to Jerusalem under Zerubbabel, Ezra, and Nehemiah. During this time frame, they rebuilt the temple. We know that, in time, this temple was eventually destroyed, and a third temple will be built during the time when the Antichrist makes a deal allowing the Jews to rebuild the temple. The Antichrist will come into that temple and cause problems, but in all of this the *King of Glory* will come back. Hold onto that picture as we tie all this together.

When Jesus came the first time, He restored us from bondage to freedom. In John 7:37–38, Jesus invited anyone who was thirsty to come to Him and drink. He said, "The one who believes in Me, as the Scripture has said, will have streams of living water flow from deep within him." So, Psalm 126:4 is a picture of Christ coming and restoring us, with the water flowing freely through us.

In Ezekiel 47:1–12, Ezekiel experienced the events described in these verses in a vision. The water described in verses 3–5 flowed from the temple—from the presence of God. The water flowing from the temple—from Jerusalem—went from his ankles to his knees to his waist. The water soon flowed deep enough to swim and became a river that could not be crossed on foot. The water flowed from the temple all the way down into the Arabah to "the sea of foul water"— meaning the Dead Sea (Ezekiel 47:6–8). When this fresh water pours into the Dead Sea, the Dead Sea becomes fresh. And since the water became fresh, there will be life everywhere the water goes (Ezekiel 47:9). This living water produces fruit—nothing dead. Each month there will be fresh fruit for food and leaves for healing because the water comes from the sanctuary (Ezekiel 47:10–12).

In Psalm 126, the people asked God to restore everything that was dry. They were coming out of bondage and wanted to experience new life. When we ask Jesus to do this for us, He gives us living water. Ultimately, we will see the temple again, and according to Ezekiel 47, it will bring life to the land. Within us is the joy of the freedom we can experience. Around us is the promise of life that is coming through Christ and the third temple. Wiersbe said, "Before us comes the challenge of work."[7] Verses 5–6 explained that those who "sow in tears will reap with shouts of joy." Farming is a hard pursuit at times. The ground is hard. It takes work to see fruit. *Nelson's Commentary* said the people of Jerusalem went to Babylon in tears, which led to repentance. Because of this repentance, at the end of 70 years, they experienced a tremendous reward.[8] The Lord truly came to

[6] Radmacher et al., 732.

[7] Wiersbe, 345.

[8] Radmacher et al., 732.

rescue His humble and repentant people. But that reward didn't come without work—confession and repentance.

## Closing

The Lord wants us to reap a harvest of rejoicing, but it only comes when we are willing to submit ourselves and do the work of asking the Lord to release us from the things that have kept us in bondage. It actually takes work. Galatians 6:9 confirms this promise. Too many of us quit before we experience the rewards in life that are around us. You have to keep walking this out to experience more of Him!

## The Daily Word

The Lord restored Zion (the nation of Israel) after years of captivity, and He desires to bring restoration to your life. You need to decide "Yes, I am willing to seek freedom, to seek life, to seek the fullness of *joy* the Lord has for me through Him!"

Just as a garden takes time—pulling weeds, plowing soil, planting seeds, waiting for seeds to grow—the same is true in your life with Christ. You can decide to just walk by the garden and do nothing—not enjoy the beauty or taste the fruit. Or you can choose to embrace the work, cultivate beauty, and seek the Lord for healing through repentance and humility. *What's your choice today?* The Lord is willing to do great things in your life and is waiting to bring you full healing! He desires to fill your mouth with laughter and shouts of joy and bring restoration. It may take time, *but it's worth it for freedom.*

**When the LORD restored the fortunes of Zion, we were like those who dream. Our mouths were filled with laughter then, and our tongues with shouts of joy. Then they said among the nations, "The LORD has done great things for them." —Psalm 126:1–2**

Further Scripture: Isaiah 61:7; Amos 9:14; Galatians 6:9

## Questions

1. When the Jews returned from captivity, other nations said, "The Lord had done great things for them." Do you think the other nations were jealous? What did Jesus say about Israel and jealousy (Romans 11:11–14)? Would someone looking into your life be jealous of what Jesus has done? How so?

2. What does Psalm 127:1 mean? Do you think Matthew 7:24–27 further describes or explains this verse? Why or why not? Is your "house" built on a firm foundation?

3. In Psalm 127:2 said it is vain to work so hard to have enough food. Where else do we see this in Scripture (Matthew 6:26; John 6:27; Philippians 2:16; Colossians 3:23–24)?

4. What did the Holy Spirit highlight to you in Psalms 126—127 through the reading or the teaching?

# Lesson 90: Psalms 128—129

## *King of Glory*: Protection of the Oppressed

## Teaching Notes

### Intro

We've been on this journey of studying the Bible in Revive School for over a year. We started in the Pentateuch, the first five books of the Bible, which set the tone for what we are going to talk about today. The psalmist writes about everything that happened between the Pentateuch and the historical books. This is a psalm of reflection that deals with how the Israelites were to cope with everything they had been through.

We are still on a Psalm of Ascent. A Psalm of Ascent was sung as the Israelites traveled to Jerusalem for either the Feast of Unleavened Bread, the Feast of the Harvest, or the Feast of Tabernacles. Three times each year, the Israelites traveled to Jerusalem, and when they did, they were singing. These times of ascent were always a time of reflection and praise. This psalm is a song of lament and trust and focuses on how to deal with persecution and suffering.

### Teaching

*Psalm 129:1–2*: These verses are going to discuss how to accept persecution and suffering. These verses are essentially the same, but the second verse declares the attackers had not prevailed. These verses are an Israelite reflecting on how God delivered them in the past. We are going to look at how Israel dealt with persecution.

- *Genesis 12:1–3*: Abraham was called. As Abraham traveled, some people would bless or curse him, and God would return those blessings or curses. Abraham had to understand that God had it taken care of. This takes us back to Psalm 19, which says to trust the word.
- *Genesis 21:8–13*: Isaac was persecuted by Ishmael. Right away, Ishmael mocked Isaac. There was always tension between them. Isaac had to come to terms with receiving constant persecution from his brother. Galatians 4:21–31 describes the tension we still feel today of Muslims (Ishmael)

verses Jews (Isaac) and Christians. There is something crazy about the fact that the Jews have not been wiped off the face of the earth. Story after story in Scripture is of leaders and countries who tried to wipe the Jews off the face of this earth. However, they did not prevail.

- *Exodus 1:9–14*: The more the Israelites were persecuted, the more they increased and molded into a nation. They were not destroyed. We see the language of deliverance from suffering in Psalm 88:15 and Hosea 11:1.

- *Exodus 14:19–31*: The *Egyptians* tried to drown the Jews, but the Lord drowned the Egyptian army instead.

- *Isaiah 37–38*: The *Assyrians* tried to starve the Israelites into surrender, but God wiped out their army.

- *Daniel 3*: *King Nebuchadnezzar* (the ruler of Babylon) tried to burn the Jews up, but the Lord delivered them.

- *Daniel 5*: Although *Belshazzar* blasphemed the God of Israel and defiled the holy vessels, that night the Medes and Persians killed him.

- *Daniel 6*: The *Persians* had Daniel thrown into the lions' den, but God rescued him, and the beasts killed the soothsayers instead.

- Hitler, in one of the worst scenarios of all time, killed over six million Jews in gas chambers, but he was eventually defeated, and the nation of Israel was formed in 1948.[1]

Why? Why is everyone wanting to wipe out a tiny nation, a little people group? Why is the enemy so concerned? Matthew states that Jesus wanted to gather His people together, but they refused and became a desolate nation, and Jesus finished by saying they would not see Him until He comes back and His chosen people say, "Blessed are you who comes in the name of the Lord" (Matthew 23:37–39)! So according to this, the enemy reasons if he destroys Israel, the Lord cannot come back as Jesus promised. But God has not let the enemy wipe out the nation of Israel no matter what persecution or adversity he tries to inflict, the Lord always prevails. And He will come back and clean house (Zechariah 14).

*Psalm 129:3*: Not only did the Israelites have to accept being persecuted, Wiersbe points out that the Israelites had to learn to benefit from the persecution.[2] This verse implies much suffering. MacArthur explains that the psalmist used "farming

---

[1] Wiersbe, *The Bible Exposition Commentary: Job–Song of Solomon* (Colorado Springs: David C. Cook, 2004), 350.

[2] Wiersbe, 350.

analogy . . . to describe the deep, but non-fatal, wounds inflicted on Israel by her enemies."[3]

*Psalm 129:4*: Constable writes that the actual reigns or things that bound Israel were now cut off.[4] This verse shows us that the affliction stopped. It was important for the Israelites to pass down their experiences with persecution down to the next generation.

*Psalm 129:5–8*: The psalmist wrote, "Let all who hate Zion be driven back in disgrace." The word "disgrace" here means shame. MacArthur explains that disgrace means embarrassed and humiliated.[5] The psalmist referred to the image of withered grass to describe the fate of those who persecute Israel. MacArthur wrote, "Grass with shallow roots . . . quickly dies with the first heat, depicts the wicked."[6]

## Closing

Satan hates Israel. He is going to do anything he can to wipe out the Jews. This is why we need to pray for deliverance. We want the enemy to be defeated. (See John 4:22.) Salvation is from the Jews; salvation is Jesus (John 4:22)! Jesus means freedom. Satan knows his time is limited. Salvation is offered to anyone. The enemy will not prevail.

## The Daily Word

The Lord has faithfully protected Israel over the years, and He promises to protect you from the enemy just the same. Remember, in Christ, there is life. In Christ, there is victory. In Christ, there is freedom. No weapon formed against you will succeed. You may be attacked over and over, but *as you stay rooted and grounded in Christ Jesus, you will find victory*. The enemy's plans will not prevail.

What does it look like to keep fighting even in the midst of attacks? Stand in confidence from the Lord. Keep walking by faith, trusting that God is victorious, and therefore you have victory in Him alone. Victory comes from fixing your eyes on Jesus and His wisdom. Seek Him. Spend time in His Word. Allow His

---

[3] John MacArthur, *The MacArthur Bible Commentary* (Nashville: Thomas Nelson, 2005), 685.

[4] Thomas L. Constable, *Expository Notes of Dr. Thomas Constable: Psalms*, 433, https://planobiblechapel.org/tcon/notes/pdf/psalms.pdf.

[5] MacArthur, 685.

[6] MacArthur, 685.

voice to lead you and guide you. But know, even when you are still, He is fighting for you. The enemy will not prevail. Remain in Christ. He is your stronghold.

**Since my youth they have often attacked me—let Israel say—Since my youth they have often attacked me, but they have not prevailed against me. —Psalm 129:1–2**

Further Scripture: Isaiah 54:17; Jeremiah 1:19; 1 John 4:4

## Questions

1. Why would someone be happy or blessed by fearing the Lord? What does it mean to fear the Lord?

2. What could be a consequence of not fearing the Lord and to continue in sin (2 Samuel 12:12; Matthew 10:26)?

3. According to Psalm 128, what was the psalmists saying will be the blessings of those who fear the Lord? Is the Lord the top priority in your home?

4. The title of Psalm 129 is "Protection of the Oppressed." Compare this psalm with Psalms 118:1–4 and 124:1–5. How do you see the Lord's protection and faithfulness?

5. How did Jesus use the image of Psalm 129:6 in the parable of the sower (Matthew 13:5–6, 20–21)?

# Lesson 91: Psalms 130—131

*King of Glory*: Having a Heart Connection

## Teaching Notes

### Intro

As we continue through our study in Psalms, remember that our phrase for how the Messiah is presented in the book is *King of Glory*. Psalm 130 is within the fifth book of the psalms (107—150) and was one of the Psalms of Ascent (120—134). The psalms give us an emotional connection and can bring back a memory of what was happening earlier. For example, I used to fish a lot with my buddy Adam. I had a fishing lure called "A Dancing Nancy," that would dance across the top of the water. While we fished, we'd listen to music, especially the song, "A Girl Named Tennessee," which had the perfect rhythm for me to get the lure to dance. Whenever I hear that song, I remember that day—standing on the boat in the sunshine, making the lure dance, and fishing with my buddy. I have an emotional connection to that song. Likewise, these Psalms of Ascent were written to create an emotional connection for the author and for the people who sang them as they went up to Jerusalem. These psalms can also create an emotional connection for us that goes much deeper than just reading the Scripture to a heart connection and a soul connection.

Psalm 130 builds a case for ultimate redemption that begins with mercy, moves into trust, and leads to hope. The psalm can be outlined in three sections: desperate cry for mercy (vv. 1–2); strong expression of trust (vv. 3–4); and deliberate decision to hope (vv. 5–8).

### Teaching

*Psalm 130:1–2*: The psalmist cried out from the depths of his soul (v. 1). How deep could this be? The *King of Glory* is ready and waiting for us to cry out to Him. Have you cried out from the depths? In my own life, I've been there. I was married before I was a believer, and things were not going well. We were in counseling, and I was praying we would have the strength to get through—even before I was believer. I cried out to God when I couldn't do it anymore.

The psalmist cried out for mercy and that God would hear him (v. 2). God has power and dominion over all, so we can cry out to Him and He will hear us! The definition of the word "mercy" is "compassion or forgiveness shown toward someone whom it is within one's power to punish or harm." I think we inherently know God hears our voice! Sometimes in our fleshly interactions, we want to make sure someone is listening to us and not just hearing us. The psalmist begged God to listen—to let God's ears be attentive to his pleas.

*Psalm 130:3–4*: These verses speak of trust in the Lord. In verse 3, the psalmist stated that if God kept record of his sin, he would be unable to stand before Him to face the judgment he deserved (Romans 5:8). In reality, it only takes one sin to separate us from the Lord. That's all He needs to count. One. But in God, there is forgiveness (v. 4). The word "fear" in verse 4 can be understood as "awe." The weight of our sin and our separation from God is heavy. But, the Almighty and Powerful God gives a way to set that sin aside—He forgives us so we can be in relationship with Him, so we can understand His purpose for our lives, and so we can tap into His power in order to live out that purpose. We can trust in God's mercy and forgiveness.

*Psalm 130:5–8*: The psalmist waited for God and he put his hope in God's Word (v. 5). He waited for the Lord with more intensity than the watchmen on the night shift waited for the morning to come (v. 6). Watchmen were tasked with keeping eye over the village at night to keep people safe. It was a lot of pressure to look for things in the darkness. Imagine the relief when the morning light appears. That is the anticipation we have as we wait on the Lord to work.

The psalmist expressed a deliberate decision to hope in God (v. 7). There is intentionality in calling on the Lord, trusting in the Lord, and putting hope in the Lord. It is active and purposeful. Our souls are waiting for something to connect with . . . to plug it and to charge it up. People find other ways to try to fill their souls—people, products, places, professions—but it should come from the Lord. I sat next to a woman on a plane recently who had a tough upbringing and didn't get the best love from her parents. She went to a church camp and was filled up but didn't have anyone to walk with after that. She was a kind person and made it a point to love others, but it was clear that she was still looking for that connection to come into alignment with her soul. We know it's Jesus. How many people in our lives "know God" but don't necessarily know Jesus? They believe in God but are missing out on the power of Jesus Christ. This woman, like a watchman, was looking for the moment when her soul would align with the Lord.

# Closing

When Erica and I were about to get married, I remember Kyle asking how he could pray for us. I told him to pray that we could live our lives like Aquila and Priscilla. We wanted to walk alongside of people who did not know the Lord or had not developed intimacy with Him. In Acts 18, Aquila and Priscilla took in Apollos, who knew a lot about the Lord through John the Baptist but had not experienced an intimate relationship with God. They showed Apollos mercy, and what it meant to trust in the Lord, and helped him find his hope in the Lord. They helped him make an emotional and soulful connection to God. After Aquila and Priscilla walked alongside of Apollos, he was able to preach with all boldness (Acts 18:24–28).

We wanted to walk along with people who were also searching for that emotional connection with God. Every Sunday, we have an open invitation to our home for dinner. We invite people to come over with no agenda, and we spend time talking and encouraging, and learning their God story. Some evenings we spend time talking about sharing the gospel or the love of Christ for the lost. In the process of talking and listening, we are asking God for discernment to know what He would have us speak into their lives, how we can bless them, and how we can help them align their hearts with His. Often, we're just helping call out the movement of God in their lives as they tell their stories.

All of us can look at the ministry of Aquila and Priscilla, the only married couple presented in ministry in the New Testament, and ask God how He can use us to pour into others who are seeking Him. We can be ministering to those seeking God for the first time, and those who haven't yet experienced fully what a relationship with Christ can be like. Ultimately, we want them to have a complete connection of their hearts with Him.

## The Daily Word

As the sun comes up over the horizon, the watchmen breathe a sigh of relief. The light of morning has come. The darkness of night and any potential attack now ends with the dawn. The light from the sun has arrived, and the watchmen feel hopeful for a new day.

As you wait today for a job, a child, joy, peace, healing, finances, or whatever it may be, find your hope in the Lord. The Son of God has come. He is your light. His Word brings forth healing, truth, joy, and salvation. Just as a watchman stands alert and waiting, you too must stand alert and waiting for the Lord to move in your life. Picture yourself waiting for the light to shine forth on the horizon. He is with you. Proclaim His love. Proclaim His light. Yes, it may be difficult to wait through the darkness . . . *but wait with hope in the Son of God, Jesus.* Wait with hope in the Lord.

**I wait for Yahweh; I wait and put my hope in His word. I wait for the Lord more than watchmen for the morning—more than watchmen for the morning. —Psalm 130:5–6**

Further Scripture: Isaiah 52:7–8; Ezekiel 3:17; Micah 7:7

## Questions

1. Psalm 130 begins with what seems to be an urgent prayer. Think of a time when you have cried out to the Lord with this intensity or a sense of urgency. What was the result of your prayer? If your urgency of prayer is going on now, keep pouring out your heart to Him.

2. In Psalm 130:5, why did the psalmist place his hope in God's Word (Psalm 119:89; Matthew 5:18; Luke 16:17; John 10:35)? How does this parallel Psalm 130:7?

3. How did God redeem His people in the Old Testament? What is the fulfillment of this redemption for believers today (Romans 8:18–30; Galatians 3:13)?

4. Would Psalm 115:3—"He does whatever He pleases"—sound disturbing and fearful if you didn't have complete confidence that God is good?

5. What did the Holy Spirit highlight to you in Psalms 130—131 through the reading or the teaching?

# Lesson 92: Psalms 132—133

*King of Glory*: David and Zion were Chosen

## Teaching Notes

### Intro

This week we finish our study in the book of Psalms. The study of Psalms has by far been the longest teaching series we've ever completed on any book of the Bible and has been a great study for me. I wasn't sure about dealing with the up and down emotional themes throughout Psalms, but it hasn't felt repetitive to me. Our phrase for the book of Psalms is *King of Glory*, but the one underlying theme that has surprised me is that the *King of Glory* is *coming to Jerusalem*. So many of the psalms point to Jerusalem—to the celebration of worship there, to the presence of God there, and to the future work of the Lord there. Psalm 132 fits into three categories. It is a royal psalm, a Psalm of Ascent, and a messianic psalm. This is the longest of the psalms of ascent.

In Psalm 132 is the excitement of going up to Jerusalem into the dwelling place of the Lord (v. 7). The Jews understood Jerusalem was God's city. Psalm 132 is similar to Psalm 89. Both psalms reference an anointed king and that applies to both the time in which it was written and the future *King of Glory*. Along with the anointed king, both psalms present an enemy to be faced. Both psalms refer to the horn of salvation and to the throne. MacArthur states that Psalm 132 "contains the nation's prayers for David's royal descendants which look ahead, even to Messiah."[1]

### Teaching

*Psalm 132:1–5*: The anonymous psalmist asked God to remember the hardships David endured (v. 1) and how he had sworn an oath to the "Mighty One of Jacob" (v. 2). This is a rare designation of God, used first by Jacob (see Genesis 49:24–25). Isaiah 1:24 uses the term "the Mighty One of Israel." Israel was the second name God gave Jacob. Both phrases were used to show that God provided protection and blessing in times of hardship. In verses 3–5, David was driven by the need to find a dwelling place for God and His Ark (2 Samuel 7:1–2).

---

[1] John MacArthur, *The MacArthur Bible Commentary* (Nashville: Thomas Nelson, 2005), 686.

This became a hardship for David (2 Samuel 24), because he was not allowed to build God a dwelling place, even though he bought the land for it. God told David his son Solomon would be the one to build the temple.

*Psalm 132:6–7:* The psalmist moved from David's hardships to David's descendants. He stated that they heard the Ark was near Bethlehem in an area called Ephrathah and found it in the fields of Jaar (also known as Kiriath-jearim). The Ark had been at Kiriath-jearim for 20 years (see 1 Samuel 7:1–2) before it was taken to Jerusalem (2 Samuel 6:1–5). MacArthur explains, "God's throne is in heaven and His footstool is on earth."[2] In this context, "His footstool," in verse 7 referred to "worship at the ark of the covenant on earth."[3] Constable describes the response to the journey of the Ark back to Jerusalem:

> The Israelite pilgrims who sang this psalm resolved to go to worship Yahweh on Mt. Zion: the place in Jerusalem where the ark rested— referred to here as God's "footstool" (v. 7). That was where God dwelt in a localized way among His people. It was His earthly "throne." The pilgrims called on the LORD to meet with them there. They spoke of "the ark of Your strength" (v. 8) because it represented Yahweh's strength in Israel's previous battles.[4]

The Ark had been through a lot, including going before the people in the wilderness and leading them across the Jordan River into the Promised Land.

*Psalm 132:8–10:* The Israelites called on God to "rise up, Lord . . . You and Your powerful ark" and meet them in Jerusalem (v. 8a). *Nelson's Commentary* points out that they asked God to send His Anointed One to them as He had promised.[5] The psalmist asked that God put everything back into place in His city—His Ark, His king, His priests, and His godly people in worship (vv. 8b–9). The psalmist begged God not to turn away from them because He had promised His Anointed One forever (v. 10).

*Psalm 132:11–18:* The psalmist reminded God that He swore to David his descendants would reign on the throne forever (vv. 11–12). *Nelson's Commentary* states

---

[2] MacArthur, 686.

[3] MacArthur, 686.

[4] Thomas L. Constable, *Expository Notes of Dr. Thomas Constable: Psalms*, 465, https://planobiblechapel.org/tcon/notes/pdf/psalms.pdf.

[5] Earl D. Radmacher, Ronald B. Allen, and H. Wayne House, eds., *Nelson's New Illustrated Bible Commentary* (Nashville: Thomas Nelson, 1999) 734.

verse 11 was "a poetic recasting of the central words of the Davidic covenant" (2 Samuel 7:8–16).[6] Sadly, we know how many of the kings who descended from David were bad kings. "The promise to David was specific in terms of God's intended blessings on faithful sons, His chastening of wayward sons, and *His ultimate fulfillment in the anticipated coming Son*"[7] (emphasis added).

God chose Zion (Jerusalem) to be His home and His resting place forever. He desired it (vv. 13–14). God would bless His people in His city, clothe His priests with salvation, and the people would "shout for joy" (vv. 15–16). To "shout for joy" literally means to "utter loudly" and was used to describe "hearty, joyful singing."[8] In Jerusalem, God would make a "horn grow for David" and prepared a lamp of authority for the coming Messiah (v. 17) (Isaiah 11:1–5). The coming Messiah would wear the crown while His enemies would be clothed in shame (v. 18).

## Closing

The psalms of ascent that were sung going up to Jerusalem were for all of us. We will all be going up to heavenly Zion (Hebrews 12:22–24). The Messiah's kingdom will be established forever (Isaiah 9:7), and His enemy will not withstand Him. The *King of Glory* is perfect. It is a song of preparation for all of us, because we will all ascend to Him in His time.

## The Daily Word

When there is unity on a sports team, the game is more likely to end in victory. When there is unity in the body of Christ, it leads to victory in the kingdom. The Lord longs for oneness and unity. The world will believe in Jesus when they witness harmony among brothers and sisters in Christ.

How do you make every effort to live in harmony with one another? Love binds everything together in perfect unity. *So put on love.* Remember love comes from above—from the love of your heavenly Father. Allow your love to overflow from the love you receive from Him. Love your family. Love your brothers and sisters in the body of Christ. Don't keep records of wrong. Forgive others and seek forgiveness. As you love others, the world will take notice and witness the oneness. Through the power of the Holy Spirit, lay yourself aside and walk in humility. If you feel a lack of unity with a brother or sister, it is time to seek reconciliation. Begin with asking the Lord how to love them today, and walk it out in obedience, trusting He will be with you.

---

[6] Radmacher et al., 734.

[7] Radmacher et al., 734.

[8] Radmacher et al., 734.

> **How good and pleasant it is when brothers live together in harmony!
> —Psalm 133:1**
>
> Further Scripture: John 17:20–23; 1 Corinthians 13:4–8a; Colossians 3:14

## Questions

1.  Why was David so insistent on finding and bringing the Ark back to Jerusalem in Psalm 132:3–5 (2 Samuel 6:12)?

2.  In Psalm 132:12, the Lord made a promise to David. Where else in Scripture was this promise made (2 Samuel 7:11–12; Psalm 89:3–4)?

3.  Psalm 133:1 speaks on how good it is to "dwell in unity." There are several instances in Scripture where unity and joining together can accomplish much. Where in Scripture are these mentioned (Deuteronomy 32:30; Romans 12:16; 1 Corinthians 1:10; Hebrews 10:25)? Are you dwelling with your brethren? If not, what can you do to spend more time with like-minded people?

4.  What did the Holy Spirit highlight to you in Psalms 132—133 through the reading or the teaching?

# Lesson 93: Psalms 134—136

*King of Glory*: His Love Is Eternal

## Teaching Notes

### Intro

Today's chapters have two common themes: name and love. Psalm 134 is the last of the 15 Psalms of Ascent that were sung by pilgrims on their way up to Jerusalem for one of the three required feasts (Deuteronomy 16:16).

### Teaching

*Psalm 134:1–3*: The psalmist mentioned people "who stand in the Lord's house at night!" One example of this was Anna: "There was also a prophetess, Anna, a daughter of Phanuel, of the tribe of Asher. She was well along in years, having lived with her husband seven years after her marriage, and was a widow for 84 years. She did not leave the temple complex, serving God night and day with fasting and prayers" (Luke 2:36–37). Matthew Henry noted,

> Some of them did by night stand in the house of the Lord, to guard the holy things of the temple, that they might not be profaned, and the rich things of the temple, that they might not be plundered. While the ark was in curtains there was the more need of guards upon it. They attended likewise to see that neither the fire on the altar nor the lamps in the candlestick went out.[1]

Other verses that describe praying:

1 Timothy 2:8: "Therefore, I want the men in every place to pray, lifting up holy hands without anger or argument."

1 Peter 2:9: "But you are a chosen race, a royal priesthood, a holy nation, a people for His possession, so that you may proclaim the praises of the One who called you out of darkness into His marvelous light."

---

[1] Matthew Henry, "Psalm 134," in *Matthew Henry Commentary on the Whole Bible*, found at https://www.biblestudytools.com/commentaries/matthew-henry-complete/psalms/134.html.

Numbers 6:24–26: "May Yahweh bless you and protect you; may Yahweh make His face shine on you and be gracious to you; may Yahweh look with favor on you and give you peace."

*Psalm 135:1–4*: The first verse in each of Psalms 134 and 135 begin similarly, by calling for praise: "Hallelujah! Praise the name of Yahweh. Give praise, you servants of Yahweh" (v. 1).

Psalm 100:4 says, "Enter His gates with thanksgiving and His courts with praise. Give thanks to Him and praise His name." The enemy's power is taken when we come before God with thankful and grateful hearts.

The psalmist declared that Yahweh chose "Jacob for Himself." While Christians have personalized this statement and made it about how we have been grafted in, God chose Israel. The entire reason we have been grafted in is because God made Israel "His treasured possession" (v. 4).

*Psalm 135:5–7*: Verse 5 parallels 136:2–3: "Give thanks to the God of gods. His love is eternal. Give thanks to the Lord of Lords. His love is eternal.
Verse 6 parallels 136:4–6: "He alone does great wonders. His love is eternal. He made the heavens skillfully. His love is eternal. He spread the land on the waters. His love is eternal."

Verse 7 parallels 136:7–9: "He made the great lights: His love is eternal. The sun to rule by day, His love is eternal. The moon and stars to rule by night. His love is eternal."

*Psalm 135:8–12*: Verses 8–9 parallel 136:10–12: "He struck the firstborn of the Egyptians; His love is eternal. And brought Israel out from among them; His love is eternal. With a strong hand and outstretched arm. His love is eternal."

*Psalm 135:13*: This verse declares, "Yahweh, Your name endures forever, Your reputation, Yahweh, through all generations."

## Closing

These chapters use several names for God:

1. *Lord*—Adonai, which means "my Lord."
2. *God*—Elohim, which simply means "God."
3. *LORD*—or Yahweh, meaning I AM, the only name given exclusively to God, creator of heaven and earth. "Then Moses asked God, 'If I go to the Israelites and say to them: The God of your fathers has sent me to you, and they ask me, 'What is His name?' what should I tell them?' God replied to Moses,

'I AM WHO I AM. This is what you are to say to the Israelites: I AM has sent me to you.' God also said to Moses, 'Say this to the Israelites: Yahweh, the God of your fathers, the God of Abraham, the God of Isaac, and the God of Jacob, has sent me to you. This is My name forever; this is how I am to be remembered in every generation" (Exodus 3:13–15).

God's love is eternal. His name endures forever. This all points to a future revelation where the kingdom of God will be fully realized and we will all join together with the Father in Zion. We are going to be with our God and delight in His everlasting love forever!

---

## The Daily Word

The psalmist reflected on God's eternal love from the time of creation to when Israel settled in the land of Canaan. God's eternal love lasted not only through the miraculous moments and times of faithfulness but also through the challenging times and seasons of discipline. Through each high and low of life, the psalmist knew God's love was eternal, His mercy endured forever, His love never quit.

Today, reflect on the word "eternal"—something that lasts forever and ever with no beginning and no end. Because God loves you, He sent His Son Jesus to save you from death so you could live eternally with Him—*a forever love*. Your citizenship now rests in heaven. Even when you walk through the valley of the shadow of death, the Lord's love abides with you. His mercies are new each morning. Through your temptations and weaknesses, God's love remains full of compassion. It is gracious, slow to anger, and rich in faithfulness and truth. His love won't quit on you. Receive it. Accept it. Rest in it. Child of God, God's love for you is eternal.

**Give thanks to the Lord of lords. His love is eternal. He alone does great wonders. His love is eternal. —Psalm 136:3–4**

Further Scripture: Psalm 86:15; John 3:16; Romans 8:35–37

---

## Questions

1. Psalm 134:2 says to "lift hands in the Sanctuary and bless the Lord." Do you lift your hands to bless the Lord? Why or why not? Will this type of worship will be done in heaven?

2. What does Psalm 135:16–18 mean in your own words? Do idols such as these still exist today? What about the ones who made them? Are there possible idols in your own life that need to be forsaken?

3. What does "His love is eternal" (Psalm 136) mean to you? Take a few minutes to meditate on that phrase and how it affects you.

4. What did the Holy Spirit highlight to you in Psalms 134—136 through the reading or the teaching?

# Lesson 94: Psalms 137—139

*King of Glory*: Maturing in Discipline

## Teaching Notes

### Intro

Our study of the Psalms of Ascent is complete. Psalm 137 is about the Babylonian captivity. In captivity, the people remembered the good days in the past in Israel. The author of Psalm 137 is unknown. The psalm's title is simply, "The Lament of the Exiles." Wiersbe pointed out that the words "remember" and "forget" are used five times in the nine verses of Psalm 139.[1]

### Teaching

*Psalm 137:1–4*: MacArthur characterized the first four verses as lamentations.[2] The exiles sat down by the rivers of Babylon—the Tigris and Euphrates[3]—and wept over their memories of Zion. The temple, which symbolized God's presence, was in Zion, so perhaps the exiles wept over a feeling of inability to connect with God. Even after the exile ended and the temple was rebuilt, the people still had this feeling: "As a deer longs for streams of water, so I long for You, God. I thirst for God, the living God. When can I come and appear before God? My tears have been my food day and night, while all day long people say to me, 'Where is your God?'" (Psalm 42:1–3). The exiles sat by the river because sitting was the official posture of mourning.[4]

As they sat by the rivers, the Israelites put away their instruments because the Babylonians jeered them to sing "the songs of Zion" (v. 3). Music was meant to be a joyful expression of Israel's worship: "Sing for joy to God our strength; shout in triumph to the God of Jacob. Lift up a song—play the tambourine, the melodious lyre, and the harp. Below the horn on the day of our feasts during the new moon and during the full moon" (Psalm 81:1–3). Now, in captivity, the

---

[1] Warren W. Wiersbe, *The Bible Exposition Commentary: Job–Song of Solomon* (Colorado Springs: David C. Cook, 2004), 363.

[2] John MacArthur, *The MacArthur Bible Commentary* (Nashville: Thomas Nelson, 2005), 689.

[3] Wiersbe, 363.

[4] Wiersbe, 363.

Israelites saw no cause for joy, especially as their captors sarcastically asked them to sing songs of their God. The setting seemed completely out of place for the Israelites to praise God. Their attitude was summarized in verse four: "How can we sing the Lord's song on foreign soil?"

*Psalm 137:5–6*: MacArthur observed a transition from lamentations to conditions.[5] The Israelites pictured Jerusalem because it was the place where they would have rather been. In the middle of their sorrow, the Israelites intentionally remembered where they came from and where their joy resided. Their desire to remember was so strong they asked God that their "right hand forget its skill" (v. 5) and their tongue stuck to the top of their mouths (v. 6) if they ever forgot Jerusalem. Forgetting Jerusalem would have been equivalent to forgetting God, so the Israelites worked to keep their eyes on Jerusalem.

Even though the Israelites were suffering, they were learning to work through their suffering. They were in exile, so their conditions were not good. However, they were learning to keep their eyes on God in the midst of their suffering. It might have felt awkward for the Israelites to keep their eyes on the Lord in this way, but they were attempting to live out Psalm 9:11: "Sing to the Lord, who dwells in Zion; proclaim His deeds among the nations." The Israelites were being refined by the Lord. They were learning how to hold onto their faith in the Lord in the midst of suffering and in the middle of things not working out like they expected.

*Psalm 137:7–9*: While this psalm started with lamentations and then moved to conditions, verses seven through nine contain imprecations.[6] Imprecations express hatred for enemies. The psalmist expressed his desire for God to step in and deal with Israel's enemies who had caused them to go into exile. Implied within the imprecatory statements is a desire for God to fight against Israel's enemies because Israel was powerless to do so themselves.

The Edomites had been allies with Babylon in the destruction of Jerusalem[7]: "So rejoice and be glad, Daughter Edom, you resident of the land of Uz! Yet the cup will pass to you as well; you will get drunk and expose yourself. Daughter Zion, your punishment is complete; He will not lengthen your exile. But He will punish your iniquity, Daughter Edom, and will expose your sins" (Lamentations 4:21–22). While Edom rejoiced over the destruction of Jerusalem, Israel asked God to repay them with a similar fate because of their own sin. The Israelites experienced God's discipline because of their sin. Constable wrote, "Believers who experience God's discipline for their sins may feel great sorrow. Sometimes

---

[5] MacArthur, 689

[6] MacArthur, 689

[7] MacArthur, 689

discipline cuts us off from the blessings of corporate worship and the joy it brings. It is always appropriate to ask God to remain faithful to his promises."[8]

## Closing

"In struggling against sin, you have not yet resisted to the point of shedding your blood. And you have forgotten the exhortation that addresses you as sons: My son, do not take the Lord's discipline lightly or faint when you are reproved by Him, for the Lord disciplines the one He loves and punishes every son He receives. Endure suffering as discipline: God is dealing with you as sons. For what son is there that a father does not discipline? But if you are without discipline—which all receive—then you are illegitimate children and not sons. Furthermore, we had natural fathers discipline us, and we respected them. Shouldn't we submit even more to the Father of spirits and live? For they disciplined us for a short time based on what seemed good to them, but He does it for our benefit, so that we can share His holiness. No discipline seems enjoyable at the time, but painful. Later on, however, it yields the fruit of peace and righteousness to those who have been trained by it" (Hebrews 12:4–11).

Chip Ingram listed five characteristics of biblical discipline from Hebrews 12:

1. The necessity of discipline is to deter destruction (v. 4)
2. The means of discipline are actions and words (v. 5)
3. The motive of discipline is to express love (vv. 6–8)
4. The goal of discipline is to teach obedience (v. 9)
5. The result of discipline is short-term pain and long-term gain (v. 10–11)[9]

When you look at Psalm 137, you have to look at Hebrews 12 to understand why God did what He did. He wants to make sure we learn. It's a refining process, and in the refining, you begin to look more like Jesus.

## The Daily Word

The God of the universe created you in your mother's womb. He knit you together. He calls you remarkable and wonderfully made. He knows your eyesight, your height, the number of hairs on your head, and even your thoughts. *Nothing is hidden from Him.* All your days were written in His book before a single one of

[8] Thomas L. Constable, *Expository Notes of Dr. Thomas Constable: Psalms*, 476, https://planobiblechapel.org/tcon/notes/pdf/psalms.pdf.

[9] Chip Ingram, "Five Characteristics of Biblical Discipline," Focus on the Family, https://www.focusonthefamily.com/parenting/effective-biblical-discipline/effective-child-discipline/five-characteristics-of-biblical-discipline.

them began for you. Isn't that amazing? From the moment of your conception, He has been at work maturing you and disciplining you into His image.

Not only is the Lord all-knowing, but His presence is also always with you to strengthen and guide you as you mature. There's nowhere you can hide, no distance you can run, no height too high, or depth too low, where He is not with you and able to move on your behalf. His hand is always there to lead you and hold on to you. As you walk through today, *believe these truths from the Lord*: You are known. God has plans for you. You, child of God, are beautifully and perfectly created. God designed you and has a specific plan for you! Hold on to these powerful promises for your life today!

**For it was You who created my inward parts; You knit me together in my mother's womb. I will praise You because I have been remarkably and wonderfully made. Your works are wonderful, and I know this very well. —Psalm 139:13–14**

Further Scripture: Psalm 139:1–5; Ephesians 2:10; 1 Peter 2:9

## Questions

1. In Psalm 137, why were the people weeping? Have you ever felt like you were in captivity or enslaved to something/someone? If so, explain.

2. Read Psalm 138:6. Explain what the statement, "He takes note of the humble," means. What about the statement, "He knows the haughty from a distance"?

3. In Psalm 139, David shared that God knows everything about us and that we cannot flee or hide from Him. How did David seem to feel about these truths? What about you? How does knowing these things about God make you feel?

4. According to Psalm 139:16, God had written in His book all the days ordained for David before he was even born. Do you think this is true about each one of us? Why or why not?

5. In Psalm 139:23, David asked God to search his heart. After describing how God knew everything about him earlier in the chapter, why do you think David worded his request this way?

6. What did the Holy Spirit highlight to you in Psalms 137—139 through the reading or the teaching?

# Lesson 95: Psalms 140—142

*King of Glory*: Protection from Sin and Sinners

## Teaching Notes

### Intro

Since we have three psalms to cover today, we'll focus on just one of them. Psalm 140 is a fascinating psalm. It is the last of the Imprecatory Psalms where the writer petitioned "God to carry out justice by bringing punishment or destruction upon evildoers, especially those who have mistreated him."[1] Psalm 142 has the unique description of being written by David when he was in a cave. Charles Haddon Spurgeon said, "Caves make good closets for prayer; their gloom and solitude are helpful to the exercise of devotion. Had David prayed as much in his palace as he did in his cave, he might never have fallen into the act which brought such misery upon his later days."[2] But today, let's focus on Psalm 141, a prayer for protection from sin and sinners. When we come to the point where we don't know what to pray, Psalm 141 gives us a framework to get us started.

### Teaching

John Chrysostom, archbishop of Constantinople in the late AD 300s, said believers need to pray this prayer every evening. "The fathers singled out this psalm . . . prescribed its recital as a kind of saving medicine and cleansing of sins so that whatever stain we incur throughout the course of the day—abroad, at home, wherever we pass the time—we might on coming to the evening expunge through this spiritual air. It is, you see, a medicine that removes all these stains."[3]

---

[1] Robert L. Deffinbaugh, "Psalm 109: A Prayer for the Punishment of the Wicked," Bible.org, May 27, 2004, https://bible.org/seriespage/psalm-109-prayer-punishment-wicked.

[2] Charles Haddon Spurgeon, *The Treasury of David*, vol. 3 (McLean, VA: MacDonald Publishing, n.d.), 323.

[3] Robert C. Hill, *St. John Chrysostom: Commentary on the Psalms*, vol. 2 (Brookline, MA: Holy Cross Orthodox Press, 1998), 276.

*Psalm 141:1–2*: The headings that will be used to describe this psalm were developed from a sermon on Psalm 141 from pastor Steve Shepherd.[4] We begin by saying, "Lord, hear my prayer." David called on Yahweh, the Lord, to hear him and hurry to help him. When we pray, it's not just the words we use, but it's the inflection in our tone. In Scripture, incense is often associated with prayer. In Revelation 5:8, John described the bowls full of incense—the prayers of God's people. In the tabernacle and the temple, the prayers of the people ascended to God as the smoke of the incense rose in the sanctuary. In Exodus 30:34, God told Moses what to include in the makeup of the incense. According to www.templeinstitute.org, the incense included a special secret herb that caused the smoke to rise to heaven in a straight column. The altar of incense can also be seen as a picture of the intercession of Christ. Placed before the mercy seat of the Ark of the Covenant, the altar pictured our Advocate standing in the presence of God (Hebrews 7:25; 9:24).

David raised his hands in prayer. At least seven times in these psalms the psalmist lifted up his hands in prayer. In 2 Chronicles 6:12–13, when Solomon dedicated the temple, he prayed with his hands spread out toward heaven. In 1 Timothy 2:8, Paul urged men to pray while "lifting up holy hands." According to Sam Storms, praying with our hands lifted up can show several things about our soul/heart before God: We lift our hands in *surrender* to a higher authority; as an expression of *vulnerability*; as a sign of *dependence*; in expectation of *receiving* a gift; to shift attention *away* from self to the Savior; or as the *beloved* of God.[5]

*Psalm 141:3*: David prayed, "Guard my mouth." What an incredible prayer! How often do we ask God to shut our mouths? James 3:5–6 points out the tongue is like a fire. We ask God to protect what comes out of our mouths because what we say reflects on Him.

*Psalm 141:4*: David prayed, "Protect my heart." Don't let my heart be drawn to what is evil and don't let anything evil come out of my life. In 2 Timothy 2:22, Paul said, "Flee from youthful passions, and pursue righteousness, faith, love, and peace."

---

[4] Steve Shepherd, "Lord, Come Quickly," Sermon Central, December 24, 2013, https://www.sermoncentral.com/sermons/lord-come-quickly-steve-shepherd-sermon-on-christian-life-181481.

[5] Sam Storms, "10 Things You Should Know About the Lifting of Hands in Worship," Sam Storms (website), December 31, 2018, https://www.samstorms.org/enjoying-god-blog/post/10-things-you-should-know-about-the-lifting-of-hands-in-worship.

*Psalm 141:5a*: David transitioned from rejecting the wicked to embracing the correction that comes from the righteous, praying, "discipline me." Spurgeon said, "Depend upon it, the man who will tell you your faults is your best friend. It may not be a pleasant thing for him to do it, and he knows that he is running the risk of losing your friendship; but he is a true and sincere friend, therefore thank him for his reproof and learn how you may improve by what he tells you." Spurgeon added, "The oil of flattery is not excellent."[6] It's important to allow God to discipline you and strengthen you. Ephesians 4:15 stresses the importance of "speaking the truth in love." Hebrews 12:7–11 states that God disciplines us as His children so we can share in His holiness. This discipline will be painful, but it will yield peace and righteousness.

*Psalm 141:5b–7*: David next asked God to "expose evil." The bottom line—let their wickedness be shown for what it is. This visual of being thrown off the sides of a cliff is poignant and powerful because there are some impressive cliffs in Israel. David prayed for severe judgment against the evildoers. When people see where evil will lead them, they will turn back to true and righteous words. In Matthew 7:4–5, Jesus told His followers to "take the log out of your eye, and then you will see clearly to take the speck out of your brother's eye." Notice David first prayed for discipline and correction and then exposure of evil. David's prayer led toward everything Jesus would preach.

*Psalm 141:8–10*: David's prayer ended with, "Fix my eyes." David asked for focus—to look to God for refuge and protection. Focus is another common theme in the psalms. The psalmist's prayer is to fix his eyes on God, to seek God (Psalms 16:8; 25:15; 119:37). To focus on God is also seen in Psalm 16:8; Psalm 25:15; and Psalm 119:37. David prayed for his focus to remain completely on God so he could stand against the distractions. When we are distracted from God, we get into trouble. David prayed his enemies would "fall into their own nets" even as he would "escape safely" (v. 10). David's trust in God was repeatedly vindicated as those who sought to destroy him were themselves destroyed. Notice the similarity of these verses with Hebrews 12:1–3. We have to fix our eyes on the Lord.

## Closing

Psalm 141 gives us an incredible outline for prayer. "Hear my prayer, Lord, as I position myself; as I cry out to You in my desperation because I need You, hear my prayer. Guard my mouth as I pray to You. Guard my mouth as I witness for You. Guard my mouth as I speak because it reflects on You. Also protect my heart—may it not be pulled aside or given to anything else. May it always be

[6] Spurgeon, 309.

only for You. Lord, discipline me and refine me. In love, speak truth into my soul so I may be strong for You. Then, Lord, expose the evil around me. Because I'm focused on You, I can expose it and show it for what it is. Fix my eyes on You so I am able to walk through this incredible journey of life."

## The Daily Word

Day after day, David turned to the Lord in prayer. His prayer life is a model for you. Are there ever times when you turn to the Lord to seek Him but don't know what to say? Today, use Psalm 141 as an outline for your prayer as you seek the Lord. David's honest words will resonate within your heart.

As you begin to pray, call upon the Lord and ask Him to hear you. Then lift up your hands in worship as a symbol of surrender, vulnerability, and honesty to the Lord. Next ask the Lord to guard your mouth and keep watch over the door of your lips. How many times in the middle of hardship is your first inclination of the flesh to spew words of hatred, jealousy, or anger? *The Lord knows the power of your tongue.* Therefore, ask Him to put a guard over your mouth. When you welcome the Lord into your situation, He will answer. He will protect you, discipline you, and expose evil. Turn to the Lord in prayer. He is faithful, and His promises are true day after day after day.

**LORD, I call on You; hurry to help me. Listen to my voice when I call on You. May my prayer be set before You as incense, the raising of my hands as the evening offering. LORD, set up a guard for my mouth; keep watch at the door of my lips. —Psalm 141:1–3**

Further Scripture: Ezra 9:5; Ephesians 4:29; James 3:5–6

## Questions

1. What does Psalm 140:3 say about the power of the words that come out of our mouths? Have you ever been verbally attacked by someone? Have you ever been the serpent, the one with poison on your lips? What does the Bible say about this (Proverbs 10:20, 31; 18:21)?

2. According to Psalm 141:2, how do you think the psalmist entered into God's presence? How do you prepare for your prayer and worship time? How do you want God to receive you?

3. As a Christian, do you ever feel as though the wicked are setting traps for you, as the psalmist described in Psalm 141:9? How do you conquer that?

4.  Psalm 142 was a psalm of David when he was hiding from Saul in a cave. Think of some of the "cave" moments in your life. Did you cry out to God as David cried out in this psalm, or were you overcome with fear and worry? What was the outcome?

5.  What did the Holy Spirit highlight to you in Psalms 140—142 through the reading or the teaching?

# Lesson 96: Psalms 143—145

*King of Glory*: A Cry for Help

## Teaching Notes

### Intro

While all three of these psalms are psalms of David, we're going to walk through Psalm 143. At some point in his life, David journaled about his situation. The psalm he wrote is considered one of the penitential psalms because he was on his knees, penitent before the Lord.

### Teaching

*Psalm 143:1–6:* David began by asking God to hear his prayer. According to Warren Wiersbe, when you pray, you have to "tell God your situation."[1] This was David's seventh and final "I'm sorry" psalm, but he didn't actually come out and say, "I'm sorry." David began by calling on God's faithfulness and righteousness even as he prayed, "Lord, hear my prayer" (v. 1). David came to God with the mentality that God answers prayer because of His faithfulness and righteousness. God is a loving Father who wants to take care of His kids (see Matthew 7:11). We too can come to God with confidence because we know Him and His character through reading His Word.

David then asked God not to judge him because "no one alive is righteous in Your sight" (v. 2). This phrase seems to indicate David had messed up, but so had everyone else. According to John MacArthur, "David admits his own unrighteousness and realizes that if he is to be delivered for the sake of righteousness, it will be because of God's righteousness, not his own."[2] But *Nelson's Commentary* points out that David didn't say he was sorry for what he had done.[3] David's statement that no one is perfect is supported by other Scripture verses. Romans

---

[1] Warren W. Wiersbe, *The Bible Exposition Commentary: Job–Song of Solomon* (Colorado Springs: David C. Cook, 2004), 372.

[2] John MacArthur, *The MacArthur Bible Commentary* (Nashville: Thomas Nelson, 2005), 691.

[3] Earl D. Radmacher, Ronald B. Allen, and H. Wayne House, eds., *Nelson's New Illustrated Bible Commentary* (Nashville: Thomas Nelson, 1999), 740.

3:23 says, "For all have sinned and fall short of the glory of God." Isaiah 64:6 says that we are all unclean before the Lord.

David said the enemy had pursued and crushed him so that he lived in darkness. According to *Nelson's Commentary*, "The biblical metaphor of light and darkness begins in Genesis 1:2–3. To live in darkness is similar to being in the pit (v. 3)."[4] David's spirit was weak, and he was overcome with dismay (v. 4). David said he had nothing left—he had no hope.

But David remembered "the days of old" and meditated on all God had done (v. 5). David combatted his season of darkness by thinking about everything God had done. David "spread out" his hands to God (v. 6), indicating his complete surrender to Him. When you go through a dry season, you have got to talk to the Lord. According to MacArthur, "As a drought-struck land yearns for life-giving water, so persecuted David longs for his life-giving deliverer."[5] In the Sermon on the Mount, Jesus said, "Those who hunger and thirst for righteousness are blessed, for they will be filled" (Matthew 5:6). If you long to experience more of God, He promises He will fill you up. In order for the parched body to be filled, you have to tell God your situation and ask for Him to answer. Looking back at Psalm 143:5, David held on to what he knew about God. We can also look back at everything God has done: "the creation . . ., the call of Abraham, the pilgrimage of Jacob, the life of Joseph . . ., the exodus from Egypt, and the conquest of Canaan."[6]

David reflected and meditated on what God had done. How do you reflect on something? Do you write it down and look at it? Journal it? Draw it? Do whatever brings it forth so that you can think on it. What do you need to do to develop the mentality of giving everything to the Lord? First Peter 5:7 says to cast "all your care on Him, because He cares about you."

*Psalm 143:7–12*: We tell God about our situations and ask Him to answer us. According to Wiersbe, we then "wait for the answer in expectation."[7] David asked God to answer him quickly because his spirit was failing (v. 7a). We need God to answer us now because we don't know if we have the capacity, the perseverance, and the steadfastness to keep going. David then got a little extreme by saying if God hid His face, he would "be like those going down to the Pit" (v. 7b). Without God's answer, David said he would feel as though he was dying. Wiersbe pointed out that David wanted the same answers we want today.[8] He wanted

---

[4] Radmacher et al., 740.

[5] MacArthur, 691.

[6] Wiersbe, 373.

[7] Wiersbe, 373.

[8] Wiersbe, 373–74.

to see God's face (v. 7). He wanted to hear God's Word (v. 8). He wanted the blessing of God's protection (v. 9). In his prayer life, David was very specific in what he asked from God. He wanted to know God's will (v. 10). David wanted to see God face to face, hear His voice, receive His protection, and know His will. Finally, David wanted to bring glory to God's great name (vv. 11–12). David was in a hard spot, and yet he modeled for us how to talk to the Lord. He cried out to God, admitting he had messed up in some way.

When we're in a tough spot, maybe it's depression, but maybe it's just a funk—a spiritual dry spell—or a season of loneliness, what should we do? Betsy de Cruz did a study on how to move from the funk to faith in God again; from the pit of despair to the fear of God. She offered ten things:

1. Let go of the guilt that you're in that place of depression (Psalm 42:5).
2. Reach out to tell someone (James 5:16 describes the process of asking people to pray for you).
3. Get professional help. Or seek counsel and wisdom from others (Proverbs 11:14).
4. Draw close to God and get real with Him (Psalm 34:18).
5. Cling to the Word of God (Psalm 23; Romans 5:1–8; 1 John 4:9–10).
6. Start your personal joy project. Do something that brings you joy.
7. Help someone else. Do something to take eyes off yourself and love somebody else.
8. Tune into worship (Psalm 59:16–17). Let the words of God minister to you through music.
9. Do something creative. It gives you the liberty to mess up as you express yourself.
10. Keep your perspective. Psalm 30:5b: "Weeping may spend the night, but there is joy in the morning."[9]

## Closing

If you are in a funk and you begin to walk through this process, joy is coming in the morning. That's what I love about David—he always kept his eyes on God regardless of where he was.

---

[9] Betsy de Cruz, "10 Ways Christians Can Fight Depression," Crosswalk.com, August 15, 2017, https://www.crosswalk.com/slideshows/10-ways-christians-can-fight-depression.html.

## The Daily Word

Friends often greet each other with, "How are you doing?" Many will smile and say, "I'm good." But what if one day you aren't good? What if that day, when someone asked how you were doing, you said, "My spirit is weak within me; my heart is overcome with dismay." David told the Lord this honest truth and even said, "Answer me quickly!" David's spirit was failing, and he didn't want to go further into the pit.

Can you relate to this place of despair, loneliness, and depression? Release your feelings to the Lord and let go of any shame or guilt. Then reach out and tell someone as you seek their wisdom. Remember, you are not alone. You don't have to stay in this place of despair. Others will relate to you. Receive and believe these promises from the Lord today: *The Lord loves you and cares for you. He is your rock, stronghold, deliverer, and shield. Take refuge in Him because the Lord is gracious and compassionate, slow to anger and great in faithful love.* Today, if your spirit is weak and your heart is overcome with dismay, *the Lord will listen* to your prayer for help.

**LORD, hear my prayer. In Your faithfulness listen to my plea, and in Your righteousness answer me. . . . My spirit is weak within me; my heart is overcome with dismay. —Psalm 143:1, 4**

Further Scripture: Psalm 143:7–8; 144:2; 1 Peter 5:6–7

## Questions

1. Psalm 143:5 says, "I remember the days of old; I meditate on all Your doings; I reflect on the work of Your hands." How often do you meditate on God's handiwork? Or reflect upon God's creation and all He has done? How big is your God?

2. Have you ever prayed what the psalmist prayed in Psalm 143:8, "Teach me the way in which I should walk," and then not listened to what God told you? If so, why, and what was the result?

3. Do you know God's will for your life, as the psalmist asked God to teach him in Psalm 143:10 (Ephesians 5:15–20)? If so, are your following what He leads you to do? If not, take a couple moments to ask God what it is He wants you to do.

4. Psalm 144 refers to God using many different names: rock, fortress, stronghold, deliverer, shield. What are some other names for God? If you wrote a psalm, what names would you use for God based on how He has worked in your life?

5. What did the Holy Spirit highlight to you in Psalms 140—142 through the reading or the teaching?

# Lesson 97: Psalms 146—147

*King of Glory*: Hallelujah!

## Teaching Notes

### Intro

Psalms 146 and 147 build upon one another. The reciprocity between the two psalms points to a Divine Architect who ordered the placement of these works within the canon of Scripture.

### Teaching

*Psalm 146:1; Psalm 147:1*: Both psalms begin with a declaration of praise to God: "Hallelujah!" Psalm 147 describes our worship as "pleasant and lovely" to God. Psalm 146 calls on "my soul" to praise the Lord. The soul can be summarized as the entirety of our being. This is a call to have all of our being engaged in praise to the Lord.

*Psalm 147:2–5*: The major theme of Psalm 147 is the rebuilding of Israel. Isaiah 61 uses similar language: "They will rebuild the ancient ruins; they will restore the former devastations; they will renew the ruined cities, the devastations of many generations." (Isaiah 61:4) Part of the rebuilding of Jerusalem would see that the Lord "heals the brokenhearted and binds up their wounds" (v. 3). Again, this paralleled the language of Isaiah 61: "The Spirit of the Lord God is on Me, because the Lord has anointed Me to bring good news to the poor. He has sent Me to heal the brokenhearted, to proclaim liberty to the captives and freedom to the prisoners" (Isaiah 61:1).

The psalmist praised the Lord for His knowledge. Specifically, the Lord not only knows the number of stars in the sky, He also has named each one. Because of this, the Lord "is great, vast in power; His understanding is infinite" (v. 5). Theologian A. W. Tozer listed 18 attributes of God:

1. All-wise
2. Infinite
3. Sovereign

4. Holy
5. Triune
6. Omniscient
7. Faithful
8. Immutable (Unchanging)
9. Eternal
10. Self-sufficient
11. Self-existent
12. Omnipresent
13. Omnipotent
14. Good
15. Just
16. Merciful
17. Loving
18. Transcendent[1]

*Psalm 146:8–9; Psalm 147:6:* The psalmist continued to declare the Lord's help for "the afflicted" and contrasted this desire with his opposition to the wicked (147:6). Again, this paralleled Isaiah 61: "to proclaim the year of the Lord's favor, and the day of our God's vengeance; to comfort all who mourn, to provide for those who mourn in Zion; to give them a crown of beauty instead of ashes, festive oil instead of mourning, and splendid clothes instead of despair. And they will be called righteous trees, planted by the Lord to glorify Him" (Isa 61:2–3).

*Psalm 147:7–9:* According to the Jewish Encyclopedia, a lyre was like a smaller version of a harp that would have been used in personal worship.[2] The psalmist praised the Lord for providing for and sustaining the creatures of the earth. Psalm 136:25 similarly says, "He gives food to every creature. His love is eternal."

*Psalm 147:10–11:* The psalmist declared that the Lord values "those who fear Him" and who hope in Him, not powerful horses or people: "Now I know that the Lord gives victory to His anointed; He will answer him from His holy heaven with mighty victories from His right hand. Some take pride in chariots, and others in horses, but we take pride in the name of Yahweh our God" (Psalm 20:6–7).

---

[1] A. W. Tozer, *The Knowledge of the Holy: The Attributes of God* (San Francisco: HarperCollins, 1961).

[2] Emil G. Hirsch and Immanuel Benzinger, "Harp and Lyre," Jewish Encyclopedia, http://www.jewishencyclopedia.com/articles/7266-harp-and-lyre.

Instead of taking pride in things of the world, the psalmist exhorted us to cling to the Lord above all else. "For everything that belongs to the world—the lust of the flesh, the lust of the eyes, and the pride in one's lifestyle—is not from the Father but is from the world" (1 John 2:16).

*Psalm 147:12–20*: The Lord was responsible for the prosperity and fortune of Israel (vv. 12–14). His sovereign power extended even to controlling the weather, specifically in His bringing snow and then clearing it from the land (vv. 15–18). The Lord gave "His Word to Jacob" (v. 19). The psalmist wrote that "He has not done this for any other nation" (v. 20). Barnes noted,

> He has favored Israel more than any other people by giving them his revealed truth. This was so. There was no nation in the ancient world so favored as the Hebrew people in this respect. There is no nation now so favored as the nation that has the revealed will of God—the Bible. The possession of that book gives a nation a vast superiority in all respects over all others. In laws, customs, morals, intelligence, social life, purity, charity, prosperity.[3]

## Closing

The simple fact that the Lord gave Israel His Word was enough for the psalmist to end this psalm with a "Hallelujah!"

### The Daily Word

What do you place your hope in? Is it in the things of this world? Your financial investments? A powerful boat or fast car? Perhaps a remodeled home or an amazing vacation? Maybe even the success of your children? Keep in mind, the things of this world will come and go. Yes, the Lord gives you good gifts to enjoy, but when these good things from the Lord begin to identify who you are, God is not pleased. You will never be truly satisfied or strengthened in the things of this world. Eventually they will collapse and fade away.

Instead, *put your hope in the Lord*. He remains faithful forever. Fear the Lord more than you place value on the things of this world. These earthly things will fall and vanish. You don't even know what tomorrow will hold, so why trust in something that may not be here tomorrow? But—Hallelujah!—*with the Lord you can stand firm. With the Lord you can have freedom and victory.* You can place your

---

[3] Albert Barnes, *Barnes' Notes on the Whole Bible*, https://www.studylight.org/commentarics/bnb/psalms-147.html.

confidence in the Lord because He will be with you forever. Seek the Lord for help daily. Fear the Lord, then you will be blessed. Hallelujah!

**He is not impressed by the strength of a horse; He does not value the power of a man. The Lord values those who fear Him, those who put their hope in His faithful love. —Psalm 147:10–11**

Further Scripture: Psalm 20:7–8; 146:5–6; James 4:13–14

## Questions

1. How does Psalm 146 compare to the conviction that Paul spoke about in Philippians 1:21 and Colossians 3:4?

2. What does it mean to live a life of praise (Romans 8:28; Ephesians 5:20; Philippians 4:6; 1 Thessalonians 5:18)?

3. Why did the psalmist say not to put our trust in a person in Psalm 146 (Genesis 12:10–13)? Who did the Israelites put their trust in instead of the Lord (Exodus 14:10–14; 16:1–3; Numbers 14:1–10)? In whom or what are you tempted to place your trust in rather than the Lord?

4. According to Psalm 147:6 and 11, who does the Lord lift up and who does He take pleasure in (1 Samuel 2:30; Matthew 23:12; Luke 1:50; James 4:10)?

5. To whom did God first give His Word (Psalm 147:19–20)? What were they supposed to do with that Word (Deuteronomy 4:7–8; 6:4–9; Romans 9:4)? We are privileged to have the Word of God so accessible to us. What does the Lord desire us to do with His Word (James 2:14–26)?

6. What did the Holy Spirit highlight to you in Psalms 146—147 through the reading or the teaching?

# Lesson 98: Psalms 148—150

*King of Glory*: Adoration Through Praise

## Teaching Notes

### Intro

We are going to wrap up our study of the book of Psalms with Psalm 150. Each of the last five psalms begins with, "Praise the Lord! Hallelujah!" Each psalm increases and builds in praise and joy until we come to Psalm 150.

"Hallelujah" is a great word! In Hebrew "Hallelu" transliterates into the English word "praise." Hallelu-jah literally means, "Praise God!" Pastor David Guzik explains,

> Each book of Psalms closes with a doxology (Psalms 41:13; 72:18–19; 89:52; 106:48). This entire Psalm can be seen as a doxology that not only closes the fifth and final volume of the collected psalms, but also closes the entire book of Psalms. Psalm 150 contains no argument, no real teaching, no real explanation. It is an eloquent, passionate cry to all creation to give Yahweh the praise due to Him.[1]

We are to position ourselves before the only One worthy of glory and honor.

### Teaching

*Psalm 150:1–2*: Pastor Joel Pankow described these verses as the "Hellelu-Why."[2] This all points to the Messiah. "In His sanctuary," is a reference to the temple, where God dwelled. Since Jesus died and rose again, God now "tabernacles" within his people, choosing not to dwell in a building. We are His temple and should therefore live out the implications of what that means.

"His acts of power" are displayed in creation. This phrase also carries with it the idea of God as champion because of the victory He has won through Jesus on

[1] David Guzik, "Psalm 150—Let All Things Praise the Lord," Enduring Word, 2020, https://enduringword.com/bible-commentary/psalm-150/.

[2] Joel Pankow, "The Last Psalm Explains What 'Hallelujah' Is All About," Sermon Central, June 12, 2003, https://www.sermoncentral.com/sermons/the-last-psalm-explains-what-hallelujah-is-all-about-joel-pankow-sermon-on-worship-definition-59218?ref=SermonSerps.

the cross (Colossians 1:19–20). It's a wonderful miracle that we stand before God as holy, something that is only possible through the forgiveness won by Christ. "His surpassing greatness" is a good reminder for us. We should praise Him simply for who He is. Our adoration of God is not meant to depend on mood, or feeling, or circumstance.

On every page of the Bible is the idea of worshipping God—that we are created and saved to the praise of His glory. But much of what passes for worship today misses the mark. Adoration is not about me and what God does for me. Adoration is all about Him—recognizing that I am for Him. I breath for Him. I live for Him. I spend my life for Him. Proclaiming God's rightful worth and position.

In Mark 12:28, Jesus was asked, "Which commandment is the most important of all?" He answered, "You shall love the Lord your God with all your heart and with all your soul and with all your mind" (v. 30). Adoration calls for concentration—not a fierce mental concentration so much as a focusing of our love, an outpouring of wonder toward God. It is not about doing our duty—pleasing our spouse or parents—it's about praising the Lord—Father, Son, and Holy Spirit—for *who* He is and *what* He has done.

*Psalm 150:3–5*: Pastor Joel Pankow described these verses as the "Hellelu-How."[3] Psalm 150 describes an incredible praise band. In Israelite worship, the music was loud and boisterous. You know I could and would love to teach on each instrument and all the varieties and textures—but that's not our purpose today. You can use anything to praise God. The psalmist made a list of a variety of musical instruments to use—trumpets, harps, lyres, tambourines, flutes—even dancing—you name it.

When the Ark was brought back to Jerusalem, David illustrated something similar to this type of praise in 1 Chronicles 15:27–28. See also this instrumental theme with other "benchmark" verses (a short list): Exodus 15:20–21; Nehemiah 12:27; and 1 Corinthians 15:51–52. The point is that we are free to worship God with variety—using our talents and instruments to praise God's name.

*Psalm 150:6*: Pastor Joel Pankow described these verses as the "Hellelu-Who."[4] Now let's not take adoration for granted. There's going to come a time when breath that comes through our nostrils will leave and won't return any more. God has given each of us breath; we're called now to breathe His praise. God does not care about eloquence, only sincerity and obedience. Your worship is acceptable as long as it comes from the heart. You don't need to meet any other mold than that.

---

[3] Pankow.

[4] Pankow.

The psalmist didn't say you have to be checked at the door with, "Let me hear your voice. Okay. I guess you can carry tune." You don't *have* to know how to play the lyre, a guitar, or a trumpet to praise God. All he asked was, "Do you have breath? Are you alive? Is your body warm? Then we'll take you." When you look at God's Word, He even accepts praise from things that aren't even human (Psalm 148:7–11; Revelation 5:13).

This song begins and ends with the command to praise the Lord. We're to praise Him everywhere, with all means possible because of His mighty acts, because of who He is. We're to praise Him with a wide variety of instrumentation and with triumphant expressions of worship. To live a lifestyle of adoration for the best instrument of praise is an individual wholly committed to Him.

*Action Step #1*: I invite you to step forward from the role of observer to participant. Adoration is not meant to be passive as if it's something we watch or listen to. We are to be fully engaged in active worship, lifting our praise to God by engaging our head, heart, and hands. Ask yourself: If I'm just a worship-observer, what is keeping me from entering in? Take this obstacle to the lord for help.

*Action Step #2*: Make it a habit in prayer to tell God how much you love Him. If you need help, try this: "Eternal Father of my soul, let my first thought today be of You, let my first impulse be to worship You, let my first speech be Your name, let my first action be to kneel in prayer. Amen."[5]

## Closing

The reason we are here, as Jesus said, is to let your light shine before men, they may see your good deeds and praise your Father in heaven (Matthew 5:16). We are here to praise the Lord. It isn't really that difficult. When we realize the Hallelu-why that we are praising a God of compassion and mercy—the rest of it all comes into place. No matter who we are or how we do it, as long as we're giving praise to God for His mercy and compassion in Christ—our light will shine and give glory to God.

> We never really adore Him until we arrive at the moment when we worship Him for what He is in Himself, apart from any consideration of the impact of His Divine Selfhood upon our desires and our welfare. Then we love Him for Himself alone. Then we adore Him, regardless of whether any personal benefit is in anticipation or not. Then it is not what He has done for us or what we expect Him to do for us, but what He has been from eternity before we existed, and

---

[5] Pankow.

what He is now even if we were not here to need Him, and what He will be forever . . . it is that which captivates us and evokes from us the selfless offering of self in worship. That is pure adoration. Nothing less is worthy of the name.[6]

## The Daily Word

Jesus said the greatest command is to love God with all your heart, all your soul, and all your mind. Love God with everything. Praising God with everything you have shows your love to God. Just as you would encourage or praise a son or daughter to demonstrate your love for them, praise the Lord for the good things He has done.

Don't let an off-tune singing voice, lack of musical gifting, or uncoordinated dance moves slow you down. You can *praise the Lord* with everything *you* are and with all *you* have. Anything that has the breath of life can praise the name of the Lord. So that includes you! Today, pause for a moment and praise the Lord. Simply say out loud, "Blessing and honor and glory and dominion to the One seated on the throne, *and to the Lamb, forever and ever!* Amen!" Life is full of highs and lows, but one thing that remains the same yesterday, today, and tomorrow is the Lord God Almighty. Hallelujah!

**Let everything that breathes praise the LORD. Hallelujah! —Psalm 150:6**

Further Scripture: Psalm 148:7–11; Matthew 22:36–38; Revelation 5:13

## Questions

1. In Psalm 148, who is to be praised in heaven and on earth, and why is He to be praised?

2. What does it mean in Psalm 148:14 that God has exalted the "horn" (NKJV) of His people (1 Samuel 2:1; Luke 1:69)?

3. Read Psalm 149:1. Why is it important to God that we gather with other believers (Ephesians 5:19; Colossians 3:16; Hebrews 10:25)? What is the primary focus of gathering together for worship?

4. Psalm 149 is a call to praise God with our worship. Why must we be careful of how we worship Him (John 4:22–24; Colossians 2:16–23)? What is one virtue that brings God great joy (Isaiah 66:1–2)?

---

[6] Albert E. Day, *An Autobiography of Prayer* (New York: Harper, 1952).

5. As the study of Psalms concludes with a psalm of praise, take time right now to praise the Lord for who He is. What mighty acts can you praise Him for in Scripture and in your own life? Be sure to praise Him for the little things.

6. What did the Holy Spirit highlight to you in Psalms 148—150 through the reading or the teaching?

# Lesson 99: Proverbs 1—2

*Wisdom*: Wisdom and Discipline

## Teaching Notes

### Intro

We are in the book of Proverbs! The author of most of proverbs is Solomon. MacArthur writes, "Proverbs pulls together the most important 513 of the 3,000 proverbs pondered by Solomon" (1 Kings 4:32; Ecclesiastes 12:9).[1] There are 31 chapters in the book of Proverbs. The word we are going to use to describe the Messiah from the book of Proverbs is *Wisdom* (Matthew 12:42). In 2 Chronicles 1:8–12, Solomon asked the Lord for wisdom. Jesus is greater than the wisdom Solomon had. When you hear the word *Wisdom*, this wisdom ultimately points to Christ (1 Corinthians 1:30).

Constable points out that "chapters 1—9 do not contain 'proverbs' as such, but longer wisdom speeches."[2] "Solomon originated or collected most of the proverbs (10:1—22:16 and chapters 25—29 definitely, and possibly chapters 1—9)."[3] In chapter 30 are the words of Agur. Finally, in chapter 31 are the words of Lemuel.[4]

### Teaching

*Proverbs 1:1*: MacArthur writes, "The word 'proverbs' means, 'to be like'; thus, Proverbs is a book of comparisons between common, concrete images and life's most profound truths. Proverbs are simple, moral statements that highlight and teach fundamental realities about life."[5] MacArthur goes on to point out that Solomon asked God for His wisdom (2 Chronicles 1:8–12) "and offered 'pithy sayings' designed to make people contemplate (1) the fear of God and (2) living

---

[1] John MacArthur, *The MacArthur Bible Commentary* (Nashville: Thomas Nelson, 2005), 695.

[2] Thomas L. Constable, *Expository Notes of Dr. Thomas Constable: Proverbs*, 1, https://planobiblechapel.org/tcon/notes/pdf/proverbs.pdf.

[3] Andrew E. Steinmann, "Proverbs 1–9 as a Solomonic Composition," *Journal of the Evangelical Theological Society* 43:4 (December 2000): 659–74.

[4] Constable, 2.

[5] MacArthur, 695.

by His wisdom."[6] This entire book takes truths and looks at how to apply them to life situations. These principals are not limited just to the book of Proverbs (Genesis 10:9; 1 Samuel 10:12; 24:13; Jeremiah 31:29; Ezekiel 12:22).

*Proverbs 1:2*: According to MacArthur, "The book reflects a threefold setting as: (1) general wisdom literature; (2) insights from the royal court; and (3) instruction offered in the tender relationship of a father and mother with their children, all designed to produce meditation on God."[7] Now, this is a cool image when we study the Old Testament: "The priest gave the Law, the prophet gave a Word from the Lord, and the sage (wise man) gave his wise counsel" (Jeremiah 18:18; Ezekiel 7:26).[8] This is the backdrop. "In Proverbs, Solomon the sage gives insight into the 'knotty' issues of life (1:6), which are not directly addressed in Law or the Prophets."[9] The two major themes throughout Proverbs are wisdom and folly. Every day we have a choice to figure out which path we are going to take.

Having said that, Solomon wrote the proverbs before he had turned away from God (1 Kings 11:1–11). Remember, Solomon eventually split the kingdom of Israel. At this point, Solomon still had to choose which path he would take. Even with all his wisdom he chose the wrong way. No one is perfect. We sometimes have an image of biblical heroes like David or Solomon having led a perfect life or being perfect people. They were not perfect. They fell because they chose a path of folly. You have to choose the path of wisdom every day. Solomon wrote Psalms 72 and 127, Ecclesiastes, and Song of Songs. MacArthur wrote, "Solomon came to the throne with great promise, privilege, and opportunity. God granted his request for understanding (1 Kings 3:9–12; 1 Chronicles 1:10–12), and his wisdom exceeded all others (1 Kings 4:29–31). However, Solomon failed to live out the truth he knew and even taught his son Rehoboam."[10] As you go through this process of understanding wisdom, please understand this: *it is an everyday battle.* Just because you have wisdom doesn't mean you should stop depending on the Lord.

*Proverbs 1:3–6*: The point of going through Proverbs is to learn what wisdom and discipline are. MacArthur explains, "To the Hebrew mind, wisdom was not knowledge alone, but the skill of godly living by wisdom and instruction (Deuteronomy 4:5–8)."[11] Wisdom is not about just being smart; it is about using what

---

[6] MacArthur, 695.

[7] MacArthur, 695.

[8] MacArthur, 695.

[9] MacArthur, 695.

[10] MacArthur, 696.

[11] MacArthur, 698.

you know to live out God's plan for your life. MacArthur defines instruction as "the discipline of moral nature," and understanding as "the mental discipline which matures a person for spiritual discernment."[12]

The book of Proverbs should lead to wisdom, discipline, and understanding. There are a lot of examples of passing down wisdom and knowledge to the simple, the naive, and the innocent, much like a father or mother passes down wisdom and knowledge to their son or daughter. A wise man will listen and increase their learning, yet they will also seek out guidance. Wisdom says, "I need more to get through everyday life." Christ is our wisdom.

*Proverbs 1:7*: We are to fear God with respect and awe yet understand He can consume us at any given time (Hebrews 12:28–29). We see a dual image of love and judgment. There is a balance between the two.

## Closing

MacArthur noted the progression in this passage: "(1) teaching about God; (2) learning about God; (3) fearing God; (4) knowing God; and (5) imitating God's wisdom."[13] This is a great example to help you understand the book of Proverbs. Once you fear the Lord, you start to know and imitate Him. I never saw the book of Proverbs as a guidebook for parenting, and yet it helps develop everyday practical life skills we all need.

### The Daily Word

Have you ever wondered: *What is the fear of the Lord?* Solomon described fear of the Lord as "the beginning of knowledge." He also wrote, "To fear the Lord is to hate evil." Solomon wisely instructed his son to search for wisdom and understanding as though it were a treasure, and by doing so, "then you will understand the fear of the Lord." Later, in the New Testament, the author of Hebrews told believers, "Hold on to grace. By it, we may serve God acceptably, with reverence and awe, for our God is a consuming fire."

As you wrestle with comprehending the fear of the Lord, *press in and seek the Lord for wisdom and understanding.* Make the choice to seek Him in all your ways like searching for a treasure. In your decision to seek the Lord for answers, for help, and for grace, you will demonstrate your reverence toward Him and your faith in trusting Him. Additionally, you will display your confidence in God as a consuming fire. The more you discover the Lord, the more you will hate evil. You will know your God is able, and this will compel you to stand in awe and

---

[12] MacArthur, 698.

[13] MacArthur, 699.

reverence at His ways. *You will find yourself walking in the fear of the Lord.* Nothing else will ever compare to the treasure discovered in seeking Him.

**The fear of the LORD is the beginning of knowledge; fools despise wisdom and discipline. —Proverbs 1:7**

Further Scripture: Proverbs 2:3–5; 8:13; Hebrews 12:28–29

## Questions

1. Who was the main writer of Proverbs? Who else contributed to this book (Proverbs 30 and 31)?

2. What do you think the purpose of Proverbs is (Proverbs 1:2–6)? How can you go about getting or receiving this wisdom?

3. An important phrase in Proverbs is "the fear of the Lord." How many times is this phrase found in Proverbs 1—2? Is there a difference in how each one is used?

4. How does Proverbs point to Jesus (Matthew 12:42; 1 Corinthians 1:24, 30; Colossians 2:3; 1 John 2:6)?

5. According to Proverbs 2:1–5, how can you understand the fear of the Lord and find the knowledge of God?

6. What did the Holy Spirit highlight to you in Proverbs 1—2 through the reading or the teaching?

# Lesson 100: Proverbs 3—4

*Wisdom*: Learning to Trust God

## Teaching Notes

### Intro

So far, we've had 100 lessons in the Wisdom books—including Job and Psalms. Today, we continue with our second lesson in the book of Proverbs. First Kings states Solomon wrote over 3,000 proverbs. God used Solomon to write down divine principles for everyday living. For the study of Proverbs, *Wisdom* is the one word that describes the Messiah (1 Corinthians 1:24). Everything Solomon pointed to as wisdom in the book of Proverbs came from God and eventually points to Jesus as the Messiah. In chapter 2, the writer referenced both God's Law and God's commands. Proverbs 3:4–6 is a classic text out of Proverbs, and it's where we'll camp out today.

### Teaching

*Proverbs 3:1–4*: Proverbs 3 continues the "our son" language from the first two chapters. Wiersbe explains verses 1–10 point out to Solomon's son the set of conditions to follow in his life.[1] Verse 2 implies that if you live according to God's Law and commands, you'll live a longer life. Is it a condition? I think he's saying that if we live our life according to God's instructions, we'll live life out to the fullest. Colossians 1:9–10 states: "For this reason also, since the day we heard this, we haven't stopped praying for you. We are asking that you may be filled with the knowledge of His will in all wisdom and spiritual understanding, so that you may walk worthy of the Lord, fully pleasing to Him, bearing fruit in every good work and growing in the knowledge of God." The first condition is that we need to "learn God's truth" of His mercy and faithfulness (v. 3)[2] (Luke 2:52). When we follow the conditions in verse 3, we're following the example of Jesus.

---

[1] David Guzik, "Psalm 150—Let All Things Praise the Lord," Enduring Word, 2020, https://enduringword.com/bible-commentary/psalm-150/.

[2] Warren W. Wiersbe, *Be Skillful: God's Guidebook to Wise Living* (Colorado Springs: David C. Cook, 1995), 47.

*Proverbs 3:5–8*: The second condition calls us to "obey God's will" (v. 5). It's not enough to learn about God; we're required to obey His will in our lives. We need to do the work by trusting God with our entire beings, rather than depending upon ourselves. We are to trust God to guide us in the right direction (v. 6). *Nelson's Commentary* defines the phrase "trusting in God" as "a conscious dependence on God, much like leaning on a tree for support."[3] We tend to think about the narrow paths—like how to pay off the mortgage in a shorter period of time or take a job because the salary is more. But God may have another path for us that we haven't even considered because we're focusing only on what is right in front of us at the moment. We ask God to bless our efforts, even when we haven't sought His plan for us. Verse 7 says not to consider yourself to be wise but to fear the Lord and turn from evil. Verse 8 states these things will bring about healing and strength.

Wiersbe brings a different picture to the concept of trust and describes it as "to lie helpless, facedown," as "a servant waiting for the master's command in readiness to obey."[4] We trust in the Lord but wait for what He wants. The instructions state to trust in the Lord, not on ourselves; to think about the Lord to guide us; and to fear the Lord and seek His wisdom to help us turn away from evil. These instructions lead to healing our bodies and strengthening our bones. Healing comes when we trust in the Lord. Our question is: are we willing to trust God with our face down before Him, waiting on Him to guide our paths? That means God can come in and do whatever He wants because *He is God*.

*Proverbs 3:9–18*: Wiersbe explains the third condition is to "share God's blessings" (vv. 9–10).[5] We are to give the Lord our possessions and the firstfruits of our harvests (v. 9), and we will be blessed with His blessings (v. 10). This goes against everything we believe in American society—take what we have and invest it for ourselves. Instead, it all belongs to God, and He blesses us in our obedience to Him. Remember we can NEVER out-give God. Wiersbe states we are to "submit to God's chastening" (vv. 11–12).[6] *Nelson's Commentary* explains, "The discipline of the Lord is the other side of His grace. We should cherish God's correction in our lives, because God disciplines only those He loves"[7] (Hebrews 12:7–10).

---

[3] Earl D. Radmacher, Ronald B. Allen, and H. Wayne House, eds., *Nelson's New Illustrated Bible Commentary* (Nashville: Thomas Nelson, 1999) 748.

[4] Wiersbe, 47.

[5] Wiersbe, 48.

[6] Wiersbe, 48.

[7] Radmacher et al., 749.

## Closing

This is a process. We have to learn God's truth so we can obey His will in our lives. We have to share God's blessings as we go, and we have to be ready to accept God's discipline, which in His love, helps us to continue to learn His truth. This is a phenomenal text about how to take God's principles and apply them to our everyday lives. And we do it so we will look more and more like Jesus every day.

---

### The Daily Word

When you lean against a tree, you place trust in the tree's ability and strength to hold you up. You believe the tree won't fall down, which allows you to keep standing. Now, imagine the tree as God. You believe that He is strong enough to hold you up. Just like the tree, you will keep standing as long as you *lean on God*, relying on His strength to keep you from falling over.

*Are you leaning on God to hold you up, or are you leaning on something else?* God has given you promise after promise, encouraging you to rely on Him in all your ways for understanding. He is with you. He is your God. He will strengthen you. He will help you. He will hold on to you. Therefore, *trust the Lord with everything*, believing in His ability, strength, and reliability to hold you up and guide you on the right paths. Lean on that tree—the Tree of Life—the Lord God Almighty. Can you picture yourself leaning on God? Rest in Him alone. He will hold you up and guide you!

**Trust in the Lord with all your heart, and do not rely on your own understanding; think about Him in all your ways, and He will guide you on the right paths. —Proverbs 3:5–6**

Further Scripture: Psalm 62:1; Proverbs 3:7–8; Isaiah 41:10

---

### Questions

1. What two words in Proverbs 3 describe God's character (Psalm 100)? How did the Apostle John describe Jesus' character in John 1:14?

2. According to Proverbs 3:1–12, what are four conditions for receiving God's guidance (vv. 1–4; 5–8; 9–10; 11–12)?

3. What are some blessings from the Lord if you trust and obey Him (Proverbs 3:13–35)?

4. Solomon reiterated in Proverbs 4:4 to "keep my commands." Why do you think this is so important (1 Chronicles 28:9; Proverbs 3:1; 7:2; Ephesians 6:1–4)?

5. What did the Holy Spirit highlight to you in Proverbs 3—4 through the reading or the teaching?

# Lesson 101: Proverbs 5

*Wisdom*: Avoid Seduction

## Teaching Notes

### Intro

Proverbs 5 especially addresses the men. What we're going to talk about today is extremely sensitive in nature. It feels like half of America has been entrenched in Proverbs 5, and truthfully, some of those in the church have been entrenched as well. This message is in no way meant to judge or condemn anyone today. I want to walk through chapter 5 right where you are today. My prayer is that God uses this lesson as a preventative to lead us to walk the right path. This chapter is about sexual temptation. Wiersbe reminds us God created sex, and He has every right to tell us how to use it.[1] Sex is one area Satan wants to influence and take what God has intended for good and use it for evil and destruction. Wiersbe explains sexual sin can lead to "disappointment and disillusionment" and cause the sinner "to search for larger 'doses' of sexual adventure in order to attain the imaginary pleasure level they're seeking."[2]

### Teaching

*Proverbs 5:1–6*: In verse 1, Solomon told his son to listen to his wisdom. As we said a couple of days ago, these chapters were written before Solomon took his eyes off the Lord. In this section, Solomon wrote about the dangers of seduction. He compared the lips of his innocent young son with those of forbidden women who would try to seduce him (vv. 2–3). Solomon knew the young man would be lured to these women who knew exactly what they were doing. Solomon understood that the women, once they had gotten what they wanted, would become bitter and sharp to the son (v. 4). Satan can use those women to cause pain, disappointment, and destruction. In fact, in verse 5, her journey will end in Sheol—in death. Constable explains, "The temptress comes with words that are sweet (flattering) and smooth (delightful, v. 3). Nevertheless, if swallowed, they

---

[1] Warren W. Wiersbe, *The Bible Exposition Commentary: Job–Song of Solomon* (Colorado Springs: David C. Cook, 2004), 407.

[2] Wiersbe, 407.

make the person tempted by them feel bitter (ashamed) and wounded (hurt, v. 4). Even flirting produces this effect sometimes."[3]

Often, it's the little things that can lead us down a dark path. Constable states the forbidden woman "has no concern with living a truly worthwhile life but only with gaining some immediate physical and emotional thrill (v. 6)."[4] People don't think about the consequences of the actions they take before they act. There's a news story of 20 men who walked into a massage parlor who were arrested for prostitution. You know they weren't thinking about getting caught and facing consequences but just wanted to satisfy physical urges at that moment.

*Proverbs 5:7–14*: Solomon moved on to talk about what unfaithfulness would cost his son. He told his son to stay away from her and not even go near the door of her house (vv. 7–8). Temptations are unavoidable and are all around us (Genesis 4:7). Solomon told his son to stay away to avoid the temptation (2 Timothy 2:22). Sadly, we've so isolated ourselves from others that no one even knows when we're hanging around a door that we shouldn't even be near. Constable states, "The price of unfaithfulness is so high that it is unreasonable. Therefore, one is wise to avoid tempting himself or herself by continuing to admire the 'merchandise.' Most marital infidelity occurs because the parties involved continue to spend time together. Here Solomon advised avoiding the company of a temptress."[5] Wiersbe stresses, "God created sex not only for reproduction but also for enjoyment, and He didn't put the 'marriage wall' around sex to rob us of pleasure but to increase pleasure and protect it."[6] This is why Solomon told his son to stay away from that door. Otherwise, going through that door would cost his son his vitality and tie him to someone who was cruel and uncaring and exploitive (vv. 9–10). Even his health could be taken (v. 11). Solomon assured his son that at the end of his life, he would recognize that he had hated discipline when it could have saved him (vv. 12–14).

*Proverbs 5:15–23*: In verses 15–23, Solomon addressed why fidelity is important. These verses are extremely graphic of a man and woman having intercourse. Solomon emphasized with the description that intercourse is meant for a husband and wife and no one else. Intercourse is not meant to be shared with strangers and prostitutes. Intercourse is meant only between husband and wife: "drink water from your own cistern" (vv. 15–17). Instead, take pleasure in "the wife of your youth." If marriage is hard, stick it out, ask God to help, and do your best to save the marriage God created you for.

---

[3] Thomas L. Constable, *Expository Notes of Dr. Thomas Constable: Proverbs*, 49–50, https://planobiblechapel.org/tcon/notes/pdf/proverbs.pdf.

[4] Constable, 50.

[5] Constable, 50.

[6] Wiersbe, 407.

In marriage, people sometimes get bored with their spouses and long for someone else to satisfy them. But Solomon told his son to be lost in his wife's body and her love forever (vv. 19–20). The word "infatuated" in verse 20 actually means "ravished" or "intoxicated."[7] Wiersbe states, "The adulterer watches the river turn into a sewer, but the faithful husband sees the water become wine."[8] Verses 21–23 point out that we cannot get away with any sexual sin without God knowing about it. God knows everything—what's on your phone and your computer. You can't hide any of it from Him. Verses 22–23 say the wicked man is trapped in the ropes of his own sin (John 8:34, 36; Romans 6:16), and he will die because he had no discipline.

## Closing

If you get seduced into a situation, it's because of selfishness. It's because you're not thinking about anyone but yourself. You become stupid, because temptation has captured you. But Christ is in the business of setting people free. Your stupidity is not too big for Christ to fix. Stay away from the seduction and keep your eyes on Jesus Christ. It's not too late for you to throw away your phone, get a new phone number, close social media—whatever it takes to burn that door.

Fight for your marriage as long as you can. Dave Willis lists ways to fight for your marriage:

- Take a break from all forms of criticism, nagging, or sarcasm.
- Find something positive to encourage and affirm in your spouse.
- Choose the right support system.
- Pray for your spouse and your marriage.[9]

I'd add one more. Every day, I pick up my wife so the kids will see that we are physically connected. When you do these things, you can close the door to temptation and the gap between you and your spouse.

## The Daily Word

Seduction from the wrong source will kill a marriage, but it can be avoided. Pay attention! Often a seductive person lures another person away from a husband or

---

[7] Wiersbe, 408.

[8] Wiersbe, 408.

[9] Dave Willis, "4 Ways to Fight for Your Marriage When You are Fighting Alone," Home Word, January 10, 2018, https://homeword.com/jims-blog/4-ways-to-fight-for-your-marriage-when-you-are-fighting-alone/#.XJlpl9EpBPM.

wife, seeking to destroy a marriage with the help of the devil, who tells you the lie that you will find happiness and satisfaction with someone else.

Heed Solomon's advice: Don't go near the door of seduction! It leads to destruction and into even deeper sin. Listen, it may look enticing and seem like everything you have ever wanted, but it won't really satisfy or last. *Make the choice* to flee, block the person's phone number, avoid places where your paths may cross, walk on the other side of the road, and even drop out of the shared committee or group. Take action and do whatever you need to do to resist the lure of seduction. Admit your weakness to the Lord and ask Him for strength. Fix your eyes on Jesus daily. Ask for help from a trusted friend. The Lord will give you strength. *He is a God of transformation and power!* But you must also make the decision to stay away and flee from seduction.

**So now, my sons, listen to me, and don't turn away from the words of my mouth. Keep your way far from her. Don't go near the door of her house. —Proverbs 5:7–8**

Further Scripture: Proverbs 5:22–23; 1 Corinthians 6:18; 2 Timothy 2:22

## Questions

1.  In Proverbs 5:4, Solomon said an immoral woman was as "dangerous as a double-edged sword" (NLT). What is so dangerous about this type of sword? Where else in Scripture is the double-edged sword mentioned (Hebrews 4:12–13; Revelation 1:16)?

2.  In Proverbs 5:8, Solomon warned: "Stay away from her. Don't go near the door of her house." What was he telling his 'son' to do (Matthew 26:41; 1 Corinthians 10:13; James 1:13–15)?

3.  When you read Proverbs 5:15, what does it mean to you? Where else in Scripture does it speak about sex with your wife (Genesis 2:24; 1 Corinthians 7:2; Hebrews 13:4)?

4.  Read Psalm 119:9; 2 Corinthians 7:1; Ephesians 5:3; and 1 Peter 1:14–16. What do you think these verses are telling us to do? Does this sound like what Solomon was trying to say in Proverbs 5? Why or why not?

5.  God tells His children to live pure and holy lives and be free of sexual sins. In your own words, what could be some of the physical and mental problems with sexual sins, premarital sex, and adultery?

6.  What did the Holy Spirit highlight to you in Proverbs 5 through the reading or the teaching?

# Lesson 102: Proverbs 6—7

*Wisdom*: Seven Deadly Sins

## Teaching Notes

### Intro

*Wisdom* is our one word for Proverbs. The book of Proverbs regularly communicates the difference between wisdom and folly. While Proverbs had a royal court perspective and wisdom literature, it also approached wisdom from a parenting perspective. All of this pointed to God's wisdom, which would ultimately be revealed in Christ: "Yet to those who are called, both Jews and Greeks, Christ is God's power and God's wisdom . . . But it is from Him that you are in Christ Jesus, who became God-given wisdom for us—our righteousness, sanctification, and redemption" (1 Corinthians 1:24, 30).

### Teaching

*Proverbs 6:1–5*: Constable pointed out the dangers of "assuming liability for the debts of others" in these verses.[1] Solomon warned against co-signing on a loan for your neighbor. This was a general admonition against becoming indebted to others. The Apostle Paul wrote: "And if he has wronged you in any way, or owes you anything, charge that to my account. I, Paul, write this with my own hand: I will repay it—not to mention to you that you owe me even your own self" (Philemon 18–19). In a seeming contradiction, Paul offered to take on Philemon's debt to Onesimus. However, Paul took on Philemon's debt in an attempt to bless Philemon, not to make a personal profit. The motive made all the difference.

*Proverbs 6:6–11*: Solomon moved on to speaking against laziness. Solomon charged the slacker to observe the ant to become wise. In this instance, wisdom would be gained from observing a creature that was obedient and dedicated to its task. Similarly, people can become wise by observing and spending time with other people who are obedient to God.

---

[1] Thomas L. Constable, *Expository Notes of Dr. Thomas Constable: Proverbs*, 53, https://planobiblechapel.org/tcon/notes/pdf/proverbs.pdf.

*Proverbs 6:12–15*: Solomon cautioned against being unfaithful. The gestures in verse 13—"winking his eyes, signaling with his feet, and gesturing with his fingers"—were all methods by which this person deceived others to get his way. This person's condemnation would come quickly and would be irreversible (v. 15).

*Proverbs 6:16–19*: Solomon listed seven things that are "detestable to Him":

1. *Arrogant eyes*—a callback to verse 13a—"Do nothing out of rivalry or conceit, but in humility consider others as more important than yourselves" (Philippians 2:3). Jesus is our example of living a humble life (Philippians 2:5–11).

2. *A lying tongue*—a callback to verse 12b—Jesus said this attitude of lying to others comes from Satan: "You are of your father the Devil, and you want to carry out your father's desires. He was a murderer from the beginning and has not stood in the truth, because there is not truth in him. When he tells a lie, he speaks from his own nature, because he is a liar and the father of liars" (John 8:44).

3. *Hands that shed innocent blood*—"You have heard that it was said to our ancestors, Do not murder, and whoever murders will be subject to judgment. But I tell you, everyone who is angry with his brother will be subject to judgment. And whoever says to his brother, 'Fool!' will be subject to the Sanhedrin. But whoever says, 'You moron!' will be subject to hellfire. So if you are offering your gift on the altar, and there you remember that your brother has something against you, leave your gift there in front of the altar. First go and be reconciled with your brother, and then come and offer your gift" (Matthew 5:21–24).

4. *A heart that plots wicked schemes*—a callback to verse 14a—an obvious example of a wicked scheme would be plotting a terrorist scheme. David's affair with Bathsheba was another example of a wicked scheme.

5. *Feet eager to run to evil*—a callback to verse 13b—Adam and Eve ran to evil: "Then the woman saw that the tree was good for food and delightful to look at, and that it was desirable for obtaining wisdom. So she took some of its fruit and ate it, she also gave some to her husband, who was with her, and he ate it" (Genesis 3:6). Adam and Eve saw temptation, were drawn to it, and intentionally walked toward it.

6. *A lying witness who gives false testimony*—While still a form of lying, this form of lying was specifically identified because of its intent to crush someone else. "Do not lie to one another, since you have put off the old self with its practices and have put on the new self. You are being renewed in knowledge according to the image of your Creator" (Colossians 3:9–10).

7. *One who stirs up trouble among brothers*—The Lord has always wanted His people to be unified.

*Proverbs 6:20–35*: The tone shifted back to parents' admonitions to their son. The son was exhorted to view their teaching "as a light" and see discipline as "the way to life" (v. 23). Solomon again warned against lust (vv. 25–26) and adultery (v. 29) by asking, "Can a man embrace fire and his clothes not be burned? Can a man walk on burning coals without scorching his feet?" (vv. 27–28).

## Closing
When we begin to go down a path that is contrary to God's wisdom, we will have to deal with consequences.

### The Daily Word

An earthly father shows his love for his children by giving instructions and setting boundaries. In the same way, your heavenly Father has given you commands and teachings to follow. Yes, He loves you unconditionally. Yes, He forgives your sins. Yes, His grace and mercy will follow you all the days of your life. *But that doesn't mean you intentionally stray from His commands, His teaching, and His Word.* His Word should guide you away from doing evil and away from the things the enemy wants you to believe are OK. The seven things the Lord hates are a good example of things to flee from: eyes that are arrogant, a tongue that lies, hands that murder the innocent, a heart that hatches evil plots, feet that race down a wicked track, a mouth that lies under oath, and a troublemaker in the family.

The Lord hates how the devil tempts you. He detests the destruction sin brings to your life, and *He wants to protect you from evil.* Therefore, it is important to read the Word of God. It will guide you as a lamp to your feet and a light for your path. The Lord will provide the strength to follow His commands as you walk, lie down, and wake up. Just take one step at a time towards following Him.

**My son, keep your father's command, and don't reject your mother's teaching. Always bind them to your heart; tie them around your neck. When you walk here and there, they will guide you; when you lie down, they will watch over you; when you wake up, they will talk to you. —Proverbs 6:20–22**

Further Scripture: Psalm 119:105; Proverbs 6:16–19; 6:23–24

## Questions

1. What is Proverbs 6:1 talking about? What are some things the Bible says about loaning money (Deuteronomy 15:1–3; 23:19–20; Proverbs 22:26)? How has borrowing and lending money changed since then? Do you think we go against God's Word by the process in which we lend and borrow today? Why or why not?

2. What are the seven things God hates (Proverbs 6)? Why do you think Proverbs 6 only points out these seven things? What are some other things that God hates (Exodus 20:3–17; 1 Timothy 1:9–10)?

3. What does Proverbs 6 say about a lazy person?

4. How does Proverbs 6 advise us to keep from falling into sin?

5. Why do you think Solomon warned so strongly against the lust of the flesh (Proverbs 7)? Do you think people take this seriously today?

6. What did the Holy Spirit highlight to you in Proverbs 6—7 through the reading or the teaching?

# Lesson 103: Proverbs 8—9

*Wisdom*: Wisdom vs. Foolishness

## Teaching Notes

### Intro

Our word or phrase to describe the Messiah in the book of Proverbs is *Wisdom*. Many times, the book of Proverbs feels like a letter from Solomon to his kids. But Proverbs 9 is a little different. There is no mention of a son, and the chapter takes on more of a feel like a party. When you have a party, you have to have something to celebrate. Then you announce it and prepare for it. Then you actually have to have the party—that's what Proverbs 9 is about. The question is, who will respond to the invitation?

### Teaching

*Proverbs 9:1–2*: Wisdom has prepared her house and prepared the feast on her table. In ancient Israel, wine was a staple part of the feast. Jesus' first miracle, recorded in the Gospel of John, was turning water into wine. Wisdom's house was carved on seven pillars (v. 1). Tom Constable gave several options for what this means: "They may be an allusion to the cosmos (Proverbs 8:22–31) that God made in seven days. Some of the ancients envisioned the world as resting on seven pillars." Others point out there are seven sections in Proverbs 2 through 7. Also, the number seven implies perfection, completion, or wholeness.[1]

*Proverbs 9:3–9*: The female servants called out to those who were inexperienced and lacked sense (vv. 3–4). As if calling from a mountaintop, the servants invited all of the people to come (v. 5). The image of the bread and wine points to the New Testament. In John 6:51, Jesus said, "I am the living bread that came down from heaven. If anyone eats of this bread he will live forever." In Jesus' discourse, the bread and the wine symbolized life. So, the servants issued an invitation to come to a banquet where they would receive life. Those who responded were encouraged: "leave inexperience behind, and you will live" (v. 6). As the church

---

[1] Thomas L. Constable, *Expository Notes of Dr. Thomas Constable: Proverbs*, 65–66, https://planobiblechapel.org/tcon/notes/pdf/proverbs.pdf.

today calls people to come to God, we need to say the same thing: leave the inexperience and lack of sense behind. You don't have to have this whole thing figured out—just come and partake. We can't earn a place at the table because we are all sinners (Romans 3:23). We hear this invitation, literally, from Golgotha and the cross. Because of what Jesus did on the cross, He invites us to His table. Through His blood and His body, He invites us to Himself. This aligns with Ephesians 2:8–9, which emphasizes that salvation is a gift from God.

When the invitation is issued, there will be mockers and scoffers and people who question all of the above (v. 7). As people respond to the invitation, they have a humble spirit and are open to receiving more (vv. 8–9). There are consequences to whether and how we respond to this message. Will we receive it in humility or walk out in arrogance?

*Proverbs 9:10–12*: "The fear of the Lord is the beginning of wisdom" (v. 10a). Hebrews 12:28–29 gives us a healthy perspective on the fear of the Lord. Since we've received the invitation, then let's come to the table in awe and reverence of who God is. Further, "knowledge of the Holy One is understanding" (v. 10b). When we respond, we gain greater respect and deeper knowledge of God. If we live according to the Word of God, the wisdom He has given us, then "years will be added to your life" (v. 11). When we respond, we experience the presence of the Lord. But if we mock the message and the presence of God, we will bear the consequences (v. 12).

*Proverbs 9:13–18*: There is another banquet that's opposite of the feast of wisdom. The woman Folly is rowdy, gullible, and knows nothing (v. 13). She also calls out from the highest point of the city to those who pass by (vv. 14–15). Notice the contradiction between Wisdom and Folly. Folly offers the same invitation to those inexperienced and without sense (v. 16). The enemy will always mask itself with light. The same message is delivered, but Wisdom's invitation brings life, and Folly's invitation leads to death. Look at the counterfeit food offered by Folly: stolen water and tasty bread eaten secretly (v. 17). The devil is a counterfeit to the truth. He makes himself attractive enough that people want him—but, then it's a trick. Folly promotes a funeral, not a feast—death, not life (v. 18).

Proverbs 9 parallels Jesus' message in Luke 14 when He invited everyone to a feast. Generally, in these feasts, there were two invitations. Some days in advance of the celebration, the host notified guests of the day and hour of the feast. Then, on the day of the feast, the host went back to confirm the guests were coming—an RSVP so that the host knew the exact number of guests so the cook could prepare the feast. In Proverbs 1:22, Wisdom called to three groups of guests: foolish ones (simple), mockers, and fools. In Proverbs 8:5, the invitation was issued only to two groups: the inexperienced (simple) and fools. Then, in Proverbs 9, the third invitation was given only to the simple (inexperienced).

In Luke 14:16–24, Jesus told a parable about a master who gave a great banquet. He issued the first invitation, then on the day of the banquet, when his slave went out to gather those invited, every guest made an excuse for not coming to the banquet. The Master of all masters then went to great effort to invite everyone—the poor, maimed, blind, and lame (the simple and foolish)—to come to His table. As these filled his house, the master stated none of those men originally invited would enjoy his banquet. Although not specifically stated in the Proverbs 9 passage, once the invitation is sent out, you have to decide whether to accept or reject the invitation. People have a list of excuses for not accepting the Master's invitation—they're not ready, their friends and their family will think they're crazy, they're having too much fun, or they've done too many bad things. The list can go on and on!

## Closing

No matter what excuses are offered, we are not exempt from going out and inviting people to the Master's table. We are not exempt from telling others what Christ has done—sacrificing His body (bread) and shedding His blood (wine) so we can accept His invitation. We are responsible to deliver the news/invitation; we're not responsible for how they respond. Who would have thought Proverbs 9 would spur us on to issue the invitation? Once people get the invitation and accept it, it's time to celebrate.

## The Daily Word

An invitation to walk on the path of wisdom is available to anyone—no experience needed. You don't have to have it all together. You don't have to have tons of knowledge. You don't have to do good works and earn your way to walk along the path of wisdom.

Jesus shed His blood and died to save the entire world from death so anyone who believes in Him may receive His grace and eternal life. But the choice to get off the path of folly, to instead walk along the narrow path of wisdom and pursue understanding, rests on you. *The Lord offers the invitation to everyone—yes, even the inexperienced.* You are welcomed and invited to come and receive Jesus, the bread of life. The choice is yours. What path will you choose to walk?

"**Whoever is inexperienced, enter here!**" **To the one who lacks sense, she says,** "**Come, eat my bread, and drink the wine I have mixed. Leave inexperience behind, and you will live; pursue the way of understanding.**" **—Proverbs 9:4—6**

Further Scripture: Matthew 7:13–14; John 3:16; Ephesians 2:8–9

## Questions

1. According to Proverbs 8, how can you show that you fear the Lord? When you fear the Lord, what do you get in return (Proverbs 9:10)?

2. Name at least three things Proverbs 8 identified as better than gold, silver, and jewels?

3. According to Proverbs 8, whom does the Lord love? How do you diligently seek the Lord in your everyday life?

4. About whom is Proverbs 8:22–31 talking (Proverbs 3:19; John 1:1–2; Colossians 1:17)? Who do you think was speaking here?

5. In Proverbs 9, what does the Lord promise for those who are wise and fear Him?

6. What did the Holy Spirit highlight to you in Proverbs 8—9 through the reading or the teaching?

# Lesson 104: Proverbs 10—11

## *Wisdom*: A Collection of Solomon's Proverbs

## Teaching Notes

### Intro

Solomon, the son of David, wrote many proverbs. Collectively, from the book of Kings (1 Kings 4:32), we know Solomon wrote at least 3,000 proverbs and 1,000 songs. While Solomon was a prolific writer, many of his proverbs are pithy sayings, little nuggets of wisdom, strung together. As we read through each chapter, sometimes it just doesn't flow in our minds and the way we teach. Tom Constable broke chapter 11 into two sections, with verses 1–15 describing "Wise Living," and verses 16–31 describing "Wise Investments."[1]

### Teaching

*Proverbs 11:1*: The word "detestable" isn't used frequently. This wasn't on the earlier list of the seven things God finds detestable, so this seems to say there are other things that God really hates. One of those is dishonest scales, using inaccurate weights in order to cheat people. Compare this with Proverbs 16:11, which also emphasizes God's concern with honest balances and scales. God has set the standard, so wise living depends on His scales. Doing business with honesty and integrity delights God. Proverbs 20:10, 23 also emphasize God that detests differing weights and dishonest scales. Scripture says cheating the system to get ahead is unacceptable.

*Proverbs 11:2–3*: This theme of wise living is based on integrity.

*Proverbs 11:4*: Let's say you cheat the system by earning money in an unethical way. That wealth won't save you on the day of judgment, the day when God's wrath comes. Wealth won't allow you to escape the penalty of death. But righteousness rescues from death. Ezekiel 7:19 also said silver and gold will not be

---

[1] Thomas L. Constable, *Expository Notes of Dr. Thomas Constable: Proverbs*, 82, 86, https://planobiblechapel.org/tcon/notes/pdf/proverbs.pdf.

able to save the unfaithful on the day of the Lord's wrath. Solomon said you have to be humble to understand this (v. 2).

*Proverbs 11:5–7*: Wise living says don't put your hope in your resources, because you can't bring it with you.

*Proverbs 11:8–11*: People celebrate when the wicked die (v. 10). This verse brings to mind Saddam Hussein and Iraq. When he died and his statue was toppled, do you remember how Baghdad rejoiced? There's something in us that rejoices when the wicked get caught. Think about situations where a dictator runs a country and takes things from its citizens; everyone rejoices when the dictator is taken down.

*Proverbs 11:12–13*: There are times when we just should not say anything.

*Proverbs 11:14*: When you surround yourself with good counsel, you can experience deliverance from things that hold you in bondage. Everyone can be delivered from something that holds them back. Counselors speak truth into your life to help you examine your life to identify those things that hold you back. You cannot hold a "lone ranger" mentality—you need people to run with you in this life. Proverbs 15:22 and 20:18 emphasize the importance of having many good counselors or advisors in our lives. Proverbs 24:6 says the same thing. Maybe this is the problem with the American church—we're afraid of counsel and guidance, so we fall into sin. Scripture says victory comes when we surround ourselves with many counselors. Counselors should not be people who are "yes" men—people who say yes to everything you propose. John MacArthur said, "The more crucial the decision, the more appropriate is corporate wisdom."[2] You are never above counsel, so humble yourself to this part of wise living. Always seek the Lord first, then consult wise counsel (the Davids, the Solomons, the Nathans) to ask them what they think about the path to take. Things get messed up when we seek counsel from others before first seeking the Lord.

*Proverbs 11:15*: Basically, if you put up money to vouch for a neighbor, you're in trouble. But if you hate these kinds of agreements, then you're safe.

*Proverbs 11:16*: Now we're switching to wise investments. MacArthur explained, "While evil people may grasp at wealth, they will never attain the honor due a gracious woman."[3] Money won't gain you honor and respect, and it won't last long either.

---

[2] John MacArthur, *The MacArthur Bible Commentary* (Nashville: Thomas Nelson, 2005), 709.

[3] MacArthur, 709.

*Proverbs 11:17–19*: "The wicked man earns an empty wage" (v. 18a) probably refers to one who used dishonest scales to gain wealth by cheating others. There are two clear paths—righteousness leads to life and evil leads to death.

*Proverbs 11:20*: "Those with twisted minds are detestable to the Lord." Where does that fit into the seven things God detests? Twisted minds could refer to someone who schemes, who has innocent blood on his hands. "But those with blameless conduct are His delight" (v. 20b). That statement goes back to the very beginning, to the one who functions with integrity and who delights to honor God.

*Proverbs 11:21–23*: All continue to emphasize that the wicked will be punished.

*Proverbs 11:24–26*: When you give freely, your storehouses will be overflowing. When you keep giving it away, God says He'll keep giving to you. Finally, you have this picture: People who live with a spirit of poverty even if they're rich, hoard what they have because they're afraid they will become poor. Instead of hoarding, open up the doors and give it away. This is the way of wise investing. God gave you the skill or talent to earn the money in the first place, so if you give it away, He'll give you more. Why? Because God wants the kingdom to advance. He wants the people of God to have what they need to continue to work.

Dr. Ligon Duncan described ten principles of giving.[4] Jesus expects and requires us to give. Jesus wants us to give for the right reasons. Jesus wants us to practice benevolent or charitable giving. Our giving is ultimately to the all-seeing Father. Christian giving is an act of worship. Giving should be done in light of the incarnation. (Because Christ gave of Himself, why are we holding back?) Giving should be in accordance with our means. The liberality of God's blessings to us is connected to our liberality in giving. Giving ought to be done with a cheerful heart. Giving should be done willingly because we freely received.

## Closing

In this proverb, we see wise living. God blessed us with the finances to get to this point. Now we need to take it one more step to wise investment. What is my wise investment? How can I keep giving this wealth away for the kingdom of God? This is an incredible nugget of truth because Solomon, who was the wisest man ever, didn't ask for money, fame, or wealth; he asked for wisdom. When he got wisdom, guess what else he got? Everything else.

---

[4] J. Ligon Duncan, "Ten Principles for Christian Giving," First Presbyterian Church, Jackson, Mississippi, October 21, 2013, https://www.fpcjackson.org/resource-library/blog-entries/ten-principles-for-christian-giving-part-1 and https:// www.fpcjackson.org/resource-library/blog-entries/ten-principles-for-christian-giving-part-2.

## The Daily Word

The Lord loves a cheerful giver. As the Lord counsels you in all your ways, He will direct your path as you steward the resources He has given you. The truth is you can't take anything with you to eternity. Wealth is not profitable on the day of judgment. The hope you place in your finances will vanish when you die. So while you are on earth, do not put your hope in earthly possessions.

Ask the Lord how to steward the different gifts He has given you: your time, your talents, and your resources. *The Lord says a generous person will be enriched and a person who sows generously will also reap generously.* Seek the Lord, and He will direct your path. It may require you to be stretched, it may require you to walk by faith, and it may seem crazy. But the Lord is faithful when you walk in obedience. Take that step and watch the Lord honor your faithful, generous, obedience! May you be flooded with His living water poured over you!

**One person gives freely, yet gains more; another withholds what is right, only to become poor. A generous person will be enriched, and the one who gives a drink of water will receive water. —Proverbs 11:24–25**

Further Scripture: Proverbs 11:4, 7; 2 Corinthians 9:6–7; Philippians 4:19

## Questions

1. Many verses in Proverbs 10 reference some form of speech (mouth, lips, babbling). How many can you find? Why do you think Solomon highlighted this so often in this chapter (Luke 6:45)?

2. Read Proverbs 10:19. The NASB uses the phrase "restrains his lips." Restraint or self-control is one aspect of the fruit of the Spirit (Galatians 5:22–23). How abundant is this "fruit" in your life?

3. According to Solomon, the righteous will never be shaken (Proverbs 10:30). As a believer, have you ever felt like you were being shaken? During these times, what truth can you stand on (Psalms 55:22; 112:6; Hebrews 12:26–27)?

4. Proverbs 10 and 11 contrast the righteous (upright) and the wicked. Do you see this contrast in our culture today? How do you interact with these two groups?

5. Read Proverbs 11:4. Consider Paul's statement in Philippians 3:9, as well as Psalm 53:3 and Isaiah 64:6. Now read 1 Corinthians 1:30; 2 Corinthians 5:21; Jeremiah 23:6; and 33:16. After reading these verses, can you see the Messiah who delivers us from death in Proverbs 11:4?

6. What did the Holy Spirit highlight to you in Proverbs 10—11 through the reading or the teaching?

# Lesson 105: Proverbs 12—13

*Wisdom*: Tame Your Tongue

## Teaching Notes

### Intro

This has kind of been a random week. Our study of the book of Proverbs has been all about golden nuggets of divine principles and practically applying them to our life skills. What I really hear throughout the book of Proverbs is a father talking to a son. From a broad perspective, Solomon gave general advice for everyone. These are practical illustrations. Our one word for this book is *Wisdom*, which we've seen throughout this entire book. This wisdom points to Christ (1 Corinthians 1:24, 30).

### Teaching

*Proverbs 13:1*: A wise son listens to the father's discipline and does not mock or rebuke it. God is dealing with us as sons and daughters (Hebrews 12:7). Fathers are expected to discipline their children. There is a value to discipline.

*Proverbs 13:2–4*: We must be careful about the words that come out of our mouths. You don't have to say everything all the time. We need to watch what we say. Do you always have to have the last word? Do you share your opinion on everything? Do you say hurtful words in the spirit of competition? Do you always have to be right? Do you hurt others with your words?

In my own family, we struggle to tame our tongues. When I tell you this, I'm trying to be transparent, and it is something my family and I struggle with. Everyone has areas in their lives that are their weak points; this is one of ours. If you struggle with the words that come out of your mouth, look at Luke 6:45 and James 3:6–8.

Whatever we say is coming from our hearts and goes to our tongues. What we do with the words on our tongues can uplift or destroy like fire. It is imperative that what comes from our mouth is of the Lord. I want to walk through ways to tame the tongue. James Fraser of Brea provided 12 ways to tame the tongue[1]:

1. Speak no sin.
   - "Keep your tongue from evil and your lips from deceitful speech." (Psalm 34:13)
2. Speak to edify.
   - "I tell you that on the day of judgment people will have to account for every careless word they speak." (Matthew 12:36)
   - "Coarse and foolish talking or crude joking are not suitable, but rather giving thanks." (Ephesians 5:4)
3. Speak sparingly.
   - "When there are many words, sin is unavoidable, but the one who controls his lips is wise." (Proverbs 10:19)
   - Be slow to speak. "My dearly loved brothers, understand this: Everyone must be quick to hear, slow to speak, and slow to anger." (James 1:19)
4. Speak with restraint.
   - Don't be loud and defiant/clamorous. "She is loud and defiant; her feet do not stay at home." (Proverbs 7:11)
   - "These people are discontented grumblers, walking according to their desires; their mouths utter arrogant words, flattering people for their own advantage." (Jude 16)
   - Jesus said He would not argue or shout. "He will not argue or shout, and no one will hear His voice in the streets." (Matthew 12:19)
5. Speak without haste.
   - "The mind of the righteous person thinks before answering, but the mouth of the wicked blurts out evil things." (Proverbs 15:28)
6. Speak reverently.
   - We can speak reverently with authority when our actions show we have been with Jesus. "Because He was teaching them like one who had authority, and not like their scribes." (Matthew 7:29)
   - "When they observed the boldness of Peter and John and realized that they were uneducated and untrained men, they were amazed and recognized that they had been with Jesus." (Acts 4:13)
   - You are an ambassador for Christ. It is hard to get to this point unless you are spending time in His presence.

---

[1] James Fraser, "12 Ways to Tame the Tongue," Reformation Scotland, February 1, 2018, https://www.reformationscotland.org/2018/02/01/12-ways-to-tame-the-tongue/.

7. Speak in faith.
   - Because we believe we have the right to speak in faith. "And since we have the same spirit of faith in keeping with what is written, I believed, therefore I spoke, we also believe, and therefore speak." (2 Corinthians 4:13)
   - "I believed, even when I said, "I am severely afflicted." (Psalm 116:10)
   - When you are struggling, ask the Lord to increase your faith.
   - You can speak about what you've seen and heard, about what God has done in your life. "What we have seen and heard we also declare to you, so that you may have fellowship along with us; and indeed, our fellowship is with the Father and with His Son Jesus Christ." (1 John 1:3)
   - We to speak so that others will come to Christ.
8. Speak prayerfully.
   - Bless what I am about to say. "Then the king asked me, 'What is your request?'" (Nehemiah 2:4)
9. Speak wisely.
   - "Let the message about the Messiah dwell richly among you, teaching and admonishing one another in all wisdom, and singing psalms, hymns, and spiritual songs, with gratitude in your hearts to God." (Colossians 3:16)
10. Speak in fear.
    - "I said, 'I will guard my ways so that I may not sin with my tongue; I will guard my mouth with a muzzle as long as the wicked are in my presence.'" (Psalm 39:1)
11. Speak with kindness.
    - "Who does not slander with his tongue, who does not harm his friend or discredit his neighbor." (Psalm 15:3)
12. Speak without self-praise.
    - Let someone else praise you. "Let another praise you, and not your own mouth—a stranger, and not your own lips." (Proverbs 27:2)

## Closing

"Dear God, I pray we would be men and women of God who would learn to control our mouths; that we can edify and glorify you. Help us to be men and women of prayer. Help us to always point others to you. Amen."

## The Daily Word

Make a specific effort to think before you speak. Before you let words out of your mouth, pause long enough to think if your words are worth the time, energy, and impact they may have on others. If it's too hard to take a breath and pause, put your hand over your mouth as a literal guard for five seconds. And then say your words.

Have you ever tried putting toothpaste back into a tube? Probably not. The process is very messy, time-consuming, and nearly impossible. When a person squeezes toothpaste out of the tube, the toothpaste remains out of the tube for good. The same is true for your words. *Once you speak your words, you can't take them back.* When you think before you speak and display self-control through the power of the Holy Spirit, you help prevent offending or hurting someone. Today, may your words speak life and love into others as you practice self-control.

**The one who guards his mouth protects his life; the one who opens his lips invites his own ruin. —Proverbs 13:3**

Further Scripture: Luke 6:45; James 3:5–6; 1 Peter 2:23

## Questions

1. In Proverbs 12:12, Solomon stated, "The root of the righteous yields fruit." What fruit should we see coming from the righteous (Galatians 5:22–23)?

2. Solomon wrote in Proverbs 12:14b, "And the deeds of a man's hands will return to him." Compare that to Galatians 6:7 (Psalm 90:17). How are these verses similar? Have you experienced this in your life?

3. Have you observed people who are living in chaos and destruction yet see nothing wrong with the path they're on (Proverbs 12:15)? Have you tried to offer advice or counsel? How do you receive counsel from others?

4. Do you see a correlation between Proverbs 12:20b and Matthew 5:9? Explain.

5. Read Proverbs 13:9. Could this verse be pointing to the Messiah (John 1:4–5; 8:12; 12:46)?

6. What did the Holy Spirit highlight to you in Proverbs 12—13 through the reading or the teaching?

# Lesson 106: Proverbs 14—15

*Wisdom*: The Gift of Speech

## Teaching Notes

### Intro

Proverbs are golden nuggets that Solomon wrote, which we just want to soak up and cherish. The problem is that, for example, Proverbs 15 has 33 verses, which is basically 33 sermons. So, this week, we're going to hang out in just a couple of areas. Today, we're going to address our talk (our tongue) and parenting. When we think about the proverbs, we think about nuggets of wisdom that one generation passes down to the next, over and over again.

### Teaching

*Proverbs 15:1–2*: A gentle answer turns away anger, but all harshness does is stir up more and more anger. *Nelson's Commentary* says, "Often it is not so much what we say but the way we say it."[1] A softer tone gets a better response. Wise people know how to respond in a way that makes people want to connect with them (v. 2a). The way they teach, interact, and communicate makes people want to know more. They draw people to what they are saying. In contrast, fools blurt out foolishness (v. 2b). Derek Kidner pointed out: "A wise man does not parade his knowledge; a fool does."[2] We want to listen to the wise people who don't say much, but when they do talk, what they say is important.

Warren Wiersbe said that Proverbs teaches us four things about human speech: "(1) Speech is an awesome gift from God; (2) speech can be used to do good; (3) speech can be used to do evil, and; (4) only God can help us use speech to do good."[3] When we depend on God for what we say, this works. When we function in the flesh, this doesn't work. As parents, we may do better at this, but

---

[1] Earl D. Radmacher, Ronald B. Allen, and H. Wayne House, eds., *Nelson's New Illustrated Bible Commentary* (Nashville: Thomas Nelson, 1999), 760.

[2] Derek Kidner, *Tyndale Old Testament Commentaries: Proverbs* (Downers Grove, IL: IVP Academic, 1964, 2008), 105.

[3] Warren W. Wiersbe, *The Bible Exposition Commentary: Job–Song of Solomon* (Colorado Springs: David C. Cook, 2004), 439.

we are nowhere near perfect. We also get to see firsthand how this works on our children. The tongue can radically impact someone's life. Based on your speech, people are either drawn to your words or repulsed by your words.

*Proverbs 15:3–4*: God is continually watching His people, and, based on the previous two verses, He's watching how they use their tongues. Will they reflect Christ in all they say and do? God's awareness of what is in our hearts is described in 2 Chronicles 16:9 and 1 Samuel 16:7. Scripture confirms that what is in our hearts is what comes out of our mouths (Luke 6:45). When we have a relationship with Jesus, then it should come out in our speech, making other people want what we have.

Verse 4 ties back with verses 1 and 2. A soft answer (v. 1) is a soothing tongue, and it is a tree of life (v. 4). But the hurtful word (v. 1) has a "crooked dealing"[4] that breaks the spirit. The tongue can bring healing when we release a good word—the gospel, the Scriptures, the truth—it takes people back to how God originally designed us. But when you give in to a devious tongue, it breaks the spirit.

*Proverbs 15:5*: Although Solomon seemed to completely change topics here, this verse almost ties back to verse 2. When you release something wise, based on how you say it, people might actually receive what you say (v. 5). "A fool despises his father's discipline" (v. 5a) may be connected to how his father says what he says.

*Proverbs 15:6*: Trouble will always follow the income that has been gained through wickedness (or illegal means).

*Proverbs 15:7*: This verse ties directly to verse 2. The word "broadcast" describes making known what needs to be known at the right time with the right tone. In contrast, the fools will broadcast whatever they know to anybody however they can be heard.

## Closing

Proverbs are practical, daily nuggets that come from the Lord. If we can take these truths and actually apply them as we interact with people, we will walk in the footsteps of Jesus.

---

[4] Radmacher et al., 760.

## The Daily Word

The Lord gave you words as an incredible gift that allows you to communicate. He empowers you to use your words to turn away anger, share knowledge, and encourage others. *And yet* words can also be used for evil. Your words can stir up wrath, blurt out foolishness, and cause hurtful wounds to those around you. The tongue can cause destruction and harm to the world, or it can spread the love of Jesus by declaring the gospel. *There is power in your words both for good and for evil.*

How can you control your tongue and use it for good and not for harm? Do you know what you want to do but have a hard time controlling what you say? Self-control is a fruit of the Spirit. Therefore, abide in Christ, walk in the power of the Spirit, and then you will demonstrate the fruit of the Spirit. Your words will become more life-giving as you abide in the love of the Lord. The Lord will strengthen you to slow down and think before you speak as you release control to Him. Ask the Lord to transform your heart and mind in Him so that your words bring love and not destruction to those around you.

**A gentle answer turns away anger, but a harsh word stirs up wrath. The tongue of the wise makes knowledge attractive, but the mouth of fools blurts out foolishness. —Proverbs 15:1–2**

Further Scripture: Proverbs 15:3–4; John 15:4; Galatians 5:16–17

## Questions

1. Read Proverbs 14:12. Have you lived or "walked" in a way that you thought was right but in hindsight you realized was a destructive path? If so, explain. How have you seen others do this? Do you think this verse could be applied to self-righteousness?

2. A wise man is cautious and turns away from evil, according to Proverbs 14:16. How does a person gain wisdom to do this (Proverbs 1:7; 2:1–6; 15:33)?

3. Solomon taught that a gentle answer turns away wrath. Have you experienced a person answering you in gentleness (humility) rather than anger and watched it diffuse the situation? What about a situation where you responded with a soft answer rather than a harsh response? Do you think keeping the words "Love, Listen, Discern, and (then) Respond" in mind could help someone master this?

4. Do you believe Proverbs 15:3? Does this verse bring fear, encouragement, peace, or another response in you? Why do you think that is your response?

5. Review Proverbs 15:8 and 1 Corinthians 13:3. Do you see any similarity between these two verses? Why or why not (1 Samuel 15:22; Psalm 51:16–17; Isaiah 1:11–17)?

6. What did the Holy Spirit highlight to you in Proverbs 14—15 through the reading or the teaching?

# Lesson 107: Proverbs 16—17

*Wisdom*: God Evaluates Our Motives

## Teaching Notes

### Intro

The writings of Solomon, the wisest man of all times, continue into Proverbs 16. Solomon pointed out to the younger generation that—with their speech—they could choose to take the harder, narrow path that is more life giving. Or they could take the easier, wider, but also darker path that included making fun of people, mocking people, and delivering words that aren't from the Lord.

### Teaching

*Proverbs 16:1–2*: You can try all you want, but until you give this over to the Lord, it will either be your flesh or the Spirit of God speaking through you (v. 1). John MacArthur said, "Human responsibility is always subject to God's absolute sovereignty."[1] In other words, man can plan, dream, and hope, but the final outcome is delivered from the Lord. This image continues to build in verse 2. People may think they're going through life with everything figured out, but God knows their motives (v. 2). God always knows why people are doing what they are doing. God becomes the ultimate judge in everything that we do. Proverbs 21:2 confirms that God evaluates our motives. Proverbs 24:12 confirms that God knows everything about why we do what we do. First Samuel 16:7 points out that people see what is visible (about another person) but God sees their heart. First Corinthian 4:4 also states that God evaluates us. This includes how we talk; what we say, and how we say it.

*Proverbs 16:3*: In verses 1–2, when we do things on our own, people don't even know Whose we are. But when we actually commit our activities to God, He'll allow our plans to be achieved (v. 3). It's going from simply being labelled a Christian to surrendering everything to Jesus to follow Him. In the Hebrew, the word "commit" actually means to "'roll upon' in the sense of both total trust and

---

[1] John MacArthur, *The MacArthur Bible Commentary* (Nashville: Thomas Nelson, 2005), 713.

submission to the will of God."[2] Proverbs 3:5–6 presents this same mentality. Psalm 22:8 says there is a true reliance on God. Psalm 37:5 urges us to commit our way to God, trust Him, and then watch Him act. *Nelson's Commentary* says, "Trusting the Lord with our decisions frees us from preoccupation with our problems."[3]

*Proverbs 16:4*: According to this text, God has prepared everything, not just for the righteous and the good, but also for the evil and the wicked. God is in control of everything, even when it doesn't make sense. Remember, God used Pharaoh to prepare things for His people. All this will bring glory to God on the day of judgment.

*Proverbs 16:5*: This verse fits when we realize that if we're not committing our activities to the Lord, then we're trying to do things by ourselves. Be assured, if you have a proud heart, you "will not go unpunished." *Nelson's Commentary* says, "Pride has everything backwards. It takes credit away from the Giver who gives graciously and awards it to the receiver who takes without thanking."[4] Instead of committing your activities to the Lord, you take credit for what you did. God hates when people rob Him of His glory.

*Proverbs 16:6*: The second half of this verse is easy. When we see the Lord, we fear Him (hold Him in awe) and turn away from evil. Even though there's wickedness, God has it covered. God's mercy, love, truth, loyalty, and faithfulness will take care of it. When we realize what God has done for us and have turned away from evil, then our wickedness is covered. But only those with a humble and contrite heart will receive this.

*Proverbs 16:7*: When our ways please God, He makes even our enemies "be at peace" with us. God can make our enemies like us. In the Sermon on the Mount, Jesus painted a picture about peacemakers: "The peacemakers are blessed, for they will be called sons of God" (Matthew 5:9). When you're intentionally making peace, you are sons of God. When you go out of your way to reflect the love of Christ, people—even your enemies—will be drawn to that.

A note on Proverbs 16:7: Even though this verse states your enemies will be at peace with you, it doesn't mean you won't deal with persecution. Second Timothy 3:12 says, "In fact, all those who want to live a godly life in Christ Jesus will be persecuted."

---

[2] MacArthur, 713.

[3] Earl D. Radmacher, Ronald B. Allen, and H. Wayne House, eds., *Nelson's New Illustrated Bible Commentary* (Nashville: Thomas Nelson, 1999), 762.

[4] Radmacher et al., 762.

*Proverbs 16:8*: Solomon loved to talk about money. He emphasized that having a little with righteousness was better than having much that was gained unjustly. Being in right standing with God is better than having great income without God. *Nelson's Commentary* reminds us, "Righteousness is the real treasure."[5]

*Proverbs 16:9*: This verse compares with verse 2 and 3. We can begin to walk out our path, but it's the Lord who plans our course. We can write out our "heart plan," but we have to trust the Lord to show us the path—to determine every one of our steps. But we have to be willing to hear Him, even if He says that's not a good fit. If we've committed ourselves to Him (v. 3) and trust Him completely by allowing Him to determine our steps (v. 9), then all of it could be achieved (v. 3). Here's the crazy thing—we may not know the timing. In Genesis 50:20, Joseph told his brothers, the ones who had sold him as a slave to the Egyptians when he was a young man: "You planned evil against me; God planned it for good to bring about the present result—the survival of many people." God took all of the wrong that the brothers planned against Joseph and worked out His plan.

Psalm 119:133 says, "Make my steps steady through Your promise; don't let any sin dominate me." This leads us to realize that God can make all of our steps steady, but based on Proverbs 16:2, we need God to weigh our motives.

## Closing

If you're putting down a heart plan, please allow God to weigh out your motives so you can see if this is of Him or if it's of you. If it's of Him, get ready. Buckle up because it's going to be an adventurous ride. If it's not, it might last for a season, but not forever. It might be bumpy; it might be smooth. But if it's not of Him, it will not last.

### The Daily Word

Do you have a plan for the day? Perhaps you wrote down some goals you hope to achieve in the years ahead. Now what? Have you thought to pray through those plans or goals and commit your steps to the Lord? God promises He has a plan for your life. Therefore, as you make plans, as you set goals, commit your activities to the Lord and ask Him to determine your steps.

Commit each moment, each activity, and each decision to the Lord with a pure heart and pure motives. Take the next step you know to do and trust the Lord will provide. *If you feel stuck, delight yourself in the Lord, ask Him for wisdom, and keep walking.* The Lord's grace will follow you because He promises to remain faithful and never leave you. Try not to overthink the plans. The end

---

[5] Radmacher et al., 762.

result may look different from or even beyond what you imagined, but if your heart is aligned with the Lord's, it will reflect His love . . . and that's the ultimate goal in everything!

**All a man's ways seem right to him, but the LORD evaluates the motives. Commit your activities to the LORD, and your plans will be achieved. . . . A man's heart plans his way, but the LORD determines his steps. —Proverbs 16:2–3, 9**

Further Scripture: Psalm 22:8; 119:133; Jeremiah 29:11–12

## Questions

1. According to Proverbs 16, how does one depart from evil? What inclines a believer to fear the Lord?

2. How do you reconcile human responsibility and God's sovereignty as it relates to our "plans" (Proverbs 3:6; 16:2, 9, 33; 19:21; 21:1)?

3. What does Proverbs 16:20 promise to those who heed God's instruction (Psalm 34:8; Jeremiah 17:7)? Are there areas in your life right now where you are not trusting God and His wisdom but relying on the wisdom of the world?

4. What is someone doing when they mock the poor (Proverbs 14:31; 17:5)?

5. How does God feel about those who pervert justice (Exodus 23:6; Proverbs 17:23; Isaiah 5:23)?

6. What did the Holy Spirit highlight to you in Proverbs 16—17 through the reading or the teaching?

# Lesson 108: Proverbs 18—19

*Wisdom*: Love, Listen, Discern, and Respond

## Teaching Notes

### Intro

Here we are, lesson 108! That is a lot of lessons in wisdom literature. The first wisdom book we talked about was the book of Job. From there we looked at the book of Psalms mostly written by David. Now we are in the book of Proverbs, which was written by David's son Solomon. Next week we are going to get into Ecclesiastes and the Song of Songs. What is interesting about the book of Proverbs is that Solomon discusses so many different topics. If you can hang in there, I think you will realize that there are practical life truths that could change your life.

### Teaching

*Proverbs 18:1*: Anyone who isolates himself for selfish desires or self-preservation will eventually be found out. Look at all the leaders, Christian and non, who have fallen in the last few years after their poor behavior was exposed. If you begin to isolate yourself and pursue selfish desires, destruction is coming. Isolation is not good. God designed us to be a part of the body. *Nelson's Commentary* states that one indicator of an isolated person is that he becomes "so intolerant of anyone who disagrees with him that he finds fault with all wise judgment."[1] If you are always right and everyone else is always wrong, step back and look at your life.

*Proverbs 18:2*: When you isolate yourself, you begin to go into this compulsive talker mentality, which keeps you from hearing and understanding other's opinions. *Nelson's Commentary* states, "A compulsive talker never listens, only pausing to plan what he will say next. Every speech confirms what a fool he is."[2] This type of talking is called cheap talk. Cheap talk is full of meaningless words that are readily available. *Nelson's Commentary* provides how to evaluate our words and stay away from cheap talk:

---

[1] Earl D. Radmacher, Ronald B. Allen, and H. Wayne House, eds., *Nelson's New Illustrated Bible Commentary* (Nashville: Thomas Nelson, 1999), 764.

[2] Radmacher et al., 764.

- "Sometimes the wisest course is to keep quiet. We need to weigh our thoughts and words carefully if we intend to be helpful (Proverbs 11:2)."[3] When you humble yourself and open yourself up to what people in your life have to say, that is wisdom.

- "The one thing we never want to talk about is a confidence with which we have been entrusted (Proverbs 11:13)."[4] You don't ever want to be the one to go around sharing information someone has given to you. We don't want to be gossips or spread rumors. A trustworthy person keeps confidences. Sometimes Christians can hide gossip in prayer requests. When in doubt, shhhhh!

- "If we know how to use words, we can accomplish noble ends."[5] We need to watch our tone in what we are saying (Proverbs 15:1–2). God has designed us with our own unique personalities. We don't want to try to be like someone else. We want to become better versions of ourselves by speaking words that are loving and kind.

- "We need to watch what we say. Our mouth can get us in trouble (Proverbs 18:6–7)."[6] When in doubt just stay quiet.

- "If we give our opinion on a matter before hearing the facts, we will tend to bring shame on ourselves (Proverbs 18:13)."[7] We act like we are the experts of everything. If there is humility, we will receive what God is saying to us and how to respond.

- "Talk is cheap, but easy talk can be expensive. Saying the wrong thing at the wrong time can lead to unfortunate consequences (Proverbs 18:21)."[8] Again, when in doubt, please just stay quiet. Just tone it down a little bit. As important as it is to speak carefully, we also need to listen carefully. If you want to grow in the Lord, you need to be open to what others are saying.

*Proverbs 18:8*: Gossip is like a poisoned Oreo cookie; it looks delicious, but it's toxic. Gossip seems fun and irresistible, but it's toxic to you and those you are gossiping about. Be careful what you release and be careful with what you've been entrusted. If someone is releasing gossip, don't receive it. You have to be strong enough to tell someone you don't want to hear it. Receiving and spreading gossip

---

[3] Radmacher et al., 765.

[4] Radmacher et al., 765.

[5] Radmacher et al., 765.

[6] Radmacher et al., 765.

[7] Radmacher et al., 765.

[8] Radmacher et al., 765.

will mess up your inner self. This is a hard truth to receive. But when we refuse to listen to gossip, that's when we start walking with integrity.

*Proverbs 18:9–11*: The lazy man runs toward destruction; the righteous man runs toward the Lord. A rich man trusts in their wealth to make them untouchable (Luke 12:13–21).

*Proverbs 18:12–13*: It is crucial that we love, listen, discern, and then respond. Sometimes with the gospel we are quick to tell people what they need without listening to their story.

*Proverbs 18:14–15*: "Sickness can be overcome, but there is no medicine for a broken spirit (Proverbs 15:4; 17:22; Isaiah 66:2)."[9] The wise keep learning. Learning to listen, to talk, to love, and to discern.

*Proverbs 18:16*: This verse speaks to my heart: "A gift opens doors for a man and brings him before the great." When you give generously, that gift gives you a window into that person's life. Whether its money, eggs, a car, or your time, a generous gift gives you an "in" with a person or group. Once that door is open or that relationship established, God can use you to share His word. This is not a motive but reality. The more you sow and start opening doors, the more God will give you opportunities to open doors. We receive gifts from the Lord to bring glory to Him.

*Proverbs 18:19–20*: Back to talking! When there is offense with a family member it is really hard to overcome. It is especially important to love, listen, and discern with your family. Americans talk a lot. How many other things do you do as much as talking during the day? Talking is pretty important. I want to encourage us to glorify the Lord with our body, including the tongue. We will be held accountable for every careless word we've spoken (Matthew 12:36). When in doubt, apologize when you have been careless with your words.

*Proverbs 18:22*: New topic: marriage! I was hoping to have more time with this; unfortunately, that is not the case. So, here is Marriage 101 in 30 seconds. A wife is a good thing. It is not good for a man to be alone (Genesis 2:18). Where do we get all these statements? From Scripture (Genesis 2:18; Proverbs 18:22; Ecclesiastes 4:9–10). Two is better than one. I don't know your experience. I just know that marriage has made my life better.

---

[9] Radmacher et al., 765.

## Closing

I love Solomon because sometimes it feels like he is writing with ADD (attention deficit disorder). That's why these verses can be applicable to everyone.

---

### The Daily Word

Stay quiet. Stay quiet. Stay quiet. Gossip, harsh words, sarcasm, lies, and foolish and quick-spoken words can lead to strife and devastation. Remember the classic saying, "If you don't have anything good to say, then don't say anything at all." Put this into practice today.

On the flip side, when you aren't talking, you're listening. Listen to understand. Listen because you truly care and seek to love. If you hear something you don't like, be slow to respond. This allows room for the Lord to move in your midst. The Lord promises to fight your battles. You need only to be still. Choose to remain quiet and see what happens today. If you get upset, *stay quiet.* If you get impatient, *stay quiet.* Even if you think you know better, *stay quiet.* Wait for the moment when the Holy Spirit prompts you to speak. *Then say something.* Speak with love. Speak with gentleness. Speak with the peace of Christ. *The key is to take your time and choose your words wisely.* So, stay quiet until the Holy Spirit says, "Go!" Then overflow like a river with God's love!

**The one who gives an answer before he listens—this is foolishness and disgrace for him. —Proverbs 18:13**

Further Scripture: Proverbs 18:4; Matthew 12:36–37; Colossians 4:6

---

## Questions

1. What does Proverbs 18:2 say about a compulsive talker (Proverbs 17:27; Ecclesiastes 10:12–14)? Which is the better route to go, according to scripture (James 1:19)?

2. What is the danger in listening to gossip (Leviticus 19:16)? Is gossip something you struggle with? How can you keep from gossiping or listening to gossip (Proverbs 11:13)?

3. How does Proverbs 19:1 describe integrity (Proverbs 3:1–12; 15:16; 16:8)? What does Proverbs seem to put an emphasis on?

4. Read Proverbs 19:6. How can this verse be seen as generosity or bribery (Proverbs 17:8; 18:16)?

5.  What is the penalty for liars as described in Proverbs 19? What leads to life? How does lying contradict the character of God (Deuteronomy 32:4; John 14:6; 1 John 5:6)?

6.  What did the Holy Spirit highlight to you in Proverbs 18—19 through the reading or the teachings?

# Lesson 109: Proverbs 20—21

*Wisdom*: The Heart is What's Important

## Teaching Notes

### Intro

As Tom and I worked through the book of Proverbs, we were trying to decide whether to teach on Proverbs 20 or 21. The first verse of Proverbs 21 made our decision easy: "A king's heart is like channels of water in the hand of the Lord; He turns it wherever He wishes" (NASB). "Channels" refers to the direction of the water. *Nelson's Commentary* states, "A person can look at a river and think that it is following a random pattern, but the water is following the direction of God's hand. So is the king. This world's apparent chaos is God's work."[1] God is in charge of any dictator, president, or prime minister. God can change that person's heart in an instant and direct it in any way He chooses.

Not too long ago, I was with a group that went to one of the countries in the Balkans and actually met with the prime minister. We had already met with the speaker of the house and the foreign minister. We went in as ambassadors of the Lord to invite them to Jerusalem and to ask them to consider putting an embassy in Jerusalem. They were considering putting an economic office in Israel, which is a miracle in itself. The prime minister called someone else in and asked him where he was looking at putting that office and was told they weren't sure yet but maybe Tel Aviv. One of the people with us graciously explained why they should put an office there, using the Word of God. In that conversation, I saw the prime minister change direction and tell them to put the office instead in Jerusalem. Right then, I went to Proverbs 21:1 because I watched God change the prime minister's mind before my eyes. Anything is possible through God's hand (Romans 13:1, 5).

### Teaching

*Proverbs 21:1–3*: Whatever a man does seems right to him, but the Lord evaluates the motives behind the actions (v. 2). Doing what is right before God is more

---

[1] Earl D. Radmacher, Ronald B. Allen, and H. Wayne House, eds., *Nelson's New Illustrated Bible Commentary* (Nashville: Thomas Nelson, 1999), 748.

important to Him than making sacrifices (v. 3). We could spend our entire time on verse 3. This is all about where the heart is in worship. The Lord is after the heart first:

> The sacrifice of the wicked is detestable to the LORD, but the prayer of the upright is His delight. (Proverbs 15:8)

> Wickedness is atoned for by loyalty and faithfulness, and one turns from evil by the fear of the LORD. (Proverbs 16:6)

> You do not delight in sacrifice and offering; You open my ears to listen. You do not ask for a whole burnt offering or a sin offering. Then I said, "See, I have come; it is written about me in the volume of the scroll. I delight to do Your will, my God; Your instruction lives within me." (Psalm 40:6–8)

Jesus explained that the Pharisees went to the temple to worship but didn't take care of their parents (Matthew 15:3–6; Mark 7:9–13). Possibly His words reflected Micah 6:8: "Mankind, He has told you what is good and what it is the LORD requires of you: to act justly, to love faithfulness, and to walk humbly with your God" (1 Samuel 15:22–23; Hosea 6:6; Matthew 9:9–13; 12:1; 15:3; 23:23).

Sacrifices can be hypocritical displays that do not reflect the true heart. God desires mercy—not sacrifice. The condition of our heart matters.

*Proverbs 21:4–8*: If the eyes, "the lamp that guides the wicked," are haughty from the attitude of an arrogant heart, it shows sin (v. 4). *Nelson's Commentary* explains that "planning typically leads to plenty, and haste to poverty" (v. 5). But profit will not last from a lying tongue (v. 6). Verses 7–8 compare the actions of the wicked and guilty to the behavior of the innocent and the righteous. This was a typical theme for Solomon—the paths of the wicked and the righteous.

*Proverbs 21:9, 19*: Verse 9 suggests that it is better to live outside in the elements than to share a house with a nagging wife. Someone who nags will beat you down over time, and it is not the way God intended the marriage relationship to be. If God can change a king's heart, he can change a spouse's heart.

## Closing

"Dear God, I pray we would be men and women of God who would learn to control our mouths. That we can edify and glorify you. Help us to be men and women of prayer. Help us to always point others to you. Amen."

## The Daily Word

Do you ever wish you could just change the course of someone's life? Maybe a cold-hearted spouse, a prodigal child, an estranged parent, or an unwise friend? The Lord sees your hurting heart and promises that He is there. Hang on to this truth: *If the Lord is able to direct the heart of a king, then the Lord is able to turn the heart of your loved one.*

What can you do in the waiting? Take your hands off the wheel, stop trying to control the rudder of their lives, and *pray*. The Lord hears your prayers. Trust He is at work. He is in control, so allow Him to guide your child, your spouse, or your friend back to Him. While you wait, continue to love the Lord your God with all your heart, all your soul, and all your mind. This way, you will remain strong in the Lord and be able to resist the enemy's plans to discourage you. Remember to trust that if the Lord is able to direct the heart of a king, then He is more than able to change and direct the heart of those you love. Hang on to this promise.

**A king's heart is like streams of water in the LORD's hand: He directs it wherever He chooses. —Proverbs 21:1**

Further Scripture: Exodus 15:6; Psalm 27:14; 1 Corinthians 10:13

## Questions

1. Read Proverbs 20 carefully. What verse is repeated? Why do you think this particular verse was repeated? Explain what you think this verse means and why it is important.

2. When you read Proverbs 21:2, what do you think it means? Where else in Scripture does this appear (1 Samuel 16:7; Proverbs 16:2; Luke 16:15)? Do you feel your way is right? Do you think the Lord would agree?

3. Proverbs 21:9 and 21:19 are nearly identical. What are the differences between them, and what do you think the author meant by them? Could it also include men, or only women, as the author stated?

4. What did the Holy Spirit highlight to you in Proverbs 20—21 through the reading or the teaching?

# Lesson 110: Proverbs 22—23

*Wisdom*: Dedicate a Child

## Teaching Notes

### Intro

This is lesson 110. You know what that means? There have been 110 days straight of wisdom literature. I hope people are feeling wise after this. So far, in the book of Proverbs, we've discussed talking too much, choosing the right wife, and taking the right path. Proverbs is made up of golden nuggets of truth. My hope is that you can take these verses and apply them to your lives in a helpful way.

### Teaching

*Proverbs 22:1*: Having a good name is better than having a ton of money. What we are talking about is reputation. You could have all the money in the world and be considered a terrible person. No one wants to be that person.

*Proverbs 22:2*: If you're rich, God made you. If you're poor, God made you. We have to be careful not to show favoritism (James 3). *Nelson's Commentary* concludes, "This means that those who favor the rich over the poor (James 2) have not only missed the point of creation, they have insulted the Creator."[1]

*Proverbs 22:3*: A sensible person is someone who is prudent or shrewd. A sensible person takes cover when in danger. The inexperienced keep going, showing no wisdom.

*Proverbs 22:4*: This verse is a cool picture of a good life: humility, wealth, honor, and life.

*Proverbs 22:5*: If you take a crooked path there is bound to be trouble and pain.

---

[1] James Fraser, "12 Ways to Tame the Tongue," Reformation Scotland, February 1, 2018, https://www.reformationscotland.org/2018/02/01/12-ways-to-tame-the-tongue/.

*Proverbs 22:6*: "Teach a youth about the way he should go; even when he is old he will not depart from it." As I teach through this passage I am thinking of my kids. The word "teach" can also be translated as the word "train." The word for "teach/train" occurs three other times in the Bible. *Nelson's Commentary* explains, "The word 'to train' (or teach) is a term related to the familiar festival name, 'Hanukkah,' from the Hebrew for 'dedication.' . . . This is the principal parental task, to receive children as a charge from the Lord, who are then to be dedicated to the way of God in their lives"[2] (Deuteronomy 20:5; 1 Kings 8:63; 2 Chronicles 7:5).

This teaching and training in Scripture represents dedication.

Jason DeRouchie from Bethlehem College and Seminary wrote, "'Train up' may, therefore, be too weak of a translation and miss the potential element of consecration to religious and moral direction."[3] We need to set apart what we are doing. This dedication includes a ceremony. DeRouchie continued, "Proverbs suggest that the act of dedicating in Proverbs 22:6 is focused more on an intentional, sustained, God dependent shepherding of our children's hearts as they grow into adulthood—one in which the children themselves are aware of the parent's trajectory-setting intentions. This is not a passive calling for dads and moms."[4]

This dedication is an ongoing process. I want my kids to understand that I want to walk them through the process of growing up walking with the Lord, and I want to do it every day. This is not an easy task, especially when we get frustrated and lose patience with our kids. There is more to dedicating your kids than having a ceremony during a service and then hoping Sunday school will supply them with the spiritual knowledge they need.

Children are a reward from God (Psalm 127:3). Our children are blessings. When do kids stop being kids and become adults? Your children will always be your kids, even when they hit adulthood. Share the truth with them daily whether they want to hear it or not (Leviticus 25:18; Deuteronomy 6:7–9; 12:28). For examples look at the relationships of Hannah and Samuel, Joseph and Jesus, Abraham and Isaac, and finally Eunice and Timothy. There is value to holding these truths in our hearts in order to teach them to a younger generation. It can be hard to teach and impart knowledge if the truth is not in us. It is important to teach our children that there are two choices in life—the way of wisdom and life or the way of folly and death.

---

[2] Radmacher et al., 771.

[3] Jason DeRouchie, "Train Up a Child in the Way He Should Go," Desiring God, September 20, 2016, https://www.desiringgod.org/articles/train-up-a-child-in-the-way-he-should-go.

[4] DeRouchie.

Part of teaching our children involves discipline (Proverbs 3:12; 29:15, 17; Hebrews 12:5–6, 10). DeRouchie wrote, "When left to themselves, the 'young' lack judgment and have hearts filled with foolishness."[5] Why is discipline necessary? The young are lacking sense (Proverbs 7:7). DeRouchie went on to write, "Without discipline the young bring disgrace on their parents."[6] It is important to correct behavior and allow kids to face their consequences (Proverbs 29:15). We have to walk out this process of discipline. We want our kids dedicated to the Lord so that they will not depart from the Him. We must pour into our children every day, not just when they are young.

This is hard; all of my kids have responded differently to the gospel. They have all accepted Christ, but they are all in their own different stages. There could be a day they turn against the Lord, I don't see that happening, but what if they did? Steven Cole wrote, "Hurting parents must demonstrate God's love and forgiveness to their children."[7] Here are a few points Cole made about the story about the prodigal son—the son who left his family wealthy and prideful but eventually came back home humble and wise (Luke 15:11–32). Cole points out:

1.  "The father was hurting."[8]
    *   "There was pain of rejection, humiliation, and guilt."[9] These are all things people deal with.
2.  "The father was loving and ready to forgive."[10]
    *   The father's love: "He relinquished without rejection, had deep concern, had heartfelt compassion, outward affection, unaffected humility, underserved generosity, and undeserved acceptance"
    *   If you don't have these things, why on earth would a child want to come back?
    *   The father's forgiveness: "His forgiveness was immediate, total, forgotten, costly, restorative, not the guilt-blame approach, and was active forgiveness, not passive."[11]

---

[5] DeRouchie.

[6] DeRouchie.

[7] Steven J. Cole, "Lesson 73: A Model for Hurting Parents (Luke 15:11–32)," Bible.org, June 14, 2013, https://bible.org/seriespage/lesson-73-model-hurting-parents-luke-1511-32.

[8] Cole.

[9] Cole.

[10] Cole.

[11] Cole.

## Closing

It is important to pour into the younger generation. For some of us we need to look no further than our family. For others we should seek out those in need of guidance. You don't have to have a perfect family. No matter what craziness you experience with your family day to day there is never an excuse to not teach, dedicate, and pour into your children. When we are constantly pouring into our family, then we can trust the word of God to come into fruition.

## The Daily Word

Parents and other adults have the responsibility to instruct children in the way they should go. The child's path begins with the parent and loving adults in their lives. Are you grounded in the Word of God and walking in love and humility as Christ walked? Do you love the Lord with all your heart, soul, and strength?

As you walk with the Lord, as you talk about the Word of God, the children in your life will learn from your example. Children will bear witness to a person following Christ. Teaching children how he or she should walk with the Lord will not just happen from a Sunday morning visit to church. *No, it comes from discipline, established boundaries, and reflecting Christ's love all week long!* Therefore, share with children how the Lord impacted your day or read a meaningful Bible verse together. Ask a child to pray for you, and then ask how you can pray for them. *Be intentional to train up children in the Lord.* Make it a priority. The Lord is faithful and will bless your efforts and sacrifice.

**Teach a youth about the way he should go; even when he is old he will not depart from it. —Proverbs 22:6**

Further Scripture: Deuteronomy 6:4–9; Ephesians 6:4; 1 John 2:6

## Questions

1. When you read Proverbs 22:6, which shows us a promise from God, do you believe this to be a true statement? Have you had any experience with this? Has God's promise come to pass yet?

2. In Proverbs 22:14 and 23:27–28, the author spoke on immoral women. Where else in Scripture, besides Proverbs, are immoral women warned against (Genesis 39:9–12; Romans 1:26; 1 Corinthians 15:33)?

3.   Read Proverbs 23:13–14. Does society as a whole follow these directions? How do you think the world would be different if these directions were followed? Do you agree with them? Why or why not?

4.   What did the Holy Spirit highlight to you in Proverbs 22—23 through the reading or the teaching?

# Lesson 111: Proverbs 24

*Wisdom*: Honey

## Teaching Notes

### Intro

Proverbs 24 is a long passage, so I asked the Lord to highlight one thing He wanted me to teach, and He did. I am nervous but excited! Today, we are going to talk about honey. We are going to look at the importance of honey, how it relates to Scripture, and how it relates to our word for Proverbs—which is *Wisdom*. We are trying something new today! I am going to present a different perspective of how honey can possibly be a foreshadowing of the coming Messiah. There is a form of encouragement here too. By the end of this lesson, I want you to know what honey means in Scripture.

### Teaching

*Proverbs 24:1–12*: Surround yourself with wisdom and knowledge. That knowledge can come from people you chose to surround yourself with. This is a powerful justice passage. It is important to take responsibility for being aware of the needs of those around us.

*Proverbs 24:13–14*: From Solomon, the wisest man of all time, his advice to his son was to eat honey. Solomon compared honey to wisdom. If honey is good and sweet, then wisdom is good and sweet. He also wrote that both honey and wisdom bring hope and a future.

What are the benefits of honey? According to "Six Verses About Honey in the Bible," the Bible says:

1. "The Promised Land to the Israelites was described as a land flowing with milk and honey." The word I would use to sum this idea up is "abundance" (Exodus 3:6–8).
2. "Honey . . . was a symbol of good health" (1 Samuel 14:24–27).
3. "Honey . . . was also an honored gift" (Genesis 43:11).
4. "The book of wisdom extols goodness of honey" (Proverbs 24:13).

5.  "John the Baptist survived on honey" (Matthew 3:1–4).
6.  "Honey is in the . . . book of Revelation" (Revelations 10:7–11).[1]

What are the types of honey? According to the *Illustrated Bible Dictionary*, four types of honey are mentioned in the Bible:

- Ya'ar—honey of the bee or honey found in the woods (1 Samuel 14:24, 27)
- Nopheth—honey that drips (Psalm 19:10; Proverbs 5:3)
- Debash—"bee honey, vegetable honey distilled from trees" (Genesis 43:11; Exodus 3:17)
- Tsoph—"cells of honeycombs, full of honey (Proverbs 16:24)"[2]

What are general facts about honey? According to Patrick Clark:

- There are 20,000 species of bees; seven species are honeybees.
- "Honeybees must seek and collect nectar from suitable flowers."
- "The nectar, a thin, easily spoiled, sweet liquid, is transformed ('ripened') by the honeybee to a stable, high-density, high-energy food."
- "Honeybees have two stomachs, a honey stomach, which is used to hold nectar, and the regular stomach."
- "Honeybees visit as many as 1,500 flowers in order to fill their honey stomachs."
- "They add enzymes to the nectar, which begins its conversion to honey."
- The honey we eat is essentially nectar that honeybees have repeatedly regurgitated (sometimes into another bee's mouth, or directly into the honeycomb) and dehydrated.
- "This drying process is accelerated through worker bees flapping their wings to drive off moisture once in the honeycomb."[3]

It is interesting how God set up this process of making honey through the bees. What if the land of milk and honey was a foreshadowing of the Word of God?

---

[1] "Honey in the Bible—Love These 6 Significant Verses!" Benefits of Honey (website), https://www.benefits-of-honey.com/honey-in-the-bible.html.

[2] M. G. Easton, *Illustrated Bible Dictionary*, 3d ed., s.v. "honey" (Nashville: Thomas Nelson, 1897), https://www.biblestudytools.com/dictionary/honey/.

[3] Patrick Clark, "Honey: A Healing Gift from the Creator," Creation.com, March 28, 2016, https://creation.com/gods-healing-gift-of-honey.

Pastor Mike Storti wrote, "We find that [honey and milk] symbolizes the Word of God which is the Lord Jesus Christ. Israel, the land of God's Word, is both the written Word of God and the living Word of God, the Lord Jesus Christ. Christ is the promised seed of Israel, from the Promised Land (Galatians 3:16)."[4] Jesus is the milk and honey of God's Word. He is the way into the Promised Land. Jesus is saying He is the honey.

Schaefer states, "Honey is the only food that includes all the substances necessary to sustain life, including enzymes, vitamins, minerals, and water; and it's the only food that contains 'pinocembrin,' an antioxidant associated with improved brain functioning."[5] Christ is saying, "I am that. I am everything you need and everything you are looking for."

## Closing

I know that some of you might think this is a stretch, but I am saying that honey is the Word of God that points to Jesus. According to Dr. Katherine Marengo, these are the top six benefits of raw honey:

1. Honey is "a good source of antioxidants, [which] help to protect your body from cell damage." This is who Christ is. He is our protector.
2. Honey has "antibacterial and antifungal properties, [that] kill unwanted bacteria and fungus." Jesus is your protector and defender.
3. Honey can "heal wounds and . . . can boost healing time and reduce infection." Isaiah wrote that Jesus is the ultimate healer.
4. Honey is a "phytonutrient powerhouse [which can] keep insects away or shield the plant from ultraviolet radiation." Jesus keeps the devil and demons away from us.
5. Honey "helps with digestive issues." When you are in the word of God there is something soothing that brings peace to your soul.
6. Honey "soothes a sore throat."[6]

---

[4] Mike Storti, "Christ—The Milk and Honey of the Promised Land," Bible Watchman, August 16, 2019, http://biblewatchman.com/milkandhoney.htm. Accessed on April 11, 2023, from the Internet Archive, https://web.archive.org/web/20190816185524/biblewatchman.com/milkandhoney.htm.

[5] Susan Schaefer, "Interesting Facts About Honey & Honey Bees," Wasatch Beekeepers Association, April 29, 2016, https://wasatchbeekeepers.org/2016/04/29/interesting-facts-about-honey-honey-bees/.

[6] Katherine Marengo, reviewer, "Top 6 Raw Honey Benefits," Organic, It Matters, May 24, 2020, https://www.organicitmatters.com/organic-food/top-6-raw-honey-benefits/; original article from Rena Goldman and Catherine Clark, "8 Raw Honey Benefits for Health," Healthline, updated February 26, 2023, https://www.healthline.com/health/food-nutrition/top-raw-honey-benefits.

What's the big deal about honey? We are going to receive the Promised Land and the honey—all through Christ. If we know we have the truth, we need to do something about it. Just as the bees are constantly working to deliver honey, we must deliver the good news to others.

## The Daily Word

In the Bible, honey often symbolizes the Word of God or a desired gift from the Lord. Just as honey can naturally help your body heal wounds and soothe sore throats, the Word of God does the same in your life. Feeling stressed, worried, angry, confused, or lonely? *Turn to the Word of God as your source of relief and help.* Read the Word and allow the Lord to transform your heart moment by moment, seven days a week.

God promises the Word will never fade away. He promises you will find a future and a hope. His Word will be soothing to your soul and healing for your bones. Christ will bring you peace. Watch what happens to your soul as you rest in the Word *every day*. Go ahead and eat a spoonful of honey while you're at it!

**Eat honey, my son, for it is good, and the honeycomb is sweet to your palate; realize that wisdom is the same for you. If you find it, you will have a future, and your hope will never fade. —Proverbs 24:13–14**

Further Scripture: Exodus 3:7–8; 1 Samuel 14:29; Psalm 119:103

## Questions

1. Proverbs 24:1 says not to be envious of evil men. Have you ever found yourself being envious? Is there danger in being envious? What else does the Bible say about envy? Can envy be a good thing (Proverbs 3:31; Mark 15:10; Romans 11:11, 14; James 4:5)?

2. Some people believe wisdom and knowledge are the same thing. What does Proverbs 24 say about them? What is the difference between them (Ecclesiastes 7:11–12; 1 Corinthians 8:1)?

3. What does Proverbs 24 say about a "just man" versus a "wicked man"? Should we rejoice when our enemy stumbles? Why or why not (Proverbs 25:21–22; Matthew 5:44)?

4. What did the Holy Spirit highlight to you in Proverbs 24 through the reading or the teaching?

# Lesson 112: Proverbs 25—26

*Wisdom*: Control the Temper

## Teaching Notes

### Intro

Proverbs 25 is titled "Hezekiah's Collection." According to *Nelson's Commentary*, "The proverbs collected in Proverbs 25—30 reflect important reforms enacted by King Hezekiah of Judah."[1] Hezekiah's father, Ahaz, had turned away from the Lord by serving idols and practicing child sacrifice. As a result, Judah suffered devastating losses to the Assyrians and the Israelites of the Northern Kingdom. When Hezekiah assumed the throne, he removed all of the idolatrous practices and centers, restored temple worship, and resumed nationwide observance of Passover. Hezekiah would have found and copied these proverbs of Solomon, which were later included in the book of Proverbs.

### Teaching

*Proverbs 25:1–5*: All of the verses in this chapter point to the last verse. When you take away the impurities, you have silver (v. 4). When you take away the wickedness, you have a king (v. 5). Hezekiah removed all the impurities and wickedness his father had allowed in Judah.

*Proverbs 25:6–7*: Don't exalt yourself because you think you're important (v. 6). Instead, it's better for the king to recognize you or call you up front (v. 7). Don't claim honors for yourself; allow the Lord to put you in that position. That takes self-control.

*Proverbs 25:8–11*: Be slow in the process of taking others to court (v. 8). It's not only a matter of speech but also a matter of self-control. Begin your talk with your opponent, but don't reveal your hand (v. 9). It's all about discernment and self-control (v. 10). "A word spoken at the right time" (v. 11a) indicates that when you release something at the right time—that text, email, phone

---

[1] Earl D. Radmacher, Ronald B. Allen, and H. Wayne House, eds., *Nelson's New Illustrated Bible Commentary* (Nashville: Thomas Nelson, 1999), 773.

call, communication—it's "like gold apples on a silver tray" (v. 11b). This takes self-control, because when you wait to release a word, it might be the perfect timing.

*Proverbs 25:12–15*: Again, when you release a wise word, in the right season and at the right time, others can receive it as if it were a golden ring or an ornament of gold. Everything is about self-control. How can a gentle tongue break a bone (v. 15)? Words used wisely and with gentleness can break the atmosphere or the situation. Someone with a gentle tongue can do more good than someone who yells and screams.

*Proverbs 25:16, 27*: Consume only what you need. Too much of anything—even a good thing—can cause illness or harm. This is yet another example of the need for self-control.

*Proverbs 25:17*: Don't overstay your welcome at your neighbor's house (v. 17). Don't be the one who is always borrowing something or lurking around. *Nelson's Commentary* states: "Too much neighborliness becomes an imposition."[2]

*Proverbs 25:18–26*: All of these verses build up to the statement in verse 28. Jesus' words in Matthew 5:43–48 reinforce the teachings of these verses. Clearly Jesus was talking about how you love your neighbors and how you interact with your enemies. In summary, love on your enemies, be careful about who you marry, share the good news with others, and don't yield to the wicked.

*Proverbs 25:28*: Without controlling your temper, you are exposing yourself to everybody and letting your guard down. Self-control comes from the Holy Spirit (Galatians 5:22–23). If you have no self-control, then you're functioning in your flesh rather than in the Spirit. The organization Focus on the Family stated these things about self-control: "Self-control is the discipline of delaying impulse or gratification for a greater purpose or cause. The ultimate goal for practicing self-control is to choose Christ over the world. The power to overcome tempta-tion and practice self-control comes from God's Spirit."[3]

Kristen Wetherell said, "We display our God and his gospel when we are self-controlled."[4] We show patience toward others. Our words become purer. We

---

[2] Radmacher et al., 773.

[3] Ted Cunningham, "Got Self-Control?" Focus on the Family, https://www.focusonthefamily.com/parenting/spiritual-growth-for-kids/fruit-of-the-spirit/got-self-control.

[4] Kristen Wetherell, "The Eternal Importance of Exercising Self-Control," Open the Bible, April 28, 2016, https://unlockingthebible.org/2016/04/the-eternal-importance-of-exercising-self-control/.

watch what we say. We're not involved in evil or wickedness when we're exercising self-control. Wetherell continued, "We protect our souls when we are self-controlled."[5] When we practice self-control, we are less vulnerable to temptation. The Greek word for self-control is *egkrateia*, which is defined as "the virtue of one who masters his desires and passions, especially his sensual appetites."[6] In other words, those desires are truly tempered. The ultimate example for us is Jesus, who had no sin in His life, though He was tempted (Hebrews 4:15). Jesus had to master those temptations; He had to use self-control. Luke 22:42 states that Jesus, before His earthly death, prayed for God to "take this cup away from Me." Jesus didn't want to go through with the crucifixion, but He submitted to the Father's will.

## Closing

An article compiled on the website WikiHow described steps to discipline or control the flesh.[7] First, go through a time of training (Hebrews 12:11). Second, put to death the lusts of the flesh (Romans 8:13; Colossians 3:5). Third, learn to love self-control (1 Corinthians 6:12). Fourth, keep the focus on yourself, not others (Matthew 7:1–3). Don't worry about whether or not other people are using self-control. Fifth, deny yourself (Luke 9:23). Sixth, keep the end goal in sight (John 12:24). Finally, understand the necessity of self-discipline and self-control (Matthew 10:38).

If you're not using self-control, you're becoming more about yourself than about Him. Let's not live in that place of functioning in the flesh. Instead, focus on functioning in the Spirit of God. When we are tempered and self-controlled, the Spirit of God can move freely.

## The Daily Word

Raise your hand if there is an area in your life lacking self-control. It's hard to stop yourself, isn't it? You don't want to scream at your kids or your spouse. You don't want to constantly judge people with harsh comments. You don't want to be in debt. You just don't know what to do, and you feel out of control. But before you know it, it's too late and the damage is done. In an effort to maintain control of

---

[5] Wetherell.

[6] James Strong, *Strong's Expanded Exhaustive Concordance of the Bible* (Nashville: Thomas Nelson, 2009), s.v. "egkrateia," Bible Tools, https://www.bibletools.org/index.cfm/fuseaction/Lexicon.show/ID/G1466/egkrateia.htm.

[7] "How to Discipline Your Flesh as a Christian," WikiHow, January 27, 2020, https://www.wikihow.com/Discipline-Your-Flesh-As-a-Christian.

a difficult situation, you lost control of yourself. *Child of God, you are not alone in this place.*

If you lack self-control right now, take a break. The Word of God says to put to death the things of your flesh. First, you need to die to yourself and surrender this area in your life to the Lord. Read the Word of God, perhaps focusing on Scripture about self-control. Let the Word of God fill you up. As you rest in the Lord, the Spirit of God will lead you. Take time to renew your mind in the Word. Not just one day, *but day after day.* Before you know it, the Spirit will guide and direct your thoughts and your actions, allowing you to bear the fruit of self-control. *God is the God of breakthrough.* Trust Him to fill you up with His fruit of the Spirit as you daily abide in Him.

**A man who does not control his temper is like a city whose wall is broken down. —Proverbs 25:28**

Further Scripture: Romans 8:13; 12:2; Galatians 5:22–23

## Questions

1. In general, the book of Proverbs gives advice and wise counsel. Do you have a proverb that you live by—original or scriptural—that you like to share with others? Walk through your week and listen to the wise people that you encounter and learn from their "proverbs."

2. Meditate on Proverbs 25:3. Does this overwhelm you? How do earthly kings compare to the heavenly King (Daniel 2:47; 1 Timothy 6:15; Revelation 17:14; 19:16)?

3. Have you ever heard the phrase, "You can't have too much of a good thing"? According to Proverbs 25:16, is this true? Why do you think having too much of a good thing can be bad? Name an example of this (Exodus 16:17–20; Numbers 11).

4. What does Proverbs 25:17 say about wearing out your welcome? In your opinion, is this always the case?

5. Where do you see advice being given to bosses in Proverbs 26? Have you ever worked for someone who has done this? How did it affect the overall department or place of employment?

6. How is flattery compared to lying in Proverbs 26? Is it a bad thing to flatter people? Why or why not?

7. What did the Holy Spirit highlight to you in Proverbs 25—26 through the reading or the teaching?

# Lesson 113: Proverbs 27—29

*Wisdom*: Iron Sharpens Iron

## Teaching Notes

### Intro

This week we will finish up the book of Proverbs. Proverbs has been the hardest book to teach, except for maybe Job. Proverbs 27 has 27 verses, and each verse could literally be a sermon. Also this week, we will begin and finish the book of Ecclesiastes. I pray the Lord guides our discussion today and helps us see the Lord's Word for us in this chapter.

### Teaching

*Proverbs 27:1–6*: The chapter begins with the admonition not to brag about what will be happening tomorrow, because we have no idea what the rest of today could bring (v. 1). There's an ancient Israeli warning about not having concern for tomorrow or that will overshadow the needs of today. All we have is today. Jesus taught on this as well, reminding His listeners that they could not change anything with worry (Matthew 6:23–34).

We are not to praise ourselves (v. 2). *Nelson's Commentary* explains, "Self-praise is also out of place for the person of wisdom and reveals an insensitivity to the fitness of things. Praise is a comely garment; and though we may desire to wear it, it is always better if others place the garment upon us."[1] We should be intentional in praising others. Verses 3–4 address aggravation, fury, anger, and jealousy. But open reprimand is better than concealed love (v. 5). And while a trusted friend can wound us, the kisses from an enemy are excessive (v. 6). *Nelson's Commentary* explains verse 6 as "correction given in love by a friend is better than insincere acts of affection."[2]

*Proverbs 27:17*: Verse 17 has been used by many men's groups in churches: "Iron sharpens iron, and one man sharpens another." Of course, this applies to

---

[1] Earl D. Radmacher, Ronald B. Allen, and H. Wayne House, eds., *Nelson's New Illustrated Bible Commentary* (Nashville: Thomas Nelson, 1999), 774.

[2] Radmacher et al., 774.

everyone. This ties to verse 6 and about a friend speaking into another friend. I want to walk through this concept of iron sharpening iron. Doug Hamilton wrote an article entitled, "The Sharpening of the Christian," in which he outlined the history and importance of iron:

- Bronze was the main metal used in weapons before 1300 BC, but the natural supply of bronze was running out. Therefore, iron, a stronger metal, was created, probably by the Philistines.

- No other armies had iron weapons because the Philistines kept the processes they used in making the weapons a secret. This is obviously one of the reasons the Philistines were such a formidable enemy (1 Samuel 13:19–22). The Israelites had to pay the Philistines to have their own weapons and farming instruments sharpened. In the process, the Israelites learned all about sharpening their tools.

- During the next decades, around the time of King David, the secret of working with iron leaked out and Israel began to make their own weapons out of iron. When Solomon wrote Proverbs 27:17, everyone in Israel knew the importance of keeping their weapons sharp because they had earned their own independence in battle.

- The process of sharpening iron was:

  1. First, the iron for the sword was pounded with an iron hammer to flatten the edges.
  2. Second, an iron file or iron-ore stone was used along that edge to make it razor sharp.
  3. Third, another piece of iron was used to rub the edge to keep it sharp.[3]

Consider these verses in understanding the concept of iron sharpening iron:

> The one who walks with the wise will become wise, but a companion of fools will suffer harm. (Proverbs 13:20)

> Do not be deceived: "Bad company corrupts good morals." (1 Corinthians 15:33)

---

[3] Doug Hamilton, "The Sharpening of the Christian," 1, http://camphillchurch.org/publication_files/the-sharpening-of-the-christian.pdf.

Wherever we are, we will rub off on someone, or someone will rub off on us. We will influence them, or they will influence us. That's why we must surround ourselves with godly men and women.

Hamilton writes, "When Christians are spending time with each other, there is incredible sharpening that occurs. . . . It is when we are around one another as the 'Holy Nation, a Royal Priesthood, a People of God's Own Possession' (1 Peter 2:9), that we gain the Spiritual Advantage the Razor Edge that is needed to be victorious in this world and leading to the heavenly realm."[4] We are designed to be in assembly with God's people so we will be effective in battle.

## Closing

Hamilton concludes his article with a list of techniques that we can use to sharpen iron with other believers:

1. Show love to one another (John 13:34–35).
2. Confess your sins to one another and pray with him/her (James 5:16).
3. Sing praises and study God's Word with someone (Colossians 3:16).
4. Show humility to someone (Philippians 2:3–4).
5. Share encouragement to someone with words and actions (1 Thessalonians 4:18; 5:11; Hebrews 3:13).
6. Spend quality time with others (Colossians 3:12–13).[5]

### The Daily Word

If you leave a piece of iron alone, it will grow dull, never fulfilling its ultimate purpose to cut things. It needs to hit against another piece of iron to remain sharp. In a similar way, people need people. When people are left alone, they tend to grow dull, unmotivated, and may even make unwise decisions. But when two people are together, they bring out the best in each other, sharing thoughts, laughter, encouragement, and wisdom. God intended for people to be with people. Jesus said the greatest command is to *love God* and *love others*. *He has a purpose for you to be with others.*

Everyone has an excuse about why they don't pursue friendships: "I'm sure he's busy" or "She won't want to." These excuses leave both people alone. You are meant for each other! Pray and ask the Lord for guidance. Then initiate something with someone. Be a friend. Just show up. And then show up again. Before long, it will feel natural, and you'll begin to sharpen one another through the love

---

[4] Hamilton, 2.

[5] Hamilton, 3.

you have for the Lord and each other. What are you waiting for? Say a prayer and contact someone today!

**Iron sharpens iron, and one man sharpens another. —Proverbs 27:17**

Further Scripture: Proverbs 27:9; Ecclesiastes 4:9–10; John 15:12

## Questions

1. What do you think Proverbs 27:14 means? Do you have any friends like this? Are you one of these friends?

2. Proverbs 27:17 says, "Iron sharpens iron, so one man sharpens another." What are some ways we can "sharpen" each other?

3. Proverbs 28:6 says, "Better is the poor who walks in his integrity than he who is crooked though he be rich." Why is integrity more important than riches (Job 8:20; Proverbs 22:1; Matthew 5:33–37)?

4. Proverbs 28:7 uses the word "glutton." What is the definition of glutton, and why would this be humiliating to a father (Genesis 25:29–34)?

5. Why do you think it is foolish to lose your temper as it is stated in Proverbs 29:11? Is there ever a case when you think it wouldn't be considered foolish (Mark 11:15–17)?

6. What did the Holy Spirit highlight to you in Proverbs 27—29 through the reading or the teaching?

# Lesson 114: Proverbs 30—31

*Wisdom*: There is a Generation

## Teaching Notes

### Intro

Proverbs is so rich that it can speak to us in a variety of ways. While these two chapters contain a lot of great truths, we will key in on two passages out of today's chapters.

### Teaching

*Proverbs 30:1*: Who were these people? The Talmud referred to Solomon by at least six names: Jedediah, Koholeth, Agur, Lemuel, the son of Jacah, and Samuel.

*Proverbs 30:7–9*: As fallen creatures, we are drawn to self-reliance, comfort, and self-protection by our sinful nature. When we find ourselves in seasons of having too much, our reliance on the Lord wanes, and we can become reliant on ourselves rather than on God. On the other end of the spectrum, when we have too little, we can doubt that God will provide for us and be tempted to sin and to provide for ourselves.

In 1 Samuel 21, David took consecrated bread from Ahimelech the priest for his men because they did not have the means to provide for themselves. David almost found himself in the predicament outlined in verse 9: "or I might have nothing and steal, profaning the name of my God."

"Because you say, 'I'm rich; I have become wealthy and need nothing,' and you don't know that you are wretched, pitiful, poor, blind, and naked, I advise you to buy from Me gold refined in the fire so that you may be rich, white clothes so that you may be dressed and your shameful nakedness not be exposed, and ointment to spread on your eyes so that you may see" (Revelation 3:17–18). The Laodiceans had lost sight of their need for God in their abundance. They found themselves on the opposite end of the predicament outlined in verse 9: "Otherwise, I might have too much and deny You, saying, 'Who is the Lord?'"

Solomon seems to have written as a natural man trying to relate to a spiritual God. Solomon knew he was not content when he was full and that he was not trustworthy when he was hungry.

*Proverbs 30:11–14*: God has revealed Himself throughout history in seven dispensations:

1. *Dispensation of Innocence:* God created Adam and Eve to be perfect in the Garden to show humanity that walking perfectly with God was fully possible. In the midst of this perfection, it was still possible for humanity to be tempted to sin. This dispensation ended when Adam and Eve ate the fruit and were banished from the Garden of Eden.

2. *Dispensation of conscience:* After Adam and Eve ate the fruit of the tree of the knowledge of good and evil, they did what was right in their own eyes. This dispensation ended because "the earth was corrupt in God's sight, and the earth was filled with wickedness" (Genesis 6:11). The flood was the ending point of this dispensation.

3. *Dispensation of human government:* After Noah and his family came off the ark, God said to Noah, "I will require the life of every animal and every man for your life and your blood. I will require the life of each man's brother for a man's life. Whoever sheds man's blood, his blood will be shed by man, for God made man in His image" (Genesis 9:5–6). Every man still did what was right in his own eyes, but now a measure of consequence was introduced to quell evil.

4. *Dispensation of promise:* The promise was given to Abraham. God determined to make a new people out of Abraham for people to see the blessing of God over the judgment of God.

5. *Dispensation of Law:* As the descendants of Abraham came out of Egypt, God gave Israel the Law to outline how to relate to Him.

6. *Dispensation of grace:* Ushered in by the crucifixion and resurrection of Jesus.

7. *Dispensation of peace:* We are all waiting for this time.

A dispensation described how God related to humanity in a specific time period. In each of the dispensations, there came a generation that ushered in the next generation because of its sinfulness. Verses 11–14 describe the characteristics of a generation that could usher in the next dispensation. Each verse described an attitude that we can observe today. Second Timothy 3:1–5 says, "But know this: Difficult times will come in the last days. For people will be lovers of self, lovers of money, boastful, proud, blasphemers, disobedient to parents, ungrateful, unholy, unloving, irreconcilable, slanderers, without self-control, brutal, without love for what is good, traitors, reckless, conceited, lovers of pleasure rather than lovers of God, holding to the form of godliness but denying its power. Avoid these people!"

*Proverbs 30:24–28*: Each of the animals described has figured out a way to live and thrive in the midst of any generation. Solomon urged us to learn lessons from them so that we could live in the generation in which we find ourselves, regardless of how wicked or sinful it may be.

## Closing

While we may be living in the generation that ushers in the dispensation of peace, God has instructed us on how we can live in it wisely.

---

### The Daily Word

God promises His Word is pure. He is a shield to those who take refuge in Him. So today, focus on taking refuge in Him. Be careful not to find security in what you will eat or in successful business deals or awards. Rather, take refuge in the Lord. Hide yourself in Him. Surrender your will to His. Depend on Him in all aspects of life. Sometimes, when you start gaining wealth, success at work, or even an ease in your regular routines, it is easy to become self-sufficient. *You can get to the point where you don't recognize your need for the Lord.*

Wealth, success, and ease here on earth are not bad in and of themselves. It's the tension of *not being consumed by it all and still seeking the Lord* as your security rather than the things on earth. God may have more for you, but perhaps you have gotten to a place of saying, "Who is God?" Continue to give thanks for your circumstances, and seek the Lord for His strength, His wisdom, and His refuge. The Lord will grant peace and guide you as you give Him honor, praise, and glory!

**Keep falsehood and deceitful words far from me. Give me neither poverty nor wealth; feed me with the food I need. Otherwise, I might have too much and deny You, saying, "Who is the LORD?" or I might have nothing and steal, profaning the name of my God. —Proverbs 30:8–9**

Further Scripture: Proverbs 30:5; 1 Thessalonians 5:18; Hebrews 13:20–21

---

## Questions

1. Who is Proverbs 30:4 talking about (Colossians 1:16–17)? Where else in Scripture do you hear a similar question (Job 38—41)?

2. Proverbs 30:8–9 compares poverty to riches. Which do you think is more dangerous? Why?

3. Does Proverbs 30:11 apply today? If so, do you think it is worse or better today (1 Samuel 2:12–17, 22–25; 2 Samuel 13:1–14)?

4. What are the four creatures we can learn from (Proverbs 30:24–28)? What can each of them teach us?

5. What are some attributes of a virtuous wife (Proverbs 31)? Which of these attributes do you think are most important in a wife?

6. What did the Holy Spirit highlight to you in Proverbs 30—31 through the reading or the teaching?

# Lesson 115: Ecclesiastes 1—2

*Eternal Throne*: The Limitations of Wisdom

## Teaching Notes

### Intro

Mindi's painting for Ecclesiastes includes seven sunflowers. Seven is commonly associated with perfection. God created everything in six days and rested on the seventh. Seven also indicates completion or the fullness of time. The Hebrew word for seven is "shevah," which means "full, satisfied, have enough of." We can rest when we look to the Son. When looking for how Christ is seen in the book of Ecclesiastes, the word we will use is *Eternal*. Ecclesiastes 3:11 implies that every single person is searching because God has put eternity in their hearts. People are searching for the *Eternal*—ultimately the Messiah.

The word "Ecclesiastes" means "teacher" or "preacher." Ray Stedman said a better translation is "the searcher," because the author had a "searching mind that has looked over all of life and observed what is behind the actions of people."[1] The Greek word, ecclesia, means "assembly." The Hebrew word for preacher is Qoheleth, which describes "one who gathers, assembles, or collects."[2] With all this in mind, we begin to see Solomon, the writer of Ecclesiastes, as a man who was constantly searching and communicating his search to everyone else. Hebrews 13:8 says, "Jesus Christ is the same yesterday, today, and forever," which means He is our eternal life.

John MacArthur listed the elements that identify Solomon as the author. The teacher is identified as "the son of David, king in Jerusalem" (v. 1) and "king over Israel" (v. 12). "The author's moral odyssey chronicles Solomon's life" (1 Kings 2–11). The teacher "taught the people knowledge" and wrote "many proverbs" (Ecclesiastes 12:9).[3] Ecclesiastes was probably written in the latter years of Solomon's life. As MacArthur said, he was probably painting a picture about not investing so much time here because there's something more.[4] Solomon was

---

[1] Ray C. Stedman, *Is This All There Is to Life?* (Portland, OR: Multnomah, 1985), 11.

[2] Stedman, 11.

[3] John MacArthur, *The MacArthur Bible Commentary* (Nashville: Thomas Nelson, 2005), 731.

[4] MacArthur, 731.

known by his father, David, to have extraordinary wisdom (1 Kings 2:6, 9). In 1 Kings 3:7–12, Solomon asked God for wisdom to rule Israel, and God granted him more wisdom than any other man. In Ecclesiastes 12:13b–14 Solomon concluded, "Fear God and keep His commands, because this is for all humanity. For God will bring every act to judgment, including every hidden thing, whether good or evil." We might talk about life being a breath, coming and going, but we are still accountable to God for how we live. We have to keep our eyes on the *Eternal*—on the Son.

## Teaching

*Ecclesiastes 1:1–2*: David served 40 years as king. Solomon also served 40 years as king. It was a time of peace and no fighting. Solomon's opening statement is "Absolute futility" (v. 2). Other translations read, "Vanity of vanities," (ESV) or "Meaningless" (NIV). Ultimately, life is a vapor; it comes and it goes. The thing to keep in mind is that even though this life passes quickly, we can be forever with Him. The question is, if everything is meaningless, then why do we focus on the temporal so much? Why are we not pointing people to the eternal rather than the temporal? This is one of the most important books of the Bible. If we understand that everything we have is worthless that it comes and goes just as a vapor, then we can put all of our focus on the eternal.

*Ecclesiastes 1:3–7*: What is the gain if you work hard every day at a factory in Indiana or at any other job? Generations of people may come and go, but only the earth remains (v. 4). Solomon describes the earth's existence as the rising and setting of the sun, the cycle of the wind, and the flow of water to the sea (vv. 5–7).

*Ecclesiastes 1:8–11*: Man is never satisfied—we always want more. Once we have something, we may be happy for a little bit, but it doesn't last. When you start a collection of something—what do you do? You keep collecting. "There is nothing new under the sun" (v. 9c), and "there is no remembrance" (v. 11). Most of us would like to say we will leave a legacy, but the likely reality is that 20 to 30 years after we've died, only our family will remember us.

*Ecclesiastes 1:12–18*: Solomon had discovered that everything he had done had been "a pursuit of the wind" (v. 14). Even gaining wisdom and knowledge had been "a pursuit of the wind" (v. 17).

## Closing

Every single one of us is searching. When we focus on life under the sun, we will find it meaningless, empty, and a breath. But when we keep our eyes above the sun, focused on the Son, Jesus, then we will find complete fulfillment. The Son is *Eternal*. Jesus brings and gives life. In 1 John 5:11, we are assured: "God has given us eternal life, and this life is in His Son."

---

## The Daily Word

Solomon labored to achieve all the pleasures in the world: wealth, possessions, fame, women, servants, achievements, and wisdom. He attained everything under the sun, and yet he called it *absolute futility*—meaning it vanished like a vapor or a breath and had fleeting value. What can you learn from Solomon?

What are you living for? Maybe it's time to shift your focus of what's most important to you. Shift your focus from attaining more and bigger and better toward things that will last for eternity. This world has more and more to offer, but *will it satisfy you and quench your thirst and hunger?* Solomon called it all futile. It's time to stop seeking and searching for contentment from things *under the sun*. Instead, focus on the *Son, Jesus Christ*, the same God yesterday, today, and tomorrow. Jesus, the Son, brings life, love, peace, and joy and will be with you through eternity. In His presence there is fullness of joy, more than anything under the sun could ever bring. Today, focus on the true Son, and His joy will last forever.

**"Absolute futility," says the Teacher. "Absolute futility. Everything is futile." What does a man gain for all his efforts that he labors at under the sun? — Ecclesiastes 1:2–3**

Further Scripture: Psalm 107:9; Ecclesiastes 2:20; 1 John 5:11

---

## Questions

1. What evidence points to Solomon as the one who wrote Ecclesiastes (1 Kings 3:12; 10:10–23; Ecclesiastes 1:1, 12, 16; 2:8)?

2. One of the key terms in Ecclesiastes is vanity. What was the author trying to communicate by using this word (Ecclesiastes 1:14; 6:12)? What should you conclude, then, about living this life without God? Why does this outlook change when you have Christ (Psalm 16:11)?

3. Read Ecclesiastes 1:8–9. Why are people not satisfied with life (Ecclesiastes 3:11)? What is the ultimate solution to find satisfaction (Matthew 11:28)?

4. There are at least three "vanities" in Ecclesiastes 2:11–26. What are they?

5. In Ecclesiastes 2, why did Solomon say he hated life? Why does this seem strange coming from Solomon (Proverbs 8:35)? Have you ever felt the

dissatisfaction Solomon described? How did you handle it? How should the healthy Christian feel about life overall (1 Peter 3:10–12)?

6. What did the Holy Spirit highlight to you in Ecclesiastes 1—2 through the reading or the teaching?

# Lesson 116: Ecclesiastes 3—4

*Eternal Throne*: Short but Meaningful

## Teaching Notes

### Intro

Reading single passages out of Ecclesiastes can be dangerous. Much of the tone of the book is negative. One of the most common words used in Ecclesiastes is "meaningless." This one word provides meaning to the entire book of Ecclesiastes.

In Hebrew, the word is pronounced, "Ha-vel."[1] "Meaningless" is first used in Genesis 4:2 as the name for Abel, one of Adam and Eve's children. In Hebrew, Abel's name literally meant "short," and gave the picture of a breath. Isaiah 57:13 uses the same Hebrew word translated as "breath": "When you cry out, let your collection of idols rescue you! The wind will carry all of them off, a breath will take them away. But whoever takes refuge in Me will inherit the land and possess My holy mountain." Proverbs 31:30 uses the same word translated as "fleeting": "Charm is deceptive, and beauty is fleeting, but a woman who fears the Lord will be praised."[2]

With all of its uses, the common picture portrayed by the word "meaningless" is that of shortness. As shared in yesterday's teaching, the true word for Ecclesiastes is *Eternal*. Ecclesiastes is meant to point us to Jesus by encouraging us to live for that which is eternal and not for that which is temporal. Job taught us that a person could lose everything and still have satisfaction in God alone. Ecclesiastes tells us the opposite. Solomon showed us that if someone had everything—wealth, treasure, wisdom, power—but were missing God, they would lose satisfaction. When we understand that a better translation than "meaningless" or "vanity" is probably "short," our understanding of Ecclesiastes changes. Psalm 90:12 says, "Teach us to number our days carefully so that we may develop wisdom in our hearts."

---

[1] *Hebrew Aramaic Dictionary of the New American Standard Exhaustive Concordance* (La Habra, CA: Lockman Foundation, 1998), 1892.

[2] Samuel Prideaux Tregelles, *Gesenius's Hebrew and Chaldee Lexicon* (London: Samuel Ragster and Sons), BlueLetterBible.org, https://www.blueletterbible.org/lang/lexi- con/lexicon. cfm?Strongs=H1892&t=ESV.

## Teaching

*Ecclesiastes 3:1*: Time is measured in different ways. Chronological time is told by our watches, and various activities are governed by seasons.

*Ecclesiastes 3:2–8*: These verses contain couplets that make the same point in different ways by expressing opposites. Each verse points out that different circumstances can call for different responses.

*Ecclesiastes 3:9–15*: Things are made beautiful when they are used at the appropriate time. God has given us opportunities in this season of life, whatever season of life that may be, that we will not have in future seasons. Time must be measured in light of eternity or we will live foolish lives. We have opportunities each day to choose things that will fade away or things that will last for eternity. Wisdom encourages us to choose the things that will last for eternity.

## Closing

Ecclesiastes encourages us to not neglect eternity for today. We only have a short time in this life and in whatever season we are in currently. These are gifts from God. We choose how we receive these gifts and how we live in them.

---

### The Daily Word

Do you ever think to yourself: *If I can just get through this season of life, then it will be better?* Or maybe you think: *I can't wait until I am at that level.* The truth is, there will always be another level above and another season you wish you were in. Late nights with crying babies, teenagers and emotions, aging parents: it's all a part of life. *There is a time for everything.* God has appointed the seasons and the moments of your life for you to grow into who you are in Christ and to give Him glory.

The key is to fix your eyes on Jesus through each season. Choose to focus on eternity with your Savior Jesus Christ. When you are changing a diaper in the middle of the night, thank the Lord and imagine eternity. There is a time for everything: *a time to weep and a time to laugh, a time to mourn, and a time to dance.* Embrace the season you are in right now. Today is a gift from the Lord. Today has purpose. The Lord has something for you to learn today. Give thanks even in the middle of the hard or the mundane. Ask the Lord what He has for you today!

**There is an occasion for everything, and a time for every activity under heaven. —Ecclesiastes 3:1**

Further Scripture: Ecclesiastes 3:4; Philippians 4:11; 1 Thessalonians 5:18

---

## Questions

1. The theme of Ecclesiastes 3 is that everything has an appointed time. In what ways did Jesus support this (Matthew 26:18; Mark 1:15; John 2:4; 7:6, 30)? What about other Scriptures (Genesis 18:14; Exodus 9:5; Matthew 8:29; Romans 13:11; 2 Corinthians 6:2; Galatians 4:2, 4)?

2. Do you agree with Solomon's statement in Ecclesiastes 3:19? Why or why not?

3. Read Ecclesiastes 4:1–3. How would you describe Solomon's outlook? Does he seem to have written words of "wisdom"?

4. Solomon claimed every skill and work comes from one person's envy of another (Ecclesiastes 4:4). Do you agree with this? If so, is having ambition wrong? How can we ensure we're not working out of envy (Galatians 5:26; James 3:13–18)?

5. What did the Holy Spirit highlight to you in Ecclesiastes 3—4 through the reading or the teaching?

# Lesson 117: Ecclesiastes 5—6

*Eternal*: God's Gift of Sleep

## Teaching Notes

### Intro

We are continuing our study in the book of Ecclesiastes 5 today. Our word for Ecclesiastes is *Eternal*. Everyone is searching for eternity, which can only be found in Christ. Life itself is temporal.

### Teaching

*Ecclesiastes 5:1–7*: Wiersbe states that the key to verses 1–7 is, "Don't rob the Lord."[3] Wiersbe explains when Solomon went to the temple, "He noted that many of [the worshippers] were not at all sincere in their worship, and they left the sacred precincts in worse spiritual condition than when they had entered."[4] That background explains Solomon's advice in verse 1: "Guard your steps when you go to the house of God" (1 Samuel 15:22). From Proverbs, this describes a "heart condition." Worship is out of obedience, not duty. Solomon also cautioned to be careful in prayers and make them sincere, not speaking them to gain attention (vv. 2–3). Don't pray because you want to be heard with empty prayers that make you feel good. We should have a heart for prayer and the words should just flow from the heart (Psalm 141:1–2; Matthew 6:7; 12:34–37). Charles Spurgeon said, "It is not the length of our prayers, but the strength of our prayers that makes the difference." In verse 4, Solomon stressed not to lie to God—do not make a vow to God and then not fulfill it. It is better not to vow at all than to give a vow and not honor it (v. 5). Do not let your mouth lead you into guilt by saying your vow was a mistake (v. 6). Stop talking in futility (v. 7).

---

[3] Warren W. Wiersbe, *Be Satisfied: Looking for the Answer to the Meaning of Life* (Colorado Springs: David C. Cook, 1990), 75.

[4] Wiersbe, 76.

*Ecclesiastes 5:8–9*: Wiersbe summarizes verses 8–9 as, "Don't rob others."[5] The perspective has moved from the temple to city hall. *Nelson's Commentary* says, "All people live by God's grace in His provision for the earth."[6] If we see oppression and perversion of justice, we are to step in against it.

*Ecclesiastes 5:10–20*: Wiersbe describes this section as, "Don't rob yourself."[7] Verse 10 emphasizes that the one who loves money will never feel like he has enough—he will never be satisfied (2 Chronicles 9:23–28; Ecclesiastes 1:8; 4:8). Solomon received 25 tons of gold each year as gifts from those who wanted to receive his wisdom. "Desire always outruns possessions, no matter how vast acquisitions may grow."[8] The abundance of wealth consumes a person, and he/she can't even sleep (v. 11).

Why is sleep necessary?

- Sleep allows us to rest our minds so we wake rested in the morning (Exodus 34:2; Psalm 5:3; Isaiah 50:4).
- God put Adam in a deep sleep (Genesis 2:21).
- God rested (Genesis 2:2).
- The Sabbath was for rest (Exodus 31:15; Leviticus 23:3).
- Sleep is a gift from God (Psalm 4:8; Proverbs 3:24).

## Closing

The average American sleeps seven hours and thirty-six minutes per night. The average bedtime is 10:55 pm, and the average time to wake up is at 6:38 am. On weekends, the average American sleeps 40 minutes longer. Fifty to 70 million Americans have a sleep disorder. Forty-eight percent snore. Sixty-seven percent of Americans report less than good sleep, and 37.9 percent fall asleep during the day. Almost five percent have fallen asleep while driving. Thirty percent have insomnia, and 25 million suffer from sleep apnea.

Jesus slept (Matthew 8:24) because He trusted God. We can rest when we give our burdens to Christ (Matthew 11:28–30). Psalm 121:3–4 states God will never slumber or sleep. When we rest in Him, we are getting prepared for the *Eternal*.

---

[5] Wiersbe, 78.

[6] Earl D. Radmacher, Ronald B. Allen, and H. Wayne House, eds., *Nelson's New Illustrated Bible Commentary* (Nashville: Thomas Nelson, 1999), 786.

[7] Wiersbe, 79.

[8] Radmacher et al., 786.

## The Daily Word

Solomon wisely said *money never satisfies*. You may earn more and more money, but it will never truly satisfy. Will you ever think you have enough? In this world, there will always be more to attain. But just when you attain that one thing, your eyes will be set on something new. Even money is futile and fleeting—here today and gone tomorrow. The Lord created your soul for eternity. The only 100-percent secure investment in life is giving yourself fully to the Lord. In Him, you have rest. In Him, you have peace. In His presence, there is joy. He meets your every need.

Money and wealth will never bring the satisfaction you search for. There may be times when you feel it is easier to trust in the security of money more than the ultimate security and promises found in the Lord. Do a heart check today and *seek the Lord* for true satisfaction.

**The one who loves money is never satisfied with money, and whoever loves wealth is never satisfied with income. This too is futile. —Ecclesiastes 5:10**

Further Scripture: 2 Chronicles 9:23; Luke 12:15; 1 Timothy 6:9–10

## Questions

1. Ecclesiastes 5:10 talks about the one who loves money. What does 1 Timothy 6:10 say about the love of money? How can a person get rid of the "root"?

2. Read Ecclesiastes 5:13; Matthew 6:19–21; and Luke 12:13–21. How do Solomon's words point someone to a better way? What about Jesus?

3. How many other parallels can you find between Ecclesiastes 5 and Matthew 6?

4. With everything Solomon owned, according to Ecclesiastes 6, how did he view it all? What might have been the cause of his viewpoint (1 Kings 3:3; 11:1–6)?

5. What did the Holy Spirit highlight to you in Ecclesiastes 5—6 through the reading or the teaching?

# Lesson 118: Ecclesiastes 7—9

*Eternal*: How God Sees Us

## Teaching Notes

### Intro

Whenever I study the book of Ecclesiastes, I put one word in front of it: "ponder." I think there is so much in Ecclesiastes that we are supposed to question why and how. I approach it through equations, usually to answer why. I ask myself if I agree with it. I consider whether or not I see where the author is coming from.

### Teaching

*Ecclesiastes 7:1–6*: This chapter begins with a reality check: What is best for life compared to what is enjoyable? Verse 1 contrasts the importance of having a good name to having wealth and the day of death being better than the day of birth. Life is our very breath, one after another. We do not think about each breath we take, but without each breath, we could not live or accomplish anything. Verses 2–3 point out that as we experience grief and hardship in life, we grow and mature. One brings about the other. What we learn in our sorrow is better and has a more lasting effect than what we learn while laughing. The times when I have learned to walk with God the best is not when life was easy and fun but when I was walking through the hard places. The lessons of life do not always come from the good but from the hard (vv. 4–6).

*Ecclesiastes 7:7*: Why does oppression make a wise man mad (v. 7a)? A wise man would typically have had a plan—a beginning, a process, and an end. To face oppression would divert the wise man's efforts—take him away from his plan. Why does a gift destroy the heart (v. 7b)? This speaks to people in a position of authority whose opinion can be swayed. This person can be flattered and can be catered to. Men must have accountability and not flattery. We are currently experiencing this in politics because money (gifts) can corrupt. This is the human experience, but we do not have to be swayed by that. Our release from this is our eternal perspective.

*Ecclesiastes 7:8*: Why is the end of something better than the beginning (v. 8a)? How many times in this life do we have a great idea that is never fulfilled? How many times have people tried to do something unsuccessfully? The point is that what is best is the big idea that has been fulfilled (the end). At the end of life, the fulfillment is to be able to say life was well-lived. Those who are patient in waiting for the Holy Spirit are better than those who are proud and move before the Holy Spirit moves (v. 8b). The patient say, "let it come in its own time," and the proud say, "it must be done now" (Romans 8:28).

*Ecclesiastes 7:9–10*: In the face of oppression or injustice, Solomon warned not to be hasty in becoming angry, "for anger abides in the heart of fools" (v. 9b). I always attach anger to ownership. Anger defends something—me, my territory, my reputation—because I have the right to defend these parts of me. But if we believe that God is the owner and the defender, we are to bless those who misuse or mistreat us. Do not ask why it was better in the "good old days" (v. 10). The "good old days" were just the days that came before.

*Ecclesiastes 7:11–12*: Wisdom comes from God. Wisdom is our protection that preserves our lives. We have to determine how to make sense of these days and work within them.

*Ecclesiastes 7:13–15*: The path of life is crooked, but God can make it straight (v. 13). We are to be joyful even as we know that the day of adversity is coming. There are good people who die young, and there are wicked people who live long lives (v. 15). This is a ponder moment; it seems unfair. We should ask God to teach us wisdom; He is not afraid of our questions. We should ponder the way of man, and we should ponder the way of God.

*Ecclesiastes 7:19–22*: Wisdom makes us stronger (v. 19). Someone who is wise can be better than many warriors because they have figured out a strategy in how to accomplish something instead of just rushing. There is no one on earth who is only good and never sins (v. 20). Do not pay attention to what others say, but pay attention to what you say. Do not put too much value in others' opinions because it is easy to be critical when you do not have the correct perspective.

*Ecclesiastes 7:29*: God has made man to be upright and righteous, but humankind has instead pursued many schemes or devises. This is why Ecclesiastes 7 is a reality check of how we think.

*Ecclesiastes 9:11–12*: First Corinthians 1:26–28 relates to verse 11. Ecclesiastes gives us the practical way to look at things—we do not have to be overqualified, over-skilled, or overly rich for God to use us. What we can do does not bring us to God. It is in our weaknesses that God chooses to use us—even under-qualified, under-skilled, and poor.

## Closing

We should put ourselves in these chapters and ask ourselves, Am I overtaken in a human experience? Am I looking at my life through the things that have been, and am I disqualifying what is ahead of me because of where I have been? Am I limiting myself by my qualifications? Am I letting others put their expectations on me or allowing something someone said to diminish me? Ecclesiastes instructs us not to consider those things and not to let that be the mantra of our lives. Instead, we should walk in the confidence that God will use, qualify, and bring us into a place of fulfillment. Let Him be the one who writes our story.

---

## The Daily Word

You may have times in life when you immediately get angry about something. It's your first reaction. You get irritated, you feel your heart race, and your face gets flushed. In this situation, do not rush to anger. You may want to, you may even have a right to, but *anger abides in the heart of fools*. Take a deep breath, say a prayer, and ask the Lord for wisdom in responding to the situation.

There are two sides to every situation, and often the Lord wants to move in ways beyond what you can see. So, give God time to move before you speak. Give time for understanding. Don't be the fool and rush toward anger. Anger often defends something—perhaps yourself, your territory, or your reputation. Anger rises within you as you defend your rights. *Just pause before you respond.* Allow the Lord to be your defender. Walk out the promise, trusting God to work all things together for His good and His purpose. His work is perfect, His ways are entirely just, and He is a faithful God. Trust Him instead of taking control of the situation and risk acting like a fool.

**Don't let your spirit rush to be angry, for anger abides in the heart of fools. —Ecclesiastes 7:9**

Further Scripture: Deuteronomy 32:4; Romans 8:28; 2 Thessalonians 3:3

---

# Questions

1. In Ecclesiastes 7:19, how can the statement "one wise person is stronger than ten leading citizens of a town" be true? How would you explain this verse?

2. When you read Ecclesiastes 8:9–14, do you believe this is true for today also? Do you think things have changed much from King Solomon's time? Why or why not?

3. In Ecclesiastes 9:5, the author wrote, "The living at least know they will die, but the dead know nothing." How would you describe this verse to someone else?

4. What did the Holy Spirit highlight to you in Ecclesiastes 7—9 through the reading or the teaching?

# Lesson 119: Ecclesiastes 10—12

*Eternal*: What Is It All About?

## Teaching Notes

### Intro

Whenever we read or teach the Word of God, we are responsible for what we've heard and taught. As you think about the last few times you've been in the Word of God, what did you do with what you learned? How were you encouraged? Studying the Word in community with others gives us the opportunity to talk about what we have learned. Today, we are looking at the end of Ecclesiastes. Our word for Jesus in this book is *Eternal*. Life only makes sense when it is connected to the *Eternal* God. This book calls us to remember our purpose and not to allow ourselves to be distracted.

### Teaching

In the world today, people seem to be trying to answer the question, "What is it all about?" The writer of Ecclesiastes was dealing with purpose and what life is all about. Today, we are at the end of the book, and we will focus on "the conclusion of the matter."

*Ecclesiastes 12:9–14*: Solomon didn't skip the content about the meaninglessness of things in order to stress the command "fear God and keep His commands" (v. 13b) because he knew that we would not blindly accept his statement. He knew each of us would go out on our own search for meaning, trying to test if this was the truth. Solomon tested several different things before concluding those things were really just a breath that didn't last very long. Let us recount some of those things:

- Ecclesiastes 1:17—chasing wisdom was like chasing after the wind
- Ecclesiastes 2:1—pleasure proved to be meaningless
- Ecclesiastes 2:2—laughter and pleasure (feeling good) also proved meaningless

- Ecclesiastes 2:3—wine and folly, but guided by wisdom, proved meaningless

- Ecclesiastes 2:4–6—made great works; built houses; planted vineyards, gardens, parks, fruit trees; made pools of water. He tried to accomplish something bigger than himself, but this was also meaningless.

- Ecclesiastes 2:7—bought slaves, amassed large herds and flocks. He was the wealthiest person around, but it proved to be meaningless.

- Ecclesiastes 2:8—gathered gold and silver and treasure, singers and concubines, again meaningless.

- Ecclesiastes 2:9—became the greatest and most powerful man in Jerusalem, remained wise, yet that was like chasing after the wind.

- Ecclesiastes 2:10—denied himself nothing he desired, refused himself no pleasure. Even indulgence did not bring satisfaction.

- Ecclesiastes 5:7—Solomon started to realize dreams and words were meaningless, but God was to be feared.

- Ecclesiastes 6:2—God gives some people wealth, possessions, and honor so they lack nothing. But God doesn't grant them the ability to enjoy them; strangers enjoy them instead. People today who have traveled to third-world countries seem surprised that people who have little can be happy. But the people in those third-world countries were never fooled by thinking such things could make them happy.

- Ecclesiastes 6:9—If every hunger were fed, wouldn't that be the definition of satisfaction? Unless there is a hunger that cannot be fed here on earth. Ecclesiastes shows there is a hunger bigger than getting every appetite fed. Without God, there is dissatisfaction and emptiness.

Reflecting on all these things led Solomon to conclude: "Fear God and keep His commandments" (v. 13). You can look at this statement as if it is two separate things: "Fear God" and "keep His commandments." Or you can read this as one connected statement: "Fear God by keeping His commandments." In this latter approach, the definition of fearing God is keeping His commandments.

The fear of the Lord is discussed throughout the wisdom literature (and throughout the Bible).

- Job 1:9—Even Satan recognized Job feared God. Satan could take away Job's wealth, possessions, family, but he couldn't away Job's fear of the Lord.

- Psalm 34:9—Those who fear God lack nothing. Why? Because you can chase everything but God, and you'll be dissatisfied. But when you fear

God, you end up satisfied. "Seek first the kingdom of God and His righteousness, and all these things will be given to you as well" (Matthew 6:33 NIV).

- Revelation 14:7—Fear God by giving Him glory. We fear God by truly worshipping Him and giving our whole lives to Him.

The fear of the Lord is a very big deal. What characteristics of God do you think are most emphasized in our modern culture? Some say it is God's love—His infinite love, His perfect love. But we need to understand that for every quality of God there are other qualities that are never diminished. Jesus is full of grace and truth. His grace does not shorten or diminish His truth. Neither does He emphasize truth so that it diminishes His grace. In God, there is both love and justice. You can have a fear of the Lord and you can have a tremendous love for the Lord. In Matthew 22:37–39, Jesus told us what it is all about: "Love the Lord your God with all your heart, with all your soul, and with all your mind. This is the greatest and most important command. The second is like it: Love you neighbor as yourself."

In Ecclesiastes, it is all about fearing God and keeping His commandments. Both statements are equally valid. The two go together completely. Loving God includes fearing Him, and fearing Him includes loving Him with everything in us. In fearing God, there is a way you can live that makes you want to run to Him instead of away from Him. When you fear God by keeping His commandments, then you are not afraid to be around Him. Conversely, when you do not fear God by keeping His commandments, then you are afraid of Him. The incredible thing about fearing the Lord—when you truly get it— is that you love Him enough to think He's made this list of commands because He loves you. He believes in you, He wants a future for you, and He has great things for you. Truly, fearing God and keeping His commandments leads us to love God with all our hearts.

## Closing

The sum of all things in Ecclesiastes—the conclusion of the matter—is do not be suckered into pleasures, do not be suckered by possessions and thinking that what you have will make you happy, and do not be suckered by your work or things you have to do. Instead, understand that fearing God, keeping His commandments, and following His directions is the sum of it all.

## The Daily Word

After all his searching, Solomon concluded that fearing God and keeping His commands was the ultimate life goal. And the same is true for us. Fearing God and keeping His commands alone will result in true satisfaction. God will bring judgment. That's not your job. Your job is to fear the Lord. You're responsible to love the Lord your God with all your heart, soul, strength, and mind and to love your neighbor the same way. Keep this as your singular focus. *Be in awe of the Lord to the point it spurs you on to keep His commands.*

Don't get suckered into the things of the world, searching to find happiness and satisfaction. Resist getting angry, impatient, and discontent. The Lord will take care of you because He sees all. As you press on to love Him and love others, and you will find the other things will work out. Stand firm and fear the Lord. God promises you will lack nothing. *This truth is amazing grace.* Today, focus on the narrow path of fearing the Lord and following Him.

**When all has been heard, the conclusion of the matter is: fear God and keep His commands, because this is for all humanity. For God will bring every act to judgment, including every hidden thing, whether good or evil. —Ecclesiastes 12:13–14**

Further Scripture: Psalm 34:9; Luke 10:27–28; Revelation 14:7

## Questions

1. Solomon spoke about foolishness or folly in Ecclesiastes 10:1. Can you think of a time in your own life or someone else's that exemplified this verse? In what ways?
2. How would you compare wisdom to an ax head? Does Ecclesiastes 10:10 make sense? Why or why not?
3. What comes to mind when you read Ecclesiastes 11:4? Could this be an example of 2 Corinthians 5:7? Why or why not? Do you feel you are an example of the farmer or the verse in Corinthians? Why?
4. What did the Holy Spirit highlight to you in Ecclesiastes 10—12 through the reading or the teaching?

# Lesson 120: Song of Songs 1—3

*Bridegroom*: The Bridegroom and the Bride

## Teaching Notes

### Intro

This is the fifth and final book in the wisdom and poetry section of Scripture. This book is also known as Song of Solomon because Solomon wrote it. First Kings 4:32 says that, in addition to writing more than 3,000 proverbs, Solomon wrote 1,005 songs. David was a composer of songs, so it's no wonder his son Solomon also wrote songs. With the title "Song of Songs" we can think of this song as the best of the best. Solomon wrote this as he ruled over a united kingdom for 40 years. The name "Solomon" appears at least seven times in the book, so there's really no question that he was the author. The only question is when he wrote it. At the time it was written, it would have been viewed as one song, not a series of little love poems or songs.

There are two main characters in the song. One of them is Solomon. The other is the Shulammite woman. Who was she? First of all, she was from Shunem, a village located about three miles north of the Jezreel Valley. The Jezreel Valley will one day be the site of the battle of Armageddon. In this song, Solomon described his love for the Shulammite woman as well as the locations around where she lived. She could have been Pharaoh's daughter (but there's no evidence of this). Maybe she was Abishag, the Shulammite who cared for David in his final years. But most scholars say she was an unknown maiden from Shunem whose family lived in the area and was employed by Solomon. More than likely, she was the one of whom Solomon said, "Enjoy life with the wife you love all the days of your fleeting life" (Ecclesiastes 9:9). Most likely, she was his first wife, because Solomon married 699 other women (1 Kings 11:3). Although Solomon had seven hundred wives and three hundred concubines, there's a really good chance this was his first love letter to his first wife.[1]

There are also a couple of minor players in the book. Some translations have the letters W or M before some of the verses. There are times when it's very difficult to figure out who is talking in the Song. Sometimes it is Solomon or the

---

[1] John MacArthur, *The MacArthur Bible Commentary* (Nashville: Thomas Nelson, 2005), 743.

Shulammite woman, but sometimes it is other minor characters. The daughters of Jerusalem, who might have been part of Solomon's household staff, speak out. There's also a small section that may contain God's blessing on the couple. Then there were the Shulammite's brothers. Before you start reading the Song, take time to distinguish (with lines or highlights) who is speaking in the different segments of the Song.[2]

- The courtship takes place in Song of Songs 1:2—3:5. Courtship involves an element of anticipation. What will it be like? How will it unfold?
- The wedding is described in Song of Songs 3:6—5:1. This includes the wedding and the consummation of the marriage.
- The marriage and celebration are described in Song of Songs 5:2—8:14. The song talks about the tough times the couple faced in their marriage. It's important to remember that sex and marital relations were designed by God. But the enemy Satan has grabbed ahold of sex and used it for his purposes. From this song, we can see what it means to have a healthy sexual relationship with the person you're married to.[3]

So how does the relationship between a man and a woman point to the Messiah? We will begin to see how the bridegroom and the bride interact. God's plan of marriage includes sexual intimacy between two people, which is ultimately a picture of Christ and the church. Solomon is a type of *Bridegroom* who points to the ultimate *Bridegroom*, Jesus Christ. In 2 Corinthians 11:2, Paul said the church, the body of Christ, was promised to one Husband, Christ. Revelation 19:7 describes the marriage of the Lamb (Christ) to His wife, who has prepared herself in fine linen—the righteous acts of the saints. On the eighth day of Passover, the Jews read Song of Songs to remind themselves of God's love for them and their love for Him. Song of Songs is about an actual relationship between Solomon and the Shulammite woman. It's a picture of the Israelites and their relationship with the Lord. It's also the ultimate picture of the *Bridegroom* and the bride, who needs to get ready because the *Bridegroom* is coming. The *Bridegroom* is Jesus.

## Teaching

*Song of Songs 1:2–4*: The Shulammite woman spoke. She longed for Solomon to kiss her. This is the anticipation of dating. She was attracted to his lips, love, lotion, and lifestyle.[4] The daughters of Jerusalem appeared to be singing in the background: "We will rejoice and be glad for you" (v. 4b).

---

[2] MacArthur, 743.

[3] MacArthur, 744.

[4] MacArthur, 745.

*Song of Songs 1:5–7*: The Shulammite woman kept talking. She was truly concerned about how weathered she looked because she had been working in the sun. *Nelson's Commentary* explained the woman compared herself to the city maidens, and she was not sure if she was what Solomon wanted.[5] Just like in any dating relationship, the Shulammite woman was worried about whether she was good enough.

*Song of Songs 1:8–11*: When Solomon spoke, he assured her she was absolutely stunning. The comparison to one of Pharaoh's chariot horses was a compliment. First Kings 10:26–29 revealed Solomon owned lots of horses. Surely as he interacted with his horses, he was trying to create a picture of her beauty. He also promised her gifts of gold and silver jewelry to highlight her beauty.

*Song of Songs 1:12–14*: The Shulammite woman responded with anticipation of the courtship. Scripture talks about different types of love, and verse 13 is talking about sexual love. The Shulammite woman intended to wear a fragrance that would truly draw Solomon to her. She refers to her love as "a cluster of henna blossoms . . . in the vineyards of En-gedi" (v. 14). En-gedi was a place where David found protection from Saul as well as refreshment and renewal. So there was something really refreshing about their time together.

*Song of Songs 1:15*: Solomon responded by calling her beautiful. The eyes of the dove pointed to her purity, innocence, and beauty.[6] John MacArthur said these were the deep smoky grey eyes of the dove.[7]

*Song of Songs 1:16–17*: The Shulammite woman responded about how handsome Solomon was. At this point, they were still dating, so this is in the mindset of thinking about what their relationship would one day be like. God has provided everything they needed, and they wanted to be with one another.

## Closing

Just to be clear, nothing has happened between Solomon and the Shulammite at this point. This is the period of their courtship. As we continue this study, we'll tie together several more elements in these verses. It's important to remember that the *Bridegroom* and the bride in this song are a picture of the *Bridegroom* and the bride—Christ and the church.

---

[5] Earl D. Radmacher, Ronald B. Allen, and H. Wayne House, eds., *Nelson's New Illustrated Bible Commentary* (Nashville: Thomas Nelson, 1999), 795.

[6] Radmacher et al., 797.

[7] Radmacher et al., 797.

## The Daily Word

Song of Songs portrays the love between the church and the *Bridegroom*, Jesus Christ, as Solomon communicated and demonstrated his love for his first wife, beginning with attraction to one another and courtship. In a similar way, the Lord sees you. He sees you as beautiful. He sees you as precious in His sight. He understands you. He knows your strengths and your weaknesses. He sought you out and pursued you. He longs to draw you into His great love. He desires for you to come to Him and be His beloved.

Look at the Lord. *Open your eyes to His great love for you.* Allow His love to draw you in. He says He will hide you under the shadow of His wings. He will cover you with His protective feathers. He is your peace, your life, your helper. Today, may you be drawn into the intimate presence and love of Jesus. Believe you are desired and wanted. Believe you are loved with an everlasting love. Believe you are God's beloved. You belong to Him.

**How beautiful you are, my darling. How very beautiful! Your eyes are doves. How handsome you are, my love. How delightful! Our bed is lush with foliage. —Song of Songs 1:15–16**

Further Scripture: Song of Songs 2:4; Jeremiah 31:3; Ephesians 5:25

## Questions

1. Song of Songs 1:3 refers to ointment. Ointment has healing properties. Could this verse be referring to Christ? Why or why not?

2. In Revelation 19:9, an angel spoke of the marriage supper of the Lamb. How, if at all, does this relate to Song of Songs 2:4? What does "his banner over me was love" mean to you?

3. Could Song of Songs 3:1–4 be pointing to the church and/or Israel? In the days of the Great Tribulation, they will search for Jesus and not find Him. When Israel "accepts" Christ, then He will be "found" by them. Is there another way to look at this verse? If so, how?

4. What did the Holy Spirit highlight to you in Song of Songs 1—3 through the reading or the teaching?

# Lesson 121: Song of Songs 4—5

*Bridegroom*: Sex in Marriage

## Teaching Notes

### Intro

Song of Songs documents the process of falling in love—the courting, engagement, wedding, and marriage. It includes the place of sex within the marriage. The language of Song of Songs is specific, especially the language in today's passage. We continue to look at Solomon and the Shulammite woman, along with the daughters of Jerusalem, God's blessing, and the brothers of the Shulammite woman. Yesterday, we looked at the courtship—the anticipation period of falling in love and leaving parents. Today, we move to the wedding and the consummation of the marriage. God designed the sexual relationship for marriage.

### Teaching

*Song of Songs 4:1–4*: Solomon described the beauty of the woman—her eyes, her hair, her teeth, her lips, her mouth, the brow of her head, and her neck (vv. 1–4). Some of this seems strange to us, but Wiersbe explains, "Ancient peoples didn't quite understand dental hygiene [so] this is an admirable trait. Healthy teeth would also affect her breath."[1] In verse 4, Solomon described the beauty of her neck as "a queenly neck and a posture with it that exuded control, power, and stability."[2] These were all words of affirmation.

*Song of Songs 4:5–7*: Solomon described her breasts as two fawns, and named them as the "mountain of myrrh and the hill of frankincense" (v. 6). Solomon sees her as perfect—"with no imperfection" (v. 7b). This foreshadows Jesus Christ, the *Bridegroom*, who will return for His pure and spotless bride. Verse 7 is really a prophetic picture of what God wants for the body of Christ—perfection (2 Corinthians 11:2). We are spotless in Christ's eyes. Constable explains, "Perhaps she

---

[1] Warren W. Wiersbe, *The Bible Exposition Commentary: Job–Song of Solomon* (Colorado Springs: David C. Cook, 2004), 546.

[2] Wiersbe, 546.

ıt really as perfect as Solomon claimed here (cf. 1:5–6). 'Beauty is in the eye
ₑ beholder.' She was perfect to him."[3]

*ɔng of Songs 4:8–10*: Marriage is first mentioned in verse 8—"my bride." This
ɔegins the transition between courtship to marriage and consummation. Solomon was clear they had restrained from having sex during their courtship and
were waiting for the wedding before consummation. Solomon told the woman it
was time to leave everything in her life so she could come be with him completely.
The woman had captured his heart at first glance and her love was delightful (vv.
9–10). Nothing compared to his love for her. "Honey and milk" describe the
blessing of God (v. 11).

*Song of Songs 4:12–15*: The tone changes in verse 12 and becomes extremely intimate. Solomon pointed out he and the woman had not yet had sex, and she was
still a virgin ("you are a locked garden"). The bride had stayed pure. Verses 13–14
describe her passionately. She was a locked garden and a sealed spring.

*Song of Songs 4:16*: The Shulammite woman responded and began to describe
what she wanted him to do in verse 16. She was open to him—no longer locked
and kept away.

Although not all studies agree, one study found the average age in which
a male loses his virginity is 16.9, and the average age for a female is 17.2.[4]
And an astounding number of women (some studies suggest as much as 74
percent) have premarital sex.[5] The National Center for Health Statistics found
59 percent of women between the ages of 20 and 59 have had at least four
different sexual partners, and men have had an average of seven.[6] That's a lot.
I think it's because we don't teach a healthy model of what God intended for
sexual relationships within marriage between two people who have committed
themselves to each other in marriage—for passion and for procreation. When
we don't wait, or when we have sex outside of marriage, we face consequences
God did not intend—STDs, unplanned pregnancies, possible physical abuse,

[3] Thomas L. Constable, *Expository Notes of Dr. Thomas Constable: Song of Solomon*, 37,
https://planobiblechapel.org/tcon/notes/pdf/song.pdf.

[4] Vera Papisova, "Find Out When Most Teens Are Losing Their Virginity," *Teen Vogue*,
September 30, 2015, https://www.teenvogue.com/story/teens-losing-virginity-age.

[5] Jacqueline E. Darroch, Jennifer J. Frost, Susheela Singh, and the Study Team, "Teenage
Sexual and Reproductive Behavior in Developed Countries," Guttmacher Institute, November
2001, 9, https://www.guttmacher.org/sites/default/files/pdfs/pubs/eurosynth_rpt.pdf.

[6] Associated Press, "New Survey Tells How Much Sex We're Having," NBCNews.com, June
22, 2007, https://www.nbcnews.com/health/health-news/new-survey-tells-how-much-sex-
we-re-having-flna1c9471437.

emotional damage, and lower self-esteem for females. Physical, emotional, and relational issues can abound.

## Closing

Why wait for sex within marriage? Why wait for the Shulammite garden that has been designed perfectly for you? First, wait because you deserve love—a heart connection. Second, wait because not everybody is doing it. Third, wait because it's not safe.

A man is to leave his father and mother to bond with one person (Genesis 2:24). We are designed to become one—in marriage and in sex (Matthew 19:5–6; Ephesians 5:31–32). This is also the picture of Christ and His church. The picture of the Shulammite garden takes us back to the Garden of Eden, where God planned for us to be with Him in the way He had designed.

## The Daily Word

The Lord designed marriage for one man and one woman. He designed sexual intercourse for one man and one woman in a marriage covenant, joining together as one flesh. This covenant is not meant to be broken—not before marriage and not with multiple partners. After great anticipation and waiting, Solomon and his wife enjoyed one another on their wedding night. It was worth the wait as they fully relished and celebrated the love and connection between each other, just as the Lord designed it.

God's original design and intent was for purity and wholeness. Anything apart from His original plan may have spiritual and physical consequences. Walk and rely on strength from the Spirit of God to resist any temptation for sex and other impure actions outside the marriage covenant. *Beauty comes as you wait, resist temptation, and rely on the Lord for strength.* God will be with you in the waiting. And then, when the time arrives for a husband and wife to "enter the garden" together as the Lord designed it, He will bless and honor your decision and commitment to one another. Intimate love is *worth the wait.*

**Awaken, north wind—come, south wind. Blow on my garden, and spread the fragrance of its spices. Let my love come to his garden and eat its choicest fruits. —Song of Songs 4:16**

Further Scripture: Matthew 19:5–6; 1 Corinthians 7:2; Hebrews 13:4

Viewing the bride as representing the Church, how would you explain Song of Songs 4:7 (Ephesians 5:25–27)?

2. The bridegroom speaks to His bride in Song of Songs 4:10 and describes the fragrance of her perfume (or oils) as better than all spices. What might that be a reference to (Exodus 30:34–36; Psalm 141:2a; Rev 5:8; 8:3–4)? What does that reveal about how the Lord views our prayers?

3. How might Song of Songs 5:2 be better understood by reading Revelation 3:20?

4. What similarities do you see between Song of Songs 5:2–6 and Matthew 25:5–13?

5. Read the description of the bridegroom in Song of Songs 5:16 and think of it as describing Jesus. Do you ever experience this kind of response in regard to Him? How do you express it? What if the Lord wants you to express your love for Him by expressing it to His body (the Church)? Would that change how you treat your brothers and sisters in Christ?

6. What did the Holy Spirit highlight to you in Song of Songs 4—5 through the reading or the teaching?

# Lesson 122: Song of Songs 6—8

*Bridegroom*: Restored Marriage

## Teaching Notes

### Intro

This is lesson 122 in the Wisdom books and the third, and final, lesson in Song of Songs. It is one of the 1,005 love songs King Solomon wrote; this one is about his first wife—the Shulammite woman—whom he desperately loved and was attracted to. Any relationship will go through stages. Within the song, Solomon describes the states of courtship, the wedding ceremony, the marriage, the apathy that can come into the marriage, and then the redemption of it. Throughout the song, others, such as the Daughters of Jerusalem (Song of Songs 1:4b; 6:1, 13; 8:5) and the brothers of the Shulammite (Song of Songs 8:8–9), added their comments and praises. And, in chapter 5, God added His blessings (Song of Songs 5:1b).

When Solomon described the Shulammite woman using metaphors of Jerusalem and armies, he was saying she was the joy of everything. This is why he fell in love with the Shulammite. As we move through these verses, notice the process. Solomon pursued her with the anticipation of the marriage and having sexual relations with her. The marriage, once consummated, did not stay in the honeymoon period but eventually moved into apathy (5:2—6:13). Tom Constable outlined this process:

1. Indifference and withdrawal (5:2–8)
2. Renewed affection (5:9–16)
3. Steps toward reconciliation (6:1–3)
4. Restoration of intimacy (6:4–13)
5. Communicating affection (7:1–10)[1]

---

[1] Thomas L. Constable, *Expository Notes of Dr. Thomas Constable: Song of Solomon*, 40–46, https://planobiblechapel.org/tcon/notes/pdf/song.pdf.

### ⸱hing

⸱g *of Songs 7:1–9*: Solomon described his wife's beauty intimately in a way that ⸱isfies Solomon (vv. 1–4). In verse 5, Solomon pointed out that she was royalty. These verses almost duplicate what Solomon first wrote when he was anticipating the physical intimacy of the marriage to come. Solomon described the blessings and gifts he received from the Shulammite woman (vv. 6–8). Even kissing her was like drinking fine wine (v. 9). With every word, Solomon created a picture of a relationship that had been revived and restored back to its beginning attraction and desire for each other.

In 6:13b, Solomon described two camps, or armies, and used the story of Jacob and Esau to explain it (see Genesis 32:1). Jacob was on his way to meet his brother after they had fallen out. God sent His army of angels to meet Esau and his army. This place of two armies coming together was named Mahanaim. This shows Solomon's wife was viewed as a helping army that fought with him, not an enemy army that fought against him.

*Song of Songs 7:10–12*: In verse 10, his wife "expressed her loyal love for the third time."[2] This speaks of her love and devotion for him—that sexual attraction was on her side as well as his. She invited him to go to the country with her (v. 11), something he had asked her earlier that was rejected (Song of Songs 2:8–17). Solomon described his wife as fine wine (v. 9), and she wanted that wine to pour from her for his pleasure and satisfaction (v. 9, 12). She promised him her love (see 1 Corinthians 7:1–7). The wife was initiating sex with her husband and promising that they would try both old things and new things together (v. 13). Mandrakes were a pungently fragrant herb considered to be an aphrodisiac.[3] Her growing desire for him increased sexual relations throughout their marriage.[4]

You may not have had godly relationships before. You may have suffered and even been abused. That is not the love that comes from Christ, and you do not have to put yourself in a position to accept that kind of abuse under the guise of love.

## Closing

Douglas Sean O'Donnell points out that when you're thinking about marriage, marriage must be pure:

---

[2] John MacArthur, *The MacArthur Bible Commentary* (Nashville: Thomas Nelson, 2005), 751.

[3] J. Cheryl Exum, *Song of Solomon: A Commentary* (Louisville: Westminster John Knox, 2005), 249.

[4] Constable, 49.

1. "Pure passion is patient." It waits for the proper time and the proper person.
2. "Pure passion is pleasurable."
3. "Pure passion is a protection against impure passion." When a husband and wife are experiencing good sexual relationships, neither will have any desire for impure passion.
4. "Pure passion is a promotion of the Passion."[5] Coming together in passion and complete love of self actually promotes The Passion of Christ. The world takes notice of our relationships! It all points to Christ.

Christ is the *Bridegroom*. He is excited to spend time with His church—His bride. "Husbands, love your wife as Christ loved the church and gave Himself for her to make her holy, cleansing her with the washing of water by the word" (Ephesians 5:25–26).

---

## The Daily Word

The bond of love in marriage is strong. Solomon and his wife displayed the balance of communication and sexual pleasure in their relationship of love. They went through a time of restoration and came back to enjoy each other like they had on their wedding night. To do so, they had to pause and *get back to their first love.*

God designed marriage for a husband and wife to enjoy pleasure and emotional and physical intimacy together like a "love so strong even a mighty river cannot sweep it away." In your marriage, do you make time to communicate emotionally and physically connect intimately as one flesh as the Lord designed? Be honest. It is easy to let kids, work, and busy schedules get in the way of pursuing love with your spouse. *But it is not an excuse.* Today is the day to pray for restoration in your marriage. Say to each other: "Where has your love gone? Come back, come back, so I may look at you." *The Lord intended for your love to remain as one, united forever.* Today, pray for a restored affection, a restored communication, and a restored intimacy. First, seek the Lord together, and He will rekindle the flame of love. Step out in faith and love one another as Christ first loved you.

**Love's flames are fiery flames—the fiercest of all. Mighty waters cannot extinguish love; rivers cannot sweep it away. —Song of Songs 8:6–7**

Further Scripture: Song of Songs 6:1,13a; Ephesians 5:25–26; 1 John 4:19

---

[5] Douglas Sean O'Donnell, *The Song of Solomon: An Invitation to Intimacy* (Wheaton, IL: Crossway, 2012), 81.

Song of Songs 6:10 describes the bride as one who was "bright as the sun." Read Matthew 5:14–16. If we are the bride, how should we "shine" so we glorify our Father who is in heaven?

2. Solomon mentioned the beautiful sandaled feet of his bride (Song of Songs 7:1a). Look at Romans 10:15 and Ephesians 6:15. Are your feet "sandaled" with the gospel of peace (Isaiah 52:7)? As part of the bride of Christ, how do you carry the good news to those who need it?

3. The love spoken about by the bride in Song of Songs 8:6–7 is "as strong as death" and cannot be quenched nor rivers overflow it. How does this compare with Romans 8:38–39?

4. What did the Holy Spirit highlight to you in Song of Songs 6—8 through the reading or the teaching?

# Contributing Authors

### Dr. Kyle Lance Martin
Kyle Lance Martin is the founder of Time to Revive, a ministry based in Dallas, Texas, whose mission is to equip the saints for the return of Christ. His heart's desire, aside from loving his wife and four kids, is to engage people with the Word of God directly in their own environment. Kyle believes when people turn to the Messiah in humility and have a willingness to walk in the Holy Spirit, they can know and experience the calling of being a disciple of Jesus Christ. Kyle received his master of biblical studies from Dallas Theological Seminary and his doctor of ministry in outreach and discipleship from Gordon-Conwell Theological Seminary.

### Pastor Gordon Henke
Gordon Henke is a pastor from northern Indiana, serving the church for 25 years. His passion is the studying of the Word. With confidence in the truth of the Word, he passionately helps people boldly share their faith.

### Pastor Tom Schiefer
Tom Schiefer is the senior pastor of Nappanee First Brethren Church in Nappanee, Indiana. Prior to accepting a call to pastoral ministry, he was a band and choir director in Ohio. In the context of these two careers, he loves to orchestrate the Word of God, and the message it contains, into harmony with people's lives.

### Pastor Fred Stayton
Fred Stayton is the lead pastor of Sonrise Church in Fort Wayne, Indiana, and has a passion for turning the hearts of fathers back to their children. Fred and his wife, Cheryl, have six children and one grandchild.

### Ryan Schrag
Ryan Schrag is the national director for Time to Revive and has a heart to "equip the saints for the return of Christ" in the United States. Prior to joining full-time ministry, he was formerly the owner/operator of a lawn care business.

### Wesley Morris
Wesley Morris is the Georgia state chairman for Time to Revive. A former construction worker turned pastor, he now trains and equips people to encounter Jesus and boldly share their faith.

### Edwards

ₗ Edwards is the Minnesota state chairman for Time to Revive and leads wor-
ₗp both nationally and internationally. For the past 20 years he has been leading
ₗorship and speaking to the body of Christ about his heart's desire to see the
church united, revived, and equipped to do the work of the ministry.

### Shawn Carlson

Shawn Carlson is the executive director for Time to Revive. He has a strong
desire to see people grow closer to Jesus through the study of God's Word and the
carrying out of His mission.

### Matt Reynolds

Matt Reynolds is the president of Spirit & Truth, a ministry aimed at equipping
believers and churches to be more empowered by the Spirit, rooted in the truth,
and mobilized for the mission. After serving as a local pastor for 13 years, Matt
responded to a missionary calling to pursue Spirit-filled renewal in the church.

### Larry Hopkins

Larry Hopkins is a businessman and entrepreneur in Dallas, Texas, who loves
studying and discussing God's Word. He has a heart for revival, which stems
from his love and desire for the Bible.

### Pastor Kyle Felke

Kyle Felke is a former pastor in northern Indiana. He grew up in a home where
both parents were teachers, which instilled in him a passion for teaching. This,
combined with a love for Jesus, led him to pursue a biblical education and pastor
a church in northern Indiana.

## Contributing Authors

*The Pentateuch*
Kyle Lance Martin

*The Gospels*
Kyle Lance Martin
Josh Edwards
Ryan Schrag
Matt Reynolds

*The Historical Books*
Kyle Lance Martin
Wesley Morris
Josh Edwards
Pastor Gordon Henke
Pastor Tom Schiefer
Pastor Kyle Felke
Larry Hopkins

*Acts*
Kyle Lance Martin
Pastor Gordon Henke
Pastor Tom Schiefer
Wesley Morris
Shawn Carlson

*The Wisdom Books*
Kyle Lance Martin
Pastor Gordon Henke
Pastor Tom Schiefer
Wesley Morris
Ryan Schrag
Pastor Fred Stayton
Shawn Carlson
Josh Edwards

*Paul's Letters*
Kyle Lance Martin
Pastor Gordon Henke
Pastor Tom Schiefer
Wesley Morris
Shawn Carlson
Josh Edwards
Ryan Schrag

*The Major Prophets*
Kyle Lance Martin
Pastor Gordon Henke
Pastor Tom Schiefer
Pastor Fred Stayton
Ryan Schrag
Josh Edwards

*General Letters*
Kyle Lance Martin
Pastor Fred Stayton
Shawn Carlson

*The Minor Prophets*
Kyle Lance Martin
Josh Edwards

*Revelation*
Kyle Lance Martin
Pastor Gordon Henke
Pastor Tom Schiefer

If you enjoyed this book, will you consider sharing
the message with others?

Let us know your thoughts. You can let the author know by visiting or sharing a
photo of the cover on our social media pages or leaving a review at a retailer's
site. All of it helps us get the message out!

Email: info@ironstreammedia.com

 @ironstreammedia

---

Iron Stream, Iron Stream Fiction, Iron Stream Kids, Brookstone Publishing
Group, and Life Bible Study are imprints of Iron Stream Media, which derives
its name from Proverbs 27:17, "As iron sharpens iron, so one person sharpens
another." This sharpening describes the process of discipleship, one to
another. With this in mind, Iron Stream Media provides a variety of solutions
for churches, ministry leaders, and nonprofits ranging from in-depth Bible
study curriculum and Christian book publishing to custom publishing and
consultative services.

For more information on ISM and its imprints, please visit
IronStreamMedia.com